Labour in Irish Politics

Labour in Irish Politics 1890–1930

The Irish labour movement in an age of revolution

Arthur Mitchell

ISBN 06–494871–4

Published in the U.S.A. 1974 by:
HARPER & ROW PUBLISHERS, INC.
BARNES & NOBLE IMPORT DIVISION

PRODUCED IN THE REPUBLIC OF IRELAND AT RICHVIEW PRESS LTD.

To my mother and father.

Contents

Preface

The intent of this study is to trace the course of the Irish labour movement in its attempt to attain political power from the period of the 1890s, when the movement was taking form, until the end of the 1920s, which marked a watershed in Irish politics. The Irish Labour Party, the instrument created by the Irish Trade Union Congress to gain political power for the workers, receives primary attention, but other worker-orientated parties and the socio-economic aspects of the nationalist parties are also treated. The industrial or the trade union side of the labour movement is considered only in relation to the development of the political side of the movement.

John W. Boyle's unpublished thesis, 'The rise of the Irish labour movement, 1888–1907', has been of great assistance to me for providing the background to the period. J. D. Clarkson's *Labour and nationalism in Ireland*, published in 1925, has been an invaluable source book for this study. In the last three years the papers of William O'Brien and Thomas Johnson have become available in the National Library of Ireland. At least four perspective monographs have appeared in the last few years: David Thornley's 'The development of the Irish labour movement', Patrick Lynch's 'The social revolution that never was', Donal Nevin's 'Labour and the political revolution' and Brian Farrell's 'Labour and the Irish political system: a suggested approach to analysis'. Two recent biographies, C. Desmond Greaves's *The life and times of James Connolly*, and Emmet Larkin's *James Larkin, Irish labour leader, 1876–1947*, have been of great help. Connolly's story necessarily ends in 1916, however, and James Larkin was outside Ireland from 1914 to 1923 and never regained his former position in the labour movement. This study concentrates on the successors to the Larkin-Connolly leadership. The problem confronting the new leaders was how could a workers' party, committed to social and economic transformation, achieve political power in a period of nationalist revolution.

I wish to offer my sincere thanks to the many veterans of the labour movement and others for allowing me to interview them. I am grateful to Mr Frank Robbins for allowing me to read his unpublished memoirs. My sincere thanks also to Donal Nevin of the Irish Congress of Trade Unions, as well as to Senator Mary Davidson, former secretary to the Labour Party, and Brendan Halligan, the present secretary. I owe a debt of gratitude to the staff of the National Library of Ireland for their unfailing courtesy and assistance over seven years. I should also like to thank the staff of the Trinity College Library for their helpfulness.

This study is based on an academic thesis prepared for submission to Trinity College, Dublin, during the years 1963–67. I shall always be grateful to Dr David Thornley, my research supervisor, for his encouragement, inspiration and guidance during that period.

I also wish to thank the following friends in Dublin for their generous advice and help: Michael McInerney, Dr John deCourcy Ireland,

John P. Feeney, Dr Christopher J. Woods, Oliver Snoddy, D. R. O'Connor Lysaght, Peter Pyne and the brothers Geraghty—Desmond, Tomás and Seamus. Many thanks also to James Watson, Brian Reynolds, Stanley Schwartz, Justin O'Mahony and Kevin O'Byrne. During the preparation of this study several of my colleagues at Curry College, Milton, Massachusetts, gave generously of their time and effort on my behalf and they shall be named: Dr Pamela Wrinch, Judson Lyon, James G. Salcucci, Robert F. Capalbo, Dr Robert Keighton, Edward H. Hastings, Arthur S. Smith, Joseph L. Schneider and Dr Franklin P. Batdorph. For assistance above and beyond the call of friendship I must cite Judson Lyon of Curry College and Oliver Snoddy of the National Museum of Ireland for their careful reading of the entire manuscript and for their many suggestions. *Go raibh míle maith agaibh.* I extend thanks also to my editor, Marilyn Norstedt, and to Seamus Cashman and Thomas Turley of the Irish University Press. Finally I must thank my wife, the former Marie O'Donoghue Leahy, for her understanding and assistance in the preparation of this study.

ARTHUR MITCHELL

Introduction

Ireland stands outside the prevailing pattern of political development in western European democratic nations in that, unlike the norm, the Irish Republic lacks a socialist party either as the governing party or as the principal opposition. Ireland, of course, is not overwhelmingly industrial, but then neither are most Scandinavian countries and there socialist parties dominate political life.

The divergence of Ireland from the general pattern first became clearly apparent in the 1930s. During that decade socialist parties achieved positions of power in most western democracies while the political labour forces in Ireland declined into insignificance. To explain this deviation in Ireland's political development it is not enough merely to repeat Mahaffy's comment that in Ireland the expected never happens and the unexpected always occurs. The deviation is, rather, the unique product of a combination of conditions existing in the country. Chief among these conditions was the long and tortuous struggle for national independence. Ireland was the last western European nation to achieve self-government. Even then, unresolved problems of nationalism remained, including partition and relations with Britain and its Commonwealth. Other factors which mitigated against the development of a major socialist movement were the slow growth of industrialization, the debilitating effect of continuing emigration, a dominant religion hostile to the socialist philosophy and a governing party with a capacity for radicalism.

A subject nation with a small industrial base presents rather barren ground for the development of socialism. This was the situation which existed in nineteenth-century Ireland. Only Belfast experienced major industrial development; the rest of the country remained basically agricultural. The principal political concern centred on the struggle to regain political rights for the majority and self-government for the country.

In rural Ireland the dominant issue was the struggle to regain control of the land by those who worked it—an issue which was the socio-economic counterpart of the Irish people's endeavour to win self-government. With the Catholic peasant population seeking to take control of the land from English and Anglo-Irish landlords, various legislation led to a massive transfer of land ownership during the two decades before the First World War; this was modern Ireland's social and economic revolution. Contrary to the expectation of the British government, this transformation did not seriously decrease the demand for political freedom.

Any lessening of the desire for independence by the farming community was counteracted by the growth of political radicalism in the urban areas. The workers of Ireland's cities and towns were a major force in the national movement from a period as early as the eighteenth century. Urban workers, mostly Protestant, were deeply involved in the agitation for restoration of parliamentary independence to Ireland in the years prior to 1782. Once this goal was attained, however, the middle-class-dominated volunteer organization used the threat of its arms to destroy assemblies of workers protesting against poor working conditions. In fact, the first general anti-combination act in these islands was the work of the newly independent Irish Parliament.[1]

Even before the repeal of the combination laws in 1824, well-organized craft unions existed in Dublin and Belfast. Although the great majority of Irish workers did not gain the right to vote until 1884,[2] there was frequent political involvement by workers particularly in Dublin, which for a time led all other cities in the United Kingdom in trades organization.[3]

The organized craft workers of Dublin were consistent supporters of Daniel O'Connell's effort to restore legislative independence to Ireland. Fergus D'Arcy points out that the Dublin workers were not motivated solely by patriotic considerations. The skilled workmen hoped that an Irish parliament would shore up their deteriorating economic position, but at the same time the Dublin trade unionists were attempting to maintain out-dated restrictions and regulations.[4] The Dublin Trades Political Union, founded in 1831, was an organization dedicated to furthering the repeal cause. Support from this quarter, however, did not prevent O'Connell from denouncing the Dublin trade union movement in 1836. He saw the craft unions of his day as restrictive combinations which were responsible, second only to the Act of Union itself, for the economic decline of Dublin.[5] The Irish leader revealed his conservative viewpoint by his opposition to minimum wage legislation and the factory acts. Speaking against a bill to strengthen the 1833 Factory Act, O'Connell warned its proponents, 'Let them not be guilty of the childish folly of regulating the labour of adults, and go about parading before the world *their ridiculous humanity*, which would end by converting their manufacturers into beggars.' It is no wonder that James Connolly termed O'Connell 'the most bitter and unscrupulous enemy of Trade Unionism' that Ireland had yet produced.[6]

The conservative Dublin craftsmen, supporters of Irish self-government, rejected radicalism in politics and in economic thought. Urban

1 Maurice R. O'Connell, 'Class conflict in a pre-industrial society', *Irish Ecclesiastical Record*, CIII (1965).

2 The Representation of the People (Ireland) Act of 1868 resulted in 'little real expansion . . . in the size of the Irish electorate . . .' David Thornley, *Isaac Butt and home rule* (London 1964), p. 27.

3 Henry Pelling, *A history of British trade unionism* (London 1965), p. 34.

4 Fergus D'Arcy, 'Skilled tradesmen in Dublin, 1800–50: a study of their opinions, activities and organizations' (M.A. thesis, University College, Dublin, 1968), p. 58.

5 J. D. Clarkson, *Labour and nationalism in Ireland* (New York 1925), pp. 135, 137–44.

6 James Connolly, *Labour in Irish history* (Dublin 1956), pp. 93–95; Giovanni Costigan, *A history of modern Ireland with a sketch of earlier times* (New York 1969), p. 160.

worker involvement in the 1848 revolt was negligible; workers were involved in the 1867 rising but were not participating as workers, and the Fenian objectives did not include labour proposals. The short-lived Irish Democratic Association of 1850, whose aims were almost entirely socialistic and revolutionary, attracted almost no trade unionist support.[7] Even the mass movement of Chartism had little success in Ireland. Arising in Britain in the late 1830s, the Chartist movement attempted to gain political rights for workers as a means towards economic security and prosperity. One of its principal leaders, Feargus O'Connor, a Corkman, hoped to join the Irish peasantry and workers with the British workers in a grand coalition to achieve both the Chartist programme and the repeal of the Act of Union.[8]

Why did Irish workers fail to respond to this appeal? The principal reason was the Liberator's opposition to Chartism. O'Connell believed that he could secure the repeal of the union by influencing the existing political parties, rather than by allying with political outcasts such as the Chartists.[9] His open hostility towards this movement was continued by his political successors, Isaac Butt and Parnell, who preferred to work through the established parties of Britain to attain their ends. Only John Mitchel and Michael Davitt supported an alliance with British worker organizations.

In addition, the organized workers of Dublin had begun a drive towards respectability in the late 1840s. By eschewing violence and intimidation, the craftsmen found that their organizations and activities were becoming socially acceptable. To have adopted radical views at this juncture, they felt, would have endangered their new-found status.[10]

Although they generally were ignored by those whose lives they hoped to transform, native socialists arose from time to time. The outstanding Irish socialist theoretician of the nineteenth century was William Thompson, of Clonkeen, Roscarbbery, County Cork, who declared in the 1820s that the solution to the problem of poverty was to be found in the creation of co-operative communities. Thompson differed from Robert Owen in that he insisted that these communities must be built and controlled by the workers themselves, rather than by wealthy patrons.[11] James Connolly awarded Thompson a prominant position among socialist theorists: Thompson 'lies . . . midway between the Utopianism of the early idealists and the historical materialism of

7 Clarkson, *Labour and nationalism,* pp. 160, 162–63; D'Arcy, 'Skilled tradesmen', pp. 74–75.

8 Donald Read and Eric Glasgow, *Feargus O'Connor, Irishman and Chartist* (London 1960), pp. 73–77, 88, 94, 128. See also Asa Briggs, *Chartist studies* (London 1959), p. 303 fn., and Rachael O'Higgins, 'Ireland and Chartism' (Ph.D. diss., Trinity College, Dublin, 1960).

9 Read and Glasgow, *Feargus O'Connor,* pp. 128, 138.

10 D'Arcy, 'Skilled tradesmen', pp. 65–66.

11 Patrick Lynch, 'William Thompson and the socialist tradition', in *Leaders and workers,* ed, J. W. Boyle (Cork 1966), pp. 9–16.

Marx. He anticipated the latter in most of his analyses of the economic system, and foresaw the part that a democratization of politics must play in clearing the ground of the legal privileges of the professional classes.'[12] A co-operative community was actually established at Ralahine, County Clare, in the 1830s. This short-lived experiment suffered from the defect of which Thompson warned: lack of worker control of the operation.[13]

Mention has been made of the socialist-orientated Irish Democratic Association of 1850, an organization founded by the soon-forgotten Bertram Fullam. There also was Thaddeus O'Malley, ex-priest and would-be politician, who attempted to gain the attention of the workers in the 1840s. An advocate of the co-operative principle, he urged that workers be given the protection of a workers' bill of rights and industrial arbitration courts. The final plea heard from O'Malley came in 1848 when he proposed that the Dublin workers should take up arms in emulation of the proletariat of Paris.[14] Branches of Karl Marx's International Workingmen's Association existed briefly in Dublin, Cork and Belfast in the late 1860s and early 1870s. In 1871 Marx selected John Patrick McDonnell as the organization's corresponding secretary for Ireland. However, McDonnell's activity was cut short by his emigration to the United States the next year.[15]

In their writings, Marx and Engels often employed Ireland as a model of a country exploited by an imperial overlord; they also examined the Irish workers in British industry, looking to this mass for the spark to ignite social revolution. No more than were British workers, the workers of Ireland were oblivious to the message of the founders of 'scientific socialism'. After the failure of the Repeal movement the organized craftsmen of Dublin shunned political issues for the next forty years. When the Dublin United Trades Association was formed in 1863, it declared that its objectives were to 'cooperate . . . for the protection of trade and the promotion and encouragement of native manufacture'. Its successor, the Dublin Trades Council, founded in 1880, had no interest in politics; its principal aim was to protect the interests of skilled workers.[16] Upon its formation in 1894, the Irish Trade Union Congress excluded political matters from its annual deliberations.

As individuals—as opposed to being members of trade unions—most Irish workers supported the home rule campaign of the Irish

12 Connolly, *Labour in Irish history*, p. 71.

13 Ibid., pp. 75–88; E. T. Craig, *The Irish land and labour question* (London 1882).

14 D'Arcy, 'Skilled tradesmen', pp lxvii–lxxiii.

15 Henry Collins, 'The English branches of the First International', *Essays in labour history*, ed. Asa Briggs & J. Saville (London 1960), p. 254; Desmond Ryan, 'When the reds came to Cork', *The Bell;* Andrew Boyd, *The rise of the Irish trade unions, 1729–1970* (Tralee 1972), p. 59.

16 Clarkson, *Labour and nationalism*, pp. 167, 175; Dublin Trade Union and Labour Council, *Dublin labour yearbook, 1930*.

Parliamentary Party. Organized workers were given a small role in the selection of candidates during the period of Parnell's leadership. But both Parnell and his party were largely indifferent to the problems of the urban workers. Michael Davitt records the Chief's hostility towards the existing craft unions: 'What is trade unionism', Parnell asked, 'but a landlordism of labour? I would not tolerate, if I were at the head of a government, such bodies as trade unions. Whatever has to be done for the protection of the working classes in a state should be the duty of the government.'[17] (This statement should be judged with the knowledge that Parnell occasionally made stern remarks merely for their shock effect or to change the subject. D. D. Sheehan credits him with being the first man to notice the degraded position of the agricultural workers, which resulted in his successful sponsorship of a labourers act.[18])

Parnell clashed with Davitt over the latter's scheme for an alliance of the home rule forces and the British labour movement. In the 1885 election Parnell urged Irish voters in Britain to support the Conservatives, whom he hoped could be brought to support home rule. Davitt, on the other hand, urged the Irish to support labour and socialist candidates.[19] Only five years later, however, during the leadership crisis in the Irish Parliamentary Party in 1890–91, Parnell made a strong bid for support from the workers. F. S. L. Lyons suggests that Parnell's action in this matter was motivated more by tactical political considerations rather than by a desire to improve the conditions of the working class.[20]

Following the overthrow and death of Parnell, Michael Davitt attained a position of great influence in the majority faction of the Parliamentary Party. From this platform of strength, he forced the nomination, for the first time, of two workers for parliamentary seats.[21] In the 1892 election two 'Labour-Nationalists', who could be considered somewhat analogous to the 'Lib-Labs' in Britain, were returned. In the elections up to and including 1910 two or three local labour personalities won seats, thus enabling the Irish Parliamentary Party to claim to represent the workers as well as other sections of the community.[22] But this was gross under-representation at best.

When the party was reunited in 1900, labour organizations were given an increased voice in the nomination of parliamentary candidates. This was doubtless due to the growing strength of the trade union

17 Michael Davitt, *The fall of feudalism in Ireland* (New York 1904), p. 637.

18 D. D. Sheehan, *Ireland since Parnell* (London 1921), p. 177.

19 T. W. Moody, 'Michael Davitt and the British labour movement', *Transactions of the Royal Historical Society*, 5th ser., vol. 3 (1953); Henry Pelling, *Origins of the British Labour Party, 1880–1900* (London 1954), pp. 66–68.

20 F. S. L. Lyons, *The fall of Parnell* (London 1962) pp. 257–58. See Parnell's address to the Irish Labour League in *United Ireland*, 21 March 1891.

21 Moody, 'Davitt and British labour'.

22 F. S. L. Lyons, *The Irish Parliamentary Party, 1890–1910* (London 1951), p. 169.

movement. In the first decade of this century the party secured passage of a body of legislation beneficial to Irish workers, including the 1906 Labourers Housing Act, a town tenant act and the 1908 Housing of the Working Class Act. But the principal beneficiaries of these measures were the rural workers, not those of the urban areas.[23] One of the most serious failures of the Irish Parliamentary Party, as Lyons has pointed out, was its consistent neglect of the terrible Dublin slums. Rather than attempt to deal with this grave problem, the party simply blamed British rule for the slums' existence and promised that all would be put right when home rule was, at length, achieved.[24]

THE FORMATION OF THE IRISH TRADE UNION CONGRESS

The major reason that the workers did not exert significant influence during the late nineteenth century was their inability to form a representative, nationally-based organization. Several attempts were made before this was achieved. The first of these occurred in 1890 when Michael Davitt initiated the Irish Democratic Labour Federation. This organization adopted an advanced social programme including proposals for free education, land settlement, worker housing, reduced working hours, labour political representation and universal suffrage. The federation attracted only a small number of trade and labour bodies in Munster, however, and it broke up during the Parnell split of the same year.[25]

Following this failure came the 'Land and Labour' national association, another Munster-based body, comprised of local 'land and labour' affiliates. This movement was designed to improve the condition of rural workers and failed to attract support from town and city workers.[26] Local 'land and labour' associations survived until the early years of the twentieth century and had considerable success in propagating labour ideals in Munster. The Irish Labour Party later was to benefit from the efforts of these associations.[27]

In 1891 another unsuccessful attempt was made to organize a national labour federation. The Dublin branch of the militant National Union of Gasworkers and General Labourers, a British-based union established two years before, was the guiding force in this effort. It issued invitations to all trade unions in the country for an organizing convention to be held in Dublin. Only unskilled workers attended; the

23 Ibid., pp. 151, 244–45, 248. Michael Davitt declared that the Labourers' Housing Act embodied 'a rational principle of state socialism'. Davitt, *Fall of feudalism*, p. xi.

24 F. S. L. Lyons, *John Dillon, a biography* (London 1968), p. 336.

25 Sheehan, *Ireland since Parnell*, pp. 172–73.

26 Ibid., pp. 168–86. Sheehan was president of the national association. In 1905 the organization split when his former associate, Dr O'Shee, formed a separate body.

27 View of Thomas Johnson, leading figure in the Irish labour movement, 1916–27 (interview, Donal Nevin), and T. J. Murphy, Labour T.D. from Cork from the 1920s to 1940s (article by Patrick Nolan, *Irish Times*, 18 Nov. 1965).

craft unions refused to join forces with the unskilled. The new organization, the Irish Labour League, adopted a radical programme going beyond that of Davitt's federation, by advocating the nationalization of land and transport. When the gasworkers failed to secure a foothold in Dublin, the labour league soon faded away.[28]

When a successful labour body was eventually established in 1894 it was almost exclusively composed of skilled workers. Irish branches of British-based 'amalgamated' unions and some craft unions had been represented in the British Trade Union Congress since its establishment in 1868. By the early 1890s the predominant view among Irish trade unionists was that this body had become too preoccupied with the expanding British movement to devote sufficient time to Irish labour questions. Despite an offer that an Irish member would have a guarateed position on the T.U.C. executive, and in the face of criticism by leaders of amalgamated unions, an Irish Trade Union Congress was formed, a very model of the British body. It immediately declared that its purpose was to 'supplement' the work of the 'parent' body' in Britain, but the establishment of an independent Irish body was the first step in the gradual separation of the two movements. The creation of a Scottish Trade Union Congress in 1897 was a different case, in that this body was comprised of trade councils and made no attempt to separate the trade union movement in Scotland from that of England. For the first twenty years of its existance, the Irish body was ignored by the British congress, except when in 1900 it was invited to merge itself with the British organization.[29] As well, the Belfast branches of British unions overlooked it.

Initially claiming to represent 30,000 skilled workers, the Irish congress showed no interest in labour political activity. Purely political issues, especially the great question of Irish self-government, were kept out of the proceedings. There was a general assumption within the congress that an attempt to take a position on such a controversial issue as home rule could very well lead to disruption of the newly-formed body. Radical and revolutionary socio-economic proposals were occasionally put before annual meetings, but for the first fifteen years the congress supported moderate, reformist measures, suitable to the advancement of skilled workers.[30]

THE BEGINNING OF LABOUR REPRESENTATION

Though not encouraged by the congress, a labour political consciousness gradually emerged. Influenced by developments within the British labour movement, it took hold first in the industrial centre of Ireland,

28 J. W. Boyle, 'The rise of the Irish labour movement, 1888–1907' (Ph.D. diss., Trinity College, Dublin, 1961), pp. 132–33; *United Ireland*, 21 March 1891.

29 Clarkson, *Labour and nationalism*, pp. 181, 187–89; Sidney and Beatrice Webb, *History of trade unionism* (London 1920), p. 473.

30 Clarkson, *Labour and nationalism*, pp. 200–201, 203. See also Emil Strauss, *Irish nationalism and British democracy* (London 1951), p. 225.

in the city of Belfast. As late as 1899 this city contained half of the trade unionists in the country. The Belfast Trades Council represented 19,000 organized workers, half of whom were in British-based unions.[31] With this strong trade union base and close ties with the British labour movement, Belfast became the vital centre of labour political activity for the fifteen years following 1892.

The struggle for labour political power was heralded in 1885 by the nomination of Alexander Bowman, flax dresser and secretary of the Belfast Trades Council, as the Liberal candidate for a parliamentary seat in North Belfast. Although he did not stand as a purely labour candidate, he was the first trade unionist in Ireland to seek election to Parliament, and he received a respectable number of votes. In 1892 the Belfast Trades Council provided an example to similar bodies in the country when it created a parliamentary and municipal election fund. Later the same year Ireland's first local Labour Party was formed in the northern city; upon the urging of Keir Hardie, it became affiliated to the newly-formed Independent Labour Party in 1893 (a year later party branches were formed in Dublin and Waterford). Belfast had the honour of electing the first Labour group to a corporation in 1897.[32]

In Dublin labour political development was slower. The local branch of the Independent Labour Party was small and without influence. Several trade unionists won election to the Dublin corporation beginning in the mid- 1890s, but they were the nominees of various nationalist groups, and only after they had secured such nominations were they endorsed by the trades council. This body moved directly into local politics in 1895 when it formed a labour electoral association. It put forward in that year the first Labour candidate for the city council; another followed in 1896. Although both men were defeated, their candidatures marked the advent of a new, and potentially powerful, factor in Dublin local politics.[33]

Interest in labour political activity was spurred throughout Ireland by the passage of the local government act of 1898, which threw open to popular election most of the public bodies previously controlled by a combination of appointed officials and members elected on a restricted franchise. Labour electoral associations sprang up in every town. Some of these were sponsored by trades councils and unions, some by 'Land and Labour' bodies and others were formed by previously unorganized groups of workers.[34] Neither the local trades councils nor the national congress attempted to draw up a

31 Strauss, *Nationalism and democracy*, p. 234.

32 Emmet Larkin, *James Larkin, Irish labour leader, 1876–1947* (London 1965), pp. 315–16.

33 Boyle, 'Rise of Irish labour', pp. 179–80, 188.

34 C. Desmond Greaves, *The life and times of James Connolly* (London 1961), p. 169.

Labour programme for local government, and they assumed no responsibility for the selection and control of Labour candidates.

The first local elections under the new act, held in January 1899, resulted in major Labour victories. Significant successes were recorded in such widely separated towns as Limerick, Dundalk, Waterford and Castlebar; six Labour men were elected to the Belfast corporation. In Dublin, where Labour men won one-fifth of the seats in the corporation, the *Freeman's Journal* commented:

> It is satisfactory . . . to find the intelligent Artisans of Dublin at last influentially represented in local affairs . . . Their position at the polls will suggest to many of them whether as regards Parliamentary representation they can be any longer put off with the pretence that in the person of William Field [a Labour-Nationalist M.P.] they are truly and adequately represented in Parliament.[35]

Alarmed at the great upsurge of labour political activity, John Redmond and the Irish Parliamentary Party urged the workers not to form separate political organizations because they might disrupt the home rule movement; the causes of 'labour and nationality must march together'.[36] James Connolly later declared that this reaction was simply an attempt to stifle the development of worker political power: 'The capitalist politicians took fright and in press and on platform the Irish workers were denounced for daring to abandon their natural leaders.'[37] The principal opponents of the Labour candidates in the election were the nominees of the United Irish League—the local organization of the Irish Parliamentary Party.

Responding to success, the Trade Union Congress warmly approved of labour representation in local government. At the 1900 meeting it passed a resolution urging the fullest possible control of local government by labour representatives.[38] But despite these victories, representation during this period accomplished little or nothing for the workers of Ireland. Labour members on many bodies became involved in jobbery and corruption and often joined forces with long-time nationalist members. In 1902 the trades congress warned Labour members not to support the nominees of 'any political party unless such nominee had been approved officially by the local trades council, trade union, or any recognised labour organization'.[39]

The situation was particularly bad in Dublin. One of the purposes of labour representation was to reform the Dublin corporation, yet 'most of the members of the Party became employees of the body they

35 *Freeman's Journal*, 19 Jan. 1899.

36 James Connolly, *Socialism and nationalism*, ed. Desmond Ryan (Dublin 1948), pp. 68, 76.

37 Article by Connolly in *Forward*, 13 May 1913.

38 Irish Trade Union Congress, *1901 report*, p. 56.

39 Clarkson, *Labour and nationalism*, p. 206.

set out to reform.'[40] James Connolly in his newspaper, the *Workers Republic*, denounced the Dublin Labour representatives:

> From the entry of the Labour Party into the Municipal Council to the present day . . . no single move in the interests of the workers was even mooted, the most solemn pledges were . . . broken and where the workers looked for inspiration and leadership they received only discouragement and disgust.[41]

In the *United Irishman,* Arthur Griffith declared that the Dublin Labour members 'had tacked themselves onto the tail of the whiskey ring and the publicans'.[42]

Labour continued to have success at the next local elections in 1900, but because of the poor service by most Labour representatives, the elections of 1902 resulted in a rebuff to Labour candidates. In 1903 Labour was routed almost everywhere, marking the failure of the initial effort to establish Labour representation in local government.[43]

This first attempt failed for two principal reasons. Firstly, little care was taken in the selection of Labour candidates, and the trade councils and the unions had no control over Labour members once they were elected.[44] Secondly, no attempt was made to clarify what Labour representation was expected to accomplish in local government. No Labour programme was drawn up and no attempt was made to coordinate the activities of the Labour members on the various bodies. On the other hand, the early successes of the Labour candidates was evidence that a properly organized and disciplined workers' party might have considerable political potential.

Belfast was the outstanding exception to the Labour debacle in local politics. Labour members there were carefully selected by and remained under the tight discipline of the Belfast Labour Party, which in turn was controlled by the Belfast Trades Council. The Labour members had avoided corrupt practices and continued to gain popular support.[45]

Besides the Belfast party, there existed for a time another worker-political party in the country. This was the small, uninfluential Irish Socialist Republican Party which had been formed in 1896 by James Connolly and a few other socialists in Dublin. Destined to be Ireland's leading socialist theorist and propagandist as well as a national martyr, Connolly was born in an Edinburgh slum in 1868. After some experience in socialist organizations in Scotland, and a spell in the British army, he

40 Article by T. Irwin, *Voice of Labour*, 14 April 1923. See also William O'Brien, *Forth the banners go* (Dublin 1969), p. 31.

41 *Workers' Republic*, 16 Sept. 1899, quoted in Greaves, *Connolly*, pp 95–96.

42 *United Irishman*, 7 Sept. 1901.

43 *Freeman's Journal*, 17 Jan. 1900; Boyle, 'Rise of Irish labour', p. 271.

44 Dublin Trade Union and Labour Council, *Dublin labour yearbook, 1930*, pp. 46–47.

45 J. W. Boyle, 'William Walker', in *Leaders and workers*, pp. 60–62; Larkin, *James Larkin*, pp. 316–17.

came to Dublin in 1896. In contrast to the 'internationalism' of the Belfast socialists, Connolly believed that the causes of socialism and national independence were complementary and should advance together. Arguing that a nation could not alter basically its social system until it had achieved political independence, Connolly carried the Fenian banner of an independent republic into twentieth century Irish politics.

In the period 1899–1903 the I.S.R.P. put forward nine candidates, including Connolly, for local office in Dublin, but none came even close to election. The party in Dublin barely held its tiny membership; its branch in Cork disappeared in 1901 when its leader, Con Lehane, emigrated to England in the wake of clerical opposition to the group. The I.S.R.P. failed to gain a political foothold because of the indifference of the dominant craft unions and the general refusal of workers to respond to its doctrinaire propaganda. In its issue of 20 April 1901, the strongly Catholic and nationalist journal, the *Leader* declared: 'We doubt if there is a native Socialist born [*sic*] in Ireland, and the third-rate hangers-on to the skirts of some cheap school of Socialism that may exist here and there are, at bottom, only victims of Anglicization . . .'. When Connolly left for the United States in 1903, the party almost disappeared. A few years later, however, its remnants joined other socialist fragments in Dublin to form the Socialist Party of Ireland in 1908. The new party eventually achieved enough stability to invite Connolly to return as its organizer in 1910.[46]

The years of Connolly's absence were years of transition for the labour movement. The emphasis on the skilled worker and reformism shifted towards an all-encompassing workers' movement and socialism; political neutrality evolved towards independent political action.

Although non-committed on the great issue of home rule, the Trade Union Congress maintained close contact with the Irish Parliamentary Party during the first decade of this century. Several 'Labour-Nationalist' M.P.s addressed the annual meetings of the congress. They generally advised the congress to maintain its reformist socio-economic outlook, to continue to avoid the perils of socialism and to support their party. In the years prior to the First World War, J. P. Nannetti, one of the 'Lab-Nat' M.P.s, acted as an intermediary between the party and the congress.[47]

In 1902 Nannetti arranged a meeting between the congress executive and John Redmond, leader of the Irish Parliamentary Party. Redmond agreed to promote most of the recommendations of the congress and called for frequent meetings between the leaderships of the two organizations. The next meeting, however, did not take place until 1909. Redmond expressed 'regret' that closer contact had not been maintained

46 O'Brien, *Forth the banners go*, pp. 2–13, 30–35, 40–44; William O'Brien papers, National Library of Ireland, MS 15672(2); Greaves, *Connolly*, pp. 62–70, 90, 110, 134.

47 Clarkson, *Labour and nationalism*, pp. 197, 201; Boyle, 'Rise of Irish labour', pp. 219–220.

in the interval but assured the congress executive that his party 'will in the future, as in the past, endeavor to fulfil for Ireland . . . the function of a Labour Party'.[48]

The congress, however, was never satisfied that the Irish Parliamentary Party gave enough attention to its recommendations and to labour matters in general. Dissatisfaction with the party grew in the first decade of the century,[49] coinciding with a demand from Belfast that the congress should establish its own political machinery. Belfast trade unionists had close ties with the expanding British labour groups, and doubtlessly were influenced by their development.[50] In the period 1900–10 there were four schools of thought in the congress concerning political activity. The first believed that trade unions should stay out of politics altogether. A second and more sizeable group held that the Irish Parliamentary Party adequately served labour's interests, and that labour political action at this time might injure the home rule effort. A third group, mostly from Belfast, declared that the congress should become an affiliated or subordinate part of the advancing British political movement. A fourth, but tiny, group under separatist influence (principally that of the Irish Republican Brotherhood and Sinn Fein) held that if the congress was to set up its own political machinery, it should be independent of any British connections.

The question of which policy the congress should adopt was a source of contention at its meetings for a decade. The separatist group took the initiative in 1902 when its leader, P. T. Daly, managed to secure congress approval of a resolution calling for the formation of a 'pledge-bound' Labour Party, controlled by and answerable to the congress. The congress executive, probably recognizing that the resolution did not reflect the true feeling of the body, failed to act on it. The executive declared that it had not done so because it 'was a most difficult matter to formulate any scheme at the present time which would be acceptable to the workers'[51] Not until eight years later was a similar proposal put to the congress.

Beginning in 1903 the congress supported a policy on political activity that was, in effect, a compromise between the proposals of the two largest groups in the body—the supporters of the Irish Parliamentary Party and the Belfast advocates of direct affiliation with British Labour. The congress recommended that Irish trade unions affiliate with the British Labour Representation Committee as a means of securing 'independent Labour representation in Ireland'. The congress itself did not set up its own political apparatus, but affiliated

48 I.T.U.C., *1903 report*, pp. 24–25; *1909 report*, pp. 9–10.

49 I.T.U.C., *1908 report*, pp. 53–54.

50 In 1904 the Belfast Socialist Party became a branch of the Independent Labour Party. William Walker became the only Irishman to serve on the latter executive. Clarkson, *Labour and nationalism*, p. 213.

51 I.T.U.C., *1902 report*, pp. 42–43; *1903 report*, p. 38.

organizations could do so if they wished.[52] With the exception of the 1906 meeting,[53] a resolution stating this policy was approved by the congress, usually by a large margin, through 1911.

Only in Belfast was the recommendation acted upon. With the support of the trades council and the unions, Labour candidates contested the North Belfast parliamentary seat on four occasions—in 1905, 1906, 1907 and 1910. William Walker was the candidate in the first three contests. These candidates polled very well but just failed of election.[54] The congress, at the same time, continued relations with the Irish Parliamentary Party, but, based on the Belfast political action, it could also appeal to the emerging British Labour Party for occasional help.

The Belfast contingent within the congress, however, was not satisfied by the mere recommendation that Irish trade unions affiliate with the Labour Representation Committee. It pressed the congress to establish its own political machinery as a subordinate part of the British organization. This course was urged by Walker, president of the congress in 1904, and John Murphy, also of Belfast, president in 1908. At the 1904 meeting Keir Hardie and Ramsay MacDonald appeared to urge the delegates to support the emerging British Labour Party. Interest in labour political activity in Ireland was stimulated by the success of the British Labour candidates in the 1906 election.[55]

The rapid growth of British amalgamated unions also helped convince the congress that it needed political machinery. The amalgamated groups absorbed many small Irish craft unions during the 1900s.[56] The Irish Trade Union Congress, however, avoided a direct statement of support to the British organization. The closest the congress ever came to commitment on this matter was in 1909. That year the congress passed a resolution not only recommending that the affiliated bodies support the British organization, but added that it 'urges upon the trades councils in industrial constituencies in Ireland the advisability of obtaining candidates to stand on labour lines and pledges itself to support such candidates if constitutionally selected'.[57] But only the Belfast Trades Council sponsored a candidate at the next general election in 1910.

The 1909 congress meeting also passed a resolution deploring sectarian and party divisions in trade unions, declaring that the 'workers

52 I.T.U.C., *1903 report*, p. 38.

53 In 1906 Nannetti made a determined plea that the congress not make this recommendation. His intervention upset the balance within the congress. The body voted against the usual resolution (17 for, 34 against), then proceeded to vote down a resolution endorsing the Irish Parliamentary Party (18 for, 33 against). I.T.U.C., *1906 report*, p. 73.

54 Larkin, *James Larkin*, pp. 37, 316–17.

55 Clarkson, *Labour and nationalism*, pp. 207, 213, 398. For a biographical sketch of Walker, see Boyle, 'William Walker', in *Leaders and workers*, pp. 57–66.

56 Clarkson, *Labour and nationalism*. p. 395.

57 I.T.U.C., *1909 report*, p. 28.

should combine with their fellows elsewhere'. This motion replaced the resolution offered by P. T. Daly which stated that the congress recognized the demand for Irish political independence and that trade unions should be 'worked' on a national basis.[58]

The Irish Parliamentary Party made a strong effort to discourage the congress from setting up its own political machinery. In 1906 Nannetti told the delegates 'the Irish Parliamentary Party were [*sic*] the Labour Party. . . . Where was the necessity of setting up new parties? . . . They could make the Parliamentary Party do everything they wished'; members of parliament could not be elected on the 'labour question alone at this time'. John Redmond said the same thing to the congress executive in 1909.[59] Joseph Devlin, who represented a Belfast industrial constituency, loudly upheld the 'rights of labour' in a 1911 strike; in 1912 he declared himself the champion of the 'workers and toilers'.[60] His statements could be interpreted as a demonstration of the party's sympathy for the cause of labour.

Two events occurred in 1909 which decisively affected the issue of political action by the congress. First, the Asquith government adopted Irish home rule as part of its programme. As the Home Rule Bill approached passage into law, the interest of Irish trade unionists in political action increased; between 1910 and 1914, home rulers among trade unionists withdrew their objections to the establishment of a congress-sponsored political party. Under home rule, they reasoned, the proposed party would not undermine the work of the Irish Parliamentary Party in London, but would be utilized to secure representation for Labour in the new Irish Parliament.

The second important event of 1909 was the emergence of the Irish Transport and General Workers Union. This union was the first to organize unskilled workers in Ireland on a large scale. It became affiliated with the congress in 1910 and soon grew to be the largest body represented in the congress. Unskilled workers previously had been very under-represented. In 1895 the Dublin Corporation Employees Union had affiliated, but only two unskilled workers' representatives were elected to the congress executive prior to 1900, one in 1895 and the other in 1896.[61] In 1906 the British-based National Union of Dock Labourers joined the congress, but this union did not have a large Irish membership. The Irish Transport and General Workers Union, however, from the date of its entry into the congress, supported four propositions which had the effect of transforming that body: it believed in the tactics of militant or 'new' unionism; it supported a socialist philosophy; it believed in Irish unions for Ireland, and it strongly believed in labour political action.

58 Ibid., pp. 50, 51.

59 I.T.U.C., *1906 report*, pp. 74–75; *1909 report*, pp. 9–10.

60 Clarkson, *Labour and nationalism*, pp. 254–55; *Freeman's Journal*, 25 May 1912.

61 Boyle, 'Rise of Irish labour', p. 156.

1

Irish Labour Creates a Political Party

THE FOUNDATION OF THE IRISH TRANSPORT AND GENERAL WORKERS UNION

The establishment of industrial unionism in Ireland and the story of James Larkin are inevitably intertwined. That demogogic, inspiring and controversial figure swept into Ireland like a human tornado, organizing, in turn, the neglected unskilled workers of Belfast, Cork and Dublin. Larkin was the commanding figure in the Irish labour movement from the creation of his union in late 1908 until he left for America in 1914. Although he did not regain his position of leadership after his return in 1923, Larkin remained a constant and important factor in Irish Labour until his death in 1947. More, he became a legend in both the Irish labour movement and the national hagiography.

Like James Connolly, Larkin was born in Britain of Irish parents and, again like Connolly, was influenced by British Labour thought. Born in Liverpool in 1876, Larkin went to work at the age of eleven. After several years' work on the docks, he became a member of the National Union of Dock Labourers and in 1906 was appointed the union's general organizer. An advocate of working-class political action from the age of sixteen, he joined the Independent Labour Party in 1893 and was active in several campaigns, most notably in 1906 when he was election agent for his union's general secretary, James Sexton, in a contest for a Liverpool parliamentary seat. Appalled by the poverty that surrounded him, Larkin became an early convert to socialism and was a frequent speaker at socialist meetings in the Liverpool area.[1]

Larkin first came to Ireland on an organizational drive for his union at the beginning of 1907. He had considerable success in organizing dock workers in Belfast, Cork and Dublin, although his initial accomplishments in the first two cities proved to be largely ephemeral. From the beginning of his work in Ireland, Larkin supported labour intervention in politics; but as an employee of a British union and as a new arrival from Liverpool, he was firmly attached to British organizations. In 1907 he supported William Walker's parliamentary candidacy in Belfast.[2] Larkin was among the group within the Irish Trade Union Congress which refuted the claim that the Irish Parliamentary Party adequately represented Irish workers. At this time he believed that the best way the workers could gain representation would be through the Labour Representation Committee in Britain. Rather than join the existing Socialist Party of Ireland, he re-established the Dublin branch of the Independent Labour Party (which lasted but a short time).[3]

1 Emmet Larkin, *James Larkin, Irish labour leader, 1876–1947*, pp. 14–17, 25–61.

2 J. W. Boyle, 'The rise of the Irish labour movement, 1888–1907', p. 376.

3 Larkin, *James Larkin*, p. 63.

Addressing the Dublin Trades Council in August 1908, he opposed the expansion of Irish-based unions.[4] By the end of this year, however, Larkin became a convert to the cause of both an Irish-based Labour Party and Irish-based unions. This change coincided with his dismissal as an organizer by the National Union of Dock Labourers.

Following a personal clash with the executive of the dockers' union, Larkin joined with a group of Dublin trade unionists to establish the Irish Transport and General Workers Union in December 1908.[5] The new union was unique in several respects. It was the first Irish union to adopt a socialist programme; seeking the nationalization of all the means of transport and 'the land of Ireland for the Irish people', it had as its ultimate object a new social and economic order—an 'industrial commonwealth'. It declared its dedication to the organization into one union of all workers—skilled and unskilled—in an industry. This objective was to be attained by means of militant union tactics, such as the boycott and the sympathetic strike, and by the use of class-orientated propaganda. The new union urged Irish Labour to end 'the policy of grafting ourselves onto the English trade union movement'.[6] The establishment and rapid growth of Larkin's union marked a turning away from the pattern of gradual amalgamation of Irish unions with British unions.

Accompanying the creation of an Irish industrial union came the introduction of syndicalism, which, very briefly, is based on the idea that organized workers, by means of militant tactics, should gradually increase their power within an industry so that eventually they would have control of the industry. Syndicalism also held that industrial and not political action was the only effective means towards the establishment of a workers' state. This doctrine was an influential force in most industrialized countries in the years leading up to the First World War, but in Ireland it had a continuing influence.

Larkin had definite syndicalist tendencies, and James Connolly, soon to be his chief lieutenant, was for a time an outspoken advocate of this approach. Yet neither could be termed orthodox syndicalists as they both were vigorous supporters of labour political activity. Both believed that industrial and political action was complementary; as Larkin once stated the case: 'I am an industrialist and at the same time appreciate the fact that Labour can accomplish a great deal through the intelligent use of the ballot. Why use one arm when we have two? Why not strike the enemy with both arms—the political and economic?'[7]

4 O'Brien notes in O'Brien papers, N.L.I., box marked MS 15677–82.

5 The union was organized in late 1908 but was not registered with the registrar of friendly societies until the beginning of 1909.

6 Irish Transport and General Workers Union, *Rule Book, 1909*, preface.

7 Larkin, *James Larkin*, p. 98; article by Larkin, 'A Labour Party here in Ireland', *Dublin Trade and Labour Journal*, 3 July 1909. See also D. R. O'Connor Lysaght's introduction to Connolly's *Socialism made easy* (Dublin 1968), pp. 1–9.

The new union experienced difficulty in winning acceptance by the Irish Trade Union Congress. The amalgamated unions, resentful of and alarmed by Larkin's success, succeeded in keeping the Transport Union outside the congress in 1909.[8] But a rapidly growing, dynamically led union could not remain outside the congress for long. In 1910 Larkin's group became affiliated with the congress, and the union and its allies immediately proposed that the congress form its own political party, independent of any British connection. The supporters of the Irish Parliamentary Party joined with the proponents of affiliation with the British Labour Party to defeat the proposal. By a vote of thirty-nine for, eighteen against, the congress adopted an amendment which stated that affiliated bodies had no authority to commit their unions financially to the proposed party.[9] The Transport Union and its sympathizers, however, succeeded in replacing craft unionists and supporters of the Parliamentary Party with Larkinites as permanent officers of the congress. P. T. Daly became congress secretary and M. J. O'Lehane its treasurer.[10]

REVIVAL OF LOCAL LABOUR REPRESENTATION

Rebuffed in its initial attempt to form a congress-sponsored Labour Party, the Transport Union and its allies turned to political activity on the local level, using every opportunity to propagate the idea of a national Labour Party. In the years 1911–15 labour representation in local government was revived and established on a solid basis not only in Dublin, but in most of the larger towns. It is well to point out, however, that political activity at this time was seen by the supporters of 'new unionism' as primarily another weapon in the industrial struggle.[11]

Despite the opposition of anti-socialist members, the supporters of Larkin won control of the Dublin Trades Council in the spring of 1911. In January of that year the council had voted to form a labour representation committee. The committee was dominated by the Transport Union and its allies; Larkin was elected acting secretary. Later that year William O'Brien, a key figure in the development of new unionism in Ireland, became secretary and served until 1915.[12] The committee declared that its purpose was to restore labour representation in order to destroy corruption and business domination in

8 I.T.U.C., *1909 report*, pp. 40–42. The union, however, won immediate acceptance from the Dublin Trades Council and within three years was the dominant force in that group. Larkin, *James Larkin*, p. 75.

9 I.T.U.C., *1910 report*, pp. 29, 48–49.

10 Ibid., pp. 2, 33, 57.

11 Interview with James Larkin, Jr., 3 Feb. 1966.

12 Larkin, *James Larkin*, p. 99. Membership on the committee was in proportion to the size of the affiliated unions. As the Transport Union was the largest union, it had the largest representation. *Irish Worker*, 3 and 10 June 1911; O'Brien, *Forth the banners go*, p. 39; O'Brien papers, N.L.I. MS 16271.

Dublin government and to ensure that trade union standards prevailed in municipal employment. The committee and the Transport Union newspaper, the *Irish Worker*, conducted a vigorous campaign to overcome the doubts of the workers concerning the value of labour representation. Many workers recalled the poor performance of labour representatives at the turn of the century; others held that trade unions should keep out of politics. The committee answered the first objection by declaring that the labour representatives on public bodies would be pledged to and controlled by the decisions of the trade councils.[13] The *Irish Worker* replied to the second objection:

> Anyone with a grain of wit knows that politics is the key to the whole labour movement. Trade Unions [are] politics, the Sanitary laws are politics, the Food and Drug Act is politics, the Old Age Pension is politics, the State Insurance Bill is politics, the Right to work is politics; so is the right to strike.[14]

Both Larkin and the business interests of Dublin viewed the entrance of the labour representation committee into the local elections as an extension of the industrial struggle into the political arena. The business interests generally supported the United Irish League, the local organization of Irish Parliamentary Party. The *Irish Worker* attacked the parliamentary party, declaring it to be a 'solely . . . agricultural party' which 'had never represented the workers, either in Parliament or out of it'. The party, it alleged, considered the workers 'as collection machines for [its] Parliamentary fund' using the United Irish League for this purpose.[15]

In its first election, in the summer of 1911, the labour committee (renamed the Dublin Labour Party in 1912) elected four representatives as poor law guardians. For the January 1912 Dublin corporation elections (20 of the 80 seats were up for election) the committee nominated seven candidates, including Larkin.[16] When the Irish Parliamentary Party warned that the defeat of U.I.L. could impair the success of the home rule movement, the *Irish Worker* replied that home rule in itself would not mean improvement in the condition of the workers; indeed, it might worsen their condition. The labour committee candidates were attacked as socialists and trouble makers in the pages of the *Irish Independent*, the property of William Martin Murphy, the leader of the Dublin business interests.[17] They were also opposed by a body of craft unionists, including E. L. Richardson and E. W. Stewart, two former officers of the trade union congress. The *Irish Worker* centred its fire on trade union candidates not nominated by the labour

13 *Irish Worker*, 3 June, 14 October 1911.

14 Ibid., 29 July 1911.

15 Ibid., 2 December 1911.

16 Ibid., 3 June 1911.

17 Ibid., 30 September 1911; *Irish Independent*, 10–15 January 1912.

committee.[18] The fire was returned in an *Irish Independent* article by a craft unionist who declared that the Larkinite candidates supported Marxism, atheism, free love and abortion.[19]

Five nominees of the labour committee, including Larkin, were elected (another seat was won in a delayed election three week later); the *Irish Worker* proclaimed 'Labour triumphant'. The *Irish Times* commented, 'Mr Larkin and his candidates achieved remarkable success.' This election also marked the revival of labour representation in other cities, including Waterford, Drogheda and Sligo where political action had been stimulated by the activity of the Transport Union.[20]

In the Dublin corporation the Labour group pressed for reform of that body and improvements in employees' wages and conditions, but were usually unsuccessful. Still, they remained watchdogs against jobbery and corruption. James Larkin was removed from the corporation because of an earlier conviction during a labour dispute.[21] Larkin charged that his removal had been plotted by William Martin Murphy and other leading Dublin employers. Richard O'Carroll, later to be killed in the 1916 rising, replaced Larkin as leader of the Labour bloc, which continued as a vocal, disciplined group.[22]

Emmet Larkin attaches considerable importance to Larkin's removal from the Dublin corporation. He argues that because of his inability to hold public office for the next seven years, Larkin concentrated on the development of his union and the organization of Irish workers for direct action, which ultimately pushed him towards syndicalism.[23] But Larkin was chiefly interested in the industrial struggle throughout this period; the Dublin corporation would hardly be likely to offer great scope for his energies. And his disbarment did not prevent him from being a strong advocate of labour political activity, as seen in the following Dublin elections and in the establishment of an Irish Labour Party by the Trade Union Congress.

When two by-elections for the corporation occurred in October 1912, the forces of 'new unionism' and Dublin business clashed once again. Both Labour nominees were unsuccessful, and Murphy's *Irish Inde-*

18 E. L. Richardson, ex-treasurer, was a candidate, and E. W. Stewart, ex-secretary, was election agent for Larkin's U.I.L. opponent. Attention centred on candidate John Saturnus Kelly of the unaffiliated Irish Railway Workers Trade Union. Kelly was elected, as was the sole Finn Fein candidate. *Irish Worker*, 6, 13, 20 January 1912.

19 *Irish Independent*, 15 January 1912.

20 *Irish Worker*, 20, 27 January 1912; *Irish Times*, 14 January 1912.

21 Larkin was removed after court action by former congress secretary E. W. Stewart. Larkin charged that Stewart had been paid to take the action by Murphy and other Dublin employers. The judge congratulated Stewart for bringing the action, 'for discharging a public benefit by coming here and instituting these proceedings'. *Irish Times*, 30 March 1912.

22 *Irish Worker*, 17 February, 22 June 1912.

23 Larkin, *James Larkin*, p. 103.

pendent claimed that 'Mr. Larkin has sustained a defeat which he will find it impossible to get over.'[24]

A group of trade unionists—mainly craft workers and non-socialists—led by E. W. Stewart continuously opposed the Labour Party in the local elections. In November 1912 Stewart published *The history of Larkinism in Ireland* in which he denounced not only Larkin but also his leading supporters. Stewart claimed that Larkinism was attempting to destroy the home rule movement and to foster revolutionary socialism. Stewart's group opposed the Transport Union during the 1913 struggle, and later, in 1916, launched a series of letters in the *Evening Telegraph* condemning the leaders of Dublin labour.[25]

In the elections from January 1913 to January 1915, Labour in Dublin made little progress,[26] although important advances were being made in larger towns, notably in Waterford, Sligo and Wexford.[27]

The difficulties Labour faced in gaining representation on local bodies were expressed by 'Enclan' in the 6 June 1914 issue of the *Irish Worker*:

> In trying to get representation . . . [Labour] has, nine times out of ten, to fight men whose sole claim for election is that they are Home Rulers. [They] choose to look upon the Labour movement as a rebel movement . . . The Labour movement is a rebel movement. It is out to teach insurrection against the tyranny of capitalism. With [home rule] coming the disadvantages which Labour suffers from, will disappear. With the rise of Home Rule comes the inevitable fall of the Home Ruler.

Nonetheless, the revival of Labour representation after 1911 marked the permanent establishment of Labour as a political force in Irish local government—an achievement which encouraged efforts to develop a political presence on the national scene.

Socialist Parties, 1908-1914

Before discussing the formation of the Irish Labour Party, it would be

24 Quoted in *Irish Worker*, 5 October 1912.

25 O'Brien papers, N.L.I. MS 15679; O'Brien, *Forth the banners go*, p. 264.

26 In the June 1912 local elections Lord Mayor Lorcan Sherlock charged that Larkin and the Labour Party were attempting to wreck the Nationalist Party. When a Labour candidate was narrowly elected to fill Larkin's seat the *Irish Independent* called it a 'Pyrrhic victory'; 'One more victory like this and Larkin is undone'. *Irish Independent*, 25, 27 June 1912.

In January 1913 seven Labour nominees went forward in Dublin, but only two were elected. Ibid., 16 January 1913.

The local elections of January 1914, which took place towards the end of the great labour struggle of 1913–14, are treated separately.

Labour polled poorly in the June 1914 poor law elections. *Irish Worker*, 6 June 1914. In January 1915 Labour held but did not increase it representation. The *Irish Worker* declared that Labour's anti-war stand was a political liability at this time. Ibid., 15 January 1915.

27 *Irish Independent*, 16 January 1913; I.T.U.C., *1913 report*, p. 31; *Irish Worker*, 6 June 1914.

helpful to examine socialist activity and its influence on labour during the period. The Irish socialist parties sought to win over the trade union movement to a socialist rather than a reformist philosophy, and they strongly favoured labour political action. There were two schools of socialist thought in Ireland: 'Belfast socialism' held that Irish labour should be part of the growing British industrial and political labour organizations; 'Dublin socialism' believed that Irish labour should develop as an independent unit.

Socialist activity in Dublin was revived in 1904 with the creation of the Socialist Party of Ireland (Cumannacht na h-Eireann) which drew together several small socialist groups, including a remnant of James Connolly's early party. The S.P.I. was propagandist rather than directly political.[28] W. P. Ryan, an original member of the party, reported it made considerable headway among Dublin workers, but it was strongly opposed by the business interests and by the Catholic Church.[29] Following his appointment as party organizer in 1910, Connolly directly attacked 'Belfast socialism', declaring that the Belfast branch of the Independent Labour Party, led by William Walker, desired that the socialist movement in Ireland should 'remain a dues-paying organic part of the British movement or else forfeit its title to be considered a part of the international socialist movement'. Connolly labeled this attitude 'false internationalism'. He claimed that the Socialist Party of Ireland was the only international socialist party in Ireland because it was a 'free conference of free people'.[30]

Connolly carried his attack to Belfast, where he established a branch of the S.P.I., winning over such prominent trade unionists as D. R. Campbell, Thomas Johnson, Joseph Mitchell and Daniel McDevitt.[31] A Cork branch, also set up by Connolly, had twenty-four members. The first national conference of the party was held in Dublin in September 1910; a national executive was set up and a party programme approved.[32]

The struggle between the two socialist positions was carried to the Irish Trade Union Congress. Connolly, having won the post of Belfast secretary of the Transport Union in 1911, was determined to turn the union to the cause of congress-sponsored political activity. Walker agreed with Connolly, but as an exponent of 'Belfast socialism' he opposed the formation of an independent Irish party. At both the 1910

28 C. D. Greaves, *The life and times of James Connolly*, p. 205.

29 Ryan was the editor of two radical newspapers, the *Irish Peasant* (1905–07) and the *Irish Nation* (1907–10). W. P. Ryan, *The pope's green island* (London 1912), pp. 15, 373–74, 276, 314.

30 James Connolly, *Socialism and nationalism*, ed. D. Ryan, pp. 12–14.

31 Other converts were William McMullen, later president of the Transport Union, and Sean MacEntee, later Fianna Fail minister and tanaiste. Greaves, *Connolly*, pp. 134, 201.

32 Francis Sheehy Skeffington was elected president and William O'Brien secretary. Among the members were Fred Ryan, Michael Mallin, R. J. P. Mortished, Peter Macken, Walter Carpenter and P. T. Daly. Greaves, *Connolly*, p. 203.

and 1911 meetings of the congress, Walker was the leading supporter of establishing the link with the British political movement. Following the 1911 meeting—where Walker had narrowly succeeded in defeating a proposal for an independent party—Connolly, who had not been a delegate, challenged Walker to debate the issue of a nationally based party versus one affiliated with British Labour. The debate took place in the pages of *Forward*, a Scottish socialist journal.[33]

In the spring of 1912 Connolly and the S.P.I. called a conference of all socialist parties in the country to establish a unified party. Walker's branch of the Independent Labour Party refused the invitation, but two other Belfast branches were represented, as well as the four branches of the S.P.I.[34] The new party, the Independent Labour Party of Ireland, not only supported a socialist programme and labour political action, it also advocated home rule for Ireland. Support for home rule was argued on a socialist basis—that it would be a step towards ending the division of Irish workers on religious-political issues.[35]

When delay was encountered in launching the new Labour Party approved by the Trade Union Congress in 1912, the political activists in the labour movement turned to the Independent Labour Party of Ireland as a vehicle of expression.[36] This party (which later returned to the name S.P.I.) continued to exist side by side with the congress-sponsored party until late 1921. The efforts of the socialist parties bore fruit when the congress condemned capitalism in 1914 and four years later accepted a socialist philosophy.

THE BIRTH OF THE IRISH LABOUR PARTY

The proponents of an independent Irish Labour Party appeared at the 1911 meeting of the Trade Union Congress in increased numbers. The annual report of the executive indicated the need for a political arm for the labour movement; it said the demands of the congress 'if not utterly ignored, are treated with scant courtesy' by the local bodies. Congress President D. R. Campbell spoke in favour of political action, without committing himself on the issue of affiliation with the British organization.[37]

The supporters of an independent, congress-based Labour Party took the initiative. Thomas Murphy of the Dublin Carpet Planners proposed, and William O'Brien seconded, a resolution instructing the executive 'to form a scheme whereby a properly federated and controlled Labour Party may be maintained in Ireland'. William Walker

33 Connolly, *Socialism made easy*, p. 29; *Forward*, 27 May, 9 June, 1 July 1911.

34 Greaves, *Connolly*, p. 224.

35 Connolly, *Socialism and nationalism*, p. 202.

36 *Irish Worker*, 22 June1912.

37 I.T.U.C., *1911 report*, pp. 16, 13.

immediately countered with the proposal that had been passed by the congress every year, bar one, since 1903: that the congress 'recommends' the trade unions and councils affiliate with the British Labour Party.[38]

The debate on differing proposals centred around Labour 'nationalism' and 'internationalism'. Walker declared that 'there was no reason why they should divorce themselves from their English and Scottish fellow workers' by establishing a 'purely local party'.

James Larkin vigorously attacked this position: 'Let the congress not be humbugged by men who talked about internationalism', he said. 'The Labour Party of the United States, Canada or Australia would not allow any English Labour Party to manage their affairs. Why should they do so in Ireland?' M. J. O'Lehane, Dublin, also was critical of this sort of internationalism; he asked, 'Why didn't they advocate affiliation with the Labour Party in Belgium, Germany or elsewhere? Why were they so enamoured of the Labour Party of England?' Some delegates supported the formation of an independent congress-sponsored party on the basis of specifically *Irish* nationalism. One spoke in opposition to 'merging his nationality with that of any other country'; another urged the congress to 'support a Party that would represent their ideals and not support those who advocated a system of education that Ireland hated'. The adherents of the Irish Parliamentary Party were not vocal at this congress, but O'Lehane charged they would once again join forces with the Belfast internationalists to defeat the independent Labour Party proposals.

By a narrow margin, thirty-two for, twenty-nine against, the congress voted for the Walker position.[39] But this was to be the last victory for 'Belfast internationalism'; at this meeting the supporters of 'new unionism' and a congress-sponsored party gained firm and permanent control of the executive. The careful preparation of William O'Brien was largely responsible for this achievement.[40]

James Connolly, who had not been chosen as a delegate, used the pages of *Forward* to lambaste the Walker group's position: 'The unborn Labour Party of Ireland was strangled in the womb by the hands of the I.L.P.ers'.[41] Another point of view was presented by the *Freeman's Journal*, the staunch supporter of the Irish Parliamentary Party:

38 Ibid., p. 36. My account of the debate and the quotations included are taken from the report, pp. 39–42.

39 Ibid., p. 42. Thomas Johnson, in his first statement to a congress meeting, supported the national party proposal, but wanted the party to be 'federated as closely as possible with the English Labour Party'. Ibid., p. 40.

40 Larkin, *James Larkin*, p. 76. The 1911 meeting saw a shift of power on the executive from Belfast to Dublin. The 1910–11 executive had four members from Belfast, four from Dublin and one from Cork. The 1911–12 executive had six from Dublin and three from Belfast. Although the executive always was to contain members from Belfast, Dublin dominated thereafter.

41 Quoted in William McMullen's pamphlet, *With Connolly in Belfast* (n.p., n.d.), p. 18.

> The necessity for the resolution or the amendment is not apparent. The [Walker] amendment implies an identity of interests which does not exist. Policies and programmes are advanced by the English Labour Party which are abhorrent to the majority of Irish workingmen. . . . The Irish Party has been a Labour Party not only for Ireland, but for Great Britain, and the most effective that the masses could desire. The fact has been admitted by the leaders of Labour of Great Britain.[42]

Undeterred by defeat and criticism, the advocates of a congress-sponsored party continued to campaign for their objective during the next year. They had at their disposal the pages of the newly founded *Irish Worker*, the first successful Labour publication. This weekly newspaper of the Irish Transport Union, under the editorship of Larkin, achieved a huge readership.[43]

But the development that swung the balance in the congress was the introduction and successful progress of the Home Rule Bill in Parliament. It was clear that under home rule a congress-sponsored party would seek representation in the Irish Parliament and would not come into conflict with the Irish Parliamentary Party. The passage of home rule also would negate the arguments of the Belfast 'internationalists' as there would be little advantage in becoming a part of the British Labour Party if there was to be an Irish Parliament. With the demand for a congress-sponsored party growing each year, however, it is very probable that the congress eventually would have set up its own party even if home rule were not imminent. It appears that the proponents of affiliation with the British Labour Party admitted defeat even before the 1912 meeting. Their leading spokesman, William Walker, had taken a job in the recently established labour exchange in Belfast and was no longer active in the labour movement.[44]

As the time for the 1912 meeting drew nearer, the *Daily Herald*, the British Labour newspaper, welcomed Irish home rule because, it said, the grip of the Irish Parliamentary Party on the country would be broken and an Irish Labour Party developed:

> From our point of view, the best thing about the bill is that home rule will bring the Irish Party into a position where it will no longer be able to claim the allegiance of the Irish workingman as a right. The possibility is created for an Irish Labour Party to develop. The present Irish Party . . . are thoroughly reactionary. . . . But the fact that they are a capitalist faction opposed to the workers can never be effectively demonstrated so long as the responsibility for Irish government does not lie on their shoulders. Put them in

42 *Freeman's Journal*, 8 June 1911.

43 W. P. Ryan, *The Irish labour movement* (Dublin 1920), p. 197; Larkin, *James Larkin*, p. 78.

44 McMullen, *With Connolly*, p. 18.

power and they will teach the wage workers of Ireland that the interests of Labour are as much opposed to those of farmers and manufacturers as to those of landlords.[45]

In 1912 the congress tackled the question of political activity once again. James Connolly, making his first appearance as a delegate, presented the resolution that the congress establish its own party. The resolution was vaguely worded, possibly in order to rally the maximum support; it proposed 'that the independent representation of Labour upon all public boards be and is hereby included among the objectives of this Congress', but included a key provision that the unions contribute one shilling per member to cover the cost of setting up political machinery. Connolly argued that since Irish self-government seemed probable, the labour movement should be ready to enter an Irish Parliament 'to represent a definite organised labour opinion' rather than tacking the movement on to a 'political party of their masters'. Because of the delaying powers of the House of Lords, it would take two years for the Home Rule Bill to become law. Both Connolly and James Larkin urged that this period be used to organize and build up the proposed party.[46]

The usual arguments were presented against political action by the congress, but the motion recommending affiliation with the British Labour Party was not put forward. John Murphy, Belfast, a past supporter of this policy, now argued that if the congress set up its own party 'political divergences' would arise; Connolly replied that there were differences of opinion among the workers in Britain and other countries. D. Milner of Dublin declared the proposal raised the issue of 'Socialism versus old Trade Unionism' and to pass the resolution would mean 'a vote of censure' on the former leadership of the congress.[47] However, no move was made to press socialist principles into the congress' programme at this time. A new issue was raised when L. Rimmer, representing the Amalgamated Society of Railway Servants, noted that the Osborne decision forbade unions from contributing funds to political organizations. W. E. Hill of the Railway Clerks Union urged the congress not to be deterred by the decision, which he said would soon be reversed, but to proceed to establish its political machinery in the meantime.[48]

45 Quoted in *Irish Worker*, 20 April 1912.

46 I.T.U.C., *1912 report*, pp. 12–13.

47 Ibid., p. 17.

48 Ibid., p. 14. In December 1909 the House of Lords ruled that trade unions were corporate bodies and could not lawfully do anything outside the purposes stated in the statute under which they were incorporated. Since political activity was not stated to be one of the purposes of unions when they were incorporated, the unions could not spend money for this purpose. The Osborne decision was negated by a new law in 1913 which allowed unions to spend money on political activity provided that members approved of such activity by ballot and that a separate political fund was established. Further, any member of a union could be exempted from the political contribution by signing a form. Irish unions often failed to make these arrangements, spending money for political activities out of general funds. Henry Pelling, *A short history of the Labour Party* (London 1961), pp. 23–24, 28.

Connolly's resolution was carried by a wide margin: forty-nine for, nineteen against and nineteen not recorded; it received a clear majority of the votes of the eighty-seven delegates. The congress also passed several other resolutions relating to political activity: greater representation for urban districts than was proposed in the Home Rule Bill, payment of members of parliament, election expenses and returning officers fees and voting rights based on adult suffrage. Female enfranchisement was supported by succeeding congresses.[49] The Nationalist press editorially ignored the congress's decision to establish a new party.[50]

Immediately after the meeting, the chief proponents of a congress-sponsored party, William O'Brien, Connolly and Thomas Johnson, set to work to get the executive to implement Connolly's resolution. Delay was encountered when Larkin, the chairman, resigned at the first meeting because members of the executive differed from a ruling which he gave as chairman. Larkin refused, for a time, to resume his chairmanship or to take the lead in organizing the new party.[51] Finally, in September 1912, the executive decided to proceed without Larkin and arranged to inaugurate the party at a Dublin meeting. O'Brien asked James Connolly to preside at the meeting, following Larkin's refusal to do so. Connolly declined because, he said, it would appear to the workers that he was being disloyal to Larkin, adding that Larkin 'must rule or he will not work and in the present stage of the labour movement he has us at his mercy'. The meeting was finally held, with O'Brien presiding, and Larkin appeared in the hall to make 'pointless' criticism of the event.[52]

C. D. Greaves says that Connolly suspected that Larkin had become luke-warm concerning the formation of the party. An opponent of Larkin's in the split in the Transport Union in the 1920s holds that Larkin was opposed to a congress-sponsored party because he was a member of the British Independent Labour Party.[53] But Larkin had been one of the strongest advocates of such a party since the entrance of his union into the congress in 1910. However, he was never a member of the Socialist Party of Ireland, or of its successor, the Independent Labour Party of Ireland. All the other leading supporters of a congress-based party—Connolly, O'Brien, Campbell and Johnson—were members of this socialist organization.

49 I.T.U.C., *1912 report*, pp. 19, 51.

50 R. M. Henry, in *The evolution of Sinn Fein* (New York 1920), points out the necessity for the labour movement establishing its own party in that the existing parties—the Unionist Party, the Irish Parliamentary Party and Sinn Fein—had little interest in the cause of the workers; pp. 102–103.

51 Larkin, *James Larkin*, p. 103; Irish Transport and General Workers Union, *The attempt to smash the Irish Transport and General Workers Union*, p. 163.

52 O'Brien, *Forth the banners go*, pp. 47–48; Greaves, *Connolly*, p. 233; Larkin, *James Larkin*, p. 103.

53 Greaves, *Connolly*, p. 232; interview with Frank Robbins, 28 November 1964.

It would appear that Larkin's resignation and the delay in organizing the new party were caused by personality conflicts within the Labour leadership. Larkin was always a difficult man to deal with, and strong differences of opinion existed long before Larkin left for America in 1914. A typical example of Larkin's behaviour occurred when the Labour executive arranged a meeting in Phoenix Park, Dublin, to present the Labour Party to the public. Two platforms were erected from which Connolly and Larkin were to address the crowd, the start of the proceedings to be signaled by a blast from a trumpet. Larkin, impatient as ever, had the trumpet sounded before the agreed time, whereupon Connolly refused to participate.[54] The differences of personality and policy within the Labour leadership were to erupt into an open split following Larkin's return in 1923. But in the years before the war, despite all the difficulties, a united leadership was maintained. Connolly, for one, recognized the vast importance of Larkin as spokesman and symbol of a dynamic labour movement.

Although Larkin eventually resumed the chairmanship of the executive, practically nothing was done to set up the new party until the 1913 meeting of the congress.[55] At that time O'Brien, now chairman of the body, proposed that the executive be given specific instructions concerning the formation of the party, increase its size from nine to twelve members, draft a party constitution, and alter the standing orders of the organization.[56] Larkin, neither on this occasion nor later, did anything to obstruct the formation of the party, and, indeed, took an active part in its propagation.

At the 1913 meeting an attempt to reverse the decision to set up a congress-sponsored party was defeated;[57] not until a decade later was any dissent voiced concerning combining industrial and political activity in one organization. The 1913 congress meeting followed the O'Brien proposals, reaffirming the decision to establish its own party, strengthening the hand of its executive and instructing it to proceed with the writing of a party constitution. Under O'Brien's chairmanship, the 1913–14 executive drew a constitution which limited party membership to affiliated trade unions and councils; groups outside the regular trade union movement, such as socialist and co-operative societies, were excluded for the present.

The proposed constitution and the control and selection of candidates were the two issues that were thrashed out at the 1914 meeting. Delegates from Belfast took the lead in seeking to allow the affiliation of

54 O'Brien, *Forth the banners go*, pp. 36–48; Larkin, *James Larkin*, pp. 319–23; Anne Marreco, *The rebel countess: the life and times of Constance Markievicz* (London 1969), p. 175.

55 The only step taken was to send out a circular urging the affiliated unions and councils to hold meetings to stimulate interest in labour representation.

56 I.T.U.C., *1913 report*, p. 38.

57 No vote is given in the 1913 report but it is assumed that this motion was defeated by a large margin. I.T.U.C., *1913 report*, pp. 31–32, 39–40, 48.

co-operative and socialist organizations with the party. They argued that the new party would be deprived of some strength if such bodies were not allowed affiliation, because not everyone could join a trade union or trades council. Secondly, they felt that the socialist groups would act as a progressive force within the party, an 'advance guard'; if they were kept out they might form their own political party.[58]

Thomas Johnson, one of the authors of the proposed constitution, warned that the congress could be 'swamped' if they allowed co-operative societies to affiliate as this would open the door to the large number of farmers' co-operatives. As for the socialist groups, Johnson declared that their 'true function . . . was propagandist merely—to educate—not to form a political party'. He said the interested non-trade unionist could participate through local Labour parties organized by the trades councils. The congress decided against allowing socialist and co-operative groups to affiliate for the present. Members of affiliated bodies, however, were allowed to continue their membership in these outside groups.[59]

Most of the enthusiasts of the congress-sponsored party belonged to such groups. Johnson said that in the case of the Independent Labour Party of Ireland, 'their propaganda was on our lines'; Connolly pointed out that the socialist organization 'through their insistent and consistent propaganda had been largely responsible for the change in the Irish Trade Union Congress. They must not be debarred from going on with such activity'.[60] The difficulties of combining the industrial and political activities of the labour movement in one organization were becoming apparent. If all 'progressive' forces were allowed inside such organization, the trade unions feared that control over industrial questions might pass into the hands of non-trade unionists. If non-trade union bodies were kept out, the political side would lose the help of many intellectuals, reform-minded individuals and campaign workers.

The British labour movement had established separate but connecting organizations for political and industrial activity;[61] in Ireland, the two functions were combined. Connolly declared that this would keep out 'the professional politician who was doing as much harm as good' in the British movement; by confining party membership to trade unionists 'the Irish Labour members would be responsible to the workers just as their leaders in the industrial fight were responsible'.[62] George Barnes, a British Labour leader, congratulated the

58 Statements of E. Mercer and D. Gordon, Belfast. I.T.U.C., *1914 report*, pp. 44, 45.

59 Ibid., pp. 45, 49–50.

60 Ibid., pp. 91–92.

61 Both the Labour Representation League (1869) and the Labour Electoral Association (1866) were sponsored by but separate from the Trade Union Congress. The Labour Representation Committee (1900) was established by both the congress and the various socialist bodies. G. D. H. Cole, *British working class politics, 1832–1914* (London 1941), pp. 151, 101–104, 113–14.

62 *Irish Worker*, 6, 20 June 1914.

Irish congress in 1914 for combining the two sides in one organization, thus 'avoiding some of the evils into which we have fallen . . . the multiplication of committees, sub-committees and joint committees that eat up the time and resources of the British Labour movement'.

In Britain the party did not limit the nominees of the Labour Representation Committee, set up in 1900, to working-class candidates—nominees were simply required to favour 'working class opinion being represented . . . by men sympathetic with the aims and the demands of the Labour movement'. According to Cole, 'the Socialists and the "Lib-Labs" were, in fact, united upon this particular issue: neither group wanted, at this stage, a purely working class movement'.[63] The Irish movement, on the other hand, voted for strict controls over Labour candidates. They had to be approved by the congress executive, and pledged to support the constitution and pronouncements of the congress. Candidates were to remain members of their unions if elected to office and were barred from supporting other parties.[64] The numerous precautions and controls put into the constitution at this time stem from the unhappy days at the turn of the century when many labour representatives failed to remain faithful to the labour organizations which first sponsored them. The political side of the labour movement had also been plagued by 'friends of labour' and unofficial labour candidates who proved to be unreliable advocates of the worker's interests.

In 1914 the congress for the first time supported a resolution aiming at the reconstruction of society: 'the Congress urges that labour unrest can only be ended by the abolition of the capitalist system of wealth production with its inherent injustice and poverty.' But palliative measures were still advocated:

> Among first steps to that end [the congress] demands legislation to secure to every person a national minimum of civilized life by measures providing for a legislative minimum wage in agriculture and all industries, the reduction of hours of labour to a maximum of forty-eight, the guarantee of a national minimum of child nurture, the prevention of unemployment, the building of healthy homes for all, and the abolition of the Poor Law.

Other resolutions called for the nationalization of Irish railways, improvements in the workmen's compensation law, votes for women, and the extension of the national health act to Ireland.[65]

The congress did not state how it believed the capitalist system would be abolished, but indicated a syndicalist philosophy in its advocacy of industrial unionism.[66] The executive was instructed to

63 Cole, *British working class politics*, p. 156.

64 I.T.U.C. and L.P., *1914 report*, pp. 49–91.

65 Ibid., pp. 95, 74–75, 78–80.

66 Connolly was a strong supporter of syndicalism, and Larkin, at the very least, was a believer in militant industrial unionism. Connolly, *Socialism made easy*, pp. 16–31; Larkin, *James Larkin*, pp. 97–98.

attempt to amalgamate the unions in each industry, but little success was achieved due to the resistance of the leadership of the smaller unions.

Though critical of the capitalist system in 1914, the congress did not formally adopt a socialist position until 1918. But the leadership of the movement was in the hands of socialists, the most prominent being Larkin, who was taken to task by the *Irish Independent* when he clashed with the anti-socialist position of Cardinal Logue:

> Mr. Larkin, at the Irish Trades Congress, preached his doctrine of rank Socialism by advocating a Co-operative Commonwealth. In contemplation of Home Rule, the Irish trade unionists are about to form a Labour Party. This is, of course, quite a proper project, but that Party will make a great mistake if it tries to force upon this country Mr. Larkin's chimerical policy. There are a variety of problems affecting labour to which the Irish Parliament must turn attention and it would be well that when dealing with these it should have the assistance of a Labour Party. But once that Labour Party goes beyond the bounds of social reforms it will not find much support among the public. Of course, the employers must, as Cardinal Logue said at Clongowes, supply the capital, but by degrees if the workmen were let in and got a small share in the concern it would give them an interest in their work and there would be far less danger of strikes. Social reforms was, he said, what they wanted. Socialism, he asserted, was impractical and could never be real. Again going back to his 'gospel of discontent' Mr. Larkin accuses Cardinal Logue of not knowing the elements of social economy. With a disregard of facts and of principles, he insists that the workers shall spoil a good cause by adopting a programme of Socialism pure and simple.[67]

In recognition of its new political role, the Irish Trade Union Congress added 'and Labour Party' to its name at this time.[68] This, then, was the structure and programme of the Irish Labour political movement as it looked forward to home rule. The Home Rule Bill was expected to be passed into law within months of the 1914 meeting, and elections seemed imminent.

RELATIONS WITH BRITISH LABOUR

The relationship between the Irish and British labour movements, never very warm, had begun to deteriorate following the successful establishment of 'new unionism' in Ireland: Larkin had ousted a

67 *Irish Independent*, 2 June 1914.

68 Answering one delegate who wanted to drop the title 'Trade Union Congress', Connolly warned that if this was done a secessionist group would adopt the title; further, 'There was a danger of warning off people who were not prepared to accept political action. . . . Let them always keep a place for those who were not as far advanced as themselves, but whose interests would bring them into line.' I.T.U.C. and L.P., *1914 report*, p. 43.

British-based union when he began the Transport Union. The executive of the Irish congress complained that the British Labour Party ignored the congress's resolutions, preferring to follow the recommendations of the Irish Parliamentary Party on Irish matters.

In the years 1912–14 three matters were at issue between the Irish congress and the British Labour Party—the relationship between the new Irish Labour Party and the British party, the composition of the Home Rule Bill and the exclusion of Ireland from British social legislation. In all three cases the Irish executive held they had not been treated fairly by the British party. In 1912 William O'Brien charged that every resolution of the Irish congress 'had been treated with contempt' by the British party. The next year Thomas Johnson declared that a congress deputation had met with 'disrespect' from George Barnes. The Irish representatives, led by Larkin, were refused a hearing at the 1913 British party conference.[69]

In 1913 both the British Labour Party conference and the Irish congress instructed their executives to conduct negotiations for a better understanding between the two movements. Two meetings were held in 1913 and one in 1914, but they only resulted in worsening relations. The Irish representatives proposed to establish a separate and independent party, 'but in all matters concerning the workers of the United Kingdom as a whole they would co-operate with the [British] Labour Party.' They requested that the political contributions of Irish members of amalgamated unions be turned over to the Irish congress. Each member was asked to make an annual contribution of one shilling. As there were several thousand Irishmen in amalgamated unions, this would amount to a considerable amount of money. The British representatives refused because, as Arthur Henderson said, the constitution of the Irish Labour Party, unlike the British, did not allow for affiliation of socialist and co-operative bodies; the differences in the constitutions made the objectives of the two parties different. The Irish delegates explained that initially the new party would only be open to trade unionists because of the different circumstances in Ireland and that other groups might be offered affiliation once the party had developed.[70]

The Irish congress was offered the alternative of becoming affiliated with the British party in the same way as the new Scottish Labour Party was. As the Scottish party was controlled and financed by the British party, this offer was declined. There the matter was left. J. D. Clarkson comments: 'The Irish Labour Party was left to shift for itself, apparently in the confident expectation that poverty would sooner or later drive it to seek accommodation with the English Party in a more amenable spirit.'[71]

69 I.T.U.C., *1912 report*, p. 18; *1913 report*, p. 34; *Freeman's Journal*, 14 May 1913.

70 I.T.U.C. and L.P., *1914 report*, pp. 7–9.

71 Ibid., pp. 9–10, 39; J. D. Clarkson, *Labour and nationalism in Ireland*, p. 408.

Efforts to influence the British Labour Party on matters of legislation also failed. The Irish congress sought greater representation for urban areas in the Home Rule Bill, the extension to Ireland of social legislation and a united Ireland under home rule.[72]

The indifferent attitude of British Labour towards the Irish movement can best be explained in practical political terms. Irish Labour had no members in Parliament; the British Labour Party and the Irish Parliamentary Party were allies—British Labour voted for home rule, while the Irish members voted for social and economic legislation supported by the British party, although they often prevented the inclusion of Ireland in such measures.[73] The estrangement between the two labour movements was aggravated during the Dublin strike of 1913 when Larkin and other Irish Labour leaders were bitterly critical of the alleged inaction of the leadership of the British movement.[74]

The Irish congress also sent delegations to the British government and to the Irish Parliamentary Party to seek greater urban representation in the Home Rule Bill and the inclusion of Ireland in social legislation. These efforts were also without result.[75] The leadership of Irish Labour for long had claimed that the Irish Parliamentary Party represented only the interests of the bourgeoise of the towns and the farming class, while it was hostile to the cause of the workers. Larkin declared that the Parliamentary Party did not seek to increase urban representation in the Home Rule Bill since it 'did not want to give the working class representation because they knew it would be to their disadvantage'.[76]

THE ADVENT OF PARTITION

During the period under consideration, the great political issue for Ireland was home rule, a policy adopted by the Asquith government in 1910 and implemented by subsequent legislation. Although all the Irish Labour leaders favoured home rule, the congress avoided commitment on this issue in order to prevent a split within the movement.[77] The anticipated coming of home rule and, with it, the creation of an Irish parliament, allowed such Belfast leaders as Johnson and Campbell to support the formation of an Irish-based, congress-sponsored political

72 I.T.U.C. and L.P., *1914 report*, p. 12.

73 See Connolly's remarks, ibid., p. 39.

74 See Chapter 2, below.

75 Interviews took place with Birrell, the chief secretary for Ireland, Redmond and Devlin. I.T.U.C. and L.P., *1914 report*, pp. 14–15, 16–17.

76 *Freeman's Journal*, 29 May 1912. Only 34 of 164 seats in the home rule parliament would have been in urban areas. Larkin presented a plan to allow 51 seats. I.T.U.C. and L.P., *1914 report*, pp. 1–2, 27–30. See also *Irish Worker*, 20 July 1914.

77 Birrell reminded the Labour delegation that the congress had not voted support for the bill. I.T.U.C. and L.P., *1914 report*, p. 16. Cathal O'Shannon pointed out (interview, 1 June 1964) that northern delegates never voiced opposition to home rule and that no Unionist ever sat on the congress executive.

party. When the Home Rule Bill was about to pass into law, the congress-party executive issued a guarded statement:

> Whilst the Bill is not altogether satisfactory to us, we must be prepared to take advantage of it and secure representation for our class in the new Parliament.
>
> In any Parliament to be elected in Ireland Labour must be represented as a separate and independent entity, having no connection with any other Party.[78]

In the spring of 1914 the Irish Parliamentary Party announced it had accepted the compromise worked out by the Liberal government with the Conservative Party and its Ulster Unionist allies, to allow certain Ulster counties to opt out of the provisions of the Home Rule Bill for six years. The Parliamentary Party set to work to win the support of Irish public opinion for this compromise, claiming that the exclusion of most of Ulster would have to be accepted if the Home Rule Bill was to become law.

The executive of the Irish Trade Union Congress immediately passed a resolution condemning the exclusion of any part of Ulster. It declared that partition 'will intensify the divisions at present existing and destroy all our hopes of uniting the workers of Ulster with those of Munster, Leinster and Connaught on the basis of their economic interest'. If Ulster were excluded, the political hopes of Irish Labour would suffer a major set-back as Belfast would contribute fourteen seats out of a total of thirty-four urban seats in an all-Ireland parliament.[79] The congress executive appealed to the Asquith government, sending a delegation to the chief secretary for Ireland, Augustine Birrell, who told the group that:

> He was haunted by the spectre called up in Ulster, and he had to try to prevent bloodshed if it were possible. When the workers realized that the exclusion was only of a tentative character, he did not believe that the movement to whom the Deputation referred as loving Ireland would plunge their country into Civil War for the sake of a few years covered by the proposal.[80]

Rebuffed by the government, the Labour delegation turned to the Irish Parliamentary Party. John Redmond told them he had accepted the exclusion of most of Ulster because 'he had to make the best provision he could in the light of the circumstances which he would not discuss, but which were ever present in the negotiations'. Thomas Johnson warned Redmond that in 'allaying the hostility of the Convenanters', the Parliamentary Party failed to realize the probability of the opposition of the 'Physical Force Party' to exclusion.[81]

78 *Irish Worker*, 8 August 1914.

79 *Irish Worker*, 21, 28 March 1914.

80 I.T.U.C. and L.P., *1914 report*, p. 16.

81 Ibid., pp. 15, 14. D. R. Campbell and P. T. Daly were the other members of the delegation.

The congress executive urged the British Labour Party to oppose the exclusion amendment and, if necessary, vote against the entire Home Rule Bill in order to prevent partition;[82] but the British party, perhaps sorely tested by the barrage of appeals and requests from the Irish movement, followed the lead of the Irish Parliamentary Party in supporting the exclusion of most of Ulster. George Barnes said the non-support of the Irish Labour position was political: 'the Nationalists of Ireland have sent men to Parliament and the Labour men have not'.[83] James Connolly replied that 'the love embraces which take place between the Parliamentary Labour Party and our deadliest enemies—the home rule party—will not help on a better understanding between the militant proletariat of the two islands'.[84]

In 'dismay and anger' concerning the progressive advance of partition, the congress executive issued a manifesto calling for a national labour demonstration in O'Connell Street, Dublin in April 1914. The meeting was declared an illegal assembly by the police but was allowed to proceed. Shortly afterwards all seven speakers at the meeting, including the presidents of the Belfast, Sligo, Cork and Dublin Trades Councils, were fined for obstructing a throughfare.[85]

A significant amount of opposition to the exclusion of most of Ulster was mustered by the Labour forces in Belfast, where Connolly led the anti-partition effort. Within days of the announcement of the compromise agreement, Connolly's branch of the Independent Labour Party of Ireland organized a protest meeting. Later, in the same hall where the leaders of the Irish Parliamentary Party had won support for the policy of 'temporary' exclusion, Connolly held another anti-partition meeting.[86] He also contributed a stream of articles warning Belfast workers that exclusion from an Irish Parliament would not only cut them off from Ireland, but would leave them still regarded by Britain as aliens.[87] An anti-partition manifesto distributed outside Belfast chapel doors declared: 'The United Irish League and the Ancient Order of Hibernians (Board of Erin) are passing resolutions in other parts of the country approving of the exclusion whilst you who will suffer by this dastardly proposal are never even consulted.'[88]

The mighty efforts of Connolly and the labour movement in Belfast were negated when sectarian strife broke out in the city. Connolly blamed Joseph Devlin, the Belfast Nationalist leader for making a solely nationalist appeal, rather than basing his politics on socio-economic

82 *Irish Worker*, 21, 28 March 1914.

83 I.T.U.C. and L.P., *1914 report*, p. 39.

84 Quoted in Greaves, *Connolly*, p. 277.

85 *Irish Worker*, 28 March, 11 April 1914; O'Brien, *Forth the banners go*, pp. 102–109.

86 Although the newspapers refused advertisements for the latter rally, the hall was filled. Greaves, *Connolly*, p. 276.

87 *Irish Worker*, 4 April 1914. See also issue of 14 March 1914.

88 Quoted in Greaves, *Connolly*, p. 276.

issues: 'Were it not for the existence of the Board of Erin', of the Ancient Order of Hibernians, which functioned as an auxiliary to the Irish Parliamentary Party, 'the Orange Society would have long since ceased to exist. To Brother Devlin and not to Brother Carson is mainly due the progress of the Covenanter Movement in Ulster.'[89] Connolly declared that this emphasis on nationalism had left the workers easy prey to sectarian appeals. But, in fact, the northern branch of Connolly's socialist party had divided on the issue of home rule.

When the Trade Union Congress met in June 1914, it voted almost unanimously against the exclusion of most of Ulster from the Home Rule Bill; the vote was eighty-four for, only two against, and eight delegates unrecorded.[90] One Belfast delegate, R. Drummond, declared that 'exclusion was one of the cleverest moves to destroy the chances of an Irish Labour Party in the first Home Rule Parliament. . . . The strongest and richest unions were in the North.'[91] The peril of partition was clear to the labour movement.

The new unionism and political activism that took hold of Irish labour from 1909 has been credited with being a contributing factor in the creation of partition. In his stimulating study, *Irish nationalism and British democracy*, Emil Strauss declares that the Ulster business interests did not fear Redmond or Devlin, who could only appeal to northern nationalists, but were concerned about the possibility that socialism and labour political action could unite Protestant and Catholic workers. Strauss implies that this was an important consideration in the decision of Unionist businessmen to oppose home rule. It is certainly true that partition created a barrier against any non-sectarian, united labour programme. But, as Strauss acknowledges, during the previous years the efforts of Connolly and Larkin to achieve this had borne little fruit:

> The failure of the new unionism, and, still more, of Irish socialism to conquer Ulster and to detach the workers of Belfast and Derry from the Unionist leadingstrings, had a critical influence on the Irish labour movement, and on Irish history as a whole.[92]

A. P. Ryan makes the unlikely suggestion that one of the factors influencing Asquith's decision to exclude the six counties from home rule was the success of Larkin in rousing the unskilled workers of Dublin and the violent events in 1913.[93]

89 *Irish Worker*, 7 March 1914. See also D. D. Sheehan, *Ireland since Parnell*, p. 269.

90 I.T.U.C. and L.P., *1914 report*, p. 72; *Dublin Evening Mail*, 2 June 1914. The resolution must have received strong support from the northern/British group: there were seventeen delegates from Belfast, three from Derry and four from Britain.

91 I.T.U.C. and L.P., *1914 report*, p. 72.

92 Emil Strauss, *Irish nationalism and British democracy*, pp. 228, 235.

93 A. P. Ryan, *Mutiny at the Curragh* (London 1956), pp. 82, 84.

The home rule argument ended with most of Ulster being excluded from the provisions of the bill. But the entire dispute was overtaken by events in Europe in the summer of 1914. With the outbreak of World War I, the Home Rule Bill, including partition, was hurriedly brought to final passage and then suspended from operation until the end of the war. With this, the efforts to develop a congress-sponsored Labour Party appeared to come to naught.

The party did not enter a general election until eight years later—in 1922. Only once—in 1915—did it contest a by-election. The congress was not to meet again for two years; the 1915 meeting was cancelled to avoid division on the issue of support for the British war effort. By the time of the next meeting the continuation of the European war and the Easter Rising had irreparably changed the political situation in Ireland. And the two great leaders of Irish Labour were gone; Connolly was dead and Larkin was in America and destined not to return until 1923.

2

The Climax of Industrial Unionism and Labour and Sinn Fein before the War

The pre-war years in Ireland were the years in which the new Irish Labour Party was attempting to find its political role. But these years also encompassed one of the greatest industrial struggles in Ireland's history—the Dublin lock-out of 1913—and saw the development of a form of nationalism that was to lead labour into a multiplicity of problems.

THE 1913 DUBLIN INDUSTRIAL STRUGGLE

In response to the 'new unionism' of Larkin and the Transport Union, the Dublin Employers Association was formed in 1911 'to meet combination with combination'. The leader of this body was William Martin Murphy, owner of both the city's tramway company and the *Irish Independent*, Ireland's largest newspaper.

By the summer of 1913 the Transport Union had succeeded in organizing a majority of the unskilled workers in Dublin. At that time the employers association demanded that their workers sign a statement that they would not join or retain membership in Larkin's union. Many workers refused and went on strike. Thereupon a large number of employers closed their businesses, locking out more workers. Because of the employers' initial move and their subsequent disemployment of other employees, the struggle that ensued would more properly be called a lock-out rather than a strike. About twenty thousand workers and over three hundred employers were involved.[1]

The lock-out lasted from August 1913 until the early months of 1914. At no time did the leadership of the Irish Parliamentary Party attempt to bring about a settlement of this tragic battle of wills. R. M. Henry says the party was in an extremely delicate position in the years 1912–14: 'On Socialism the Church could not be expected to smile (and did not smile) and its attitude determined that of the Irish Parliamentary Party'; at the same time the party dared not offend the British Labour Party whose votes were necessary for home rule.[2] The Dublin employers had declared that their battle was against 'Socialism', so the party that claimed to be 'Leaders of the Irish Nation' did not want to get involved. Only one nationalist member of parliament, Thomas Kettle, made a serious attempt to bring about a compromise settlement, and his efforts failed.[3] In his biography of John Dillon, F. S. L. Lyons

1 Estimate of William O'Brien, secretary of the strike committee; *Liberty*, January 1954. C. D. Greaves contends that the employers attacked the Transport Union in 1913 to ensure that they and not Labour would be in a position of power when home rule arrived, (*The life and times of James Connolly*, pp. 246, 261). But surely the clash was bound to occur, given the makeup of the two sides, whether home rule was in the offing or not.

2 R. M. Henry, *The evolution of Sinn Féin*, p. 102.

3 See article by Kettle in *Irish Review*, November 1913; also B. Mac Giolla Choille, *Intellegence notes, 1913–16* (Dublin, 1966), pp. 49–50.

points out Dillon's intense dislike of Irish socialism and the movement led by Larkin; Dillon's enmity towards Larkin 'was instinctive and went deeper, perhaps, than he wanted to admit even to himself'.[4] Dillon was a property owner, as were most of the members of the Irish Parliamentary Party, and in a class struggle he doubtlessly would be found on the side of the men of property.

Supporting the position of the employers were the Irish Catholic hierarchy, the British administration in Ireland and the press. Archbishop Walsh of Dublin criticized the workers' cause; the police attacked the workers and made numerous arrests; the daily press was united in condemning the 'strikers' as 'Socialists' and destroyers of society. D. P. Moran's weekly, the *Leader*, a staunch champion of the Catholic Church and capitalist industrial development in Ireland, had frequently denounced socialism, syndicalism and the co-operative movement. Once the industrial conflict began, Moran declared that the issue was not the admittedly bad standard of living of masses of the workers, but the use of the sympathetic strike, which would result in class war and the breakdown of industry. In November 1913 the *Leader* warned: 'The leaders in Liberty Hall have been inoculating the people for the last few years with a set of new ideas which in their aggregate amount to a new religion.'[5] The Larkinites also had to contend with two new weeklies, the *Toiler* and the *Liberator and Irish Trade Unionist*, both of which claimed to uphold the interests of the workers but condemned Larkin and his dangerous, alien ideas. It would seem to be more than a coincidence that two such publications should appear at the beginning of the struggle. The *Irish Worker* summed up the situation:

> It would really seem as if the Priest, the Press and the Police in Dublin had combined to aid the life-crushing, blood-squeezing, sweating employers of this city in forcing upon a section of the citizens conditions that are degrading and damning.[6]

The workers received unexpected support when the leaders of Dublin's intelligentsia and the advanced nationalists rallied to their cause. Almost every prominent name in Irish arts and letters was to be found on the labour side: George Russell (AE), William Butler Yeats, Maud Gonne, Paidraic Colum, James Stephens, Seamus O'Sullivan, William Orpen, Susan Mitchell and, in London, George Bernard Shaw. In various articles they condemned the attitude of the employers as cruel and selfish; Russell was the most active of all, his best effort being the widely published open letter to the 'Master of

4 F. S. L. Lyons, *John Dillon, a biography*, pp. 335–36.

5 *Leader*, 19 and 26 Oct. 1912; 13 and 27 Sept., 15 Nov. 1913. Liberty Hall was the trade union headquarters.

6 *Irish Worker*, 27 Sept. 1913. For the position of the church, see Emmet Larkin, 'Socialism and Catholicism', *Church History*, XXXIII (Dec. 1964).

Dublin'.[7] Commenting on their assistance, Connolly declared that nationalism had previously absorbed the attention of this group, just as it had hindered the development of class consciousness among the workers, but 'the 1913 strike brought intellectuals and workers together, as is common in other European countries.'[8]

Most of the advanced nationalists—or those who were to become so—were also aligned against the employers. The seven signatories of the 1916 proclamation, Patrick Pearse, Joseph Plunkett, Thomas MacDonagh, Eamonn Ceannt, Sean McDermott, Thomas Clarke and, of course, Connolly, together with The O'Rahilly, sympathized with the workers. The Irish Republican Brotherhood monthly, *Irish Freedom*, to which Pearse, McDermott and Plunkett were frequent contributors, lent support to the workers' position, as did Plunkett's more literary *Irish Review*.[9] But the I.R.B., as an organization, did not become involved, nor did the Sinn Fein leader, Arthur Griffith, who criticized the workers and their leadership.[10]

Curiously, the Irish Trade Union Congress played no part in the struggle, even though its executive was dominated by Dublin men, all of whom are actively engaged in the fight. Why was it not called upon to organize sympathetic strikes? If this was not considered to be practical, why did it not issue a statement of support for the workers? Surely such a statement would not have divided Irish trade unionists. Perhaps it was because the congress was considered to be little more than a platform on which workers of the north and south could meet once a year. (One nationalist opponent of Labour, James Gallagher, later lord mayor of Dublin, declared, 'The Irish Trades Congress haven't enough influence to turn a herring on a gridiron!')[11] It must also be remembered that strong trade union organizations did not develop outside Dublin and Belfast until after 1916; in 1913 the power of the movement was centred in these two cities. At the 1914 congress meeting, Larkin and the Dublin workers were treated to high praise, but by then the fight was over.

Like the Irish Trade Union Congress, the British T.U.C. took no official stand on the events in Dublin. Nonetheless, the workers were supported by many labour leaders and unions in Britain. Larkin and others made frequent speaking appearances from British platforms, and some sympathetic—but unofficial—strikes took place. A voluntary fund was established to aid the Dublin workers.

7 These articles were published in the *Irish Worker*, the *Irish Homestead* and elsewhere in 1913, and are collected in Donal Nevin, ed., *James Larkin and the Dublin lock-out* (Dublin 1964). See also Alan Denson, ed., *Letters from AE* (London 1961), pp. 85–96.

8 James Connolly, *The reconquest of Ireland* (Dublin 1917), p. 329.

9 Nevin, *Larkin and the Dublin lock-out*.

10 R. M. Fox, *Green banners* (London 1938), pp. 124, 126; J. D. Clarkson, *Labour and nationalism in Ireland*, p. 272. The young Sean O'Casey urged the I.R.B. to take the workers' part: see letter of Eamon Martin in *Evening Press*, 10 Feb. 1966.

11 William O'Brien papers, National Library of Ireland, MS 13913(2).

The lock-out attracted attention outside Ireland and England. The American labour agitator, William Haywood, came from Paris to England and Dublin to speak on Larkin's behalf. The French Confederation of Labour sent a token contribution to display their solidarity with the strikers. And the Russian revolutionary exile, V. I. Lenin, believed that the upheaval would have a lasting effect on Irish politics:

> The Dublin events mark a turning point in the history of the labour movement and of socialism in Ireland. Murphy has threatened to destroy the Irish trade unions. He has succeeded only in destroying the last remnants of the influence of the Irish nationalist bourgeoisie over the Irish proletariat . . . [footnote:] The Irish nationalists are already expressing the fear that Larkin will organize an independent Irish workers' party, which will have to be reckoned with in the first Irish national parliament.[12]

The leaders of Dublin Labour twice made use of elections as aids during the industrial struggle. In the first instance they were successful. In September 1913, the government, in full co-operation with the employers, arrested James Larkin for, in Larkin's words, attacking the Empire and the divine right of kings, and for declaring that the employers lived off profits and rent; the charge was sedition. Assuming the leadership during Larkin's absence, Connolly called upon the workers in three English constituencies where by-elections were pending to vote against the government candidates in protest against the imprisonment of Larkin, in particular, and the behaviour of the government and Dublin employers in general. A manifesto from the Dublin workers declared 'locked-out Nationalists workers of Dublin appeal to British workers to vote against Liberal jailors of Larkin and murderers of Byrne and Nolan'. The president of the Dublin Trades Councils, William Partridge, was sent to England to aid in the campaign.[13] The Irish Parliamentary Party was caught in the middle of this manoeuvre as it was supporting the government candidates. When the Liberals were defeated in two of the by-elections and had their majority slashed in the third, the prestige of the Parliamentary Party plunged.[14]

The defeat of the government in the by-elections, combined with sympathetic strikes conducted in Britain—also induced by the Connolly manifesto—achieved the release of Larkin. The Liberal government was in an exposed position. In the second election in 1910 it had

12 *Severana Pravda*, 29 August 1913, quoted in Lenin, *Collected works* (Moscow 1964), XIX, 335.

13 Connolly, along with Johnson and Campbell, had come from Belfast to support the strike. Byrne and Nolan were killed by the police during a baton charge on O'Connell Street. The text of the manifesto is found in Greaves, *Connolly*, p. 260. See also *Irish Worker*, 1 Nov. 1913, and Fox, *Green banners*, p. 123.

14 The by-elections were in Keighley, Reading and Linlithgar. Greaves, *Connolly*, p. 261.

only won as many seats as had the Conservative Party and had taken office with the support of the Irish Parliamentary Party and the Labour Party. Since that time the liberals had lost several by-elections and held less seats than the Conservatives. Lloyd George declared that the government had suffered reverses in the by-elections at the time of the Dublin conflict for various reasons, 'the most prominent of which is Jim Larkin'.[15]

The Labour leadership hoped to use the January 1914 municipal elections as a public vote of solidarity with the strikers. The Dublin Labour Party, at first proposing to run candidates in all wards, finally nominated eleven, the largest number it had ever put forward. One of the candidates, Walter Carpenter, stood as a socialist as well as a Labour nominee. The party had two allies in Laurence O'Neill (later Lord Mayor) and Dr McWalter, both members of the corporation.[16] Labour's opponents were the nominees of the local organization of the Irish Parliamentary Party—the United Irish League—and other candidates standing as 'Nationalists'. The Labour threat was considered so serious that some nationalist candidates withdrew in order not to split the vote; one such candidate urged 'the Nationalist and Catholic electors to vote' for the remaining nationalist 'and thus put down Socialism in the ward'.[17]

As in past elections, the Labour Party did not preach socialism in the campaign, but instead pointed to the social and economic conditions prevailing in the city. It also urged the voters to support the cause of the strikers by voting Labour. The *Irish Worker* exhorted:

> Tho' we are in the throes of a desperate industrial battle we feel compelled to call upon you to prove your faith in the Cause. The Dublin Labour Party, a Working Class Party . . . believe that the hour is approaching to strike a deadly blow at the corruption prevailing in the city.

The party programme called for increased corporation powers to build new housing, sanitary and housing reforms, health visitors and medical inspection of school children.[18]

William Martin Murphy's *Irish Independent* lent its full support to attacks on the Labour candidates. Referring to the *Irish Worker*, it declared that the Labour nominees were 'recommended by the English official Socialist organ'. Long editorials condemned the 'Larkinites': 'the Liberty Hall contigent and their sympathisers are out for a whole-sale raid upon the rates.' Labour representation itself was not evil as long as it was undertaken

15 *Irish Worker*, 1 Nov. 1913; Arnold Wright, *Disturbed Dublin* (London 1914), p. 233.

16 *Irish Independent*, 7 and 8 January 1914.

17 Ibid., 13 January 1914.

18 *Irish Worker*, 27 December 1913.

> as it was years ago, by men who had some sense of their responsibilities not only to their class but to the community of which they were a part. Mr. Larkin's fraternity recognizes no duty to the city or to the country. The Transport Union's policy is one of organized revolt against society, of pure destructiveness. Constructive programme it has none.[19]

The 'Nationalist' candidates charged that the Labour Party was anti-Catholic, anti-home rule and stood for 'socialistic-syndicalism'. Lord Mayor Lorcan Sherlock warned:

> Socialism was gradually making its way into Dublin. There was a growing feeling to disrespect even religious institutions. Clever Socialists were prostituting the labour movement and dragging it along the road to perdition. (cheers) ... Flouting the Archbishop's warning, insulting the priests, deporting the children, attacking the nuns, indifference to whether there were thirty-nine gods or one; these were the measures by which men sought to forward the workers' interests. (shame!)[20]

Alfred Byrne, later a long-time lord mayor, quoted someone who said Larkin had favoured secular education at a Belfast Trades Council meeting nine years before; the 'Larkinites' proceeded to break up Byrne's meeting. Pamphlets were distributed outside church doors, purporting to be issued by the 'American Labour Party', parodying the Christian catechisms; Larkin called them 'a foul and vicious libel'. He declared that he intended to ask the clergy if any labour leader in Dublin ever said anything that was 'contrary to Christian teaching or human feeling.'[21]

Arthur Griffith in *Sinn Fein* did not directly oppose the Labour candidates in the election; he told the voters to make up their own minds. But he did have critical comments about some Labour nominees; one was 'a disciple of the Divine Missioner from England', another a 'Syndicalist', a third an 'Englishman'. In February 1914 Griffith wrote, 'Employers and employed we shall have always with us and Socialist humbug too until it is recognized that every man who is not a wastrel or a criminal is entitled to labour and live decently in his own country.' Warning the workers of 'the howlings of demogogy', he declared that they were entitled to a 'subsistence' living.[22]

The Labour Party carried on a vigorous campaign, complete with open-air meetings, demonstrations and parades led by bands and the Citizen Army. But the outcome of the election was a defeat for the party and the hopes of the strikers. The popular vote in those wards

19 *Irish Independent*, 7 and 13 January 1914.

20 *Irish Times*, 15 January 1914. For Labour reaction to Sherlock's statement see *Irish Worker*, 31 January 1914.

21 *Irish Independent*, 13 January 1914.

22 *Sinn Fein*, 10 January, 7 and 28 February 1914.

contested by Labour was fairly close: the combined nationalist vote was 15,854, Labour and its allies received 12,547, and nationalist-labour candidates, not endorsed by the Labour Party, polled 1,649 votes. Almost all other wards in the city were carried by the United Irish League and the nationalists. Although the results showed a rise in the Labour vote over past returns, only two of the eleven Labour nominees, along with their two allies, were elected.[23] The *Irish Worker* pointed out that if proportional representation had been used there would have been six Labour candidates returned instead of two,[24] but there was no concealing the fact that the Labour Party had been rejected by a majority of the voters in the wards contested. Further, the party even lost seats it had formerly held. Labour had not made the advances it had hoped for; the results were not the 'dazzling display' that Connolly and Larkin hoped would turn the tide in the industrial struggle.

The Dublin press interpreted Labour's set-back as a further weakening of the party's industrial effort. Archbishop Walsh saw the results as a victory 'over a combination of influences which . . . have done no little harm in blunting, if not deadening, the moral and religious sense of not a few among the working population of our city'.[25]

Within days after the election Larkin advised some of the workers to return to their jobs. The *Irish Times* commented, 'The funds are said to be running out. Public opinion, as reflected in the municipal election, has pronounced against the strike.'[26]

The local elections of January 1914 also found Labour candidates seeking office in Cork, Wexford, Sligo and Castlebar. In these cities local affairs, rather than the situation in Dublin, were of prime interest. But here too the Labour candidates generally suffered defeat. The party's losses in Cork were laid to the 'jobbery' indulged in by the Labour representatives in the corporation.[27] The Wexford candidates suffered from the political reaction to the labour dispute of the previous year. One successful nationalist candidate pointed out that 'the workers of the town who endured six months' privation because of their trust in the promises of Mr Larkin's deputy [P. T. Daly] learned wisdom by bitter experience.' Only in Sligo did Labour score a significant success when a Labour man and Transport Union member was elected mayor.[28]

Both Larkin and Connolly recognized that Labour's lack of political power weakened the cause of the industrial struggle in 1913–14. Larkin

23 *Irish Independent*, 16 January 1914. C. D. Greaves claims that Lorcan Sherlock had a narrow escape, but actually Sherlock was returned by an overwhelming vote, polling 1,672 votes to 716 for his Labour opponent. Greaves, *Connolly*, p. 271. Emmet Larkin (*James Larkin, Irish labour leader, 1876–1947*, p. 167) does not directly connect the election with the 1913 strike. Arnold Wright (*Disturbed Dublin*) does not mention it.

24 *Irish Worker*, 24 January 1914.

25 *Irish Times*, 17 January 1914.

26 Ibid., 19 January 1914; *Leader*, 24 January 1914.

27 *Irish Worker*, 30 May 1914.

28 *Irish Independent*, 17, 24 January 1914.

declared that the strike demonstrated the need for 'one big union' and for the building of

> the new Labour Party, in which there would be no room for the old lines of cleavage, no sectarian politics . . . a working class party that would concern themselves with seeing to it that sufficient food, clothing and shelter were enjoyed by women and men and children.[29]

Connolly also urged the need for immediate political organization: as a result of the lock-out, he said, 'The philosophy of an injury to one is the concern of all is the yard-stick by which all Labour Organizations and political parties in the future will be measured . . . '[30]

The failure of Labour in the Dublin elections was crucial in ending the lock-out. The lack of support for the party made it clear that a majority of Dubliners accepted the image of Larkin, Connolly and the other leaders as anti-clerical socialist revolutionaries—the picture painted by the nationalist politicians, the press and the church. The refusal of the British T.U.C. to support sympathetic strikes or to assist the Dublin workers in anything but a voluntary way also weakened Labour's position. An obvious error by the workers' leadership was the move to send children of the unemployed (mostly Catholic) to Protestant England for the duration of the strike. This plan gave the nationalists and others an excuse to attack the 'Larkinites' by raising the sectarian issue and thus avoid the basic social and economic causes of the struggle.

LABOUR AND SINN FEIN, 1898–1914

Among the various groups of nationalists in pre-war Ireland, one small organization was of importance in its relationship to the labour movement. Arthur Griffith's Sinn Fein was by no means often in the pro-Labour camp, but the influence of Griffith and his ideas—and Labour's reaction—were of first-rank significance in deciding the course of Irish labour.

Sinn Fein was a political philosophy, developed and forwarded by Griffith, which rejected the parliamentary approach to Irish self-government; rather it called for self-reliance on the part of the Irish people, the building up of the nation from within. Griffith suggested that the Irish members of parliament should withdraw from Westminster and set up an Irish assembly which, together with the local bodies, would form the basis of an Irish government. This idea, which was a middle course between the parliamentary home rulers and the revolutionaries, was perhaps the most original and attractive part of Griffith's philosophy.

Griffith was never a complete separatist; he wanted to see Ireland assume a relationship to Britain as Hungary had to Austria in the

29 I.T.U.C., *1914 report*, p. 37.

30 *Irish Worker*, 30 May 1914.

Austro-Hungarian Empire.[31] By 1914 his position marked him out from the growing republicanism of the leaders of the labour movement and the advanced nationalists. Griffith accepted most of the conventional capitalist ideas of the time, seeking a revival of Irish industry by means of low wages for the workers and small profits for the investors. But he opposed any social or economic issues which would hinder the attainment of his primary goal—self-government: 'The time for Ireland to decide whether national development should be on lines of Collectivism or on the lines of private enterprise will be when Ireland has gained her political independence.'[32]

Griffith began his activity in Ireland with the establishment of a weekly newspaper, the *United Irishman*, in 1899 (about a year after Connolly had begun the *Workers' Republic*). Although Griffith was not a republican, the Irish Republican Brotherhood helped finance the venture, feeling that any anti-Dublin Castle propaganda would contribute to the achievement of their goal.[33] Griffith opened the columns of the *United Irishman* and its successor *Sinn Fein* to nationalists of all opinions. He printed many articles on the labour movement and socialism and gave some publicity to Connolly's Irish Socialist Republican Party at a time when the other Dublin papers refused to do so. He specifically applauded the participation of that party in the international socialist conference because it obliged an international body to recognize Ireland's national aspirations.[34] Although differing on social and economic issues, Connolly and Griffith joined forces in opposition to the Boer War, serving on the Irish Transvaal Committee and participating in the agitation against recruiting for the British Army.[35]

When popularly elected local government was instituted in 1898 Griffith welcomed Labour representation on the local bodies, but warned Labour members to 'avoid allying themselves with any of the existing political factions' and encouraged them 'to carry out the work for which they were chiefly elected. They should only intervene when the great underlying principal of Nationalism is at stake.' When the Labour members failed to be effective worker's representatives and became involved in corruption, Griffith strongly condemned their actions; before the 1903 municipal elections the *United Irishman* declared, 'Shoneenism and traitorism disguised as piety or in the garb of "labour" cannot always hood-wink the workers.' Nevertheless, Griffith endorsed Connolly's candidature: 'We are not Socialists, but we would be intensely grateful to see a man of Mr Connolly's character returned to the Dublin corporation.'[36]

31 P. S. O'Hegarty, *The Victory of Sinn Fein* (Dublin 1924), pp. 30–31; Greaves, *Connolly*, pp. 93–94.

32 *United Irishman*, 12 March 1904.

33 Greaves, *Connolly*, p. 93.

34 Ibid., pp. 94, 102.

35 Other members of the committee were Michael Davitt, Maude Gonne, John O'Leary and J. J. Nannetti, M.P. Ibid., p. 94.

36 *United Irishman*, 4 March 1899, 7 September 1901, 10 January 1903.

As a member of the printers' union (the Dublin Typographical Providential Society), Griffith was not adverse to craft unionism so long as it was strictly Irish-based.[37] He deplored the merging of small Irish unions with British amalgamated unions as an attempt to 'de-nationalize' the workers of Ireland. In 1908 Griffith announced that Sinn Fein intended to establish arbitration courts in order to keep out 'English intervention' in Irish industrial disputes. The same year he proposed an ambitious housing programme for Dublin slum-dwellers.[38]

Though by no means generally antagonistic to the labour movement, Griffith was utterly opposed to 'new unionism' in Ireland as epitomized by James Larkin and the Transport Union. It appears that he disliked Larkin for personal as well as political reasons; Griffith maintained relationships with other labour leaders, such as Connolly, William O'Brien and Thomas Johnson, while often disagreeing with their ideas. When Larkin first became active in Ireland, Griffith attacked him for representing an English union, but when Larkin established an Irish-based union, Griffith continued to be critical:

> We wish well and will give all our assistance to any genuine Irish organization of transport workers, but to assure the public that it is genuine the first essential of such a body is that those connected with it are not suspended or dismissed officials of the English Union which they formerly lauded as the one and only union to which Irishmen should belong.[39]

Robert Brennan, an associate of the Sinn Fein founder, says Griffith 'was bitterly hostile to the Larkin type of labour leader, whose aim was not true trade unionism at all, but a sort of proletarian dictatorship through the instrument of one big union dominated and directed by one man'.[40]

In the strikes and industrial battles before the world war Griffith always pointed to the harm being done to the Irish economy and to the influence of English unions and socialists; he expressed little sympathy for the grievances of the workers. In his view the 1913 struggle was caused by forces who wanted 'to use Dublin as a cockpit for deciding whether the Syndicalist method of discussing industrial disputes might be hereafter tried in England without any danger of causing English trade to go elsewhere.'[41]

'New unionism' gave as good as it got. The first issue of the *Irish Worker* denounced Sinn Fein as well as the other existing political parties; Sinn Fein, it said, was

37 Robert Brennan, *Allegiance* (Dublin 1950), says that Griffith was a 'staunch trade-unionist'; p. 218.

38 *Sinn Fein*, 30 June 1906, 12 December 1908; Sean O Luing, 'Arthur Griffith and Sinn Fein' in *Leaders and men of the Easter rising: Dublin 1916*, ed. F. X. Martin (London 1967), pp. 61–62.

39 *Sinn Fein*, 28 November 1908, 23 January 1909.

40 Brennan, *Allegiance*, p. 218.

41 *Sinn Fein*, 18 October 1913.

> a party or rump which, while pretending to be Irish of the Irish, insults the nation by trying to foist on it not only imported economics based on false principles, but which had the temerity to advocate the introduction of foreign capitalists into this sorely exploited country. Their chief appeal to the foreign capitalists was that they would have freedom to employ cheap Irish labour.[42]

Connolly declared that an Irish industrial revival built upon the sacrifices of the workers would not be worth the effort. Other observers also commented on Sinn Fein's apparent lack of concern for the working class and general hostility toward the aims of Labour. W. P. Ryan attributed this attitude to the Sinn Fein leadership's 'dim understanding of Socialism'.[43] Griffith had taken most of his social teachings from the German economist List; Connolly rejected these but supported Griffith's principle of self-reliance.[44]

Beginning about 1910 a republican wing of Sinn Fein developed. Among its spokesmen were Patrick Pearse, Joseph Plunkett, Eamonn Ceannt and Sean McDermott—all future leaders of the rebellion of 1916. They entered the world of partisan journalism in 1910 with the *Nation*, which was followed by *Irish Freedom.* Unlike Griffith, the leadership of this branch of Sinn Fein were all members of the militant Irish Republican Brotherhood; they sought to make Sinn Fein a republican movement within the context of Griffith's main policies.[45]

Also unlike Griffith, the republican branch was strongly favourable to the labour movement. *Irish Freedom* supported the workers' cause in the strikes from 1910 through 1914, including the Dublin lock-out of 1913.[46] It also gave cautious welcome to the revival of Labour representation in local government and the establishment of the Irish Labour Party.[47] Griffith's attitude toward James Larkin and the Transport Union was severely criticized by Eamonn Ceannt:

> The [Transport Union] appears to include one Englishman, who went to jail recently for uncomplimentary references to King George V; Mr. P. T. Daly, ex-prominent Sinn Feiner, still presumably a Nationalist; James Connolly, who you know to be a Nationalist of long standing; . . . Mr. Larkin is a newcomer, whose son learns Irish at Scoil Ite . . . It is the business of Sinn Fein to use the grievances of the various classes in this country as a whip with which to lash the English tyrant out of Ireland . . . Have you

42 *Irish Worker*, 27 May 1911; also 9 and 30 September 1913.

43 W. P. Ryan, *The labour revolt and Larkinism* (London 1913), p. 10. See also Ryan's *The pope's green island*, p. 317; R. M. Henry, *The evolution of Sinn Fein*, p. 103, and the Sinn Fein 1905 programme in Fox, *Green banners*, p. 70.

44 Greaves, *Connolly*, p. 187.

45 Henry, *Evolution of Sinn Féin*, p. 104.

46 *Irish Freedom*, October-December 1913. See also Clarkson, *Labour and nationalism*, pp. 281–85.

47 *Irish Freedom*, 4 January 1912, July 1912.

no condemnation of the Employers Federation, or is there one law for them and another for their servants?[48]

Although strongly opposed by Griffith, the republican wing of Sinn Fein urged Labour to join with it in an alliance of the progressive forces of political freedom and emancipation of the workers. 'The two movements rest upon the same foundation, they are but different manifestations of the same principle and would form a natural and mutually helpful alliance.'[49] *Irish Freedom* generally did not go so far as to accept the socialist programme of the labour movement, but it did support a rather vague co-operatism. As to a republican-labour alliance, correspondent 'Raparee' declared it should not be necessary to 'bribe workers to support nationality' by supporting social and economic reform. In reply to Ernest Blythe's warnings about the dangers of a 'servile State' and socialism, Sean O'Casey wrote: 'Surely there should be union between the Separatist and the railway labourer, the factory hand and the transport worker. Surely Democracy follows hard on the heels of Republicanism.'[50]

Connolly had been interested in the possibility of a Labour-progressive Sinn Fein alliance even before his return to Ireland in 1910, but no alliance developed in this period. Attacked by official Sinn Fein, the labour movement drew back from closer ties with the advanced wing, although it doubtlessly welcomed support in industrial struggles. In order to avoid a split within Sinn Fein, the republicans did not press the idea further at this time.[51]

Sinn Fein had very little political success before 1916. In 1900 it set up a political party, Cumann na nGaedheal, and in 1905 a national executive. It gained new support when the Liberal government, returned to power with a huge majority in 1906, failed to propose an Irish Home Rule Bill. At this time a group of trade unionists, including P. T. Daly and other members of the Dublin Trades Council, attracted by its policy of national self-reliance, joined the organization. When a Nationalist member of parliament resigned his seat in 1908 and stood again in the Sinn Fein interest, it appeared that a new party was rising to threaten the supremacy of the Irish Parliamentary Party. But the Sinn Fein candidates received only one-third of the vote and the party receded to insignificance.[52]

From about 1910 until 1916, Sinn Fein was in decline. Griffith proposed, in 1910, that Sinn Fein merge with William O'Brien's 'All for Ireland League,' a break-away from the United Irish League. This proposal, and the founding of the Socialist Party of Ireland, caused most

48 *Sinn Fein*, 30 September 1911.

49 Article by 'Northman', 'The economic basis of a revolutionary movement', *Irish Freedom*, January 1913. For Griffith's opposition, see Greaves, *Connolly*, p. 189.

50 *Irish Freedom*, January, November 1913; March 1914.

51 Greaves, *Connolly*, pp. 187–89; Henry, *Evolution of Sinn Féin*, pp. 106–107.

52 Fox, *Green banners*, p. 74; Greaves, *Connolly*, p. 187.

trade unionists to leave the organization.[53] When the Liberal government introduced a Home Rule Bill in the same year, Griffith, as well as Connolly and Pearse, agreed to give the Irish Parliamentary Party a 'free hand' in its efforts to restore self-government in Ireland.

Sinn Fein's political activities dwindled. Very few of their candidates stood for municipal office in the years 1911–15, and, therefore, no conflict arose between Sinn Fein and the new Labour candidates. There were only one or two Sinn Fein members in the Dublin corporation at this time, in contrast to the many Labour members of local public bodies throughout the country. It was Labour, and not Sinn Fein, which was the principal opponent of the United Irish League in the Dublin municipal elections after 1911. The Sinn Fein newspaper had an average circulation of about 2,000 copies; the *Irish Worker* sold from 20,000 to 30,000 copies per week.[54] The leaders of Irish Labour could lead strikes and demonstrations involving thousands; Sinn Fein could rally little public support. The small Socialist Party of Ireland (or the Independent Labour Party of Ireland) was considerably more active in propagandist policies than was Sinn Fein. While the Irish Trade Union Congress was constructing its political party, Sinn Fein's political apparatus remained largely imaginary. All this evidence points to the fact that Irish Labour was politically much stronger than Sinn Féin in 1914, and, indeed, until 1916; while political Labour was expanding, Sinn Féin was in decline. 'At the time of the insurrection', P. S. O'Hegarty wrote, '[Sinn Fein] was practically confined to one central branch in Dublin; while it survived as a political policy through Mr. Griffith's paper, *Nationality*.'[55]

The issues of partition and world war were to bring Labour and Sinn Fein closer together. In March 1914 Labour representatives were invited, for the first time to a Sinn Fein gathering, to discuss united action against partition.[56] When the war broke out, James Connolly and Arthur Griffith found themselves, as in the Boer War, united in opposition to Irish involvement in a British conflict.

53 Greaves, *Connolly*, pp. 189–90.

54 Larkin, *James Larkin*, p. 78.

55 O'Hegarty, *Victory of Sinn Féin*, p. 7.

56 Greaves, *Connolly*, p. 275.

3

War and Rebellion Confront Irish Labour

THE ISSUE OF THE WAR

The onset of the European war in 1914 transformed the political situation in Ireland. The Home Rule Bill received final passage but its execution was first delayed for six months, and later set back until the end of the war. Thus the political party set up by the Irish Trade Union Congress was to find no immediate outlet.

The shelving of home rule did not prevent the Irish Parliamentary Party from joining the Irish Unionists in support of the Allied cause. Nationalist members of parliament and officers of the United Irish League held recruiting meetings throughout Ireland, urging young men to join the armed forces of the United Kingdom. Sinn Fein took a completely different position; it held that Ireland had no business becoming involved in the conflict.

No significant Irish-based labour organization actively supported Britain's cause. The leaders of Irish labour—Larkin and Connolly—as well as Dublin labour organizations strongly condemned the war and denounced support for the British war effort. In Belfast and in country districts labour bodies generally took no position at all on the war issue. The official Labour attitude, expressed by the executive of the Irish Trade Union Congress and Labour Party, did not directly oppose Irish support for Britain, but was critical of the war in general and declared that Ireland's interests should be considered first. On 10 August the executive issued a proclamation, 'Why should Ireland starve?', in which it declared that 'a war for the aggrandisement of the capitalist class has been declared' and warned the women of Ireland:

> It is you who will suffer most by this foreign war. It is the sons you reared at your bosom that will be sent to be mangled by shot and torn by shell; it is your fathers, husbands and brothers whose corpses will pave the way to glory for an Empire that despises you.

Admitting that there were differences of opinion within the executive,[1] the manifesto skirted the main issue—Irish support for Britain—but urged all workers to 'aid us in this struggle to save Ireland from the horrors of famine' by means of control of foodstuffs, prevention of profiteering and the preservation of sufficient food for the Irish people.[2] The national executive, of course, did not want to offend the many Belfast workers and the smaller groups of nationalist workers who followed Redmond in supporting Britain's cause.

In expectation of a short war, the executive decided against holding

1 Thomas Johnson, chairman of the executive from 1914 to 1916, saw the war as a struggle for democracy and liberty. I.T.U.C. and L.P., *1916 report*, p. 24.

2 *Irish Worker*, 22 Aug. 1914.

the 1915 meeting of the Trade Union Congress in order to avoid dissension. The *Workers' Republic*, the Transport Union newspaper, declared that 'it was apprehended that the position of many delegates from Unions in the North would be seriously compromised and the adhesion of the Unions to the Congress endangered', if, almost inevitably, the war issue arose.[3]

It is the view of C. D. Greaves that Larkin was at first confused by the war crisis, 'making contradictory speeches in which recurred the theme of Irish support to Britain in return for a guarantee of dominion status', but that he had moved to a position of complete opposition to Irish participation by the time he left for America two months later.[4] Yet as early as 16 August 1914 Larkin proclaimed his opposition to Irish participation in the war at a mass meeting at Croydon Park. On 27 August, speaking at an anti-war meeting sponsored by the Dublin Trades Council, Larkin again opposed the war, declaring that 'the Irish workers, as a class, are taking no part in this hellish crime'. In his parting message to the Transport Union in October 1914, Larkin said, 'Our convictions have been strengthened in that matter by failure of the labour movements of Great Britain, Germany, France and Belgium of stemming the wave of jingoism and the worship of the God of Militarism by our comrades in those several countries.'[5]

James Connolly thought that the labour and socialist movements in the various European countries should have taken action to prevent their governments from going to war, by means of 'proceed[ing] tomorrow to erect barricades all over Europe, to break up bridges and destroy the transport services that war might be abolished'. Irish Labour's opposition to the war, he said, was firmly based on international labour principles:

> The Irish working class sees no abandoment of the principles of the Labour movement in the fight against this war and all it implies, sees no weakening of international solidarity in their fierce resolve to do no fighting except if it be in their own country to secure the right to hold that country for its sons and daughters. Rather do they joy in giving this proof that the principles of the Labour movement represent the highest form of patriotism, and that true patriotism will embody the broadest principles of Labour and Socialism.[6]

He condemned Redmond and the Irish Parliamentary Party for pledging their support to the British. He refuted the party's claim that Ireland already had home rule, which he called 'ruling by fooling'. The leaders of the Parliamentary Party, said Connolly, 'are prepared to sacrifice all

3 *Workers Republic*, 15 April 1916.

4 C. D. Greaves, *The life and times of James Connolly*, pp. 288–89.

5 *Irish Worker*, 22, 29 Aug., 24 Oct. 1914. Larkin also opposed the war at a meeting in Cork. Ibid., 12 Sept. 1914.

6 Ibid., 8 Aug., 31 Oct. 1914.

the sons of the poor and the soul and honour of their nation for the deferred promise of a shadow of liberty?'[7]

The Dublin Trades Council declared against Irish involvement in the war in September 1914, but there are no reports of the provincial trades councils following suit. Also in Dublin, the branch of the Independent Labour Party of Ireland strongly objected to support for Britain and organized a series of anti-war lectures in the fall of 1914. The Belfast branch, however, split on the issue of opposition to the war. Objections were raised to Connolly's anti-war propaganda; some members believed his statements should not be issued under the name of the party. Connolly commented that the objectors 'do not seem to think I ought to express an opinion on the greatest crisis that has faced the working class in our generation'. As the war continued the party fell apart, some members becoming pacifists while others joined Connolly in plans for revolt.[8]

There thus develops a picture of general anti-war feeling among the principal labour and socialist organizations. No representative labour body officially supported the British war effort, while the movement's major figures were strongly opposed. Most of the opposition, however, was based on nationalist considerations rather than socialist principles. This consideration explains why the Irish movement was the only labour movement in a belligerent country not to support the war.

The strength of Labour's anti-war feeling can best be seen in its determined opposition to military conscription as well as to 'economic conscription'—that is, enforced enlistments following dismissals by business concerns. In September 1914 the national executive of the Trade Union Congress passed a Larkin-sponsored resolution condemning economic conscription. The resolution stated Irish Labour's firm disapproval of 'the insidious and cowardly action of employers in dismissing men from their employment with a view to compelling such dismissed men, by a process of starvation, to enlist volunteers'.[9] The labour movement continued its very effective opposition to conscription of any kind until the end of the war.

In Dublin, Labour took the lead in opposing recruitment and enlistment in the armed forces. When the prime minister came to Dublin on 25 September 1914 to speak at a recruiting rally at the Mansion House, the Dublin labour leadership organized a counter-demonstration in Saint Stephen's Green. Addresses by Larkin, Connolly, P. T. Daly and Constance Markievicz were followed by a Citizen Army-led parade down Grafton Street and another meeting in College Green. The Labour speakers 'were guarded by a large body of men of the Citizen Army with rifles (which they discharged from time to time into the air during the meeting)'. The demonstration and the resulting

7 Ibid., 19 Sept. 1914.

8 Greaves, *Connolly*, pp. 286, 310.

9 *Irish Worker*, 5 Sept. 1914.

excitement largely succeeded in negating the purpose of Asquith's visit.[10] Although no republican or Sinn Fein leaders participated in the demonstration, the October issue of *Irish Freedom* applauded its purpose.

Labour, of course, was not alone in its opposition to the war—the Irish Volunteers and Sinn Fein also opted for neutrality. Joint action obviously was called for, but because of the hostility between Larkin and Griffith, no positive steps were taken until Larkin's departure for America.[11] In October 1914 the short-lived Irish Neutrality League was established, with Connolly as president, Sean T. O'Kelly of Sinn Fein as secretary and Thomas Farren, president of the Dublin Trades Council, as treasurer. A Labour-Irish Volunteer demonstration against recruitment was held the following month.[12]

A year later—November 1915—a group of Dublin employers under William Martin Murphy's leadership held a meeting to encourage enlistment. The Dublin Trades Council accused the employers of being 'recruiting sergeants', only interested in getting 'rid of ardent trade unionists, in order to fill their places with women and children at lower wages'. With the Irish Volunteers, the trades council organized an anti-enlistment demonstration.[13]

Conscription was introduced in Britain in January 1916. Labour members of the Dublin corporation spoke against its application in Ireland, and the trades council previously had advised workers that joining either the Citizen Army or the Irish Volunteers was a good way to avoid conscription.[14] This brought the various republican groups and Labour into an even closer co-operation which continued until Easter Week. Conscription in Ireland, however, did not become a major threat until the spring of 1918.

ELECTIONS, 1915

The last local government elections held during the war took place in January 1915. In Dublin the issues arising out of the great lock-out of 1913–14 dominated the campaign. Although James Larkin was now in America, the Labour candidates were labelled as 'Larkinites' and the Dublin Labour Party as the 'Larkinite Party' by their opponents. Supporters of the United Irish League urged the voters 'to sweep the last remnant of Socialiam and Larkinism' away and to defeat 'Socialism and Anarchy'.[15] The *Irish Independent*, true to form, repeatedly de-

10 Ibid., 3 Oct. 1914; *Irish Citizen*, 3 Oct. 1914; article by William O'Brien in *Labour News*, 1 May 1937. The armed force at the Labour-sponsored rally consisted of forty members of the Citizen Army and about eighty Irish Volunteers.

11 Greaves, *Connolly*, p. 219.

12 William O'Brien, *Forth the banners go*, pp. 269–71; *Irish Worker*, 17 Oct., 7 Nov. 1914.

13 *Workers Republic*, 27 Nov., 18 Dec. 1915; O'Brien Papers, National Library of Ireland, MS 15673(1).

14 *Workers Republic*, 15 Jan. 1916.

15 *Evening Telegraph*, 7, 11, 13 Jan. 1915.

nounced the 'Socialist' candidates. It declared that the elections of a year before

> resulted in a series of smashing defeats to the wreckers. This year, however, it would appear that an amnesty had been granted to one or more representatives of Liberty Hall, for the opposition is suspiciously weak. The performances of Mr. James Larkin in America should surely make the ratepayers more strongly resolved than ever before to give no quarter to his henchmen and other sympathizers with his policy.[16]

As in previous elections, the Dublin Labour Party did not advocate socialism or revolution; rather, it stressed the need for public housing, social services and educational reforms. Also as before, one candidate, Walter Carpenter, ran as both a socialist and a Labour nominee.[17] The party had to fight the election without the help of the *Irish Worker*, which had been suppressed by the authorities for its anti-war propaganda.

The results showed Labour in the same position as it was before the election; it lost two seats but gained two others, both Labour incumbents being defeated by trade unionists who stood as nationalists. One satisfying victory for Labour was the defeat of E. L. Richardson, who had been ousted as a congress officer and had since become a bitter opponent of Larkin and the party. The leader of the Labour Party in the corporation, Richard O'Carroll, and the two Sinn Fein candidates, Sean T. O'Kelly and William T. Cosgrave, were returned unopposed. The *Irish Independent* declared that the Labour Party's 'campaign was disastrous to their pretensions', but certainly the results do not show a general destruction of the party, as was advocated by its opponents. Making a short-lived reappearance, the *Irish Worker* said the loss of the Labour newspaper during the campaign had been 'the chief handicap' to Labour candidates, and that personation and dishonest vote-counting were rife. But it also admitted that Labour's anti-war stance had been injurious: 'The effect of the war in general, the calling up of working class reservists, the resulting hopes for British victory, and the Labour Party's anti-war stand had damaged Labour's political appeal'.[18]

Labour candidates were also returned in other parts of the country. The *Irish Worker* reported that three Labour men were elected in Wexford (marking the rise of the most successful local Labour Party in Ireland), two each in Sligo, Waterford and Tullamore, and that party candidates were also successful in 'many of the smaller towns throughout the country'. The editor asked for reports of further Labour successes because 'the Dublin capitalist press systematically

16 *Irish Independent*, 6 Jan. 1915. See also ibid., 8, 15 Jan. 1915; *Evening Herald*, 7 Jan. 1915.

17 *Irish Citizen*, 17 Jan. 1915.

18 *Irish Independent*, 16 Jan. 1915; *Irish Worker*, 30 Jan. 1915.

National Executive, Irish Trade Union Congress and Labour Party, 1914. Standing: James Connolly, William O'Brien, M. J. Egan, Thomas Cassidy, W. E. Hill and Richard O'Carroll.
Sitting: Thomas MacPartlin, D. R. Campbell, P. T. Daly, James Larkin and M. J. O'Lehane. Also a member, not in group, Thomas Johnson.

P. T. Daly (Daily Sketch 1913)

Councillor Partridge (Daily Sketch 1913)

The Daily Mirror

THE MORNING JOURNAL WITH THE SECOND LARGEST NET SALE.

No. 3,139. FRIDAY, NOVEMBER 14, 1913 One Halfpenny.

PEACE OR A SWORD? LARKIN SET FREE THREATENS TO RAISE THE FIERY CROSS.

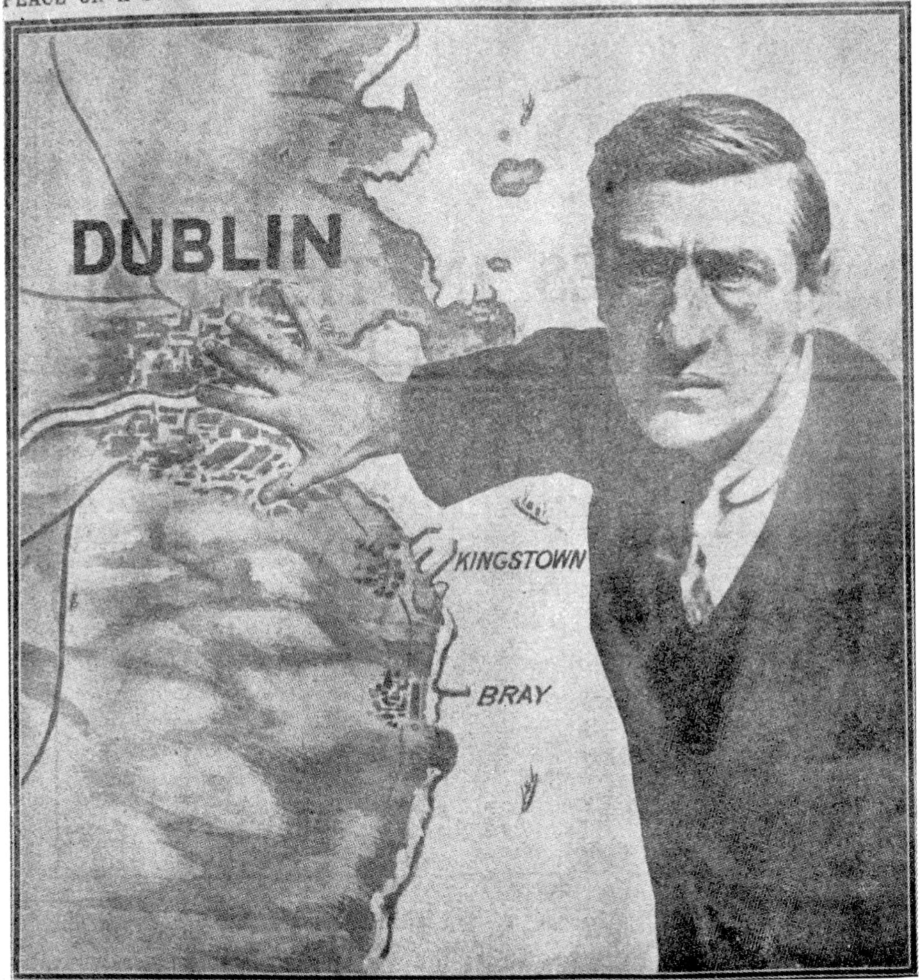

(The Daily Mirror 14 November 1913)

James Larkin (Daily Sketch 1913)

Mr. Larkin's Army (Daily Mirror 1913)

BRITISH TRADES UNION CONGRESS &
DUBLIN TRADES COUNCIL.

BRITISH TRADE UNION FUND.

Give Bearer Parcel Bread, &c.

Apply—South Wall. From 12 noon to 6
p.m. Saturday, 27th Sept., 1913.

J. A. SEDDON,
T. MacPARTLIN.

O'KEEFFE, Trade Union Printer, 8 Halston St., Dublin.

A Food Voucher 1913

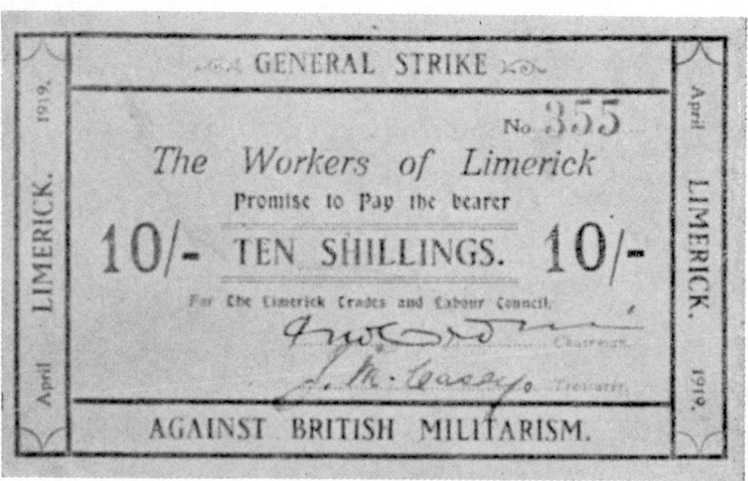

GENERAL STRIKE

No. 355

The Workers of Limerick
Promise to Pay the bearer

10/- TEN SHILLINGS. 10/-

For The Limerick Trades and Labour Council.

Chairman.

Treasurer.

AGAINST BRITISH MILITARISM.

LIMERICK. April 1919.

A Limerick Strike Note of Exchange 1919

A view of Liberty Hall after the bombardment 1916

A group at Head Office Liberty Hall, in January 1919
Standing: William O'Brien, Cathal O'Shannon;
Sitting: Thomas Foran, Nora Connolly, David O'Leary, Seamus Hughes, Patrick O'Kelly

Thomas Johnson, Thomas Farren and J. H. Thomas investigate hunger strike (Irish Independent 1920)

Ald. Richard Corish, T.D. (Mayor, Wexford)

suppresses all references to Labour candidates and when any Labour man or woman wins the victory is recorded, but the nature of the candidature is hidden'.[19]

The most important advance in Labour's political activity in this period occurred in a Dublin parliamentary by-election when a Labour candidate stood against a nominee of the Irish Parliamentary Party. The death of J. P. Nannetti, in May 1915, created the first parliamentary vacancy in Dublin (in the College Green division, a largely working-class area) since the establishment of the Irish Labour Party in 1912. Nannetti had originally been a delegate to the Dublin Trades Council and a Labour member of the corporation, and was generally held to have done valuable work for the Irish workers in the House of Commons. The Irish Parliamentary Party convention nominated John D. Nugent, national secretary of the Ancient Order of Hibernians, for the vacancy. Nugent had been a bitter opponent of 'new unionism' in Dublin, and had been accused of supplying strike-breakers in the industrial struggle of 1913–14.[20]

The Dublin Trades Council declined the invitation of Joseph Devlin to send delegates to the Nationalist convention; the council supported independent labour representation. In Connolly's opinion, 'Nobody would go there [to the Nationalist convention] in the interests of labour, unless they wanted to sell the interests of labour. The Irish Party had sold them and their country.'[21]

Nugent's nomination was taken as a challenge to Labour's political aspirations. The council unanimously passed a resolution urging the national executive of the Irish Trade Union Congress and Labour Party to approve the nomination of a Labour candidate. Although the national executive was reluctant to do so, the council's opinion prevailed, and one week before the election, on June 4, Thomas Farren, president of the council and a Transport Union member, was nominated in the Labour Party interest. Farren was not as well known as Larkin or Connolly but had been a consistent supporter of 'new unionism' in Dublin.[22]

Farren's election address, written by Connolly, stressed Labour's anti-war position: 'Under the conditions at present ruling in Ireland many of us would have preferred to let pass unnoticed the election . . . because we deprecate any act turning the eyes of Irishmen to England in the present International crisis.' Ireland 'had been left out of the best provisions of every measure of social reform and such deliberate injury' would not cease until Irish Labour achieved direct parliamentary representation.[23] During the campaign Farren charged his oppon-

19 Ibid. Newspapers in this period generally did not state in what capacity candidates were standing outside Dublin.

20 Statement of William Partridge; ibid., 14 Nov. 1914.

21 *Workers Republic*, 5 June 1915.

22 William O'Brien, '1913—its significance', in *Fifty years of Liberty Hall*, ed. Cathal O'Shannon (Dublin 1959), p. 59; I.T.U.C. and L.P., *1916 report*, p. 5.

23 *Workers Republic*, 12 June 1915.

ent with being a 'malevolent enemy of Trade Unionism' and 'instrumental in making the Home Rule Party cringe and surrender before every assault of the enemies of Ireland'; Connolly said that Nugent's party had 'given support to the Government that brought in Carson to divide and dishonour the Irish people'.[24] Labour's position on votes for women led to support for Farren from the Women's Suffrage League. The league newspaper, the *Irish Citizen*, edited by Francis Sheehy Skeffington, also endorsed Farren's social and economic ideas and his anti-war position.[25] The *Freeman's Journal* on 12 June 1915 declared that Farren was also supported by 'well-known Sinn Feiners' although no names were mentioned.

Nugent fought the election on issues arising from the 1913 strike and the war, declaring that opposition to his candidature was based on 'Larkinism and Syndicalism combined with pro-Germanism'. He asserted that Farren was opposed to enlistments, and anti-Catholic. Farren was not endorsed by Arthur Henderson or the British Labour Party, while he, Nugent, had always been a supporter of 'genuine labour' and the Irish Parliamentary Party was a 'most powerful agent for reform'. One Nugent supporter declared that Farren did not represent trade unionism or the British Labour Party but 'Larkinism, which means Syndicalism and Sinn Feinism and the pro-German intrigue that is going on in Dublin'.[26]

Nugent's campaign received strong support from members of parliament and local public officeholders, from the *Freeman's Journal* and its afternoon paper, the *Evening Telegraph*.[27] On election day the leadership of the Irish Parliamentary Party sent messages of support to Nugent; Joseph Devlin (who was considered a 'friend of Labour' and represented a working-class area in Belfast) said that Nugent supported the 'social causes for the uplifting and elevation of the working classes'.[28]

Farren did surprisingly well in the election, polling 1,816 votes to Nugent's 2,445. This vote had been achieved, said Farren, in spite of the fact that the election had been purposely rushed and that 'the presiding officers were known to be bitter and hostile opponents of the labour movement.' Thomas Johnson charged the Nationalists with corrupt practices and asserted that Nugent's 'real vote was . . . ridiculously small'.[29]

24 *Evening Telegraph*, 10 June 1915.

25 Ibid., 9 June 1915; *Freeman's Journal*, 12 June 1915; *Irish Citizen*, 12 June 1915.

26 *Evening Telegraph*, 9, 10 June 1915; *Irish Independent*, 9, 14 June 1915.

27 The *Irish Independent*, labour's usual adversary, did not take sides in this election because of a disagreement with the Irish Parliamentary Party.

28 *Evening Telegraph*, 11 June 1915. On the day before the election this newspaper featured two cartoons, one showing Larkin trampling on trade unions, contracts and 'people's faith'; the second showed Nugent defending a mother and child from Larkin's attack and was entitled, 'Nugent saved the faith and morals of the workingman's children.' Nugent employed posters and leaflets of a similar nature in his campaign. See also *Irish Citizen*, 19 June 1915, and leaflet collection in National Library of Ireland.

29 *Irish Times*, 13 June 1915; *Workers Republic*, 19 June 1915. See also O'Brien, *Forth the banners go*, p. 263.

Nugent's less-than-overwhelming victory led several newspapers to comment on the strength of the opposition to the Parliamentary Party and on the weakening of the party's machine. Certainly, Farren's vote showed that anti-war feeling did exist and could be rallied in an electoral contest.

In September a by-election occurred in another Dublin working-class division—the Harbour constituency. The Dublin Trades Council wanted the national executive to put forward a candidate, but Connolly was opposed to contesting the seat. He argued that it was not proper to turn attention toward Westminster at this time and, further, that Labour could take the Harbour seat whenever it wanted.[30] (At the time, of course, Connolly was involved in plans for a military revolt and probably did not want to divert the energies of the Labour militants towards electoral activity.) James Larkin sent a telegram declaring his interest in standing for the seat, but when the deposit money did not arrive, his name was not put forward. Several members of the Railway Clerks Association suggested that their branch secretary should be the Labour candidate, but no action was taken on this proposal.[31]

There was no Labour contender in the Harbour by-election. In fact, there were no Labour parliamentary candidates for seven years. Nationalism, not workers' rights, remained the commanding issue in Irish politics.

LABOUR AND THE 1916 RISING

The revival of the Citizen Army had begun in the spring of 1914 with the establishment of an army council and subsequent approval of the organization's structure by the Dublin Trades Council.[32] The army's original purpose was to protect workers from police attacks, but following the outbreak of World War I, this purpose was expanded to include the attainment of national independence.

The idea of rebellion was not ruled out by the leaders of 'new unionism'. Between August and October of 1914, Larkin spoke several times on the theme of England's difficulty being Ireland's opportunity. He offered the services of the Transport Union to help land rifles in Ireland, and before he left for America he told the Dublin Trades Council he hoped to 'bear a pike for Ireland' before he died.[33]

In late October, Larkin went to the United States to raise money for the Transport Union. He apparently intended to stay away from Ire-

30 *Workers Republic*, 28 Aug., 25 Sept. 1915; O'Brien, *Forth the banners go*, p. 71. O'Brien wanted Connolly to be the Labour candidate.

31 I.T.G.W.U., *The attempt to smash the Irish Transport and General Workers Union*, pp. 70–71, 133; *Evening Telegraph*, 15 Sept. 1915.

32 *Irish Worker*, 28 Mar. 1914; Dublin Trades Council, *Minutes*, 6 April 1914.

33 *Irish Worker*, 29 Aug., 5 Sept., 24 Oct. 1914. This contradicts Greaves's judgement that Larkin 'overlooked the English in Ireland in favour of the international unity of the working class' and that he talked about the economic enemies of the workers within Ireland and 'was not inclined to berate the British Occupation of the nation'. Greaves, *Connolly*, pp. 291–92, 310.

land for about a year, but the continuation of the war and subsequent events caused him to remain in America for over eight years.[34] In Larkin's absence the leadership of the Transport Union and the Citizen Army fell to Connolly, who was an active exponent of the idea of an Irish rising while the war was in progress.

With a view toward ultimate co-operation, Connolly established contacts with the Irish Volunteers and the secret Irish Republican Brotherhood, and it was with these groups that the Citizen Army later participated in rebellion. Sean O'Casey resigned as the army's secretary in protest of this alignment with the middle-class-dominated Volunteers. Later he was to write:

> It is difficult to understand the almost revolutionary change that was manifesting itself in Connolly's nature. The Labour movement seemed to be regarded by him as a decrescent force, while the essence of Nationalism began to assume the finest element of his nature. . . . The high creed of Irish Nationalism became his daily rosary, while the higher creed of international humanity, that had so long bubbled from his eloquent lips, was silent forever and Irish Labour lost a leader.[35]

Connolly, however, hoped a rising would not only achieve national independence but also a major social and economic change in Ireland; that a national revolt in Ireland would result in the overthrow of the capitalist system in Europe. In October 1915 he warned his future comrades-in-arms in the Irish Volunteers that the Citizen Army reserved the right to push forward on its own should its allies falter. And shortly before the rebellion Connolly told the Citizen Army that he foresaw the possibility of conflict with the Volunteers if the rising were successful, because, 'We are out for economic as well as political liberty.' He therefore advised his men, 'In the event of victory, hold on to your rifles, as those with whom we are fighting may stop before our goal is reached.'[36]

Connolly was co-opted to the military council of the Irish Republican Brotherhood in January 1916. Most members of this inner circle—especially Pearse, Ceannt and McDermott—were not socialists but were committed to social and economic reform. The 1916 rebellion, however, had very little socio-economic content, although Connolly hoped it would lead to more than just political independence. The rebels' proclamation declared that 'the right of the people of Ireland to the ownership of Ireland and to the unfettered control of Irish destinies' was absolute and that the republic would cherish 'all the

34 Frank Robbins claims that there was a danger that if Larkin returned to Ireland he would have been deported to England because of his anti-war stand. Interview with Frank Robbins, 28 Nov. 1964.

35 *The story of the Irish Citizen Army*, pp. 45–47, 52. This booklet was published in Dublin in 1919 under the Irish name of O'Cathasaigh.

36 Donal Nevin, 'The Irish Citizen Army', in *1916: the Easter rising*, ed. O. Dudley Edwards and Fergus Pyle (London 1968), p. 129.

children of the nation equally'. But the overriding objective of the insurgents was national independence.

Shortly before the rebellion Connolly urged the leaders of the I.R.B. group within the Volunteers to state its social programme in order to rally popular support. As the I.R.B. was a secret organization, however, it could not speak out, and the Volunteers were officially guided by moderate men, such as Eoin MacNeill, who knew nothing of the planned revolt. Similarly, the executive of the Trade Union Congress had no idea that a rising was being planned. During March and April the executive was concerned principally with the organization of the 1916 congress meeting, which was scheduled for June.[37] Connolly's increasing nationalist militancy was not well received even in his own union. When he heard of Connolly's activities, James Larkin indicated his opposition: 'the boys', he said, were 'not to move.'[38] When Connolly announced in April 1916 that the Citizen Army would raise a green flag over Liberty Hall, their headquarters, a majority of the Transport Union executive objected. Connolly overcame this opposition by informing certain members that an insurrection was to take place and that the ceremony was part of the preparation for it.[39]

Thus, relatively isolated from his union colleagues, Connolly was the only leading labour figure active in the Citizen Army or involved in the rising. The Transport Union president, Thomas Foran, and P. T. Daly were only nominal members of the army and did not take part in the rising. Michael Mallin, secretary of the Dublin stonemasons union, and Councillors William Partridge, Richard O'Carroll and Peadar Macken were active army members and participants in the fighting, but they were secondary men in the labour movement. When the call for revolution was sounded, there were two hundred Citizen Army men to answer—not exactly a show of strength considering union membership in Dublin.[40]

In January 1916 Connolly declared, 'We realize that the power of the enemy to hurl his forces upon the forces of Ireland would be at the mercy of the men who controlled the transport system.' He acknowledged, however, that his men alone could not dominate Irish transport.[41] There was, for example, the British-based National Union of Railwaymen, and Connolly could not influence the leadership of this union. But, given Connolly's commitment to industrial action, it is curious that he did not make preparations to call a general strike once the rebellion began. Trustworthy figures like O'Brien and Foran were available to make the appeal, and—hopefully—the rank and file would

37 *Workers Republic*, 25 Mar. 1916. For Connolly's participation, see ibid. 11 Mar. 1916. Connolly was the only member of the fourteen-man executive to participate in the rising.

38 I.T.G.W.U., *Attempt to smash the I.T.G.W.U.*, p. 135; Emmet Larkin, *James Larkin, Irish labour leader, 1876–1947*, pp. 211–13; Greaves, *Connolly*, p. 292.

39 *Irish Worker*, 8 April 1916; O'Brien, *Forth the banners go*, pp. 280–82.

40 R. M. Fox, *The history of the Irish Citizen Army* (Dublin 1943), p. 144.

41 *Workers Republic*, 8, 22 Jan. 1916.

respond, even over the heads of their leaders. Connolly was prepared to use his union for the transport of arms: shortly before the rising he sent William Partridge to organize members of the Tralee Transport Union to move the arms that were expected from a German ship. Connolly certainly was occupied in organizing the Citizen Army for action, but his failure to attempt the disruption of the transport system remains a puzzling factor in the wild, magnificent venture of 1916.[42]

The Easter Week rebellion left the labour movement in disarray. With Connolly's execution, labour lost its most capable tactician and its only socialist theorist. Michael Mallin was also executed, Richard O'Carroll and Peadar Macken were killed in the fighting and William Partridge died the following year, allegedly from mistreatment while jailed in England.[43] Material destruction was considerable. Liberty Hall, the symbol of dynamic unionism in Ireland, lay in ruins. The printing press and equipment of the *Workers Republic* was destroyed; its successor did not appear until December 1917. The files of the Trade Union Congress and the Transport Union either were destroyed or seized. Many other unions also suffered damage to their premises. It was estimated that the unions had to pay four to five thousand pounds to repair damage to their halls.[44]

The government arrested all trade union leaders who had shown any nationalist tendencies, although few of these had taken part in the revolt. Those incarcerated included Foran, O'Brien, Farren, P. T. Daly, Michael Mullin, Cathal O'Shannon, a Transport Union aide in Belfast, and M. J. O'Gorman, secretary of the Tralee Trades Council. The government's belief in Irish labour's direct involvement in the revolt was shared by some sections of public opinion; the initial reaction of many was that the revolt was a 'Larkinite-Labour affair'.[45]

The response of European labour and socialist opinion was an almost unanimous condemnation of Connolly's action in leading a section of his labour movement into a nationalist revolt. Anticipating the reaction, Connolly earlier commented, 'They forget I am also an Irishman.'[46] Britain's Independent Labour Party declared Connolly was 'terribly and criminally mistaken'. Thomas Johnston, the Scottish labour leader, said that he could not understand Connolly's motivations for actions which 'could not possibly secure . . . the Socialist ownership and control which he spent the best part of his life in advocating'.[47] In Russia most of the leading social democrats condemned

42 Fox, *History of the Citizen Army*, pp. 140–41; see commentary of Col. Eoghan O'Neill, *Irish Times*, 3 Jan. 1966.

43 *Dublin Saturday Post*, 18 Aug. 1917.

44 I.T.U.C. and L.P., *1916 report*, p. 36.

45 The Dublin Trades Council protested the arrests. *Dublin Saturday Post*, 16 June 1916; see William O'Brien's account of his internment in *Forth the banners go*, pp. 123–33. For public reaction, see Greaves, *Connolly*, p. 336, quoting various newspapers; Roger McHugh, ed., *Dublin 1916* (London 1966), pp. 86–87.

46 Greaves, *Connolly*, p. 338.

47 P. J. Musgrave, *A socialist and war* (London 1940), p. 16.

the rising as 'alien to the interests of the working class', a mere 'putsch'. Leon Trotsky was critical of the nationalist character of the revolt, but because a majority of the rebels were from the working class, he thought the historical role of the Irish proletariat was only beginning.

Lenin, however, praised Connolly's action. Both Connolly and Lenin sought to turn the anti-war position into a positive effort—to use the upheaval of the war for the purpose of social revolution and the overthrow of imperialism. Lenin wrote:

> The centuries-old Irish nationalist movement . . . manifested itself . . . in street fighting conducted by a section of the urban petty bourgeoisie *and a section of the workers* after a long period of mass agitation, demonstrations, suppression of newspapers, etc. Whoever calls *such* a rebellion a 'putsch' is either a hardened reactionary or a doctrinaire hopelessly incapable of envisaging a social revolution as a living phenomenon.

Acknowledging the role of the urban middle class in the rising, Lenin commented, 'Whoever expects a "pure" social revolution will *never* live to see it.' 'It is the misfortune of the Irish', he concluded, 'that they rose prematurely, before the European revolt of the proletariat had *had time* to mature.'[48]

AFTERMATH OF THE RISING

The 1916 rebellion did not have the effect in international affairs or in Ireland that Connolly had hoped. Anti-imperialist revolts did not follow in other countries; post-rising Ireland would have disappointed Connolly. No labour leader came forward as Connolly's true successor in the continuing national struggle.

At the time of his succession to the leadership of the Transport Union, Connolly wrote to Larkin:

> We are at present in a very critical stage for the whole of Ireland as well as for the Labour movement. One result of this is that we have an opportunity of taking the lead of the Nationalist movement and a certainty of acquiring great prestige among Nationalists outside of the Home Rule gang, provided our own movement is in charge of somebody in whom the Nationalists have confidence.[49]

Connolly realized that the labour movement would suffer as a result of the almost certain failure of the revolt, but he was prepared to gamble

48 For Russian views on the rising, see Nickolay Bogdanov, in *Irish Times 1916 Supplement*, April 1966. Trotsky's opinions are expressed in 'Lessons of the Dublin events', *Nashe Slovo*, 4 July 1916; reprinted in *Voina i Revolyutsiya*, 2nd ed. (Moscow-Petrograd 1923), vol. 1 (trans. Brian Pearce). Similarities between Lenin and Connolly are given by G. D. H. Cole, *Communism and social democracy* (London 1961), part 1, pp. 35–36. Lenin's thoughts on the nature of the rebellion are from 'The discussion of self-determination summed up', *Sbornik Sotsial-Demokrata*, no. 1 (Oct. 1916), in *Collected works* (Moscow 1964), XXII, 354–58.

49 Quoted by E. A. MacLysaght, *Irish Press* supplement, 9 April 1966.

that it would profit from it even more. The leaders who followed Connolly, however, rejected the alliance he had created with advanced nationalism.[50]

It is important to remember that no representative labour organization ever approved Connolly's action in joining forces with the militant nationalists. The Trade Union Congress took no position on the issue of home rule. No doubt most Irish trade unionists supported self-government for Ireland, but the congress had avoided taking a stand in order to preserve unity with the Protestant workers in Belfast who feared Catholic domination under a home rule parliament. After 1916 moderation and unity were still the watchwords of the executive. By concentrating on social and economic issues, while avoiding the national question, the trade union movement was held together during very difficult times, but this policy severely handicapped Irish Labour in its quest for political power.

Given the problem of maintaining unity, it is understandable why the congress did not follow Connolly's lead. What is less easy to understand is why a significant section of the movement in Dublin did not do so. Dublin Labour was strongly nationalistic, and both the leaders and the average union members were familiar with Connolly's teachings and example. But Connolly's successors to the leadership had not taken part in the rebellion. Had a national figure emerged from the Citizen Army such as emerged from the Volunteers (i.e., de Valera and others) the situation might have been quite different. But any such potential figure—Mallin or O'Carroll, for example—perished in the rising. Constance Markievicz became famous for her part in Easter week, but although she was a member of the Citizen Army council, she was not in a leadership position in the labour movement, and her 'socialism' was more emotional than theoretical. In Sean O'Faolain's words, Connolly's only lieutenant who survived him 'was a woman who, with the best will in the world—"ignorant good-will" in Yeats's phrase—had only the vaguest idea as to what her leader had for so long been talking about'.[51]

The Dublin leadership fell to a group consisting of William O'Brien, Thomas Foran, P. T. Daly and, to a lesser degree, Thomas MacPartlin, Cathal O'Shannon and Thomas Farren. With the exception of Daly, this group controlled Dublin Labour for the next decade. All of these men were nationalists and socialists of some sort, but they had not stood with Connolly in the revolt.[52] They were primarily trade unionists, and they believed that their first responsibility was the revival of the trade union movement. They were prepared to use their association with Connolly as an aid in rebuilding and expanding the

50 For commentary, see David Thornley, 'The development of the Irish labour movement', *Christus Rex*, XVIII, no. 1, p. 19.

51 Sean O'Faolain, *Constance Markievicz; or, the average revolutionary* (London 1934), p. 207.

52 Cathal O'Shannon unsuccessfully attempted to get to Dublin at the time of the rising.

movement, but they did not attempt to maintain the organizational ties with the militant nationalists, and they made no attempt to revive the Citizen Army at the time when the Volunteer organization was being rebuilt. For the next two years, the leadership concentrated on the economic side of the labour movement. These men believed that political power could be gained by means of an advanced socio-economic programme which would appeal to the workers; the national issue played a very small part in their calculations. Clearly they grossly underestimated the impact of nationalism on the workers. The Dublin labour leaders also worked under a very practical disability. They had to give primary attention to their trade union responsibilities, while the nationalist political group, now gathered under the banner of Sinn Fein, was able to devote the greater part of its energy to political work.

The immediate aftermath of the rising created a unique circumstance in the Irish labour movement. The Dublin Labour leadership had been arrested and deported. While martial law prevailed, trade union meetings were illegal. The immediate responsibility for the movement in this crisis fell upon those members of the congress executive then at liberty—those who were considered to be non-nationalists. The two members from Belfast, Thomas Johnson, president, and David R. Campbell, treasurer, stepped into the breach. Although their position of leadership initially was assumed to be temporary, pending the release of the Dublin leaders, these two men, especially Johnson, were to be powerful figures in the Irish Labour leadership for the next decade. Both had long been active in the Belfast Trades Council and had served as council officers. Although neither, at this time, could be termed nationalists, in the sense of being separatists, they had supported the creation of the Irish Labour Party as a means towards unifying the workers of north and south. Both were Protestants and could be termed home rulers; certainly they bitterly opposed partition.

Davy Campbell, born and raised in Belfast, had been a leader of the trades council and delegate to many congress meetings. Treasurer of the congress executive since 1912, he continued as an active member of the executive through the 1920s. During the period of the national struggle Campbell courageously and skillfully worked to maintain labour unity in strife-torn Belfast.

Johnson was born in Liverpool in 1872. Unlike Larkin and Connolly, who were also born in Britain, Johnson was not of Irish stock; he once said his heritage was 'Liverpool English'—a fact which eventually became a serious impediment to his political career in Ireland. His father was a skilled worker, and Johnson left school at twelve years to work as an office boy and messenger. He was introduced to socialism through membership in the Independent Labour Party's local branch. Johnson first came to Ireland in 1892 to work for a fish merchant in Kinsale, County Cork. In 1901 he moved to Belfast where he became a commercial traveller for a cattle food firm, a position he held until 1918. Almost immediately on arrival in Belfast, both Johnson and his wife, Mary, became active in the labour movement. He joined the National Union of Shop Assistants and Clerks in 1902. From 1902 until 1918 he was a member of the Belfast Trades Council and was active, with his wife, in the pioneering Belfast Co-operative Society. He also supported the Belfast Labour Party, standing unsuccessfully in 1908 as a Labour and home rule candidate for a corporation seat in a Unionist ward. He played an active role in the 1907 Belfast general strike, being a member of the strike committee, and he also helped in the 1913 struggle in Dublin. In 1911 Johnson first appeared as a delegate to the Trade Union Congress where he supported the creation of a congress-sponsored Labour Party. His rise to a position of prominence was rapid: he was elected vice-chairman of the executive for 1913–14 and chairman for 1914–16.

Johnson was neither the leader of a trade union nor a dominant, magnetic personality; he was a moderate, careful, hardworking man, an asset on the executive. According to William McMullen, Johnson's hesitant, thoughtful speaking manner would have prevented him from becoming a leader of Belfast Labour. Johnson himself admitted he had become the Labour spokesman only by accident; he maintained his position by his complete devotion to his responsibilities. For the next decade he worked under a number of handicaps. His English background presented difficulties, but a more serious obstacle was that Johnson was a non-violent socialist operating in a time of revolution and armed struggle. While Irish Labour generally did not support the British war effort, Johnson at this time saw the war as an Allied defence of western democracy and freedom. Finally—and most importantly—he did not fully understand the deep-rooted nationalist feelings of most Irish workers.[53]

The immediate situation facing Johnson and Campbell was described by Louie Bennett, head of the Irish Women Workers Union:

> The Dublin Trade Union movement was at that time shaken to its foundations, its leaders in jail or on the run. Thomas Johnson and D. R. Campbell were coming backwards and forwards from Belfast and working like blacks to retrieve the scattered forces of the workers.[54]

Johnson quickly launched an avalanche of correspondence at the government and the parliamentary Labour Party in an attempt to obtain the release of the imprisoned labour leaders. He specifically sought the release of O'Brien and Daly and protested against the arrest of Francis Sheehy Skeffington, the friend of the labour movement who was later shot by the British forces. In a letter to Prime Minister Asquith, Johnson sought compensation for families of working men killed during the rising (but not connected with the rebellion) and for

53 *Irishman*, 27 Aug. 1927; *Weekly Irish Times*, 18 June 1927; interviews with Mrs Mary Johnson, William McMullen.

54 *Irish Economist*, August 1922.

damage done to workers' houses by the military.[55] In July a delegation made up of Johnson, Campbell, M. J. O'Lehane and Thomas MacPartlin interviewed government and labour organizations in London. These efforts did not achieve the immediate release of the arrested leaders, but did succeed in recovering some of the Dublin Trades Council and Transport Union records. All questions of compensation were referred to a government commission; in the end, none of the national executive's requests were met.[56]

The protest activities of the new leadership did not include any reference to the leaders of the rebellion. Johnson's letters to Arthur Henderson did not mention Connolly's imprisonment; on the day of Connolly's execution, Johnson wrote to the British Labour leader about O'Brien and Daly. At its first post-rising meeting (10 June), the executive passed a resolution 'regretting the loss' of Connolly and Richard O'Carroll, who had been a delegate to congress meetings in past years. The Dublin Trades Council did not condemn the executions when it resumed its meetings in July 1916.[57]

In future political campaigns the Labour Party would be severely criticized because its parent executive had not protested the 1916 executions, which did so much to swing public opinion to the nationalist side. Perhaps the executive did not wish to endanger the early release of the arrested trade unionists, or feared the suppression of trade unionism at this time. Perhaps the leadership did not understand the significance of the executions. With the wisdom of hindsight, one can only remark that this lack of initiative on the part of Connolly's own party was regrettable in the light of future events.

By the time the Trade Union Congress gathered (for the first time in two years) on 7 August 1916 at Sligo, the leadership of the executive was no longer in the hands of Johnson and Campbell alone. Both O'Brien and Foran were released and attended as delegates. P. T. Daly, the congress secretary, was still imprisoned, but he made no known objections to the line of policy pursued by the executive and accepted by the congress.[58] The congress had avoided taking a position on the question of home rule and, by cancelling the 1915 meeting, had avoided the issue of the war, but in 1916 there was no way it could avoid the rebellion without another cancellation. The Labour conference therefore became one of the first representative bodies to pronounce on this event.

In his chairman's address, Johnson announced the position on the rebellion adopted by the executive. 'This is not a place to enter into a discussion as to the right or wrong, the wisdom or the folly, of the revolt,'

55 I.T.U.C. and L.P., *1916 report*, pp. 7–8, 9, 11, 13.

56 Ibid., pp. 7–12; *Dublin Saturday Post*, 15, 22 July, 5, 19 Aug., 2, 30 Sept. 1916. This newspaper gave excellent coverage to Labour during the period April 1916–Dec. 1917 when no Labour paper existed.

57 *Dublin Saturday Post*, 17 June, 15, 22, 29 July 1916.

58 Ibid., 5 Aug. 1916, 17 Feb. 1917.

he declared. 'As a trade union movement, we are of varied minds on matters of historical and political development.' He asked the delegates to stand for a minute to honour the memory of Connolly, O'Carroll and Macken, whom he said had participated in the rising 'purely with a passion for freedom and a hatred of oppression'. At the same time the delegates were asked to remember those who had died in the war, 'also for what they believed to be the cause of Liberty and Democracy and for Love of their country'. Johnson followed with a personal declaration of support for the Allied cause:

> The Cause of Democracy, the defence of such liberties as the common peoples of the Western nations had won was bound up with the success of France and Britain. I had held to that opinion with some enthusiasm and, despite the efforts of our Government to prove that the governing methods of all ruling classes are much alike, I hold the same opinion still, for France is still a Republic— more firmly established.

The report of the executive followed Johnson's uncommitted line on the rebellion: the loss of Connolly and O'Carroll was mourned but 'without for a moment pausing to consider the rightfulness or otherwise, of recent events in our land'. This was Johnson's compromise: the pro-war workers were not offended by a favourable reference to the purpose of the rising, while the workers of Dublin were given Connolly's memory to revere. The fact that this position was accepted without objection is due as much to the bewildered condition of the delegates as it is to the cleverness of the compromise.

The executive also attempted to dissociate the Transport Union from the Citizen Army, stating that 'not more than half' of the army participants in the rising were members of the union and that the army was simply a tenant in Liberty Hall. The executive report complained that Sir Mathew Nathan, the Irish under-secretary, and 'certain Dublin employers' had sought to give the impression that the two organizations 'were scarcely distinguishable'.[59] Most likely, the executive took this line in order that union might collect compensation for the distruction of Liberty Hall.[60] But the contention was challenged by W. E. Hill, a London-based delegate from the National Union of Railwaymen. He thought the Transport Union and the labour movement itself would be held up to ridicule if the attempt at dissociation was carried any further. The evidence was clear: 'The Citizen Army was the direct outcome of the struggle in which the Transport Workers

59 I.T.U.C. and L.P., *1916 report*, pp. 12, 17, 21–24. That the Citizen Army was positively linked to the Transport Union was the view of the Dublin Employers Federation whose annual report, published in July, stated that the 'significance of the rebellion . . . was unquestionably industrial as well as political, as the practical side of the movement was undoubtedly supported by a body which had its origins in the strike of 1913–14' (newspaper article in O'Brien papers, N.L.I., MS 15673(I).

60 During the following year the congress secretary used this argument in an unsuccessful attempt to win such compensation. I.T.U.C. and L.P., *1917 report*, pp. 28–29.

Union had been involved; it was formed and officered by the Transport Workers Union.' Hill demanded to know whom the executive thought they were 'deceiving by that report'? In reply, Thomas Foran, president of the union, asserted, 'The Transport Workers Union was proud of the actions taken by the Irish Citizen Army. There was no attempt to repudiate it.' But the executive admitted that the union had not participated in writing that section of the report, and Foran did not attempt to have it changed. The report was allowed to stand.[61]

Following the 1916 meeting, Johnson's leadership of the congress was given high praise. Louie Bennett later summed up the post-conference feeling. The meeting, she said, 'was a wonderful success, and quite the most inspiring Congress I have attended . . . Johnson's opening address as chairman outlined a constructive programme for Ireland which was truly audacious in its hopefulness; it put courage in the heart of the congress. The Irish Labour movement was launched on a new road from that date.'[62] Still, in his attempt to find a middle position acceptable to workers of both north and south, Johnson had not indicated clearly what policy the national labour organization should pursue. On one hand, he referred to the organization as simply 'a trade union movement' which need not get involved in political questions, such as the issue of the rebellion. On the other hand, he declared that 'the circumstances of the time now compel us to take action or lose the chance of assuming our rightful place in the political life of this country'.[63] The refusal of the Johnson-led congress to accept any responsibility for the rebellion, and the awkward attempt to dissociate the Transport Union from the Citizen Army, indicates that Johnson and the other leaders planned to build up a Labour Party that would stress social and economic issues on which there was no disagreement. In a period of rising nationalism, could an Irish party avoid this issue and still win significant political support? In an editorial entitled 'Is a Labour Party possible?', the *Dublin Saturday Post* of 2 September addressed itself to this question:

> Generally speaking, Labour in other countries is always democratic and nationalist. We, unfortunately, in this country are an exception. There is, no doubt, a large Labour Party in Belfast, who are thoroughly united on Labour questions with the Labour Party in Dublin, but who on many other questions are entirely opposed to them. Should, therefore, the programme of the new Labour Party be confined strictly to Labour questions, leaving members to think and act as they please on all other political questions?

61 I.T.U.C. and L.P., *1916 report*, p. 36, 37.

62 *Irish Economist*, Aug. 1922. See also *Dublin Saturday Post*, 12, 19 Aug. 1916.

63 I.T.U.C. and L.P., *1916 report*.

4
Post-Rising to the 1918 Election

By far the most important post-rising figures to emerge in the Labour leadership were Thomas Johnson and William O'Brien. These two, together with David Campbell, Thomas Foran, Thomas MacPartlin, Thomas Farren and Cathal O'Shannon, controlled the congress-party executive almost without opposition until 1923.

O'Brien's experience in the labour movement was unparallelled. A member of a Dublin tailors' union and an active socialist since the turn of the century, he had been president of both the Dublin Trades Council and the congress. He joined the Irish Transport and General Workers Union in January 1917, quickly becoming an officer and, within a year, a member of the executive. With Foran, Farren and Thomas Kennedy, O'Brien put his organizational and administrative abilities to work to revive and expand the union. In 1919 he became acting general secretary as well as treasurer of the union, while Foran continued as general president. O'Brien held the key position of secretary for the next thirty years.[1]

Under the O'Brien-Foran leadership the Transport Union concentrated on industrial organization, generally avoiding political issues although they were prepared to take advantage of Connolly's name and connection with the rising to build union membership. Union members who had been interned with Volunteers established valuable contacts throughout the country. Organizers received friendly receptions in provincial towns, and often Volunteer members became union branch officials. The Transport Union was generally considered to be the industrial or trade union side of the national movement.[2] Following its reorganization after the rising, membership grew rapidly, especially outside Dublin. Starting with 5,000 members in six branches in and around Dublin (and £100 in funds), the union grew to 30,000 members in sixty branches (and £12,000–£13,000 in funds) by January 1918, and to 50,000 members by the following September.[3]

The National Union of Railwaymen also experienced rapid growth, and with expansion, national feeling expressed itself in the demand for autonomy for the Irish branches of this British-based union. Through the pages of the *New Way* (which commenced publication in March 1917), a section of the Irish members called for the establishment of an autonomous Irish council and a separate political fund, demands which were finally conceded in June 1918. Despite many

1 *Irish Times* obituary, 31 October 1968; Cathal O'Shannon, 'A tribute to Bill O'Brien', *Evening Press* (Dublin), 8 November 1968. Sean O'Casey, no admirer of O'Brien, described him as a self-important man with a 'clever, sharp, shrewd mind of white heat behind the cold, pale mask'.

2 Interview with Cathal O'Shannon, 1 June 1964.

3 *Dublin Saturday Post*, 19 January 1918; *New Ireland*, 21 September 1918.

Irish members' interests in self-determination, a proposal was made in the spring of 1917 that the union withdraw from affiliation with the Irish congress-party. The *New Way* commented adversely, and the Dublin district council of the union declared, 'If any withdrawal is necessary, it should be a withdrawal from the English organization, so far as the membership here is concerned.' There were reports of a plan to set up a separate Irish railwaymen's union. The London executive thereupon decided to continue the affiliation with the Irish congress-party.

As with most other unions, the N.U.R. had a strong Belfast representation and was non-committal on the issue of nationalism. The first conference of Irish members of the union, held in December 1917, made no declaration on the national question, but did support the strengthening of the Labour Party. Although the N.U.R. attained a large Irish membership (about 15,000 in 1918), it was not a powerful factor in the leadership of the congress-party. Only two N.U.R. delegates were sent to the 1917 congress-party meeting, and the union was without representation on the 1917–18 Labour executive. But once Irish autonomy was gained, N.U.R. participation increased: twenty-one delegates attended the 1918 meeting, and one of these, T. C. Daly, was elected to the executive.[4]

THE CITIZEN ARMY AFTER 1916

The Citizen Army survived the rising and continued to exist until 1922, but it never again was an important or influential organization. The new leadership of the Transport Union was interested in spreading the union; a militant army under its wing would attract the attention of the authorities and bring injury to the union and its programme.

An army reorganization meeting was held immediately upon the release of the interned members in August 1916, and a new army council was formed the following February. James O'Neill, a rather ineffectual man, was appointed commandant, a post he held until 1921. The council decided that the army should be an independent organization, but that the members should be trade unionists if possible. Differences soon arose between the army and the Transport Union. When the union recovered control of Liberty Hall, the militants in the army wanted to commemorate Connolly by placing a banner across the front of the building. This they did despite the objections of apprehensive union officials, who feared reprisals by the government. Some union officers opposed allowing the army to use Liberty Hall for drilling and for concerts. Army-union relations deteriorated, and some of the new recruits were openly hostile to the union. This attitude was encouraged by Delia Larkin, Jim's sister, and by P. T. Daly, both of whom had fallen out with the union leadership by 1918.

4 For a fuller discussion of the N.U.R. in this period, see issues of *New Way*, especially March, June, July, November, December 1917 and June and October 1918.

The army was opposed to being absorbed into the revived Volunteer organization, yet it played a passive part in the national struggle of 1919–21. Thus, any worker who wanted to be active in the struggle was forced to turn to the Volunteers. The army was unanimously against the 1921 Anglo-Irish Treaty and supported the republican cause in Dublin at the beginning of the Civil War.[5]

LABOUR PARTY POLICY AND ORGANIZATION, 1916–18

In the post-rising period it was increasingly difficult for the congress-party to maintain its non-committal position on the national question, which by 1918 was clearly the dominant issue in Irish politics. Nevertheless, the Labour leadership attempted to construct a political party based on social and economic issues, hoping that the question of the future government of Ireland would be settled by others, but knowing that effective labour unity could not be attained 'until something is settled in respect of Irish government'.[6]

Although most trade unionists recognized the national question as a barrier to Labour political development, the 1916 meeting decided that an independent Labour Party, heralded by every meeting since 1912, should be brought into existence. The executive was instructed to compose a 'national labour programme'—which they did, advocating social and economic reforms demanded by successive labour meetings as well as the need for intensive trade union organization.[7] Yet, little was accomplished towards the construction of an effective political party in the years 1916–18.

The congress-party executive drew up a scheme for political organization which was sent to affiliated bodies late in 1916, but this met with a half-hearted response. Almost everyone in the labour movement was more concerned with building membership than creating a political party. And more important, the burning political issue of the day was 'out of bounds' so far as Labour was concerned. By pushing nationalism to the side, the movement was indeed gaining members, but the political allegiance of these new members was certainly not to an embryo party that took no stand on the most important aspect of contemporary Irish life.

The Labour leadership euphorically assumed that power was flowing into the hands of the workers. With Larkin and Connolly, they shared the view that industrial organization, not political activity, was the crucial undertaking leading to the triumph of the working class. When the Labour Party declared its intention to put forward candidates

5 My interview with Frank Robbins, 28 November 1964, yielded much information on the Citizen Army during this period. Mr. Robbins served in the army both during and after the rising. See also R. M. Fox, *The history of the Irish Citizen Army*, pp. 177, 199, 203–10, 211–26.

6 Thomas Johnson, quoted in *New Way*, July 1917.

7 I.T.U.C. and L.P., *1917 report*, pp. 4–5, 52–53.

in 1918, its subordination of political to industrial activity was clearly stated:

> It is upon the power of this industrial organization that the working masses must in the main rely to win their emancipation. . . . Whatever part Labour is destined to play in the political life of Ireland, its part in the industrial and economic life must always take precedence, since in Ireland as everywhere else economic power must precede and make possible political power.[8]

The belief of the labour leaders that the workers were bound to attain power doubtlessly was also influenced by the success of the two revolutions that swept Russia in 1917. With leaders of worker organizations in many other countries, the Irish labour movement hailed the revolutions as great victories for the workers and peasants of Russia and as examples to the rest of the world. Johnson declared that the first revolution was the greatest event in history since the French Revolution. The second or Bolshevik revolution was supported by the Irish Labour leadership until the totalitarian nature of the regime became apparent.[9]

Coinciding with the first Russian revolution was the revival of the Socialist Party of Ireland (Cumannacht na hEireann). The only other Irish socialist organizations at this time were the Belfast branches of the Independent Labour Party which had existed since before the war. The S.P.I., organized in March 1917, declared itself to be the successor to Connolly's earlier party and saw itself as the advanced guard of the moderate congress-party. Most of the congress leaders—Foran, O'Brien and Johnson—were also S.P.I. members, as were Cathal O'Shannon, P. Coates and Thomas Kennedy (as well as Sean O'Casey, a critic of the new Labour leadership).

Centred in Dublin, the party had little discernable influence. The 1918 programme of the Labour Party was socialist in philosophy and objectives, but this change is only indirectly attributable to the S.P.I. The congress-party, like the British labour movement, was moving towards a socialist position in any case. The S.P.I. attracted considerable attention from conservative organs who warned that the socialists were bent on a Bolshevist revolution in Ireland.[10] At the time of the Anglo-Irish treaty, control of the S.P.I. was taken over by a Communist group, led by Roderic Connolly, which rallied to the republican side in the civil war of 1922–23 (see Chapter 6).

THE LABOUR PARTY AND THE NATIONAL MOVEMENT

In the middle of January 1917, William O'Brien was approached by Arthur Griffith with a proposal to bring together the various groups

8 I.T.U.C. and L.P., *1918 report*, p. 165. See also Emmet Larkin, *James Larkin, Irish labour leader, 1876–1947*, pp. 77–88; James Connolly, *Socialism made easy*, pp. 16–31.

9 I.T.U.C. and L.P., *1917 report*, pp. 5, 30; *1918 report*, pp. 45–49; *New Way*, July 1918; Dublin Trades Council, minutes, 2 December 1918.

10 For example, see *Irish Nation*, 9, 16, 23 February 1918.

opposed to both the Unionists and the Parliamentary Party. Among those groups mentioned by Griffith were the Volunteers, Sinn Fein, Labour and the anti-partitionists in the north. In his memoirs, O'Brien says that he did not offer to work for the acceptance of this proposal by Labour because 'I did not believe that they, the Labour Movement, would have anything to do with parliamentary elections. . . .'[11] Labour, however, was not opposed to participation in parliamentary elections; indeed, it was looking forward to the next general election. The most probable reason why O'Brien declined this invitation was that Labour had declared its independence from other political parties. It is apparent that knowledge of the Labour position quickly spread among advanced nationalists. The 20 January edition of *New Ireland* stated, 'The formation of a new party, consisting of the old Sinn Fein, the Irish National League, with a friendly understanding with the new Irish Labour Party, is practically inevitable.'

The advanced nationalists were presented with a challenge when in February 1917 a by-election occurred in North Roscommon. This group decided to put forward Count Plunkett, father of the martyred Joseph Plunkett. O'Brien felt free to support the Count, whose election was a landmark victory for the nationalist movement. In the May by-election in South Longford, O'Brien and Thomas Farren were asked by Count Plunkett to help in the campaign to elect Joseph McGuinness (then still in prison). O'Brien also had a hand in the nomination of Eamon de Valera for the East Clare by-election in July 1917.[12] In effect, both O'Brien and Farren helped to lay the foundation for Sinn Fein, which was the eventual beneficiary of these victories. It is unfortunate that a by-election did not occur during this period in an industrial district in Dublin. Had this happened, the political aspirations of Labour would have been put to an early test.

In April 1917 Count Plunkett issued invitations to a 'national assembly' at which various groups would be represented. Every labour organization invited refused. In declining its invitation, the Dublin Trades Council declared, 'As a component part of the Irish Trade Union Congress and Labour Party, which is organized to obtain control of the country for the workers, we cannot send delegates to any but a Labour conference.'[13] O'Brien, Farren and Thomas Boyle were sent to explain the council's position to the meeting. Sean O'Casey, in a letter to the press, later charged that the Labour emissaries remained at the meeting and voted, even though they had been instructed to retire after explaining the council's stand. O'Brien admitted in his memoirs that he participated in the meeting and was even appointed to a committee to draw up a statement of principles for the new organization. Plunkett's convention, however, failed to become the beginning

11 William O'Brien, *Forth the banners go*, p. 144.

12 Ibid., pp. 144–46.

13 *Dublin Saturday Post*, 21 April 1917. See also issue of 28 April.

of a new national movement—too many Volunteers were still interned, and the assembly was unrepresentative without them.[14]

The reviving Volunteer organization could have established a new party, but it instead turned to the existing Sinn Fein body. Although Sinn Fein had not officially taken part in the rising, some of the insurgents, such as W. T. Cosgrave and Sean T. O'Kelly, were prominent members of the party, and the press had labelled the rising as a Sinn Fein rebellion. Griffith's party had a programme which was largely in line with the Volunteers' objectives: Irish self-government, the building up of the nation from within, abstention from the British parliament. The fact that Sinn Fein did not advocate the republican form of government was not considered to be a major problem by the advanced nationalists.[15]

The Sinn Fein reorganization meeting was held in October 1917. Eamon de Valera became president, replacing Arthur Griffith, who became vice president. (A month later de Valera also became president of the Volunteers.) The new Sinn Fein organization said that it was not a political party but, rather, a national movement for Irish independence.[16] From the beginning it proclaimed its sympathy with labour. But as Peadar O'Donnell declared many years later:

> Nobody noticed that Connolly's chair was left vacant; that the place Connolly purchased for the organized Labour movement in the leadership of the independence struggle was being denied; or reneged.
>
> It was made easy for de Valera to call Griffith in and shut Labour out, for the Irish Labour Party did not want a share in the leadership. James Connolly's work, teaching, martydom left no imprint on the policy of Irish working-class movements.[17]

Despite the many pro-Labour statements of de Valera and the other Sinn Fein leaders, the new party's programme on social and economic matters was quite similar to that of Sinn Fein before the rising. It pledged itself to support 'fair and reasonable' wages for the workers, and urged Irish trade unionists to sever connections with British unions.[18] Referring to Sinn Fein wage resolution, *Irish Opinion*, the new Labour weekly, commented, 'It was a resolution to which the assent of even William Martin Murphy might have secured. It does not go far enough. . . . The Labour demand today goes rather beyond fair

14 For O'Brien's role, see *Forth the banners go*, pp. 149–52, 184; O'Brien papers, N.L.I., MS 15680; leaflet, O'Brien papers, no. 2, book LOP 114. O'Casey's letter was in *Dublin Saturday Post*, 22 September 1917.

15 Dorothy Macardle, *The Irish republic* (London 1968), pp. 215–17.

16 *New Ireland*, 13 October 1917.

17 Peadar O'Donnell, *There will be another day* (Dublin 1963), p. 14.

18 *Freeman's Journal*, 26 October 1917; Macardle, *Irish republic*, p. 839, has the term 'living wage' rather than 'fair and reasonable' wage.

and reasonable wages.' *Irish Opinion* was also critical of de Valera's 'Labour policy':

> We agree that 'to free the country' is an objective worthy of all the devotion that men can give to it, but at the same time we would urge that pending this devoutly-to-be-wished-for consummation, men and women must live. . . .
>
> What Mr. de Valera asks in effect is that Labour should wait until freedom is achieved before it claims 'its share of its patrimony'. There are free countries, even Republics, where Labour claims 'its share of the patrimony' in vain. We can work for freedom and we will, but at the same time we'll claim our share of our patrimony when and where opportunity offers.[19]

The Labour leadership also took exception to Sinn Fein's proposal that Irish workers leave British-based unions. It pointed to the wide dispersal of skilled workers in Ireland and the fact that many workers had a financial stake in their British union's pension and benefit funds. R. M. Henry says Labour 'flatly ignored' this Sinn Fein proposal, but Irish-based unions, especially the Transport Union, were strong advocates of the reorganization of all unions on an Irish basis.[20]

LABOUR AND SINN FEIN IN POLITICAL COMBAT

In the years 1917–18, with the Irish Parliamentary Party faltering, Sinn Fein and the Labour Party competed for public support and political position in anticipation of the next general election. Sinn Féin had the advantages of a strong, emotional, well-established issue—national independence—and a leadership which had the aura of Easter week about it. Probably the weakest part of its platform was social and economic policy. As it could not afford to ignore the trade union movement, Sinn Fein attempted to blunt Labour political aspirations by declaring that it had every sympathy with labour, but that the national question was paramount.[21]

The Labour Party was handicapped in that its leaders had to devote their first energies to trade unionism, rather than to political organization. Any political hopes were seriously compromised by the party's failure to take a clear position on the national question. None of the Labour leaders were major public figures. While Labour was strongest on social and economic issues, the party was driven by political expediency to support positions it would not have held under normal circumstances. Sinn Fein's insistence on the sole issue of nationalism undoubtedly influenced Labour's position on the 1917 Irish Convention, on self-determination and on abstention.

19 *Irish Opinion*, 1 December 1917.

20 Warre B. Wells and N. Marlowe, *The Irish convention and Sinn Féin* (London 1917), pp. 68–69; R. M. Henry, *The evolution of Sinn Féin*, p. 307; I.T.U.C. and L.P., *1917 report*, pp. 55–58.

21 See de Valera's statement in *Dublin Saturday Post*, 19 January 1918, and Sean O'Casey's reply.

From the time Sinn Fein was reorganized, the two parties attacked and counter-attacked through the columns of nationalist and Labour publications. Sinn Fein supporters hammered at Labour's lack of commitment to direct action and the party's failure to take a stand that might not meet with the approval of 'a hopeless minority' of Unionist workers. Labour responded with the charge that Sinn Fein favoured capitalism; that in emphasizing the single issue of nationalism, Sinn Fein was conveniently overlooking the aims of a large number of influential workers in the north and the very real social and economic needs of all Irish workers.[22]

Already in the autumn of 1917 Sinn Fein was organizing its electoral machinery. Labour's P. T. Daly claimed the new party was selecting candidates for Dublin constituencies—including the constituency contested by Labour in 1915 (College Green)—without paying Labour 'the courtesy of asking us whether we agreed or disagreed'.[23] Labour's political infirmity was demonstrated when a non-Labour man was co-opted to fill the seat of a deceased Labour member in the Dublin corporation. Although the Sinn Fein executive had decided not to oppose the Labour candidate, the Sinn Fein members of the corporation voted for the other man.[24] The Dublin Trades Council protested this action, and William O'Brien charged that P. T. Daly, as a corporation member, had not worked to get the Labour man a seat. The episode marked the beginning of an open break between the two Labour leaders.

Commenting in a newspaper letter on Labour's powerlessness and the trades council's outraged reactions to the corporation fiasco, Sean O'Casey said the affair proved it was impossible to hold the position that Labour must remain away from 'all other political parties'. He advised Labour to stand boldly for its rights, because 'the Labour movement will never clash with Sinn Fein for . . . Sinn Fein would never dare clash with the Labour movement.'[25]

DOMESTIC ISSUES

The 1917–18 Irish Convention

In the spring of 1917, the British government, anxious to demonstrate to world opinion that progress toward the solution of the 'Irish question' was continuing, called for a convention of representative Irish groups to seek a plan for internal self-government. The scheme received a major setback when Sinn Fein refused to participate. The advanced nationalists held that a convention would be useless: the British had already assured the northern Unionists that they would not be forced

22 'Lector' in *Irish Opinon,* 16 March 1918 (James Carty, *Bibliography of Irish history, 1912–21* [Dublin 1936], p. 104, identifies Alfred O'Rahilly as 'Lector'); Stanislaus Smith in *Voice of Labour*, 20 April 1918; E. Guff in *Irish Opinion,* 16 February 1918; *New Ireland,* 2 March 1918.

23 Report of Dublin Trades Council meeting in *Dublin Saturday Post,* 15 September 1917.

24 The Labour candidate was Thomas Lawlor.

25 *Dublin Saturday Post,* 22 September 1917.

into an all-Ireland government against their wishes, and the convention simply would be a propaganda device to give a false impression to the United States and other countries.[26]

Labour was offered seven of the ninety-five convention seats, divided among the trades councils of Dublin and Cork and the trade unions of Belfast.[27] The national labour organization, however, was not invited to participate. Thomas Johnson's proposal that the congress-party should ask for an invitation was defeated by the deciding vote of the chairman, William O'Brien. With this, the Dublin and Cork Trades Councils proceeded to reject the invitations, but the Belfast unions decided to send delegates. In an attempt to negate the rejections from Dublin and Cork, the British government secured acceptances from two well-known, non-Belfast trade unionists—James McCarron, past chairman of the trades congress, and J. Murphy of the Dublin branch of the N.U.R. Although five of the six labour delegates presented a statement supporting limited self-government and the creation of a fully democratic parliament, the labour group played an insignificant role in the proceedings of the convention.[28] Yet the British government could claim that 'labour' was represented.

The manner in which this affair was handled clearly indicates a lack of unity within the Labour Party both on the question to the right of self-government and the means by which this should be achieved. The movement showed itself incapable of creating a united front in the face of an important political decision.

Food for the Irish People

The problem of ensuring that sufficient food remained in Ireland during the period of the war had been recognized by Labour since the beginning of the conflict.[29] At a special meeting on food control held in December 1916, a resolution was adopted calling upon the government to set up a system of food and price control and to require the tillage of all unused land. Some delegates, however, thought the resolution relied too much on government action and that the unions should act independently.[30] Sinn Fein, scorning to turn to the government, proceeded to organize its own food control committees.

26 Wells and Marlowe, *Irish convention and Sinn Fein*, p. 43.

27 Labour was originally offered five seats, but this number was raised to seven to induce labour participation. Ibid., p. 46.

28 R. B. McDowell, *The Irish convention, 1917–18* (London 1970), pp. 85–86. The Dublin Trades Council queried how Murphy had received his nomination. A protest was sent to the general secretary of the N.U.R., J. H. Thomas, who was probably Murphy's nominator and who was then serving as a privy councillor. *Dublin Saturday Post*, 18 August 1917; O'Brien diary 24 September 1917, in O'Brien papers, N.L.I., MS 15705. See also O'Brien's *Forth the banners go*, p. 153.

29 The congress had called for food control in its 1914 manifesto, 'Why should Ireland starve?' See Chapter 2. The 1916 congress repeated the demand. I.T.U.C. and L.P., *1917 report*, pp. 15–18.

30 The delegates were Thomas Irwin, M. J. O'Lehane and Richard Corish. Corish declared that 'the resolutions before the meeting were of no use unless they decided what they were going to do.' I.T.U.C. and L.P., *1917 report*.

When the government established a control committee in the autumn of 1917, labour representatives participated.[31] They soon demanded that the committee be given executive powers to meet the food situation. 'As the Labour Party was quick to point out', R. M. Henry wrote, '[the situation] could not be met by unofficial organization, however energetic, such as the Sinn Féin food committees, but required official action.' Henry continued:

> The Labour Party's criticisms, were, from the economic point of view, perfectly sound. An Irish Food Control Committee with executive powers . . . in the hands of locally-elected bodies to conserve and distribute local supplies of food, was ideally the proper scheme: but the proper scheme was, as usual, unattainable and Sinn Fein was doing what was perhaps the only thing that could be done under the circumstances.[32]

Labour participation on the committee was short lived. In December the Labour members resigned, denouncing the committee as 'only a fake and a fraud'. The party then joined forces with the Sinn Fein committees.[33] The Cork Trades Council, criticizing this action, 'would have preferred that the Trade Councils and the Irish Labour Party Executive had operated without Sinn Fein',[34] for by joining the Sinn Fein committees Labour gave credence to the idea that Sinn Fein's stand had always been correct.

The Spectre of Conscription

The Irish congress-party had been opposed to military conscription since the beginning of the war (see Chapter 3)—an opposition based on the belief that conscription would restrict the freedom of trade unions and lead to subsequent labour conscription. Sinn Féin was also opposed, but on the grounds that Ireland was a separate nation.

As the need for more troops increased, and as Irish enlistments fell, the British government took action to force enlistments. In the spring of 1917, it decreed that vacant civilian positions should not be filled by men between the ages of sixteen and sixty-two. The Labour leadership was criticized for not opposing this scheme, but by the autumn, when conscription appeared imminent, the Labour executive exhorted 'all trade unions to prepare to resist by every means'. Among the means recommended were strikes and the withdrawal of bank accounts.[35]

31 The Labour members were T. Farren, P. Lynch and R. Waugh of Belfast (who was also a delegate to the 'Irish convention'). I.T.U.C. and L.P., *1918 report*, p. 52.

32 Henry, *Evolution of Sinn Fein*, pp. 276, 278.

33 The labour and co-operative movements joined forces with Sinn Féin at a conference held in Dublin. *Dublin Saturday Post*, 19, 26 January 1918, Thomas Johnson papers, N.L.I. MS. 17113.

34 *New Way*, February 1918.

35 I.T.U.C. and L.P., *1918 report*, p. 37. See also H. B. C. Pollard, *The secret societies of Ireland* (London 1922), pp. 167–71; Johnson papers, N.L.I. MS. 17115. A Sligo Labour leader, John Lynch, was imprisoned in September 1918 for his opposition to conscription. *Freeman's Journal*, 10 October 1918.

The following spring the government took definite steps to implement conscription in Ireland. Thereupon, the congress-party executive, represented by Johnson, O'Brien and M. J. Egan of Cork, joined with the leaders of Sinn Fein and the Irish Parliamentary Party at the anti-conscription conference held in the Dublin Mansion House. The three Labour men became part of the nine-man 'national cabinet' which continued in existence until the crisis passed.[36]

Labour also committed itself to independent action on conscription. Labour protest meetings were held in various cities. Four days before the Mansion House conference, an anti-conscription meeting was held in Belfast, where Johnson and Campbell addressed a crowd estimated at 8,000–10,000. Next, the congress-party executive called a national Labour convention for 20 April 1918.[37] With 1,500 delegates attending, the conference was the largest of its kind held in Ireland. The meeting decided to call on all Irish workers to participate in a twenty-four strike on 23 April. The purposes of the strike were to demonstrate 'fealty to the cause of Labour and Ireland', to give 'a sign of their resolve to resist' conscription and to allow 'every man and woman' to sign an anti-conscription list.

The strike received near-total support. Only in Belfast and vicinity was it not a complete success. The two largest groups who did not participate were the workers on the Great Northern Railway and members of the British-based Postmen's Federation. Nonetheless, the economic life of the country came to a standstill; even pubs and small shops closed. The strike was a great show of strength, not only for the anti-conscription cause, but for the labour movement as a whole. According to Wells and Marlowe, it was the 'first general strike in any country in Western Europe', and, with no incidents occurring, 'its very restraint was an additional demonstration of the strength, solidarity and determination of organized Labour in Ireland.'[38]

The Labour leadership had also made contact with British Labour leaders to discuss the problem of conscription. On 10 April Johnson and O'Shannon met with their counterparts from the British party and the T.U.C. The statement issued after the meeting was solidly in favour of the Irish stand: conscription in Ireland was not possible; it it would affect needed food supplies from Ireland and would raise objections from Irishmen in the British Army and from 'all over the world. . . . Though men have doubted whether after all Ireland is a

36 The first meeting of the conference was on 18 April 1918. *Dublin Saturday Post*, 20 April 1918. For William O'Brien's account of the activities of the conference, see *Forth the banners go*, pp. 163–69.

37 Two members of the executive refused to sign the manifesto for the meeting. Campbell claimed the call was 'of an unduly alarmist nature'. J. H. Bennett of the Seamen's Union (British-based) said, 'There should not be any politics in the Trade Union Movement.' Later, however, Bennett did not see 'politics' in his union's refusal to transport British Labour delegates to the Stockholm conference. I.T.U.C. and L.P., *1918 report*, p.54.

38 *Irish convention and Sinn Féin*, pp. 153–54. For charges that violence and intimidation were used during the strike, see Wilmot Irwin, *Betrayal in Ireland* (Belfast n.d.), pp. 40–41.

nation, no one who knows the state of the country today can still doubt, for the passage of the Conscription Act has done more to cement the National unity than any other act could have done.' The Irish executive felt that British Labour's statement 'helped considerably to make up the mind of the Government on the unwisdom of conscripting the Irish'.[39]

Because of his anti-conscription position, Johnson was dismissed from his job in Belfast. His London employer wrote, 'In these stirring and alarming times, when our Nation is fighting for its very existence, we strongly discourage anything in the shape of disloyalty.' Johnson replied:

> Such steps as I have taken in connection with the opposition to conscription in Ireland were inspired not by what you call 'disloyalty' but by love of Ireland and her freedom. To me, tyranny is equally detestable, whatever the name of tyrant, be he Kaiser, Tzar, Sultan or British statesman. . . . Your own attitude towards me is a parallel of England's conduct towards Ireland.

The correspondence was published in the *Freeman's Journal* on 19 April and, as a result, Johnson became nationally known. He accepted the invitation of the Mansion House conference to become its secretary and thereafter was centred in Dublin. In later years, Johnson viewed his fight against conscription as his most significant public achievement.[40]

Although the threat of conscription remained until the end of the war, the general strike marked a high point in Labour's struggle for political recognition. The entire anti-conscription effort was a demonstration of the power Labour could wield when it took the lead in furthering national causes. But it also demonstrated that the Unionist workers of Belfast were not prepared to follow the leadership on these matters. Thereafter, when the leaders attempted to strike a middle position to appease both nationalist and Unionist workers, it lost the political support of the nationalists and failed to gain the backing of the Unionists.

THE INTERNATIONAL LABOUR SCENE

Facing any Irish movement—nationalist or Labour—was the problem of international recognition of Ireland as a nation. Sinn Fein followed the lead given by Woodrow Wilson: the achievement of peace based on self-determination of peoples. The nationalist objective was to unite the country in preparation for presenting Ireland's case to the post-war peace conference. While Labour also supported the principle of self-determination, the movement concentrated on achieving

39 I.L.P. and T.U.C., *Ireland at Berne* (Dublin 1919), p. 30. On the day following the general strike the congress-party executive had sent a manifesto to the British workers which declared that 'bloodshed' would come about if conscription were attempted in Ireland. See I.T.U.C. and L.P., *1918 report*, pp. 42–44; British Labour Party, *1918 report*, pp. 15–16.

40 Interview with Mrs Thomas Johnson.

separate Irish representation at the proposed international labour conference. If a successful case for separate membership were made, the result could be an indirect recognition of Ireland's claim to nationhood.

The call for an international labour conference originated with a Dutch-Scandinavian socialist committee and the Petrograd soviet. The Irish Labour leadership responded to the idea, unanimously voting to send a delegation to the conference, which was scheduled to meet in Stockholm during the summer of 1917.[41] The instructions to the delegation stated first, that it should 'seek to establish the Irish Labour Party as a distinct unit in the International Labour Movement', and second, that it support 'a real democratic peace without annexations and indemnities on the basis of the right of the people to dispose of their own destinies'.[42]

No Irish delegates appeared at the Stockholm conference. As was the case of the British Labour delegates, they were denied passports by the British government.[43] The executive's action in regard to the conference nevertheless became an issue at the 1917 meeting of the congress-party. Interestingly, the decision to seek separate Irish representation was not challenged; the controversy centred on its action in appointing delegates and its support of a peace without indemnities.[44]

On the first point—the selection of delegates—many representatives held that the leadership should have called a special conference to decide on the matter, or at least should have consulted the congress. H. Whitely, a labour delegate to the 'Irish convention', attacked the executive's willingness to appoint delegates to the Stockholm meeting, but not to a convention 'that was likely to evolve some form of government for their own country'. For the executive, Thomas Johnson replied: 'if they had thought there was a marked difference of opinion' on the matter, the executive would have called a special conference.

The peace issue—the second point—raised the general issue of the war, a matter that the congress-party previously had gone to great lengths to avoid. In a 'heated discussion', various Belfast members insisted that Germany, the alleged aggressor in the war, should pay indemnities. But Johnson warned that if indemnities were demanded

41 In February 1917 the Dublin Trades Council passed a resolution supporting self-determination and separate Irish representation at 'all International Labour' conferences (*Dublin Saturday Post*, 17 February 1917). The national executive, congratulating the revolutionary government in Russia on its successful establishment, pressed for self-determination of all peoples. I.T.U.C. and L.P., *1918 report*, p. 45.

42 I.T.U.C. and L.P., *1917 report*, p. 45.

43 The Irish delegates, O'Brien and Campbell, with O'Shannon of the Socialist Party of Ireland, met the representative of the Russian government, Litvinov, in London. Litvinov promised Russian support for Ireland's admission as a separate entity to the conference. I.T.U.C. and L.P., *1917 report*, p. 30; *1918 report*, p. 45; *Dublin Saturday Post*, 11, 18 August 1917; *New Way*, May, September 1917.

44 For a discussion of the controversy, see I.T.U.C. and L.P., *1917 report*, pp. 40–43, 45, 48, and *Dublin Saturday Post*, 11 August 1917.

Russia might be required to pay, and this would be a blow to the revolutionary government which had just 'won for Labour one of the greatest victories in the world's history' (a reference to the first revolution in Russia).

A motion to repudiate the executive's instructions was defeated by a vote of twenty-four to sixty-eight. J. H. Bennett, Irish secretary of the Sailors and Firemen's Union, was 'glad that there are twenty-four Britishers in the room anyway'. (A year later Bennett's union was expelled from the Irish body when its London headquarters refused to transport British Labour delegates to the international labour meeting). The executive's action and instructions were approved by a vote of sixty-three to twenty-eight.

Although Irish Labour was prevented from sending delegates to Stockholm, it did send representatives to the next conference, held at Berne in January 1919. Irish labour was recognized there as a separate national entity, and Sinn Féin congratulated the congress-party for this achievement.

THE GENERAL ELECTION OF 1918

In the spring of 1918, during the period when it was leading the fight against conscription, the congress-party executive announced its intention to put forward Labour candidates at the next parliamentary election. Writing in the *Contemporary Review* in April 1918, Michael MacDonagh commented on the Labour Party's declaration of intention:

> This novel and incalculable turn in public affairs has naturally caused uneasiness amongst the leaders of the three existing parties. It has given the gravest concern to the . . . Sinn Feiners . . .
>
> Thus crossing the Sinn Fein agitation, disturbing and to some extent confusing it, is this new movement for social betterment . . . It may disappoint the hopes so boastfully indulged in by Sinn Feiners, before this new development made its appearance, that they would sweep the country at the next General Election.

Certainly Sinn Fein criticism of the Labour Party increased after the executive's announcement. De Valera responded 'in terms of mingled apprehension and menace', said MacDonagh, who reported the Sinn Fein president as saying, 'Their enemies were trying to get Labour and Sinn Fein opposed to each other and put them in different camps. . . . Labour would find it would have a better chance of having its aspirations achieved in a free Ireland than in an Ireland tacked on to Britain.'

Sinn Fein criticism was also of a meaner nature. De Valera 'was aware that an Englishman had helped to subsidize a new Labour paper, and he asked Labour to see that it was not used to divide a united Nationalist Ireland'. Thomas Johnson responded that Malcolm Lyon's loan to set up *Irish Opinion* was made without 'strings', but this denial of English influence did not end such remarks. 'Spalpin', in a pamphlet entitled *Sinn Fein and the labour movement*, critized the influence in the labour movement of 'men with English accents', 'English subsidized papers and pamphlets' and 'English Socialists coming over to Ireland'. He warned of men who had earlier been expelled from nationalist organizations who now were active in the labour movement and opposed to Sinn Fein (probably a reference to P. T. Daly who had been ejected from the Irish Republican Brotherhood before the war). Labour's anti-conscription fight also received criticism. 'Spalpin' asked why Labour had not called national walk-outs during Thomas Ashe's hunger strike or when nationalist leaders were arrested. Sinn Féin attacks on the Labour Party, both in regards to policy and personalities, increased in tempo as the election drew near.

The three other political parties in the country made concerted efforts to win working-class support—a novel experience for the workers, according to MacDonagh. Sinn Fein as we have seen, constantly declared it had the best interests of the workers at heart. The labour spokesman for the Irish Parliamentary Party, Joseph Devlin, unveiled a 'New Democratic movement' which advocated a 'living wage for all workers' and 'full participation in the fruits of their labour' by means of participation in control of industry and profit-sharing.[45] The Sinn Fein paper *New Ireland* heaped scorn on 'Devlin, the Larkinite', but *Irish Opinion* welcomed his proposals: 'If Mr. Devlin talks Labour today, Mr. de Valera will probably follow the day after and not to be outdone, Sir J. Lonsdale [Unionist] will enter the competition next week.'[46]

The Unionist Party indeed was prepared to appeal to working-class voters. In 1917 Edward Carson said that, after the war, 'Labour must have its fair share in the body politic.' In 1918 his party set up the 'Ulster Unionist Labour Association'.[47] To prove its sympathy with the workers, the Unionist Party put forward three trade unionists in Belfast, who stood as 'Unionist-Labour' candidates. Commenting on the upsurge of interest in the cause of the workers, *New Way* in December 1917 declared, 'The ordinary political parties are competing with one another either to bribe or to suppress' the Labour Party.

Fresh from its success in defeating conscription, the annual congress-party meeting gathered in Waterford in August 1918. According to the executive, the organization 'found its prestige heightened, its enthusiasm disciplined, its membership far beyond that of any previous Congress. Its hour of destiny had struck and it found the movement ready.'[48] While hailing the growth in trade union membership, Chairman William O'Brien acknowledged that the political side of the movement had lagged behind, and urged the need for immediate action in developing of the party's electoral machinery. The conference re-

45 McDonagh article, *Contemporary Review*, April 1918.

46 *Irish Opinion*, 15 December 1917. Johnson also said he welcomed Devlin's proposals.

47 *New Way*, December 1917, August 1918. See also issues of September and November 1918.

48 *Ireland at Berne*, p. 20.

sponded by establishing a committee to create an election programme and instructed the executive to remodel both the congress-party constitution and political structure; these proposals would be presented to a special conference for approval later in the year.

But at its 'hour of destiny' all was not well in the Labour camp. The long-simmering quarrel between O'Brien and P. T. Daly had become public earlier in the year. The origin of the dispute dated to 1914: when Larkin decided to go to America, he proposed that Daly be appointed to take his place in the Transport Union. At the urging of O'Brien, Thomas Foran and others, Larkin agreed instead to appoint Connolly acting general secretary, and Daly was made head of the union's insurance section. Following the rising Daly once again aspired to be acting secretary, but the post eventually was won by O'Brien. In the period after 1916 O'Brien was very much a leader of both the congress-party and the Transport Union; Daly was not—and his exclusion deliberate. Back in 1910 Daly had been expelled from the Irish Republican Brotherhood amid muted charges of misplaced funds. O'Brien, warned that Daly was untrustworthy, alleged he was also inefficient and neglectful of his duties. Foran wrote to Larkin in America that Daly was not doing his work in the Transport Union.

The tension between Daly and the O'Brienites in the Transport Union became an open, but still internal, conflict in 1917 when Daly accepted a sum of money in the form of a testimonial from some Dublin workers, a practice frequently condemned by labour bodies. This matter was quickly brought before the Dublin Trades Council, but it declined to censure Daly directly. In February 1918, however, O'Brien called for a tribunal of council members to investigate a variety of charges against Daly: that he had failed to support fully a Labour candidate for a vacant corporation seat (see above, p. 85), was in the pay of a 'foreign Power' and had received a message in 1916 'from foreign parts' which he failed to deliver to James Connolly. Although the tribunal was not set up, the quarrel was now public. What followed was a series of internal electoral contests from which Daly consistently emerged as the loser. In March the supporters of O'Brien and Daly clashed in the Dublin Trades Council presidential election. Thomas Foran defeated Daly by a vote of forty-six to forty. Next, Daly's fire brigade union was suspended from the council because it allegedly was not a genuine, representative union—Daly charged the suspension was to prevent him from being a delegate to the 1918 congress-party meeting. (Coincidently, O'Brien was expelled in August from his union, a British-based tailors' body, on the charge that he had attempted to establish a rival union. His Dublin branch then proceeded to establish an Irish-based union.)

Daly was correct in his concern about the 1918 meeting. O'Brien's forces decided to replace Daly as secretary with Thomas Johnson. O'Brien later said, 'Daly got to know this. He was an astute canvasser and he put it about that it would be a terrible thing to have an Englishman secretary of the Congress.' At the last moment—and as part of the strategy—O'Brien himself replaced Johnson and defeated Daly by the very close vote of 114 to 109. Johnson replaced the retiring D. R. Campbell as treasurer, and three years later O'Brien and Johnson exchanged positions.

To carry the story to its conclusion: still more grief was to come Daly's way. In January 1919 he not only was overwhelmingly defeated by O'Brien for the post of treasurer of the Transport Union, but he was also ousted by Foran as head of the insurance section. At this, Daly went into bitter and lasting opposition to the leadership of the labour movement. He joined forces with Delia Larkin, who was in controversy with the Irish Women Workers Union, and presented himself as the spokesman of the 'Larkinites'. Later in 1919 he regained control of the Dublin Trades Council when he was elected secretary, but this victory proved to be short-lived as the trades council was replaced by the Transport Union-sponsored Dublin Workers Council in the congress-party two years later. Although the dispute blossomed once again when Jim Larkin returned in 1923, it did not have a significant outward effect upon the fortunes of the Labour Party in 1918.[49]

After the 1918 conference, the Labour leadership was faced with major difficulties in deciding upon an election programme and a policy. The principal issues in the forthcoming election had been framed by Sinn Fein: the election would be a plebicite on the question of Irish self-determination, Sinn Fein would refuse to enter the British Parliament but would establish an Irish assembly, and they would present the united nationalist case to the post-war peace conference. The Labour Party, therefore, was forced to take positions on the questions of self-determination and abstention.

In mid-September the executive issued a manifesto declaring the party's commitment to fight the election but to abstain from Westminster. During the same month, the executive presented proposals for a revised constitution. Both subjects were to be considered by a special Labour conference, scheduled for 1 November.[50]

The carefully worded manifesto indicated Labour support of the principle of self-determination for all peoples but did not say whether or not the party favoured Irish independence; it merely stated that

49 For the story of the O'Brien-Daly dispute at this time, see Larkin, *James Larkin*, p. 261; O'Brien, *Forth the banners go*, pp. 65–69, 164; letters from Foran to Larkin, 9 June, 16 September 1919, in O'Brien papers, N.L.I., box marked MS 15677–82 (also MS 15657); *Dublin Saturday Post*, 16 February, 2 and 16 March, 1 and 8 June, 6 July, 3 and 10 August 1918; I.L.P. and T.U.C., *1918 report*, pp. 2, 77–78; *Voice of Labour*, 26 July, 2 and 23 August 1919.

50 Although the majority of the executive favoured abstention, Thomas Foran believed the party should participate in Parliament. Thomas MacPartlin was against Labour's contesting the election. When the abstention agreement was made—on 10 September—MacPartlin and Joseph Mitchell of Belfast were absent from the meeting. I.L.P. and T.U.C. national executive, minute book, 10 September 1918, O'Brien diary, 27 August, 7 September 1918, O'Brien papers, N.L.I., MS 15705; circular of national executive of I.T.U.C. and L.P. to the secretary of each affiliated organization, dated September 1918.

Labour would 'yield to none in determination to win for Ireland freedom',[51] which has a different meaning than 'freedom for Ireland'. The party leadership apparently decided this was as far as it could go without causing a rebellion among the Unionist workers in the affiliated organizations.

As with self-determination, the abstention issued was forced by Sinn Fein. If Labour failed to take a position on this question, Sinn Fein could accuse it of being favourable to the continuation of the political union with Britain. The Irish Parliamentary Party had been abstaining from Westminster since the conscription crisis—probably having been driven to this position by the propaganda of Sinn Fein—but it was prepared to enter the new parliament. If Labour adopted the Sinn Fein position of permanent abstention, trade unionist supporters of either the Unionist Party or the Irish Parliamentary Party would object and possibly split the labour movement. So while executive declared for abstention from Westminster, the manifesto carried the qualification that successful Labour nominees might go to parliament some time in the future 'if special circumstances warranted it' and if a special congress-party meeting approved.[52] There was no mention of Labour participation in the national assembly that Sinn Fein proposed to establish following the election; apparently the Labour members would be abstaining from everything.

While Sinn Fein said it would not go to the Westminster Parliament because it did not recognize British authority in Ireland, the Labour Party's position was based on different grounds: it would abstain as a protest against recent government actions in Ireland—the conscription menace, 'daily deportations, imprisonment without trial, suppression of public opinion, of free speech and the right of meeting'.[53] Although the Dublin Labour leaders supported abstention, only two organized groups, the Mullingar Trades Council and the Irish Clerical Workers Union, are known to have given unqualified approval to the policy.[54] In some quarters the executive decision was considered a fatal blunder; Belfast Labour refused to stand on the party's programme, and, in general, the abstention issue was a divisive one.

Throughout October the Sinn Fein press continued to attack the Labour stand, accusing Johnson's party of failing to support a republican form of government for Ireland, of deserting the legacy of Connolly and of dividing the national movement at the time when unity was essential.[55] Yet Sinn Fein was prepared to negotiate with the Labour

51 I.T.U.C. and L.P., *1918 report*, p. 166.

52 Ibid., p. 168. See commentary in *New Way*, November 1918, and *Voice of Labour*, 12 October 1918.

53 Irish Labour Party and Trade Union Congress, *1919 report*, p. 12. The quote is from Thomas Cassidy.

54 *Nationality*, 26 October 1918.

55 On the question of republicanism, Johnson held the Labour manifesto to be 'republican in essence' (it called for the 'abolition of all powers and privileges based on property

Party on candidates for the election, particularly for a few seats in Dublin. As early as December 1917 the Labour journalist L. P. Byrne told Johnson, 'Sinn Fein is out for a deal' but wanted to know the probable Labour Party position on abstention.[56] By mid-August 1918, with the election apparently not far away, the Sinn Fein Standing Committee (the body directing the party during the absence of de Valera and Griffith who had been arrested earlier in the year) decided to contact 'representative Labour men', appointing Harry Boland to arrange a conference for this purpose. A Sinn Fein delegation consisting of Boland, Father Michael O'Flanagan, Robert Brennan and Alderman Thomas Kelly was selected to meet with Labour. Although the Labour men declined to attend the meeting, Boland was able to inform the standing committee that the Labour Party intended to contest fifteen seats and would support abstention on the basis of expediency, not as a matter of principle.[57]

A second attempt to arrange a meeting was successful: on 22 September, Boland and Brennan met with William O'Brien, Cathal O'Shannon and Tom Farren. The Labour group wanted Sinn Fein to stand aside for their party in four Dublin constituencies; they also stated their intention to contest as many as fifteen seats throughout the country. Following this meeting, the Sinn Fein committee, which was under great pressure to complete their list of nominees, still hoped that agreement could be reached with Labour. But the Sinn Fein constituency organizations continued to press for action, and there were objections to the negotiations with Labour. On 30 September, the Sinn Fein Standing Committee ratified candidates for three of the four Dublin seats.[58]

The Labour leadership decided to make a modest claim for representation rather than to present a major challenge to Sinn Fein. They would run a small number of candidates only in those places where they thought they had the best chance of success. Even with this limitation, there was significant opposition within the labour movement to any party participation whatsoever. In the Dublin Trades Council, P. T. Daly moved that Labour candidates should not be put forward. The motion was defeated by a vote of nine for, twenty-seven against, but several council members declared that many trade unionists would not support Labour in the election. Nevertheless, a conference sponsored

---

and ancestry'). Many people, he charged, were using the word 'republican' without giving thought to its implications, and it was 'well known that several of the most influential and active members of the Sinn Fein leaders are avowed monarchists'. See 'T.J.' (Johnson) in *New Ireland*, 26 October 1918, also issues for 12 and 19 October.

56 Letter from Byrne to Johnson, 18 December 1917. Johnson papers, N.L.I. MS 17239.

57 Minute book of the Sinn Fein Standing Committee, 16 and 23 August, 12 September 1918, cited in Brian Farrell, 'Labour and the Irish political system: a suggested approach to analysis', *Economic and Social Review*, I, no. 4 (July 1970), p. 496.

58 Ibid., 19, 22, 30 September 1918; O'Brien diary, 22 September 1918, O'Brien papers, N.L.I., MS 15705.

by the council nominated four candidates (there were seven constituencies in Dublin): O'Brien for Saint Michan's constituency, Farren for Saint Patrick's, MacPartlin for College Green and James Larkin for Harbour. Daly refused the nomination for Saint James's, but Larkin telegraphed from New York his acceptance of the nomination.[59]

In other areas of the country the appeal for Labour candidates met with a negative response. In Kilkenny, North Kildare, East Wicklow, Wexford, Waterford and Cork—centres of trade union membership—no candidates were put forward.[60] The same was true in Belfast, but here the decision was a reaction to the Labour Party's stand on self-determination and abstention. A few independent candidates and two nominees of the British-based Independent Labour Party belatedly entered the contest. A Dublin Labour Party rally in the Mansion House was disrupted by heckling from Sinn Fein supporters and Citizen Army members.

While the Belfast labour organizations refused to support the Labour Party because its position was too nationalistic, workers in the rest of the country were largely drawn to the ultra-nationalist policy of Sinn Fein. The *Dublin Saturday Post* of 26 October was not overstating the case when it said, 'There is little unanimity as to the advisability of putting forward Labour candidates,' and there was the likelihood that certain unions would 'not support the nominees of Labour'.

O'Brien apparently was not dissatisfied with the situation. In two cases he even discouraged attempts to put forward candidates. Speaking to a body of Meath trade unionists on 1 October, he advised them not to nominate a Labour candidate in their area. A week later, Capt. Jack White wrote to O'Brien offering himself as a Labour candidate. White had been the organizer of the Citizen Army before the war and, although long absent in England, had kept his nationalist record clean: he had not joined the British forces during the war and had been arrested while attempting to bring Welsh miners out on strike as a protest against the execution of the 1916 leaders. O'Brien rebuffed White, declaring that he could only be a Labour nominee if he was a member of a trade union or other labour organization and if he was nominated by one or more affiliated bodies. O'Brien does not mention in his memoirs why he discouraged these candidacies. Perhaps he realized that the nomination of numerous Labour candidates in areas where they had little chance of election would only enrage Sinn Fein and make the

59 According to M. Slevin, only six of forty-three members of his branch of the N.U.R. would vote Labour. J. Quinn said many trade unionists had decided to 'vote politically'. The Dublin tailors' union, however, by a vote of forty-six to twenty-seven, endorsed the party's decision to stand 'so long as they stood by the national principle of self-determination.' *Freeman's Journal*, 1 October 1918; *Voice of Labour*, 26 October 1918. For Larkin's acceptance, see I.T.G.W.U., *The attempt to smash the Irish Transport and General Workers Union*, p. 72, and O'Brien papers, N.L.I., MS 13961 (1).

60 See P. S. O'Hegarty in *Irish World*, 7 September 1918; *Dublin Saturday Post*, 5 October 1918; *Freeman's Journal*, 16 October 1918; *Voice of Labour*, 26 October 1918; *Cork Examiner*, 14, 17, 18, 26, 28 October, 1 November 1918.

possibility of any arrangements between the two parties more unlikely.[61]

Although the Labour Party had received nothing like enthusiastic support from trade unionists or from the public, Sinn Fein nevertheless was concerned about Labour's influence on the election. It was commonly held that only Labour's participation could prevent Sinn Fein from sweeping most of the country. The Irish Parliamentary Party appeared ready to admit defeat: its campaign lacked conviction and vigour; it surrendered twenty-five seats without a fight. Only if the opposition were divided might the Parliamentary Party survive. When Labour announced it would contest the election, the Parliamentary Party was 'openly jubilant that there might be a split between Sinn Fein and Labour'.[62]

Still attempting to avoid a clash with Labour, Sinn Féin continued confidential negotiations with the trade union leaders throughout October. The standing committee decided to offer the Labour candidates the following oath:

> I hereby pledge myself to work for the establishment of an Independent Irish Republic and that I will accept nothing less than complete separation from England in settlement of Ireland's claim; that I will abstain from attending the English Parliament and that if I am ordered by the Labour Congress to attend the English Parliament I will place my resignation in the hands of my constituents.

If the Labour candidates took this pledge, the committee would ask the Sinn Fein candidates to stand down.[63]

It is obvious that this pledge designed to allow the Labour Party to participate in the election without dividing the forces opposed to the Parliamentary Party. The pledge even dealt with Labour's official stance on abstention. Within Sinn Fein the arrangement would cause little disruption, as it would affect only the four Dublin constituencies (the candidate in Derry was overlooked) where Labour candidates were already announced. Labour apparently had found a wedge to a measure of political power.

The Sinn Fein-Labour negotiations and the pledge did not become public until the very end of October when the Sinn Fein ard fheis was held. Before then, however, there were adverse rumblings on both sides over Labour's participation in the election. The pledge was revealed to the Labour delegates at a meeting on 14 October. Sean T. O'Kelly later claimed to know of one candidate who had signed the pledge. This was probably O'Brien who had said that, if elected, he would never go

61 *Freeman's Journal*, 1 October 1918. White's brief note to O'Brien and O'Brien's reply are in the O'Brien papers, N.L.I., MS 15673. For White's background, see J. R. White, *Misfit: an autobiography* (London 1930).

62 Mrs Sheehy Skeffington said this was the reaction of a leading member of this party, John D. Nugent. *Freeman's Journal*, 31 October 1918. See also issue of 10 October and *1918 report*, p. 117.

63 Standing committee minutes, 7 and 10 October 1918, cited in Farrell, 'Labour and the Irish political system', p. 498.

to Westminster and would resign his seat if the congress-party instructed him to go. Another Labour candidate, William MacPartlin, said he had refused to sign, but Sinn Fein records show its constituency organization had declined to offer him the pledge. It is not known if Farren agreed to take the pledge, but his past record indicates he would have had no objections to it. Larkin almost certainly would have signed.[64]

The Sinn Fein ard fheis was to be held on 30–31 October and two days later the special Labour conference would convene. In Europe the German armies were in full retreat and the end of the war appeared imminent. A general election could not be far away, and the Labour Party was under constant pressure to remove itself from the contest. At the Sinn Fein gathering the agreement with Labour was criticized: 'Sinn Fein is the dominant party', said Sean Forest, 'it [is] not for them to go to any section, but for that section to come to Sinn Fein.' O'Kelly told the meeting he hoped Labour would 'stand aside to allow the election to be fought on the clean issue of Ireland vs England'.[65]

The morning the Labour conference was due to begin, the executive met. Over the objections of Farren and O'Shannon, it decided to recommend that the party withdraw from the election.[66] Johnson was given the task of presenting this decision to the conference. He began by speaking of the rapid course of events. When Labour had announced in September its intention to contest the election, the prospects were that first there would be a 'war' election and then a 'peace' election, but the 'sudden call for an armistice' had radically altered the situation. He then acknowledged the primacy of the national question:

> A call comes from all parts of Ireland for a demonstration of unity on this question [of self-determination] such as was witnessed on the Conscription issue. Your Executive believes that the workers of Ireland join earnestly in this desire, that they would willingly sacrifice for a brief period their aspirations towards political power if thereby the fortunes of the nation can be enhanced.

Continuing, he deprecated the importance of the election:

> The main purpose of the Irish Labour Party [is] not the election of one or two or two dozen members of Parliament, but the building up of an organized political labour consciousness in this country, definitely democratic, not on a single issue, but on every democratic policy that [arises].[67]

64 See standing committee minutes, cited ibid., p. 499; O'Brien diary, 14 October 1918, in O'Brien papers, N.L.I., MS 15705; *Freeman's Journal*, 31 October 1918; *Dublin Saturday Post*, 19 October 1918; *Irish Times*, 2 November 1918.

65 A 'Dublin trade unionist' declared that 'the vast majority of labour would vote Sinn Féin.' Rev. Fr. Delahunty, another delegate, stated that Transport Union members in Kilkenny would support Sinn Féin. *Freeman's Journal*, 31 October 1918.

66 I.L.P. and T.U.C. national executive, minute book, 1 November 1918; see also O'Brien's diary, 1 November 1918. O'Brien papers, N.L.I., MS 15705.

67 *Voice of Labour*, 9 November 1918; *Irish Times*, 2 November 1918.

Several delegates took exception to Johnson's explanation. D. R. Campbell could not 'follow the subtle distinction' between a 'war' and a 'peace' election; withdrawal would be a retreat from the position adopted by the last several congresses. T. Murphy of Dublin characterized the executive's recommendation as a 'big sell-out'. O'Shannon, D. Houston and P. Coates feared Ireland would not get full representation at international labour meetings if it had no parliamentary representation. To all this Johnson replied somewhat bitterly:

> If the North had made up its mind to run candidates on the programme of the Irish Labour Party . . . the Executive's decision would have been a very different one. If the South had responded heartily to the decision of the Irish Labour Party Executive five or six weeks ago the decision might have been different.

After extensive debate, the executive's recommendation was accepted by a vote of ninety-six to twenty-three. The Labour Party had bowed out of the election, exclaiming on its selflessness and hoping its sacrifice would be appreciated by the nation.[68]

As was expected, the decision was greeted with gratitude by Sinn Fein and with rage by the Irish Parliamentary Party. Republican papers were eloquent in describing the 'natural bonds' which existed between Sinn Féin and Labour, the party which had done 'the right thing at the right time'.[69] On the other side, the *Freeman's Journal* and the *Irish Times* saw the spectre of Russian influence. As the latter paper commented, 'Sedition and Bolshevism will go hand in hand to the polls.'[70]

The conference, having decided to withdraw the Labour candidates, proceeded to adopt a programme it would not need immediately for election purposes. The programme is of interest, however, because it shows that by 1918 the party was prepared to stand for a socialist, collectivist, re-construction of society. In its three most important aspects, the party programme supported action

> (a) to recover for the Nation complete possession of all the national physical sources of wealth . . .
> (b) to win for the workers of Ireland collectively the ownership and control of the whole product of their labour.
> (c) to secure the democratic management and control of all industries and services by the Nation and subject to the supreme authority of the National Government.

Delegate J. T. O'Farrell sought to insert definite socialist terminology, such as 'the common ownership of the means of production', into the programme. Johnson objected; the executive was 'asking the Congress

68 For a discussion of this aspect of the convention, see I.T.U.C. and L.P., *1918 report*, pp. 105, 107–15, 117; *Irish Independent*, 1 December 1918.

69 See issues of *New Ireland*, *Nationality*, and *Irishman* for 9 November 1919, and Selma Sigerson's pamphlet, *Sinn Fein and socialism* (Dublin 1918).

70 Full comment by both papers was given in their issues of 2 November 1918.

to subscribe to James Connolly and George Russell rather than to Sydney Webb and Arthur Henderson'. The reason the executive's draft had referred to national control, rather than workers' control, was because, in Ireland, 'the working-class was only half of the nation', the other half being mostly of the 'peasant proprietary class'. O'Farrell's amendment received only two votes.

The conference also re-affirmed the decision to house both the industrial and political branches of the labour movement in one organization. Although the political wing would be open principally to trade unionists, non-unionists would continue to be encouraged to join local labour organizations as individual subscribing members.[71]

Even after the Labour Party had withdrawn from the election, it continued to receive attention, as did the cause of 'labour' and of the 'workers' generally. The Parliamentary Party stuck the 'socialist' label on Sinn Féin, and warned the workers that the nationalists would abstain, whereas the Parliamentary Party 'would go to Parliament and help the Labour Party there to get the workers their full rights'.[72]

In Belfast the Unionist Party nominated three 'Unionist-Labour' candidates. In response, the Independent Labour Party branches put forward two candidates, one of whom stood against a 'Unionist-Labour' nominee. There were also three Trade Union candidates (the four constituencies involved were almost entirely Protestant). The Labour campaign was on the usual lines—shorter working hours, improved factory conditions, conciliation boards, an improved educational system—but avoided the issue of Irish self-government. Labour won second place in all four constituencies, but polled only a small vote. Their campaign was hurried and financially strapped, but it demonstrated that at least some of the Belfast Protestant workers were not prepared to follow the Unionist Party.[73]

The Labour Party withdrew from the election, according to the executive, in order to give the electorate a chance to decide on the question of self-determination. As the party was already committed to the principle of self-determination for all nations, this explanation is not very convincing. In reality the party was forced out of the election by negligible support: most workers had already decided to support Sinn Fein as the vehicle party to attain Irish nationhood, and Labour's latter-day conversion to self-determination and abstention came too

71 I.T.U.C. and L.P., *1918 report*, pp. 122, 131, 134, 136, 139–51, deals with the party programme. See also, *Irish Times*, 4 November 1918.

72 Leaflet supporting John D. Nugent, in the collection of pamphlets in the National Library of Ireland.

73 All three were trade unionists. The 'Unionist-Labour' candidates were Thompson Donald (Victoria), S. McGuffin (Shankill) and T. H. Burn (St. Anne). Donald was opposed by trade unionist Robert Waugh, McGuffin by I.L.P. nominee Sam Kyle. R. C. Porter (I.L.P.) and J. H. Bennet (trade unionist) stood in Pottinger and J. Freeland (trade unionist) in Cromac.

late. Sean O'Casey viewed the political situation following Sinn Fein's victory in the 1918 election:

> While the ultimate destiny of Ireland will be in the hands of Labour, it would be foolish to deny that the present is practically in the hands of the Sinn Fein Organization. Its activities are spread over the land, and Labour comes halting very much behind. This is explained by two reasons: Sinn Fein is not yet democratic, though Irish; while Labour, though fundamentally democratic, is far from being National. As Parliamentarianism was a poor copy of English Liberalism, so is Irish Labour a poorer reflex of English Trades Unionism. Its boasted Irish characteristics are far from being apparent . . . and the Irish Labour leaders are all painfully ignorant of their country's history, language and literature. It is because of these self-evident facts that Sinn Fein possesses a tremendous advantage over the Labour movement. Persecution has deepened our sympathy with our Irish origin, and the Irish Labour leadership, sooner or later, will be forced to realize that they must become Irish if they expect to win the confidence and support of the Irish working-class.[74]

In view of Sinn Fein's readiness to co-operate with Labour candidates who pledged themselves to permanent abstention, the Labour Party's complete withdrawal is somewhat surprising. It is not known for certain why the Labour leadership gave up after it had supposedly arrived at an agreement. There is no suggestion that Sinn Fein withdrew the offer, but Labour was under continuous pressure to leave the field to the separatists.[75]

Most likely, the Labour leadership decided that acceptance of the Sinn Fein offer would bring more problems than were justified by a few parliamentary seats. Acceptance would publicly ally the two parties, and in this alliance Labour clearly would be the subordinate partner. The Labour leadership was not willing to chance the disruption of the congress-party, whose fragile unity had been created by hard work and devotion. The Unionist-orientated workers would not have accepted the tie with Sinn Fein.

We should also remember the party leaders' syndicalist conviction that economic power precedes and makes possible political power.[76] They may have reasoned that it was better in the circumstances to avoid politics and throw their energies into the continuing drive for trade union expansion. But this outlook could only have brought retrospective comfort. The fact of the matter is that the Labour Party attempted to win a measure of political power in 1918 and failed, with

74 O'Casey, *The story of the Irish Citizen Army*, pp. 66–67.

75 Sinn Fein came to an agreement with the Irish Parliamentary Party regarding seats to be contested in Ulster.

76 I.T.U.C. and L.P., *1918 report*, p. 165.

most serious consequences both for the party and for the labour movement. In the 1918 election, almost two out of three electors were new voters.[77] At this decisive election they began the process of forming political allegiances, many of which lasted for a lifetime. The Labour Party was not to be in the first bidding for these votes.

77 A result of the Representation of the People Act of 1918. The Irish electorate was 701,475 in 1910 and 1,936,673 in 1918. Farrell, 'Labour and the Irish political system'. p. 487.

5

Labour and the National Struggle, 1919–21

From the beginning of 1919 to the middle of 1921 militant nationalists, led by Sinn Fein, successfully challenged British control in Ireland. Sinn Fein used its limited resources most effectively, in the end making impossible British rule in most of the country. Confronting the British-controlled police, soldiers and government officials were the small, scattered guerilla forces of the Irish Republican Army supported by a first-rate intelligence system. Sinn Fein had established a governing body—Dail Eireann—a viable judicial system and a large measure of control of local government. It successfully conveyed the impression that it was extending its governing power, and by 1921 a majority of the people supported the national movement.

When one compares the enormous power of the British in Ireland with the meagre resources of Sinn Fein, the support provided by the labour movement emerges as a crucial factor in the survival of the insurgents and in the partial achievement of their objectives. The labour movement contributed to the national struggle in a variety of ways; it did things that Sinn Fein alone could not do. Labour could, and did, launch crippling railway strikes which prevented the movement of British armed troops and munitions. It organized strikes to hinder road transportation, disrupt civil authority and force the release of imprisoned rebels. Because Labour was not directly involved in the conflict, its condemnation of British policy and practice could be presented as the views of an objective organization, with some influence in the international labour movement and in the British labour movement. Labour became Sinn Fein's ally in the local government elections, which resulted in the commitment of most local bodies to Dail Eireann and national independence. The labour movement was neither troublesome politically nor self-serving; it put aside its national ambitions. When approached by representatives of the British government concerning terms for a political settlement, Labour leaders referred them to the Dail government.[1] In short, the steady and wholehearted support of the labour movement was indispensible to the national movement in the struggle with Britain.

The Labour relationship with the political and military arms of the national movement was close but unofficial. Cathal O'Shannon, Johnson, William O'Brien, Thomas Farren and Thomas MacPartlin co-operated with Sinn Fein and the Irish Volunteers, and meetings of the leaders of the two movements were often held in Liberty Hall.[2]

1 William O'Brien, *Forth the banners go*, pp. 211–15; Frank Gallagher, *The Anglo-Irish treaty* (London 1965), pp. 28–29.

2 Cathal O'Shannon, writing in *Irish Times*, 31 January 1944 (see also issue of 18 January 1963); O'Brien, *Forth the banners go*, pp. 185–86, 189–90, 200–201; interview with Frank Robbins, 28 November 1964.

The Labour-Sinn Fein bond existed at all levels. In country districts as well as in Dublin, union rooms were used for I.R.A. meetings. James Everett, a Transport Union member and Labour public official at this time, had said that Labour Party and union meetings, especially those of the Transport Union, were often used as 'fronts' for I.R.A. gatherings.[3]

Despite close co-operation, the relationship between Sinn Fein and Labour was somewhat ambivalent. The congress-party never *officially* recognized Dail Eireann, and the Labour leaders were suspicious of the socio-economic views held by many within Sinn Fein. The labour movement, although it had temporarily put aside political hopes, continued to work towards the extension of united trade unionism and the creation of a social democratic state.

During these years of turmoil in Ireland, the trade unions and the congress-party functioned as open and legal organizations. The British authorities were aware of the co-operation between the Labour leaders and the national leaders, but they could do little except put various forms of pressure on the unions. Raids on union offices, arrests of suspects and destruction of property became commonplace. The first major raid occurred in March 1920 when six union offices were invaded and records seized; O'Brien and O'Shannon were among those arrested.[4] In November, following 'Bloody Sunday' (the day when fourteen British intelligence officers were killed by the I.R.A.), another big raid took place. The next month the *Watchword of Labour*, an outspoken supporter of Irish Independence, was suppressed for printing a full-page appeal for the Dail Eireann loan. The paper did not reappear until October 1921, long after the Anglo-Irish truce was declared. The pressure on the Transport Union is reflected in its annual reports. The 1920 report refers to 'the forces of the British Government, which chose out the union as a special object for its malignity' (p. 8); its 1921 report complained of 'the fierce hostility of the forces of the British Government, which everywhere singled out the union, its officials and active members for special attack' (p. 5).

The Citizen Army which continued to have its headquarters in Liberty Hall, played a most insignificant role in the national struggle. As mentioned above (Chapter 4), the leadership of the Transport Union had not encouraged the revival of the army after the rising, but both Peadar O'Donnell and Frank Robbins believe that James O'Neill, the commandant after 1916, was at least partially responsible for the

3 Interview with James Everett, 24 June 1964. Everett was a Transport Union official in Wicklow from 1918 and a Labour member of the Dail from 1922 until his death in 1967. See also Peadar O'Donnell, *There will be another day*, p. 17.

4 According to Bonar Law, 'O'Brien was arrested on suspicion of being implicated in a murder conspiracy that has resulted in the deaths of so many loyal servants of the Crown in Ireland.' Irish Labour Party and Trade Union Congress, *1920 report*, p. 20. For descriptions of the raids, see *Irish Bulletin*, 3 March 1920 (the *Bulletin* was the official publication of the Dail government); Cathal O'Shannon, ed., *Fifty years of Liberty Hall* (Dublin 1959), p. 77; O'Brien, *Forth the banners go*, pp. 198–200.

failure of the army to revitalize itself.[5] During 1919–21 the Citizen Army generally restricted its work to collecting intelligence and smuggling arms and ammunition.

Workers who wished to participate more actively in the fight against the British thus were forced to join the Volunteers, after 1919 the Irish Republican Army. This situation resulted in the unions losing the services of many of their most militant leaders, such as O'Donnell, Archie Heron and Eamonn Rooney, to the I.R.A. Ernie O'Malley portrayed the worker's position at this time:

> In the country the small farmers and labourers were our [i.e., the I.R.A.] main support and in the cities the workers with a middle-class sprinkling; the towns we could not count on. The countryman, sympathetic enough where a land revolution was concerned, was hostile to the revolution of organized labour. The farm labourers could understand the city workman, and was organized in labour unions with him. The movement as a whole was hostile to labour claims even though labour had helped to prevent conscription, had not contested the last election and was now refusing to carry armed troops.[6]

Viewing developments from America, James Larkin criticized the Labour leadership for failing to secure proper acknowledgement of its contribution to the national struggle. 'Why are the Party', he wrote, 'not demanding recognition and representation?' He was suspicious of a republic that had Arthur Griffith, his old adversary, as its vice-president (and, for almost a year, its acting president):

> I see that Sinn Fein wants a Republic in Ireland now. What is to become of Arthur's Kings, Lords and Commoners? Does he not want the foreign capitalists to come and start up industries in Ireland because land is cheap and labour cheap and unorganized . . . Not only do we demand a free Ireland, but we demand a free Ireland of free men and women. Certain forces in Eire seem to be exploiting the struggle for their own ends.

Thomas Foran wrote to Larkin in 1919 to assure him that although Griffith remained a leader in Sinn Fein, the pre-1916 conservative views of that organization on social and economic matters no longer applied:

> The old policy in its essentials is as dead as Queen Anne, and Griffith has had to move with the times. The [national] movement

5 Interviews with Peadar O'Donnell, 21 November 1964, and Frank Robbins. O'Donnell viewed O'Neill as a poor organizer; Robbins considered him a man of some organizational ability but self-serving and untrustworthy.

6 *On another man's wound* (London 1935), pp. 129–30.

> here is more advanced than you seem to think, and every day becomes more infected with Bolshevik propaganda . . . A big section of Sinn Fein is favourable to our propaganda and we are getting recruits every day from that quarter.[7]

The very effectiveness of Labour's contribution to the attainment of Irish self-government hindered its own political development. The success of the national movement meant, in practical political terms, the success of Sinn Fein. Great reputations, both political and military, were being built by the leaders of the national movement. Irish Labour helped to create these public personages who became Labour's political adversaries after 1922. William Norton, Labour Party leader from 1932 to 1959, once complained:

> In the welter of confusion and acrimony which followed the signing of the Treaty in 1921 and the civil war in 1922–23, the part played by the working-class in the national struggle from 1916 to 1921 has been somewhat obscured and its significance not fully appreciated.[8]

THE 'DEMOCRATIC PROGRAMME' OF 1919

Following its sweeping victory in the 1918 election, Sinn Fein prepared to form the national assembly it had promised the electors. The inagural public meeting of the assembly, Dail Eireann, was set for 21 January 1919. Only twenty-four of the sixty-nine successful Sinn Fein candidates were free to attend; most of the rest, including de Valera and Griffith, were in prison. The Labour congress-party, of course, had no part in the organization of the Dail, which was, in effect, a one-party body. Yet Labour had an important influence on the inaguration of the assembly, because the Labour leadership shaped the most significant document to emerge from the revolutionary Dail—the 'democratic programme'.

Prior to the opening of the assembly, the acting Sinn Fein leaders prepared a declaration of independence and a message to the 'free nations of the world'. They also decided that a statement of the social and economic aims of the new state should be presented in order to rally support within Ireland. For guidance on this matter, they turned to the Labour leadership. That Sinn Fein should do this is indicative of a lack of ideas and of confidence to deal with socio-economic questions. It is probable that the move was at least partially motivated by a desire to give Labour some role at this time. For its part, the Labour leadership was eager to undertake the task. The result was the 'democratic programme', a term first used in the Dublin Trades Council the previous March when a resolution was put forward urging the inclusion

7 Undated letters from Larkin to Foran in I.T.G.W.U., *The attempt to smash the Irish Transport and General Workers Union*, pp. 167, 168, see also p. xxi; letter from Foran to Larkin, 9 June 1919, O'Brien papers, N.L.I., box marked MS 15677–82.

8 R. M. Fox, *Labour in the national struggle* (Dublin n.d.), foreword.

of such a programme in the constitution of the future Irish state. The principal architect of the programme was Thomas Johnson; William O'Brien and Cathal O'Shannon assisted in the Labour draft.

O'Shannon later pointed out that this document 'was the only instrument which was fashioned outside the Dail and its Deputies'. Johnson's draft was not an official Labour statement, but, as O'Shannon commented, 'It was fairly representative of Labour opinion of what should be the social content of an Irish Government's fundamental legislation.'[9] Although the document was altered considerably before it was presented to the Dail, Johnson's basic provisions for a welfare state remained.

As the new government would claim to be a continuation, at least in spirit and philosophy, of the Easter week republic, the Labour leaders incorporated Patrick Pearse's socio-economic views from *The sovereign people*:

> The Nation's sovereignty extends not only to all the men and women of the Nation, but to all its natural possessions; the Nation's soil and all its resources, all the wealth and all the wealth-producing processes within the Nation.[10]

From this, they wrote a radical statement of the role of the modern state based on Pearse's premise.

When Johnson's draft was handed over to Sinn Fein, it aroused considerable opposition. According to P. S. O'Hegarty, the Irish Republican Brotherhood, that shadowy body within the national movement, objected to its radical nature, and Michael Collins, the I.R.B. leader, declared that he would suppress it. O'Hegarty believed the principal objection to the Johnson statement was that Sinn Féin's purpose in setting up the Dail was to use it 'to get the English out of Ireland', and 'all internal and arguable questions like [the democratic programme] should be left over until the English had actually been got out.'[11]

The content of the Johnson draft certainly was completely different from any socio-economic statement authored by Sinn Fein. Yet the document was not rejected; rather, it was revised by Sean T. O'Kelly.[12] Johnson's statement 'the nation must ever retain the right and the power to resume possession of such soil or such wealth whenever the trust is abused or the trustee fails to give faithful service' was removed. Also

9 Articles in the *Irish Times*, 31 January, 1 February 1944. In his memories, O'Brien does not mention either the democratic programme or his role in its creation.

10 Patrick Pearse, *Collected Works* (Dublin 1922), p. 336.

11 P. S. O'Hegarty, *A history of Ireland under the union, 1801 to 1922* (London 1952), p. 727. O'Hegarty further commented, 'It is not without significance that Mr Johnson . . . is by birth, rearing and temperament a doctrinaire English radical.'

12 Cathal O'Shannon, articles in *Irish Times*, 31 January, 1 February 1944. O'Kelly acknowledged the contribution of Johnson and O'Brien. *Seanad debates, XXVIII*, cols. 243–44. See also Patrick Lynch, 'The social revolution that never was', in *The Irish struggle, 1916–1926*, ed. T. Desmond Williams (London 1966) p. 45.

eliminated was his syndicalist-flavoured view that the government should 'encourage the organization of people into trade unions and co-operative societies with a view to the control and administration of the industries by the workers engaged in the industries'. And his plainly socialist conclusion was omitted:

> Further, the Republic will aim at the elimination of the class in society which lives upon the wealth produced by the workers of the nation but gives no useful service in return, and in the process of accomplishment will bring freedom to all who have hitherto been caught in the toils of economic servitude.

Even Patrick Pearse, in 1916, was too radical for Sinn Fein in 1919. Pearse's statement, 'No private right to property is good against the public right of the nation,' was diluted to 'all rights to private property must be subordinated to the public right and welfare' in the final draft. O'Kelly's task was to remove the obviously revolutionary socio-economic statements and to tone down the remainder of the document. The only new statement he inserted proposed the abolition of the Poor Law system and its replacement with a more humane welfare structure—a proposal that the labour movement for long had advocated. Even in its edited form, the democratic programme reflected the ideas of both Johnson and Irish Labour.[13]

The declaration of independence, the statement to the free nations of the world and the democratic programme were passed by the Dail without comment or debate. Piaras Beaslai, who read the programme to the assembly, later wrote:

> It is doubtful whether the majority of the members would have voted for it without amendment had there been any immediate prospect of putting it into force. . . . If any charge of insincerity could be made against this First Dail, it would be on this score. . . . Many would have objected to the communistic flavour of the declaration.[14]

Writing in 1944, O'Shannon declared that, although there had been an attempt to dismiss the programme as 'mere window dressing, as a gesture to help to keep Labour in good humour', it 'was given equal status and equal importance with the other two declarations adopted, as much solemnity and with as much display of earnestness'. In 1964, however, O'Shannon concluded that Beaslai's statement doubtlessly reflected the thinking of many in the first Dail.[15]

In his Marxian study of modern Ireland, the British historian Emil Strauss presents the view that the programme was passed only because

13 Michael McInerney, articles in *Irish Times*, 28 November 1966, 15 March 1967, 21 January 1969; Johnson papers, MS 17124.

14 *Michael Collins and the making of a new Ireland, vols.* (Dublin 1926), I, 259.

15 *Irish Times*, 31 January, 1 February 1944; interview with Cathal O'Shannon, 1 June 1964.

of the enforced absence of the moderate Sinn Fein leaders, principally Arthur Griffith.[16] Certainly it would be hard to imagine Griffith approving the programme's philosophy; he never publicly referred to it. But it is undeniable that the social ideas of Connolly and Pearse lived on not only in the labour movement: they also had some influence on Sinn Fein. In a penetrating study of the founding of Dail Eireann published in 1971, Brian Farrell has suggested that the strong socialist flavour of the programme could be attributed to the desire of the organizers of the new government to give the Labour leaders the leverage necessary to win recognition of Ireland's claim to national representation at the pending meeting of European socialists, the first since the war. Without parliamentary representation, the Irish movement would be placed at a disadvantage, but its delegation could point to the democratic programme to show that Ireland was moving in a socialist direction. Labour's success in this enterprise would support Sinn Fein's claim to national independence.[17]

Beyond all controversy is the fact that the programme was approved by the first Dail on 21 January 1919 and thus became implanted as a fundamental document in the national tradition. Sitting next to Johnson in the gallery of the Mansion House during the presentation of the programme, O'Shannon noted that Johnson, usually the most unemotional of men, was greatly moved, and, he, O'Shannon, had all he could do to prevent Johnson from standing and cheering.

Although the Labour Party made continuous reference to the democratic programme, it recognized that the government of 1919–21 was in no position to implement it. The succeeding government of the Free State held that it had no responsibility to do anything about the programme. To Kevin O'Higgins it was 'largely poetry' and the section dealing with natural resources was simply 'Communistic doctrine'.[18] But commitment to the programme was included in the Labour Party constitution of 1922 and in that of Fianna Fail when the party was founded in 1926. Granted that it was passed without parliamentary deliberation and with no immediate prospect of implementation, the programme still stands as the acknowledged social philosophy of the Irish revolutionary government.

IRISH LABOUR AT THE SOCIALIST INTERNATIONAL

Shortly after the first public meeting of Dail Eireann, a Labour delegation proceeded to Berne, Switzerland for the first international socialist conference since the war. For this gathering the British government provided passports, probably because the meeting, unlike the Stockholm conference of 1918, was held in peacetime under the sponsorship of moderate, constitutional socialists.

16 *Irish nationalism and British democracy*, p. 263.

17 Brian Farrell, *The founding of Dail Eireann: parliament and nation building* (Dublin 1971), pp. 56–61.

18 Dail Eireann debates, vol. I, cols. 573, 707 (21, 25 September 1922).

Johnson and O'Shannon were the two Irish delegates, representing both the congress-party and the Socialist Party of Ireland. They prepared a pamphlet which effectively presented Ireland's case for recognition as a separate nation.

This claim was based on precepts of 'the historic nationality, separate and distinct, of the Irish people', the 'continuous and unceasing struggle of the Irish people for its manifestation in sovereignty', and 'the present . . . demand of the people of Ireland for independence under a Republican form of government'.[19] The pamphlet created considerable interest among the delegates and was extensively quoted by the press. As there was no opposition, Ireland was seated as a national entity at the conference. This action meant that a delegation from the socialist conference would present Ireland's national claim at a hearing at Versailles.

During the course of the Berne meeting, O'Shannon proposed a resolution which demanded 'free and absolute self-determination for the Irish people and recognition by the powers at the Peace Conference . . . of the Republican declaration of Independence at Easter Week, confirmed by the people at the General Election'. For British Labour, Ramsay MacDonald immediately put forward a resolution calling for Irish home rule within the empire. The British and Irish delegations then compromised: The former agreed to support self-determination for Ireland, and the latter omitted mention of the republic and the general election. The conference passed two resolutions referring to Ireland, one supporting self-determination and the other calling upon the peace conference 'to make good this rightful claim of the Irish people'.[20]

On the principal political issue before the conference, the Irish delegation chose to stand on the far left. They opposed a resolution which supported parliamentary democracy because it 'tended to condemn the Soviet system of Government'. Instead they voted for the minority resolution calling for the 'dictatorship of the proletariat' and rejecting 'any kind of stigma which may be applied to the Russian Soviet Republic'. This vote, of course, did not mean that the Irish labour movement was revolutionary—time was to show it was not. Irish Labour was favourably disposed toward the Soviet government which had supported Ireland's national claims from the time of the Bolshevik takeover.[21]

Two months after the Berne meeting O'Shannon attended the international trade union conference in Amsterdam, where he again succeeded in obtaining recognition for Ireland as a separate nation.

19 Irish Labour Party and Trades Union Congress, *Ireland at Berne*, p. 40.

20 The Australian delegation joined in advocating the resolutions. I.L.P. and T.U.C., *1919 report*, pp. 23–27. The Irish delegation supported self-determination for Egypt, Indo-China and India. I.L.P. and T.U.C., *Ireland at Berne*, p. 47.

21 I.L.P. and T.U.C., *1919 report*, p. 31; *1918 report*, pp. 45, 48–49; *Irish Opinion*, 9 February 1918.

The resolutions approved by the two European conferences of 1919 did not directly support Dail Eireann, but they were important fillips to the fledgling republic. The achievement at Berne increased in importance when it became apparent that British opposition would not allow the Irish claim at Versailles. Speaking in April 1919, Eamon de Valera, now Dail president, declared, 'When we wanted the help of Labour in Berne, Labour gave it to us and got Ireland recognized as a distinct nation.'[22] But this recognition was of little lasting value to either the Labour movement or to the Irish government as the Berne meeting did not result in the creation of a new united socialist international. The attempt to do this was defeated by the ensuing dispute between the constitutional and revolutionary socialists. Rather than take sides, the Irish movement stood aloof. The congress-party turned down an invitation to the Second International in 1920 from which communists or supporters of the Soviet Union were to be excluded, and also declined to join the Third International, sponsored by the Soviet Union, although there was a sizeable minority within the Irish body who urged participation.[23] As a result, the Irish movement, almost alone among European labour, remained outside any labour or socialist international in the 1920s.

LABOUR AND DAIL EIREANN

The Labour congress-party never recognized the legitimacy of the Irish government, principally because the Labour leadership saw the preservation of a united trade union movement as its primary responsibility. It foresaw that recognition of the rebel republic would be objectionable to many northern trade unionists and would likely cause the suppression of the congress-party by the British administration in Ireland. Rather than acknowledge the existence of an Irish government at this time, the Labour leadership preferred to work toward their own objective, a workers' republic. Although the words, 'workers' republic', were not put into the party constitution until the 1930s,[24] the 1918 constitution was, as Johnson said, 'republican in essence' and it advocated the transformation of the economic system from capitalism to socialism. Both Connolly and Larkin had supported the goal of a workers' republic; since 1916 this ideal had been promulgated by leading Labour spokesmen and the Labour press. But the possibility of attaining a workers' republic in a country lacking signifi-

22 R. M. Fox, *Green banners*, p. 307. See also *New Ireland*, 5 April 1919; *Voice of Labour*, 29 March 1919; *Irish Independent*, 9 April 1919.

23 I.L.P. and T.U.C., *1920 report*, pp. 33, 97, 106–109.

24 In 1936 the following statement was inserted into the Labour Party constitution: 'The declaration of Democratic Principles and Sovereign Nationhood proclaimed at Easter 1916 . . . can be fulfilled only through the establishment . . . of a Workers Republic founded on equal justice and equal opportunity for all.' Following clerical objections, the final part of the statement was amended in 1940 to read: 'a republican form of government pledged to Social justice and equal opportunity for all citizens'. Irish Labour Party, *1936 report*, p. 173; *1940 report*, p. 169.

cant industrial development must have appeared remote even to its most enthusiastic supporters. Peader O'Donnell held that it was a grievous error for the labour movement to stake its hopes on the illusion of a future workers' republic rather than to throw its support behind the existing Dail republic and attempt to utilize it for the advancement of the workers.[25] The Nelsonian eye turned on the Dail republic by the congress-party was severely criticized by the supporters of the republican ideal both before and after the Anglo-Irish treaty.

As it had since 1916, the Labour leadership continued to trail behind public opinion on the national issue. In 1919 the congress-party cautiously advanced its position on the national question: the labour meeting that year declared in favour of the evacuation of British troops from the country. But it gave no indication who or what should be the governing authority after the troops had been withdrawn. At the same meeting a resolution was put forward welcoming the passage of a bill in the Commons which established the principle of government control and co-ordination of transport services. J. Duffy of Cork protested; the resolution 'assumed that this country was a domestic province of the British Government'. Notwithstanding, the resolution was approved overwhelmingly.[26]

The following year's labour conference took a stronger position on the national issue, confronting the question of who would govern following military evacuation. A lengthy resolution called for the government of the country to be left in the hands of the elected representatives and the civil servants. It also unequivocally asserted the right of the Irish people to decide not only what form of government they desired but what relationship a united Ireland would have with Britain. To this point it appears that the resolution upheld the authority of the Dail. A later passage, however, stated that the future government should be determined by a plebicite. Although this was the official position of Sinn Fein, the proposal set off a debate on the legitimacy of the government. Eamonn Rooney, an I.R.A. officer as well as a Transport Union organizer, proposed an amendment deleting the reference to a plebicite. This would 'emphasize the present position of the country', he said, 'The resolution would then affirm what the people had already declared.' P. T. Daly felt the recent local government elections had shown 'there was absolute unaminity in elected representatives pledged to the demand for a republic.' Cathal O'Shannon disagreed. When the question of future came to be settled, he said, Labour should stand for an 'out and out' workers' republic. Rooney's amendment was defeated, ninety-nine to thirty-three,[27] and once again Labour had refused to commit itself on the issue of the government's authority.

The Labour executive eventually found it necessary to refer, at least indirectly, to the existence of the Dail. Its statement to the British

25 Interview with Peadar O'Donnell.

26 I.L.P. and T.U.C., *1919 report*, pp. 130, 136, 141.

27 I.L.P. and T.U.C., *1920 report*, pp. 130–32; see also p. 37.

Labour Party's commission on Ireland in December 1920 acknowledged the existence of a government in Ireland other than the British government:

> It was clear to the [British] delegation that the vast majority of the workers in Ireland were in full and complete agreement with the National demand for complete political freedom and were prepared to take their share in the building of *the Irish state now in the course of construction*. Their demand was that *these building operations should be allowed to proceed* without interference by British armed forces. . . .[28]

The executive's manifesto, 'The country in danger', issued at Easter 1921, explicitly referred to the government, but only to draw attention to the fact that the Dail had done nothing to implement its 'democratic programme'. And the 1921 Labour conference, although informally addressed by de Valera, proposed no resolution of recognition or support for that government. To all appearances the congress-party leadership viewed the 1921–22 republic merely as a transient vehicle towards national independence.

Even the strongly nationalist Transport Union avoided the issue. Its annual reports, reflecting O'Brienite prudence, contained no mention of the Dail (the 1920 report even failed to mention the munitions transport strike, which involved many union members). But in its 1921 report, published after the Anglo-Irish truce, the union took credit for Labour's role in the national struggle and even referred to the government.

L. J. Duffy, a member and later chairman of the Labour executive, summarized the relationship between the labour movement and the Dail in his address to the 1924 Labour conference:

> The working class as a whole were in the struggle and were part of the force that sustained it. The great majority of the delegates were fully conscious of this and gave the alliance, informally, no doubt, their benediction; some went very much further and submerged their own identity in the Nationalistic movement, but Congress never formally, officially or specifically took any cognisance of that arrangement. By its silence it acquiesced in the part that was being played, and tolerated the visible association of the official Labour movement with Sinn Féin, although, in fairness, let it be said, some delegates felt the situation embarrassing from time to time.[29]

Sinn Fein was still publicly grateful to the labour movement for its unofficial but significant support. Speaking at the 1921 congress-party meeting, after the Anglo-Irish truce, de Valera praised Labour's contribution:

28 Ibid., p. 37. Emphasis added.

29 I.L.P. and T.U.C., *1924 report*, p. 120.

> It is not necessary for me to say—you know it so well . . . that were it not for the solidarity of Labour behind the national cause . . . the Irish cause would not be where it is today. . . . We who are in a position to gauge the advance of the Irish cause . . . know what your support has been to us and what your refusal to put forward even your own interests has meant to the cause of Ireland in the past two years.[30]

Nevertheless, Sinn Fein and Labour kept a critical eye on the other. When members of the Transport Union repaired an R.I.C. barracks in Enniscorthy in October 1920, the Dail ordered a special court to investigate the affair. The British authorities, it was alleged, allowed the court to meet in the hope that the investigation would result in hostility between Labour and the government, but the ploy failed. Another incident concerned a case before a republican court in Wexford involving the Transport Union and a Sinn Fein farmer. The authorities again allowed the proceedings to continue. Michael Collins learned of the British action and contacted William O'Brien who headed off trouble between the union and the Dail. Shortly before the 1921 truce Collins warned O'Brien of a British attempt to infiltrate spies into the unions, but he was careful not to issue orders to O'Brien:

> I will not suggest to you how you can meet it as, of course, you will know far more about that aspect of the case than I do, but I would say that as a first step on your part a couple of reliable branch secretaries should be informed—I mean put on their guard with a view to immediate discovery when the attempt is made. From what I know of the way the enemy regard the unions I am sure that the Transport would be the first body to be dealt with.[31]

On its side, the Labour leadership was sensitive to conservative tendencies of the government. When two Dail ministers, Griffith and MacNeill, were quoted in the *Financial Times* in September 1920 as saying that investors had nothing to fear from the insurgent government, the Labour newspaper reacted sharply:

> In the assurances given by Messrs. Griffith and MacNeill we see a ready and willing acceptance by these spokesmen of the present Republican Government of all that is essential to the continuance of British supremacy in Ireland.
>
> Unless the Irish Republic is going to carry out the principles of the Proclamation of 1916 and the Democratic Programme of

30 I.L.P. and T.U.C., *1921 report*, p. 82.

31 O'Brien, *Forth the banners go*, pp. 200, 216–18. See also J. L. McCracken, *Representative government in Ireland: a study of Dail Eireann, 1919–48* (London 1958), p. 38. On one occasion in September 1920, Deputy D. Kent of East Cork complained that 'men on the run' were being denied work by the Transport Union because they were not members of the union; the Labour minister promised to discuss the matter with the union. *Dail Eireann proceedings, 1919–21*, p. 218.

> 1919, unless it is going to enthrone Pearse's Sovereign People as ruler in a Workers Republic, independence means the replacement of French [the lord lieutenant] and Greenwood [secretary of state for Ireland] by Messrs. Griffith and MacNeill—and nothing more.[32]

In his study of the modern Irish Parliament, J. L. McCracken has made the point that the revolutionary Dail was largely middle class; urban workers and farmers were grossly under-represented, and the Dail 'had no claim to be a cross-section of the whole community'.[33] The leaders of the labour movement often criticized the lack of direct worker representation in the virtually one-party assembly. Shortly after the next general election, in which the Labour Party again gave a clear field to Sinn Fein, the executive wrote to de Valera: 'The Dail does not reflect the will of the people on any question but one, viz; the demand for national freedom.' Then, having acknowledged that the Dail *was* representative on this question, the Labour leaders contradictorally declared that their party 'reserves the right to oppose any scheme of settlement that may be proposed until it had been sanctioned by a freely elected National Assembly or by a plebiscite of the people'.[34]

Seeking the best of both worlds, the trade unions accommodated to a situation in which two governments claimed authority. The unions employed the arbitration and mediation services of both the Dail and the British governments.[35] They continued to participate in the British health service scheme because the funds were held in Britain, but they were prepared to withdraw if the Dail would finance an alternative programme. O'Brien and Foran accepted membership on the British-sponsored Irish Coal Commission; Johnson served on the Dail's Industrial Resources Commission, acting as chairman of the food sub-committee.

Although limited in resources and in freedom of action, the government made several progressive departures in labour matters. It established a separate ministry of labour, which formed a national conciliation board as early as 23 August 1919.[36] A 'Labour Arbitration Tribunal', as envisaged by the 1917 Sinn Fein programme, was set up in September 1920. Entering disputes where both parties agreed to arbitration, this institution had a creditable record. The ministry launched a plan for conciliation boards for local government bodies and their employees in March 1920. Of the eighty-eight bodies that

32 *Watchword of Labour*, 25 September 1920.

33 McCracken, *Representative government in Ireland*, pp. 33–34.

34 O'Brien papers, N.L.I., MS 15680.

35 Interview with Archie Heron, 30 November 1964. Heron was both a Transport Union organizer and an I.R.A. officer at this time.

36 The three Labour ministers during 1919–21 were Constance Markievicz, Thomas Kelly and Joseph McGrath. Countess Markievicz and McGrath had been active in the Labour movement, and Kelly had a pro-labour voting record on local bodies in Dublin.

considered the scheme, seventy adopted it, but the Transport Union did not find the plan to be particularly useful.[37] The ministry also attempted to alleviate the mounting unemployment problem. At Easter 1921 the Labour leadership proposed radical measures to promote more jobs—the ending of reductions in wages and in tillage, the surrender of idle land to 'those who are willing to work it', the creation of government-sponsored industry, the temporary suspension of rents and annuity payments. The ministry's plan stressed the need for 'the production and manufacture in Ireland of goods presently manufactured in England'. It also established an employment bureau and arranged a Labour-Farmers Union conference at which the farmers' organization agreed to some of Labour's proposals.[38]

The British presence in Ireland prevented the government from carrying out more than a fraction of its declared social and economic reforms. As President de Valera commented, the democratic programme contemplated a situation somewhat different to that in which they actually found themselves.[39] The Labour leadership clearly recognized the existing difficulties.

THE STRIKE WEAPON AND THE STRUGGLE FOR IRELAND

The labour movement initiated several strikes which were major factors in the undermining of British authority in the country. Of the four work stoppages discussed here, only the munitions transport strike was positively directed towards the achievement of national independence. All the strikes, however, helped to weaken British control.

The Limerick General Strike

The first of these strikes occurred in Limerick in April 1919, when the British authorities proclaimed Limerick a special military area and imposed a system of permits for access to the city. The Limerick Trades Council responded by calling a city-wide general strike. That the council should organize a work stoppage in these circumstances was not exceptional; what was surprising was the effect and the length of the strike. Beginning on 14 April, Limerick was in the hands of the strike committee for twelve days. With support from the public, the local leaders of the I.R.A. and Richard Mulcahy, I.R.A. chief of staff, the committee organized food distribution and issued notes of exchange, which were accepted by local merchants. Visiting foreign newsmen labelled the situation created by the strike the 'Limerick soviet'. Indeed, workers delegated by the committee were in control of the public life of the city. They took charge of observing the operation of shops, controlled food queues and directed traffic. A strike committee

37 *Dail Eireann rep., 1921–22*, p. 27; I.T.G.W.U., *1921 report*, p. 10.

38 There were about 100,000 persons unemployed at this period. See I.L.P. and T.U.C., *1921 report*, p. 2; *Dail Eireann proc., 1919–21*, p. 285; *Dail Eireann rep., 1921–22*, pp. 21, 27; *Irish News*, 28 May 1921; *Irish Bulletin*, 20 August 1920.

39 McCracken, *Representative government in Ireland*, p. 68.

member, James Carey, wrote: 'It was generally admitted that the city was never guarded or policed so well previously. The people, for once, were doing their own work, and doing it properly. There was no looting and not a single case came up for hearing at the Petty Sessions.'[40]

The committee appealed to the Labour national executive for assistance, and five days after the strike began Tom Johnson arrived in the city. He proposed that the workers evacuate Limerick, leaving the British forces with an 'empty shell'. When this suggestion was rejected, he left the direction of the strike in the hands of the local committee. Shortly after Johnson's visit, however, the national committee assumed responsibility for the paper notes of exchange and issued an appeal for contributions to the strike fund. The executive estimated that £7,000–£8,000 per week would be needed to support the Limerick action, but the response was disappointing: only £1,700 was raised, £1,000 of which came from the Transport Union and £500 from the Mansion House Conference. When the British indicated that they might change the permit order, the strike committee (on 26 April) instructed all who could return to work without permits to do so. Shortly thereafter the British order was withdrawn, and all Limerick workers resumed their jobs.[41]

The Motor Permits Strike

The following autumn saw another strike against a British decree, this time the requirement that all motor vehicle drivers obtain a permit. The reason for the strike was stated by a union official: 'The object of the Order was to get at one class of people only and these were of the Republican Party, because it sought to deprive them of the use of motors.'[42] But the efforts of the trade unions to defeat the order were characterized by dissention and disunity. There were two rival unions organizing vehicle drivers—the new, small Automobile Drivers Union and the Transport Union. The new union decided to call all its members out on strike on the day the permit order went into effect, whereas the Transport Union agreed to allow its members to continue working but not to seek permits. The Automobile Drivers Union did not inform the congress-party executive of its decision to strike, but did secure the approval of the Dublin Trades Council.[43] In an attempt to secure

40 James Kemmy, 'The Limerick soviet', *Irish Times*, 9 May 1969. Kemmy's article introduced much new material.

41 At the 1919 Labour conference Johnson and the other leaders were criticized for their hesitant response to Limerick's appeal and for their failure to organize a national strike. William O'Brien declared that a campaign of 'lying and innuendo' was being conducted against the executive. Unexpected support came from socialist Walter Carpenter, who claimed that a national protest would have been inappropriate 'unless they were prepared to use guns and hoist the Red Flag from one end of the country to the other'. See I.L.P. and T.U.C., *1919 report*, pp. 57–58, 73–74, 80–82, 117; letter from James Byrne to P. T. Daly, 28 April 1919, in O'Brien papers, N.L.I., MS 15657.

42 I.L.P. and T.U.C., *1920 report*, p. 87.

43 Rivalries within the labour movement were responsible for this situation. The Automobile Drivers Union was a rival of the Transport Union. O'Brien was secretary of the

agreement on tactics, the Labour executive met with leaders of the two unions, together with spokesmen from the Stationary Engine Drivers Union. When the Automobile Drivers refused to alter its policy, the executive agreed to support its action.

The ensuing strike had an immediate effect in Dublin—the *Dublin Evening Telegraph* (2 December) reported, 'Except for a comparatively few private cars . . . and military wagons, there was almost a complete absence of motor traffic'—and throughout the country road traffic was greatly reduced. The secretary of state for Ireland complained, 'The only argument the strikers were able to advance was that they objected to any restrictions being placed on them by an alien Government.'[44]

Two weeks after the strike began a special Labour conference was convened to consider the situation. The Automobile Drivers Union advocated spreading the strike to other unions, culminating in a general strike. This plan was rejected in favour of a policy restricting the strike to motor vehicle drivers and collecting a strike fund from other unions. The Automobile Drivers Union, however, refused to co-operate; it set up its own strike fund and continued its efforts to spread the strike, with some success—the Steam Engine Drivers Union and the Amalgamated Society of Engineers struck in sympathy.

The strike ended in failure after ten weeks. It revealed disunity within the labour movement, and, as in the Limerick strike, the national executive was accused of negligence and inaction. The Automobile Drivers Union, overlooking its own behaviour, continued to claim that the congress-party had given only half-hearted support.[45]

The Political Prisoners Strike

There was no evidence of disunity and lack of purpose in Irish Labour's next strike. On 5 April 1920 one hundred political prisoners went on hunger strike in Mountjoy jail. The Irish viceroy, Lord French, declared that they could die if they chose to do so. As the hunger strike continued, the Labour executive decided on a dramatic demonstration for the release of the men involved. On 12 April it issued a manifesto for a general strike which declared that the prisoners 'are suspected of loving Ireland and hating her oppressors. . . . These men, for the greater part [are] our fellow workers and comrades.' It urged Irish officials of British-based unions to demand support from their parent executives. The general strike began the next day and lasted two days; it was completely effective in all parts of the country barring the Belfast

Transport Union and also of the congress-party. The secretary of the Dublin Trades Council was P. T. Daly, whose opposition to O'Brien has been discussed in Chapter 4. For information on the motor permits strike, see I.L.P. and T.U.C., *1920 report*, pp. 11–18, 82, 88, 91.

44 *Irish Bulletin*, 11 December 1919.

45 During the munitions transport strike, an official of the Automobile Drivers Union claimed that had the permits strike been fought to the end there would have been no need to fight the munitions issue. The union shortly collapsed and many of its members joined the Transport Union.

area. The strike ended only after the British authorities had changed their policy toward the prisoners.[46]

The Munitions Transport Strike

The munitions transport strike, which began a month later, was Labour's most effective contribution to the independence movement. It arose out of the refusal of British dock workers to load munitions on the *Jolly George* because the arms were intended for the support of the Polish government, then at war with the Soviet Union. Seizing on this precedent, Dublin and Dun Laoghaire dockers refused to unload a British munitions ship. The Transport Union supported the men in their refusal.[47]

The strike soon spread. When the British used troops to unload the munitions, the railway workers refused to move them. The railwaymen, members of the British-based National Union of Railwaymen, also used the Polish case as a precedent; the N.U.R. national executive had directed the members not to move military goods destined for Poland. But it soon became apparent that the executive did not approve of the action of its Irish branch. The N.U.R. attempted to bargain the men back to work. It would call for a special meeting of the British Trade Union Congress to consider the Irish question if the railwaymen would move the munitions. But the Irish members not only refused to carry any military goods, they also refused to transport troops carrying arms. The special British conference was held; by a three to two vote it condemned the continued military occupation of Ireland and urged its unions to consider strike action if the government did not change its policy. Few strikes resulted, but the resolution was the strongest position yet taken by British Labour on the Irish question. The N.U.R. executive, however, paid no union benefits to those who refused to move munitions or armed troops, only to those who were dismissed for lack of work.[48]

The congress-party executive, on its part, quickly moved to support the dockers and railwaymen. It appealed to 'all who profess and call themselves Nationalists, Republicans or Trade Unionists' to contribute to a fund for the disemployed. Over £120,000 were raised, allowing for a weekly payment of £3 to each jobless man, a figure considerably higher than that paid during an ordinary industrial dispute.[49]

Rather than call a strike of all railwaymen, the executive decided on a policy of allowing individual dismissals in order to force the railway companies and the British authorities to deal with each and every case of refusal by railwaymen. The transport of troops and munitions would stop, but most of the 17,000 railwaymen could remain on the

46 I.L.P. and T.U.C., *1920 report*, pp. 34–37; O'Brien, *Forth the banners go*, pp. 190–92.

47 O'Brien, *Forth the banners go*, pp. 194–95; interview with Frank Robbins.

48 J. D. Clarkson, *Labour and nationalism in Ireland*, pp. 418–22.

49 *Watchword of Labour*, 12 June 1920; see also issue of 19 June; I.L.P. and T.U.C., *1921 report*, p. 86; O'Brien, *Forth the banners go*, pp. 195–97.

payroll, and the British would have no convenient reason for stopping all rail traffiic, as was threatened.

Over five hundred men were dismissed. The British forces were accused of attempting to close down the railways. Their tactics were described by Thomas Farren:

> It was a common practice for the military authorities to get up upon the footplate of an engine and say to the driver, 'you have got to drive this train,' put a revolver to his head and say, 'you will get the contents of this if you don't drive,' and to the everlasting credit of the railwaymen they said no.[50]

Railwaymen who continued to move munitions and armed troops were dealt with by the I.R.A., who used tarring as one of their methods of persuasion.[51]

With the threat of a general stoppage of all rail traffic hanging over the country, a special conference of labour organizations was held on 16 November 1920. The conference overwhelmingly approved the actions of the dockers and railwaymen, and denounced as a forgery a document—circulated by the British authorities—purportedly from the 'Minister of War of the Republic of Ireland' ordering the strike.

Though the conference voted to continue the strike, the executive decided on the 14 December that it was time to pull back. Military activity had intensified: Cork city was partially destroyed, martial law had been declared in Cork, Limerick, Tipperary and Kerry. The financial situation of many strikers was becoming desperate, and the British forces had broken up the food committees and the road transport arrangements made by local authorities and labour groups, arresting many of the participants. The executive therefore advised the railwaymen to carry anything that the British were 'willing to risk on the trains'. The N.U.R. executive recommended a resumption of work and generally succeeded in preventing workers from being victimized by the railway companies. In March 1921, the union granted £3 to each man dismissed for refusing to work trains carrying munitions or armed troops.

Thus ended a campaign that very considerably disrupted British attempts to put down the Irish revolt. Troops had to be taken from military duty to unload the munitions, and motor transport had to be used to supply stations which had been cut off by the railway stoppages. 'This state of affairs . . .', admitted General Macready, 'was a serious set-back to military actions during the best season of the year.'[52]

50 I.L.P. and T.U.C., *1921 report*, p. 88; see also *Irish Bulletin*, 29 June 1920.

51 See Sylvain Briollay, *Ireland in rebellion* (Dublin 1922), pp. 65–66; Florence O'Donoghue, *No other law* (Dublin 1954), pp. 79, 132.

52 Neville Macready, *Annals of an active life* (London 1924), p. 472. Macready was appointed British commander-in-chief in Ireland in 1920. The munitions strike is discussed in I.L.P. and T.U.C., *1921 report*, and in Clarkson, *Labour and nationalism*, pp. 418–24.

All four of these strikes were directed, at least in part, at breaking down British authority in Ireland, and they achieved a considerable measure of success. The prisoners' strike and the munitions dispute were particularly aided by the fact that public opinion, as well as opinion in the labour movement and the congress-party executive itself, had shifted almost completely in favour of the demand for national independence.

LOCAL ELECTIONS OF 1920 AND PARLIAMENTARY ELECTIONS OF 1921

The Labour Party had removed itself from the 1918 general election; it was to remain aloof from the 1921 parliamentary elections—but it did not abstain from all electoral activity. On Johnson's recommendation, Labour concentrated its political energies on the long-delayed municipal and urban council elections which, after long delay, were set for January 1920. In order to counteract a Sinn Fein sweep, the British government introduced the proportional representation, single transferable vote system. The only organization other than Sinn Fein that was national in scope was Labour, but British hopes of a conflict between the two in the local elections were to be dashed. The Labour executive, however, appreciated the fact that proportional representation would injure the chances of unauthorized and unofficial labour candidates.

Local Elections of 1920

The party's programme for local government was hammered out at a special conference in October 1919. Most of the platform was composed of items that the labour movement had supported for many years—medical treatment of school children, provision of school meals, scholarships, direct labour on municipal works and trade union rates and conditions for public employees. There were some new, more radical proposals as well. The housing plank advocated the immediate commencement of local housing schemes, without waiting for financial negotiations, and proposed that the unused house room of the wealthy should be rated. Another plank suggested the creation of municipally owned dairy farms, the creation of a single municipal milk supply and co-operative restaurants. A truly revolutionary proposal called for municipal occupation and utilization of land, buildings and machinery whenever they were 'unreasonably withheld from use'. Other points in the programme stressed combined action by the councils for providing house-building materials, organization of coal supplies, promotion of electrical power schemes, development of natural resources and a variety of public projects. It was clear that many of the Labour proposals could not be put into effect without going beyond the bounds of existing laws, but, read today, the programme gives the impression that the elections would be held in the most peaceful of times. This certainly was not the case; this was a period of violent conflict between the forces of the I.R.A. and the British military.

The certainty of Sinn Fein participation in the election forced Labour to consider, once again, the relationship between the two movements. The Labour conference urged its candidates not to become involved with other political parties, yet there is much evidence of agreement between Labour and Sinn Fein on the local level as to the number of candidates each should put forward. In Cork, for example, the Transport Union and Sinn Fein completely merged their political forces; as a result the Cork Trades Council only nominated three candidates. In many parts of the country, a working alliance between the two parties was practical and necessary. Both sought to oust the Nationalists who had controlled the councils the last six years. Both agreed to use the local councils as levers towards independence. Neither party could ignore the presence of the other in the election; both had large numbers of candidates. If conflict developed between them, control of many councils would be lost and the national cause thereby injured. Many adherents of Sinn Fein were workers who, although trade unionists, did not follow the political leadership of the Labour movement. The Sinn Fein nominees, of course, were pledged to support the Dail and to make the local bodies units of that government, while the Labour candidates were not so pledged. This difference did not have any serious effect on the election alliance. As far as is known, the Labour executive did not directly advise local Labour candidates to stay clear of co-operation with Sinn Fein.

Labour candidates were nominated in all parts of the country, even in the smallest towns and in the rural areas—in several places there were more Labour than Sinn Fein nominees. Nationally, Sinn Fein put forward 717 candidates; Labour 595; Unionists, 436; others, 588 (of whom about three-fifths were nationalists), for the 1,470 seats vacant. In Cork, Derry, Wexford, Belfast and Dublin, individual unions backed candidates independent of those selected by the trades council.

Division in Dublin

The Labour forces in Dublin faced the elections in a state of disarray brought about by the Daly-O'Brien conflict. Daly, defeated by O'Brien in the 1918 election for congress-party secretary and in 1919 for the post of Transport Union treasurer, was then beaten by Foran for the secretaryship of the union's insurance section. Charged by O'Brien with incompetance and dereliction of duty, Daly twice threatened to bring suit against his opponent. Following his defeat by Foran, Daly began a public attack on the leaders of the Transport Union.

With the support of Jim Larkin's sister Delia and Michael Mullen, Daly first organized protest meetings in the leading cities outside Dublin. Then, on 20 July 1919, he faced his opponents before 4,000 Transport Union members (and others) in the Mansion House. Both Daly and Delia Larkin argued that because Daly had been appointed to his union post by James Larkin, he could not be removed from this position without Larkin's consent. When a union official cited charges of financial mismanagement against Daly, 'a man produced a revolver and threatened to shoot him.' The report of the *Irish Independent* (21 July 1919) continued: 'This produced a general stampede. . . . Then the scene shifted to the platform, where in the course of a scuffle, Mr. William O'Brien was struck, and bowled over from his chair.'

The controversy went on, with Daly and his supporters producing abusive handbills as well as a weekly paper, the *Red Hand*, which contained unstinted praise for Larkin and general condemnation for the new rulers of the Transport Union. The latter fired back in the pages of the *Voice of Labour*. From New York, Larkin ordered an end to the quarrel and the restoration of Daly to his insurance position. The *Red Hand* ceased publication, but the union executive rejected Larkin's instruction as improper—an action that would be remembered when Larkin returned in 1923. But Daly was not completely luckless. Later in 1919 he succeeded in being elected secretary of the Dublin Trades Council (a position he held until his death in the early 1940s).[53]

The point that divided Dublin Labour prior to the elections was a matter in which Daly had been involved in 1917: the acceptance of a testimonial from public employees by a Labour member of the Dublin Corporation. The Dublin Trades Council executive demanded that the Labour member surrender his seat, but this was not upheld by the membership. The executive resigned, and a new executive was elected, with Daly in control. With this, the Transport Union withdrew from the council, and the three union members on the Dublin Board of Guardians resigned their seats in protest of the trades council's position.

In the local elections, the trades council put forward ten candidates, including Daly; the Transport Union put forward a slate of its own, nominating six union members and three members of the Socialist Party of Ireland. The union nominees—one of whom was Walter Carpenter, an active socialist propagandist—campaigned as 'Labour Republicans'. The Transport Union's action was contrary to the rules established for local elections and approved by the Labour conference. In its defence, the union said it was preserving 'the good name and fair fame of Dublin Labour'.[54]

In the election, held 15 January 1920, six of the trades council nominees were successful; eight Transport Union 'Labour Republicans' were elected, Walter Carpenter being the sole loser.

Unity in Belfast

The Belfast Labour Party, sponsored by the Belfast Trades Council, put forward a strong field of candidates. The Unionist Party, realizing the threat of a Labour victory, nominated 'a good selection' of Unionist labour candidates who went forward under the banner of

53 *Voice of Labour*, 2 August 1919; O'Brien papers, N.L.I., MSS 15657, 15676; *Red Hand*, 19 July–16 August 1919. See Chapter 4 and Chapter 7 ('The Larkin Split').

54 *Watchword of Labour*, 17 January 1920.

the Ulster Unionist Labour Association. The 'good selection' consisted of eight candidates out of a Unionist total of fifty-five.

The Unionist organization urged the workers to vote against 'Sinn Fein trade unionism' as represented by the Belfast Labour Party. The president of the Belfast party discounted this. 'Home rule', he said, held no fears in his party. 'We consider that the progress of Ireland is more to be considered than remaining as we are between the barriers of religious bigotry.' Unionist J. C. Craig replied that outside the Ulster Unionist Labour Association there was no political party in which trade unionists could 'exert an influence on parliamentary or municipal elections . . . unhindered by the power of the Church of Rome'.[55]

Against the Unionists fifty-five candidates, the Belfast Labour Party put forward twenty-two; Nationalists, nineteen; Sinn Fein, thirteen; Independent Labour, ten; Socialists, three. The outgoing city council contained fifty-two Unionists and eight Nationalists; Labour had no representation.

The election results were a serious setback for the Unionists. They lost fifteen seats in the council, reducing their membership to thirty-seven. Thirteen Labour candidates, both regular and independent, were elected, Unionist solidarity was broken in almost every ward of the city.

The Labour members of the new city council nominated D. R. Campbell for mayor. With the support of the Sinn Fein members, Campbell received eighteen votes, the Unionist candidate, thirty-six. The Labour representatives called for improvements in the tramway service and minicipalization of coal distribution. They proposed evening meetings of the council so as to allow working people to attend. Their political leanings were soon indicated: Assistant Police Commissioner Redmond, an Ulsterman recently transferred to Dublin, was assassinated. The Labour councillors opposed a resolution condemning the shooting, proving to the *Belfast Newsletter* that they were 'Tinged with Sinn Feinism'.[56]

The Unionist Party proceeded to cripple the development of effective opposition by abolishing proportional representation for local government elections in Belfast and environs before the next local elections were held. The return of the simple majority system reinforced the traditional sectarian rivalries; as the Nationalists only represented a minority, they would always be only the opposition. The change greatly hindered the development of the Labour Party in Belfast.[57]

55 *Belfast Newsletter*, 31 January, 7 February 1920. The Ulster Unionist Labour Association was formed in June 1918. P. Buckland, *Ulster unionism and the origins of Northern Ireland* (Dublin 1973), p. 138.

56 *Belfast Newsletter*, 23 January 1920. The *Newsletter* also thought it disgraceful that Labour Councillor James Baird was present in his 'dongaree shirt, cap in pocket'.

57 McCracken believes that the abolition of proportional representation did not hurt Labour, but had the effect of preventing Unionist splinter groups from gaining significant

National Results

The country-wide results gave Labour about one-fourth and Sinn Fein one-third of the seats. Labour returned 324 candidates, Sinn Fein 422, Nationalists 213, Unionists 297, and independents 128. One hundred and sixteen trade unionists were elected by parties other than Labour. Labour elected ninety-seven candidates in the province of Ulster, Sinn Fein and Labour combined won 250 seats to the Unionists 329 in Ulster. Nationalist incumbents were defeated in great numbers. In Dublin, where Sinn Fein won forty-two seats and the combined Labour membership was raised to fourteen, the majority of Nationalists were swept from office. The same happened in Cork: thirty Sinn Fein-Transport Union candidates were elected, but only fourteen Nationalists along with three trades council nominees.[58]

In most cases, co-operation between Labour and Sinn Fein continued after the election. The Sinn Fein-Labour majority on the Enniscorthy urban council voted to rip out of the minute book a resolution, passed in May 1916, condemning the 1916 rising. In Thurles both the Labour and Sinn Fein councillors were arrested before the first council meeting. The Labour members of the Dublin Corporation voted for the Sinn Fein nominee for mayor. Only on the Ballinasloe council was conflict reported. There Sinn Fein joined with the Ratepayers Party to gain control of the council, although Labour had elected the largest number of members.

Two of three lord mayors, seven of eight mayors and sixty-two of ninety-nine urban council chairmen pledged allegiance to the Dail republic. Because of the large number of Labour representatives elected, it appears that the great majority of these supported this policy. The Wexford Urban Council, controlled by Labour, was one that pledged allegiance to the Dail. The Dublin Corporation 'acknowledged the authority of Dail Eireann as the duly elected Government of the Irish people,' by a vote of thirty-eight to five, indicating the concurrence of a majority of Labour members.[59]

As a result of the 1920 municipal and urban elections Labour became a significant force in local administration. Next to Sinn Fein it had the largest share of representation; combined with Sinn Fein it helped form a majority in every municipal and urban board in Leinster,

---

parliamentary representation. J. L. McCracken, 'The political scene in Northern Ireland, 1926–37', in *The years of the great test*, ed. F. MacManus (Cork 1967), p. 157.

58 Some additional results (from *Tipperary Star*, 24 January 1920):

	Sinn Fein	Labour	others
Clonmel	14	6	4
Drogheda	13	3	6
Kilkenny	9	5	6 (Nationalists)
Limerick	20	4	4
Waterford	20	3	14 (Nationalists)
Wexford	2	11	9 (Ratepayers)

59 *Irish Bulletin*, 4 May 1920; *Watchword of Labour*, 17 January 1920.

Munster and Connacht. The organ of the government, the *Irish Bulletin*, spoke in January 1920 of 'the sweeping success of Sinn Fein' as an expression of the will of the Irish people in favour of a republic without acknowledging the inclusion of Labour victories as Sinn Fein successes. But in a further analysis of the election in May 1920, the *Bulletin* explained that 'under the heading "Republican" are included Sinn Fein Councilors and Labour Councillors in favour of Ireland's Independence'.[60]

What is particularly significant in this election is the strong support received by Labour in the six north-eastern counties and the relatively poor showing there by Sinn Fein. The Labour success plus Sinn Fein's more limited attainment, severely damaged the Unionist contention that the great majority in Ulster opposed any change in the position of Ireland in the United Kingdom. The *Irish Times* of 24 January said the election results proved that the need for partition was fallacious, and the *Irish Bulletin* (20 January) gave some acknowledgment of Labour's successes in the north: 'Over the six counties the tale is practically the same story of a Carsonite debacle under the assaults of Nationalism and Labour'.

Taking the Labour and Sinn Fein vote together, the election was a confirmation of the demand for national independence. The *Watchword of Labour* surely exaggerated in its interpretation of the results: 'As Labour stands almost solidly with Sinn Fein on the National question, the election really means that the Empire is in danger and with it the whole capitalist system.'[61]

Following on its success in the January elections, the Labour Party prepared for the June county council and rural district elections. This time the difficulties would be greater, as most of the councils were in rural areas where the party was weakest. However, the Transport Union had been relatively successful in organizing farm labourers, and it was hoped that the union's rural branches could be used as election organizations in the campaign. Labour looked upon the Farmers Union, composed of farm owners, as an enemy, together with the 'Farmers Freedom Force', an extremely conservative body of farm owners opposed to trade unionism. The F.F.F., organized by Loftus Bryan, put forward candidates in several districts, particularly in County Wexford where it was matched against the strongest Labour Party organization in Ireland.

The objectives of Labour in the June elections were the same as in January: to win control of the councils, first as levers towards national independence, and second to further the interests of the workers. Also as in the January elections, two groups of Labour candidates contested the elections in Dublin. At least two Transport Union candidates were

60 *Irish Bulletin*, 19 and 24 January, 17 May 1920. McCracken quotes the earlier *Bulletin* statement without realizing Labour's contribution to the success of the national movement.

61 24 January 1920.

defeated by the trades council nominees. In County Wexford, Labour defeated Bryan's F.F.F., but in general the party did not achieve an outstanding success. Many Labour candidates ran as 'Labour-Republicans', and it appears that trade unionists frequently contested the elections under the colours of Sinn Féin. Most of the candidates elected solely as Labour nominees were in the six north-eastern counties.[62] Nevertheless, Labour representation—in some form—was established in rural areas for the first time. Sinn Fein, with the support of Labour, won control of twenty-nine of thirty-three county councils.

Most of the new Labour members joined their Sinn Fein colleagues in pledging allegiance to Dail Eireann. As a result of the republican sweep in January and June, the majority of local governing bodies ignored British authority in Ireland and recognized only the Local Government Department of the Dail. In practical terms, this was not always easy. James Everett, elected chairman and paymaster of the Wicklow County Council, tells how the British authorities offered him very tempting inducements if he would co-operate with them. When Dublin Castle cut off the county's grants, the council issued credit receipts for welfare payments, salaries and the like. The receipts were accepted by shopkeepers, and the system was successfully maintained until the British evacuation in 1922.[63] In Dublin the Sinn Fein-Labour majority dismissed the city clerk for his refusal to accept a member who had signed her nomination papers in Irish. Dublin Castle claimed that he could not be dismissed because he was a permanent official, whereupon the council withheld his salary.[64]

In the attainment of its second local government objective—the implementation of its social and economic proposals—Labour had little success. Only in Cork did the Transport Union alliance with Sinn Fein produce a minor result: the council appointed a committee of inquiry to study 'the standard of living and a living wage for the Cork working man'. The *Watchword of Labour* (4 December 1920) attacked 'reactionary republicans' in local government: the lavish promises given to the working class were only promises. The Sinn Fein-controlled Roscommon County Council for example, closed down all road work, disemploying hundreds of workers. The Limerick Councy Council, also with a Sinn Fein majority, increased the load on horse carters, 'in effect decreasing wages'.

By 1922 it was quite clear to the Labour leaders that essential agreement with Sinn Fein on the national issue did not necessarily mean

62 *Irish Bulletin*, 15 and 19 July 1920, gave the figures: of 362 Labour candidates elected to rural district councils, 325 (90%) ran as Labour-Republicans; of 460 Labour candidates elected to boards of guardians, 382 (83%) ran as Labour-Republicans. Sinn Féin polled 75·1% of the vote; Sinn Fein and the Labour-Republicans combined secured 80·9%. Ibid., 11 June 1920.

63 Interview with James Everett (see footnote 3, above). Everett said most Labour members took the oath of allegiance even though they had not been pledged to do so before the election.

64 O'Brien, *Forth the banners go*, pp. 172–75; *Watchword of Labour*, 13 November 1920.

agreement on social and economic issues. 'Labour has learned from its experience of Rural, Urban and County Councils that the enemies of the Workers are to be found in all political parties, no matter what labels were attached to them when seeking election. Political war-cries are used by men to cover their anti-labour prejudices.'[65]

The 1921 'Southern Ireland' Election

The 1920 Government of Ireland Act partitioned Ireland into two 'home rule' areas. In the spring of 1921 the British government arranged elections for the new parliaments: it set the election for the twenty-six counties of 'Southern Ireland' for 19 May 1921; the election for the six counties of 'Northern Ireland' would be held five days later. Lloyd George emphasized that the act would be enforced; it would be 'war to the knife' with the rebel forces. The reaction of the Irish government was to treat the pending contests as elections for a second Dail Eireann. Yet, as in 1918, Sinn Fein agreed to divide the seats to be contested in the north, and the Unionists put forward a few 'Unionist-Labour' candidates.

The Labour Party decided to abstain from the elections. The executive explained that non-participation made clear Labour's rejection of the partitioning act, which had 'no valid sanction, being in contravention to the declared will of the Irish people'. The executive also desired to defeat what it saw as 'the obvious design of the British Prime Minister to divide the democratic forces'. It advised workers 'to demonstrate their loyalty to Ireland and freedom by voting only for those candidates who stand for the ownership and government of Ireland by the people of Ireland'.[66]

The Labour statement was mere window-dressing: the party stayed outside the elections because it would have been disastrous for it to try to force its way into them. Ireland in 1921 was a country at war. Labour's natural constituency—the working class—had been drawn to the militancy either of Sinn Fein or of Unionism. In this period of conflagration no one would have noticed if Labour had attempted to light a spark. As in 1918, Labour was forced into a highly principled but impotent position.

The Dublin Trades Council taunted the Labour leadership for not attempting to obtain a share of seats from Sinn Fein. The congress-party's support of the national movement during the preceding two and a half years justified a claim, but Sinn Fein would never make an agreement unless the Labour nominees promised to enter Dail Eireann after the election. Such an arrangement would be vigorously opposed by the Unionists within the congress-party and might well splinter the organization. National elections were for another time; for now, Labour would continue its unofficial but effective support of the national movement.

65 Irish Labour Party, *Address to the electors* (pamphlet, pub. June 1922).

66 I.L.P. and T.U.C., *1921 report*, p. 18.

The decision not to take part in the election was breached by one prominent Labour figure. It is little wonder that Sinn Fein in Wexford turned to Richard Corish: by 1921 he was mayor of Wexford, chairman of the county council and the dominant politician in the area. Before accepting the Sinn Fein nomination, Corish received approval of this step from the Wexford Trades Council, the only organization to which he considered himself pledged. He neither sought the permission of the Labour executive, nor told them of his decision. The executive termed Corish's action a breach of the spirit of the party's constitution, but this mild reprimand suggests that the Labour leaders had been forewarned of his decision, or at least were prepared to live with it.

Corish's move was a topic of debate at the 1921 Labour conference. In his defence it was said that the Wexford Trades Council had agreed to let him go forward because the Dail was the government of the country and the Dail deputies would have an important part in the independence struggle. Cathal O'Shannon reminded the conference that he had urged Labour participation in 1918 because he had foreseen how other parties would use popular Labour men to further their own political fortunes if Labour stood aside. But, unlike many others, Corish was not permanently lost to the Labour Party.[67]

The Northern Parliamentary Election.

Labour's non-participation in the elections also applied to the contests for the first parliament of 'Northern Ireland'. While the Anglo-Irish war raged in the south, the northern part of Ireland was rent by sectarian conflict. Riots in July and August 1920 had driven 20,000 Catholic workers from their employment. By the time violence subsided in Belfast two years later, 455 people had been killed (267 Catholics, 185 Protestants) and 2,000 wounded. The American Commission on Conditions in Ireland, a group committed to Irish independence, found that 'the Ulster pogroms were not primarily due to a spontaneous flare-up of smoldering bigotry, but were rather promoted by those whose economic and political interests were opposed both to strong labour unionism and to Irish Republicanism.' It reported that 'certain manufacturers and Unionist politicians' became alarmed about both the Catholic-Protestant worker solidarity in the 1919 shipyard strike and the Labour and Sinn Fein successes in the local elections.[68] It is a fact that the riots began a month after the county council elections of 1920. It is also a fact that the Transport Union experienced rapid growth in Belfast in 1919, but by 1921 the results of sectarian warfare were clear. The Belfast branch could report only that it still was in existence.[69]

In preparing for the parliamentary elections, the Ulster Unionist Council made provision for a few 'labour' candidates in order to draw

67 For the Corish case, see ibid., pp. 18, 110.

68 American Commission on Conditions in Ireland, *Report* (New York 1920), p. 69.

69 The Belfast branch grew from 500 to 3,000 in 1919. See I.T.G.W.U., *1919 report*, p. 5; *1921 report*, p. 7.

worker support. Unionist politicians made the most of the previous election of three 'Unionist Labour' candidates to the House of Commons in 1918. A Unionist publication proclaimed:

> [The Ulster workers] are the only organized workers in Ireland who have representatives in Parliament; three of their members have been returned directly on the Labour ticket, an event that has no parallel in the history of Irish Nationalism.[70]

The 'Labour' label was merely a façade; the three consistently voted with the Conservative Party. After the passage of the 1920 Partition Act, the Ulster Unionist Council assigned its 'Labour' seats in the Northern Ireland Parliament only.

The Belfast Labour Party did not officially contest the election, but there were five 'Independent Labour' candidates—four in Belfast and another in County Down. It appears that these candidatures had little organized support; the nominations were put forward at the last moment. The nationalist candidates were apportioned between Sinn Fein and the Nationalist Party. Leading figures in Sinn Fein—de Valera, Griffith, Michael Collins and Eoin MacNeill—stood for election; the Nationalist Joseph Devlin contested two seats for his Party.

Both the Nationalists and the Unionists appealed to the workers as champions of labour. Of the forty Unionist candidates, five stood as 'Unionist Labour' including William Grant, one of the founders of the Ulster Unionist Labour Association. Grant campaigned on the platform that 'the Loyalist labour people in the North of Ireland had been misrepresented, and . . . steps should be taken to show people that Labour in the North of Ireland was not like labour in any other part of the British Empire.' To Grant, 'There was only one issue and that was Protestantism versus Sinn Feinism.'[71] For the Nationalists, Joe Devlin claimed credit for securing unemployment compensation benefits for Ireland. The nationalist *Irish News* supported Devlin and his colleagues as 'the best representatives of labour in the absence of official Labour candidates. The Sinn Fein candidates are, so far as Labour is concerned, in the same category.' The paper warned the workers 'against the machinations of pseudo-labour advocates'; one could vote for the unofficial labour candidates 'if you sincerely think of them as friends of Labour'.[72]

The four Belfast Independent Labour candidates attempted to organize a rally in the Ulster Hall on 17 May 1921 (the hall had previously been denied to the Sinn Fein candidates). Before the meeting began, Unionist shipyard workers stormed the hall. In County Down, the Independent Labour candidate was accused of attempting to split the Unionist Labour vote; pressure was repeatedly brought to bear to

70 Ulster Unionist Council, *The Labour Party and Ireland: analysis and criticism* (Belfast 1921). P. Buckland, *Ulster unionism*, pp. 136, 143.

71 *Belfast Newsletter*, 6, 7 May 1921.

72 *Irish News*, 24 May 1921.

force him out of the election.[73] Against a background of anti-nationalist rioting on several nights leading up to the election, the *Irish Bulletin* (24 May) reported that the campaign

> has been notorious by the use of British armed forces to cow the Nationalist and Sinn Fein electors. The Special Constabulary formed out of the Carsonite Volunteers . . . was fashioned to break the spirit of the Nationalist and Republican minority in Ulster. . . . Of nineteen Sinn Fein candidates eight are in jail, seven others are 'on the run'.

Concerning polling day, 24 May 1921, the *Irish News* declared, 'It is no exaggeration to say that thousands of Catholic voters were forced and brutally prevented from exercising the franchise.' It reported mob action, knifings, shootings, fighting and general violence. The *Belfast Newsletter*, on the other hand, saw the arrest of four Sinn Fein poll workers as the only extraordinary happening of the day.[74]

The results showed two Independent Labour candidates at the bottom of the poll with the other three receiving very few votes. All forty Unionists were elected, along with six Nationalists and six Sinn Feiners. Political Labour was indeed in poor shape in Belfast, and events of the next few years brought little improvement. No Labour candidates were nominated in Belfast for the British parliamentary elections in 1922. The Labour Party (Northern Ireland) was not organized until January 1924. By the middle twenties Labour began to revive, and among the men responsible for this was Harry Midgley, one of the unofficial labour candidates swamped in 1921.

Once partition was established, the Irish Labour Party made no attempt to continue as an all-Ireland party. The decision no doubt was a necessary one: to attempt to deal with two political situations and two parliaments would have been far beyond the party's capacity. It viewed the Labour Party (Northern Ireland) as a fraternal body, always of course with the hope that the political barriers to unity would someday be removed.

BRITISH LABOUR AND IRISH INDEPENDENCE

The Irish Labour leadership constantly sought to influence British Labour opinion on Ireland. Following the Berne conference, when the British delegation had supported Irish self-determination, the Irish Labour leaders set out to win the British labour movement as a whole to this position.

In the spring of 1919 the congress-party executive urged Irish workers in Britain to 'bring all their influence to bear' upon the labour

73 Ibid., 19 May 1921. The disturbances at the Ulster Hall, according to the *Irish Bulletin* (24 May), were 'under the direction of officials of the local branches of the British Empire Union and the Ulster Ex-servicemen's Association'.

74 *Irish News*, 25 May 1921; *Belfast Newsletter*, 28 May 1921. See also *Irish Bulletin*, 26 May 1921.

organizations there. The message was sent to Irishmen on the Tyne and the Clyde; contacts were sought with Irish workers in Lancashire and South Wales. Further, an appeal was made to all British workers 'to use the forces at their command to compel their Government to withdraw the Army of Occupation'.[75] In the spring of 1920 Irish Labour was given an opportunity to make a practical political gesture in Britain. During his imprisonment in England, William O'Brien was nominated by a group of Irish workers to stand in a parliamentary by-election at Stockport, near Manchester. Before the May polling date, Irish Labour figures and members of the Dail addressed election meetings. O'Brien received only three hundred votes, but his candidature gave notice to the British Labour Party that the Irish issue could become a factor in British Labour politics and that the party's position on this issue could come under attack on home grounds.[76]

The leaders of Irish Labour made repeated trips to London to urge a more advance position on the British leadership. Following one unsuccessful mission in October 1921, the party-congress executive reported:

> It was clear . . . that the political ideas, the social and parliamentary systems of English government and the exigencies of party politics in England were dominant in the minds of the English [Labour] representatives while cutting little or no ice with the Irish.[77]

One shift in the British stance occurred in May 1920. The small Independent Labour Party, going beyond the self-determination position of Irish Labour, passed a resolution urging 'the recognition of the Irish Republic'. The Scottish Trade Union Congress at its 1920 meeting supported self-determination for Ireland and the withdrawal of the 'Army of Occupation'.[78]

At last, on 11 November 1920, the parliamentary Labour Party announced it had altered its position on the issue of Irish government. The occasion was the third reading of the 1920 Government of Ireland Bill.[79] The party had three demands:

1. All British forces be withdrawn from Ireland.
2. The responsibility for maintaining order be placed on the local authorities.

75 I.L.P. and T.U.C., *1919 report*, pp. 56, 136. See also *Watchword of Labour*, 12 June, 28 August 1920.

76 *Watchword of Labour*, 15 May 1920; O'Brien, *Forth the banners go*, p. 190; O'Brien papers, N.L.I., MS 13961; Dail Eireann, 1919–21, papers, DE 2/174.

77 *Watchword of Labour*, 27 October 1920.

78 Appearing as the fraternal delegate from the Irish T.U.C., Johnson urged the Scots to this course. I.L.P. and T.U.C., *1920 report*, p. 39. The action of the Independent Labour Party was reported in *Watchword of Labour*, 12 June 1920.

79 Earlier, the Irish Labour executive had been asked by the secretary of the British Labour Party to suggest amendments to the bill. The executive recommended that the British party ignore the proposed legislation, 'as we shall probably do even when it becomes an Act'. I.L.P. and T.U.C., *1920 report*, p. 31.

3. An entirely open constituent assembly be immediately elected on the basis of proportional representation. This assembly would be charged to work out, without limitations, whatever constitution the Irish people desired.

Two conditions were included, however: first, the constitution must protect minorities; second, Ireland would not allow itself to be used as a military or naval menace to Britain.

A special congress-party meeting on 16 November 1920 accepted the British party's policy. What both organizations chose to overlook was the de facto republic already in existence. Yet they must have realized that if the British army was withdrawn the Dail would become the ruling authority, and the constituent assembly they recommended would, very probably, have come into conflict with the Irish government.

The Parliamentary Labour Party demanded the establishment of a government commission to inquire into the situation in Ireland. When this request was refused the party appointed its own commission, headed by Arthur Henderson, the party leader. The delegation arrived in Dublin on 30 November 1920, the end of the most horrible month of the Anglo-Irish war. With Johnson as their guide, they toured the country viewing conditions and gathering evidence. After studying the origin and effect of the Belfast riots, the commission found that 'in the North, Labour is influenced far too much by religious animosities to take an unprejudiced view of the situation.' It rejected the Ulster Unionist Labour Association's claim that it was a bona fide labour organization.

The commission arrived in Cork shortly after the city had been partially destroyed. A well-documented booklet, *Who burnt Cork city?*, (which was published under the name of the congress-party but probably written by Alfred O'Rahilly) held the British forces responsible for the destruction, charging:

> [That] outrages similar to the sacking of Cork have been previously committed by the Crown forces in Ireland is admitted by everyone except Sir Hamar Greenwood. The British Government absolutely refused to allow any judicial civilian inquiry into the Cork outrages . . . The investigation is to be conducted by the defendents themselves, by the very persons whom thousands of men and women in Cork wish to charge and incriminate.[80]

The Labour commission concurred with these conclusions, and even made several unsuccessful efforts to bring about a truce between the British and Irish forces.[81]

Reporting to a special British trade union conference on 31 December 1920, the commission urged support for Irish self-determination, and in the following month the British Labour Party began to campaign

80 I.L.P. and T.U.C., *Who burnt Cork city?* (Dublin 1920), p. 13.

81 British Labour Party, *Report of the Labour Commission to Ireland* (London 1921), pp. 59, 60. The commission's report was challenged by the Ulster Unionist Council in their booklet, *The Labour Party and Ireland*.

against the government's repressive policy in Ireland. The 1921 party conference supported, albeit by a narrow margin, the position of the parliamentary Labour Party. An amendment explicitly limiting Irish self-determination to freedom within the empire, forcefully argued by J. H. Thomas, was rejected.[82]

What caused British Labour to change its position? One factor surely was its recognition that the Irish revolt was not the work of a small band of revolutionaries, as was the 1916 affair, but was a movement with mass support. Another factor was the realization that as long as there was no acceptable solution to the Irish question the issue would bedevil and disturb British Labour. There was the influence of the many cadres of Irish workers within the British labour movement. Perhaps the leadership was concerned about the possible effect of the Irish question on future elections; the O'Brien candidature in Stockport had been in reality a revolt against both its policy and authority. A change of front at this time made good political sense as public opinion was becoming increasingly critical of Lloyd George's failure to arrive at a solution. Irish Labour's sustained campaign to influence the policy of British Labour also must have had an effect. The fact that one of the great parties in Britain now supported Irish self-determination was an important element in bringing an end to the Anglo-Irish war and the eventual attainment of self-government in most of Ireland: Irish Labour can rightly claim at least a modest share of credit for this achievement.

THE REVOLUTIONARY FEVER

In the wake of the world war the question of social and economic change was raised in all European countries, and Ireland was no exception. Most of those concerned in Ireland agreed that the pre-war socio-economic situation was unacceptable and, therefore, some type of change was necessary: opinion divided, however, upon what system was best suited to Ireland.

Among the many systems advocated was that based on co-operation which, of course, incorporates features of both the capitalist and socialist systems. It will be recalled that Connolly and Larkin had supported the ideal of a co-operative commonwealth, as did the 1918 constitution of the Labour Party. After 1918 George Russell (AE) and Aodh de Blacam became the leading spokesmen for co-operation, but both emphasized the small rural enterprise and its individual aspects while Labour looked to the urban industrial sector and urged the need for worker control and the democratic management of industry. Labour's co-operative ideal would require state participation; Russell and de Blacam did not foresee this as being necessary.[83] In agreement with

82 Clarkson, *Labour and nationalism*, p. 433.

83 Russell presented his co-operative ideas in his book, *The national being* (Dublin 1916), in the magazine he edited (*Irish Homestead*), in the *Irish Statesman* and in an article in the *Voice of Labour* (19 May 1919). See Chapter 9 and Arthur Mitchell, 'The economic

Connolly, de Blacam favoured a co-operative commonwealth similar to the social and economic system of the old Gaelic state. In *Towards the republic* he urged the Dail to move in this direction, arguing that co-operativism was not against Catholic doctrine and that the 'good sense and deep faith' of the Irish people would preserve this system from deteriorating into 'rash Red-flaggery' of which 'the danger is very small'.

The government gave several indications of support for advanced social and economic ideals. The 'democratic programme' declared that it was the duty of the republic to ensure the development of Irish industry 'on the most beneficial and progressive co-operative industrial lines'. In August 1919 President de Valera spoke of the principle of the co-operative commonwealth 'as the best social and economic framework for the nation'. *New Ireland* (23 August) commented, 'This statement will receive a very different welcome to the scowls which hailed Jem Larkin when he said something like this six years ago.' In creating the Department of Labour and in its relations with the labour movement, the government appeared to have progressive tendencies.

The British saw more than progressivism in the rebel regime; it saw the hand of the Bolsheviks. Drawing on the Irish Unionist Alliance's alarmist pamphlets linking Bolshevism, Sinn Fein and revolutionary inclinations in the Irish labour movement, the Lloyd George government published in June 1921 a white paper which attempted to prove that Sinn Fein had become a partner to the Communist regime in Russia.[84] Indeed, inconclusive negotiations between the Soviet Union and the Irish republicans had taken place in Washington, D.C. The Russians became the only national government to recognize the 1919 republic. For its part the Dail, on 29 June 1920, passed a resolution authorizing the dispatch of 'a Diplomatic Mission to the Government of the Russian Socialist Federal Republic with a view to establishing diplomatic relations with that Government'. But the mission was not sent and no formal recognition of the Soviet government was accorded.[85]

It soon became apparent that the Irish government was not to be an agent for social and economic revolution. A test of its intentions came in the spring of 1920 when land seizures began in the western counties. The land purchase acts and old age pensions had done much to improve economic conditions in rural Ireland, yet there continued to be a discontented, impoverished and landless population. The disruptive

---

philosophy of AE', *Irish Times,* 17 April 1967. De Blacam's views are in his *Towards the republic* (Dublin 1918). Another co-operative advocate was L. P. Byrne (A. E. Malone); see *New Ireland*, 19 April 1919; Dublin Trades Council, *minutes*, 26 Aug. 1918.

84 *Irish Times,* 10 June 1921. A letter from Thomas Johnson, ibid., 11 June 1921, declared that the document contained many errors.

85 Dail Eireann, 1919–21, papers, DE 2/15; statement of Lev Sedin, Russian journalist, *Irish Times,* 21 March 1966; *Dail Eireann proc., 1919–21,* p. 174. In 1966 the minister for external affairs, Frank Aiken, claimed that the Dail formally recognized the Soviet government by the 1920 resolution. *Irish Times,* 17 March 1966.

conditions of the time—the weakening British authority, unemployment, shortages—provided the opportunity for the agricultural labourers to make their own revolution by seizing the land on which they worked. Nearly 50,000 land workers had joined the Transport Union, but the labour leadership did not become directly involved in the land conflict.

The Dail ministry quickly condemned the seizures: 'The present time when the Irish people are locked in a life and death struggle with their traditional enemy is ill-chosen for the stirring up of strife amongst our fellow countrymen,' ran a government proclamation of 29 June 1920. To deal with the unrest, the Dail established land courts and a land commission, while using its armed forces to squelch land seizures. According to Peader O'Donnell, 'Many an I.R.A. man in jail in '22 and '23 cursed his use as a defender of pure ideals to patrol estate walls, enforce decrees for rent, arrest and even order out of the country leaders of local land agitations.'[86]

During the same period, the leaders of the labour movement, both in the congress-party and the Socialist Party of Ireland, sought answers to the economic and social problems besetting the country. The Soviet system of government by councils of workers, soldiers and peasants was appealing, and, as has been noted, Irish labour was friendly toward the new Russian regime. But the congress-party flatly denied British press accusations that it was being financed by the Soviet government.[87]

The Labour leaders had behind them the growing power of the trade unions: in 1914 there were 110,000 workers in unions affiliated with the congress; by 1920 the figure was 250,000, with the Transport Union alone claiming 130,000 members. The peak was reached in 1921 when 300,000 workers were in affiliated unions.[88] An awareness emerged that this growing industrial strength combined with a collectivist philosophy could lead to social revolution—a situation conservative observers found alarming. In its major national strikes—from the anti-conscription demonstration of 1918 to the munitions transport strike of 1920—the labour movement demonstrated the potentialities

86 *There will be another day*, pp. 19–20. See also Strauss, *Nationalism and democracy*, pp. 26, 64–65; *Dail Eireann proc., 1919–21*, pp. 177–80, 277–78; *Constructive works of the first Dail*, no. 2, pp. 199–202; statement of Ministry of Labour, June 1920, Dail Eireann, 1919–21, papers, DE 2/5, and Kevin O'Shiel's memoirs, *Irish Times*, 14–26 Nov. 1966.

87 A London newspaper quoted the *Russian Press Review*, 15 October 1920, which said that Russian trade unions had sent aid to Irish railwaymen then refusing to carry munitions and armed troops. The congress-party said it had not received the aid, but if any help had arrived, it would 'gladly have accepted it'. I.L.P. and T.U.C., *1921 report*, p. 15. For other aspects of the party's relationship with the Soviet Union and Soviet ideology, see *1919 report*, p. 31; *1921 report*, p. 175; *1922 report*, p. 10; I.L.P. and T.U.C., *Ireland at Berne*; speech by Thomas Johnson, 'If the Bolshevists came to Ireland', in *Irish Opinion*, 23 February 1918; S.P.I. celebrations of the second anniversary of the Bolshevik revolution, *Watchword of Labour*, 15 November 1919.

88 *Watchword of Labour*, 26 June 1920; I.L.P. and T.U.C., *1921 report*, p. 75.

of its power. Following the general strike for the release of the hunger strikers, the *Irish Times* (19 April 1919) commented:

> Organized Labour in Ireland has won a victory which will stimulate it to further efforts. . . . The clever men who lead it have a definite programme—far more definite indeed than that of Sinn Fein. Labour, for instance, not only is Republican, but it knows exactly the sort of Republic that it wants. It proposes gradually to capture many of the essential functions of government. A continuation of the fight which ended yesterday might have witnessed the establishment or attempted establishment of Soviets of workmen in all parts of Ireland. We are on the eve of a critical struggle between Socialists and anti-Socialists in this country.

The Labour newspaper (the *Voice of Labour*, after October 1919 the *Watchword of Labour*), under the able editorship of Cathal O'Shannon, enthusiastically supported revolutionary change in the social and economic order. Food committees organized by workers were labelled 'soviets'; large estates should be divided and given to landless farm labourers.[89] Johnson, O'Brien, Foran and Farren, in fiery public speeches, expounded similar ideas. Warre B. Wells, British journalist and observer of Irish events, had the mistaken view that Johnson was a man coldly capable of employing violence: 'If the occasion arose and the purposes of his movement could not otherwise be served, he might hang you politely but firmly from a lamp-post—with a graceful gesture of regret for the unhappy necessity withal.' Wells went so far as to project Johnson as the Michael Collins of the labour movement (the de Valera would be Larkin and the Griffith, Connolly).[90] In Liberty Hall sat William O'Brien, quiet, calculating, determined, considered to be the keeper of the Connolly heritage and the director of the largest and most revolutionary union in the country. But, as events were to prove, none of the Labour leaders had any intention of formenting a violent socio-economic revolution. Referring to this period, Joseph Deasy wrote, 'The militancy of the Larkin and Connolly leadership was gone. Leaders like William O'Brien, Thomas Farren and Cathal O'Shannon expressed themselves very radically at times, but in their actions caution prevailed.'[91]

Beginning in 1919 the congress-party took measures which appeared to herald the start of social revolution. In February a special Labour conference demanded higher pay, shorter hours and a national minimum wage for all workers. In a militant statement to the employers, the executive warned, 'Any remedy we could suggest must inevitably involve a complete alteration in the basis of your system, must end in giving control of the process of wealth production and distribution to the people engaged in those processes in the interest of the community.'

89 *Watchword of Labour*, 1 May 1920; *Voice of Labour*, 12, 26 July, 2 August 1919. The paper was suppressed in December 1920.

90 *Irish indiscretions* (Dublin 1923), pp. 172, 158, 171. A general picture of the labour movement at this time is found in pp. 154–86. Interestingly, Wells barely mentions O'Brien.

91 *Fiery cross: the story of Jim Larkin* (Dublin 1963), p. 29.

But the employers were not terrified by this threat to their property; the May Day deadline for the concession of the demands passed without general compliance, and the congress-party did not move. In effect, Labour's bluff had been called.[92]

The annual congress-party meeting of 1919 urged the unions to organize worker councils in all cities and towns,[93] but the revolutionary intentions of Irish Labour were not directly tested again until the spring of 1920. In May striking creamery workers at Knocklong, County Limerick, all members of the Transport Union, seized control of the plant, ran up the red flag and continued operations, declaring, 'We make butter, not profits.' The men were led by three union organizers—John McGrath, Jack Hedley (pseud. Sean O'Hagan) and John Dowling. Probably the inspiration for this tactic came from Britain where similar events were taking place. It is apparent, however, that this and following seizures were the result of initiative by union field organizers and did not represent official union policy. Further, the seizures were essentially defensive in nature in that the workers involved were trying to prevent wage reductions.

Seeking markets for their products, the Knocklong workers called upon the trade unions to become buyers. The Belfast Co-operative Society agreed to take a regular supply of butter; otherwise, responses were few. After five days the owners agreed to the workers' wage claim, and the workers handed back control.[94]

Not until a year later did a similar seizure occur. At Arigna on the Leitrim-Roscommon border, a dozen mine employees, also members of the Transport Union, were faced with a pay cut. They took control of the mine and sold the coal locally. Their inspiration was neither the example of Knocklong nor the Russian revolution; they told a police investigator that their justification was in the decision of the the Irish Coal Commission of 1920 which declared that if owners failed to maintain mine production the workers involved had the right to do so. After two months the owners agreed to continue the existing wage rate, and the workers surrendered control.[95]

Both seizures received scant attention in the daily press, but the events and their meaning were a central topic at the 1921 Labour conference. John McGrath, the Knocklong leader, saw the revolutionary possibilities in the developments:

92 The Labour demands included a 44-hour week, a 150% increase over pre-war wages (about 20% real increase due to inflation) and a 50s per week minimum wage. I.L.P. and T.U.C., *1919 report*, pp. 44–49; *Voice of Labour*, 15 February, 17 May 1919.

93 Similar councils were established in Britain in August 1920 to fight the government's anti-Soviet actions. A. J. P. Taylor (*The trouble-makers: dissent over foreign policy, 1792–1939*, p. 153) claimed the councils marked the nearest point to revolution ever reached in Britain.

94 The seizure at Knocklong was not the first takeover by workers. In January 1919, Transport Union organizer Peadar O'Donnell led the employees of the Monaghan asylum in taking control for two days. See *Freeman's Journal*, 30 January 1919.

95 Report dated 6 June 1921, Chief Secretary's Office Registered Papers, 1921, State Paper Office, Dublin; see also Clarkson, *Labour and nationalism*, p. 436.

> The agricultural labourers have wakened up and the men in the factories have wakened up and if the bosses say they want a reduction of wages and so on then the workers of the South of Ireland are prepared to say to the bosses 'If you cannot carry on we will and we will show you how to do it'.[96]

Thomas Foran held that because the seizures were 'absolutely successful' in achieving the workers' demands this method should be widely applied in future. It was Helena Molony, together with Louie Bennett, who brought forward the central issue—what was the congress-party going to do on the matter of seizures? They urged a committee or department 'to help other bodies of workers to conduct industries which they might have to take over . . . ' Characteristically, Johnson had carefully considered the significance of the events; the seizures, he said, were

> the most important question that could be raised in the Labour movement or in Social Economy. . . . It is a challenge—let us make no mistake about it—to the rights of property. It says: though you happen to have a parchment which allots to you the right to use or possess this machine or that particular factory . . . henceforth that is not enough. We, as responsible to the workers, say these material things shall be continued in use so long as the community requires the product. That is the issue raised, and it is a contention that the Labour Party in Ireland, I hope, will continue to expound and put into operation.

No one addressed the question of whether seizures should be short-term or permanent, or whether seizures should merely be a weapon to force worker demands or should be based on the Labour principle of worker control. In any case the Labour leadership did not encourage the line of action adopted at Knocklong and Arigna; no committee was established but the matter was kept on the conference agenda until 1924 when it was quietly dropped. The executive's reference to the 'smaller country towns' as being the places where the seizures took place gives the impression that it believed the naive countrymen had been swept off their feet by the shouting of the leadership and the Labour newspaper, and had somewhat clumsily proceeded to put the words into action. The trade unionists of Dublin understood that the leaders were only talking revolution.

Other events in 1921 showed up Labour's inactivity. At Easter the executive issued a manifesto, *The country in danger*, presenting a series of demands to the employers. At the 1921 conference Johnson admitted that the employers had ignored the demands. What was the executive going to do about it? Nothing. 'Our responsibility has ceased,' said Johnson, 'It means that we may have to face a definite social revolu-

96 I.L.P. and T.U.C., *1921 report*, p. 92. The following discussion of the seizures is based on this report, pp. 91–94.

tion.'[97] The Labour executive assumed that this upheaval would be spontaneous; clearly, it was not going to organize the revolution. The Easter pronouncement stirred the government to the extent that the cabinet on 6 April instructed the ministers of trade and commerce, labour and agriculture to confer 'with a view to taking any steps necessary to prevent the starting of a class war'. But a proposal of the Labour ministry to call a conference to draw up a national labour policy came to nothing.[98]

With the Anglo-Irish truce of July 1921 came new seizures, invasions of land and violent farmer-labour conflicts. Seizures occurred in such widely separated places as Cork, where the harbour board was taken over, Drogheda, where workers seized a foundry, and Dublin, where the Rotunda theatre was occupied for three days by a Communist-led group of unemployed men. One of the leaders of the Dublin action was Liam O'Flaherty, who, like Sean O'Casey, was to earn an international literary reputation within a few years.[99]

It sometimes seemed that the Irish social fabric was beginning to come apart. McGrath, Hedley and Dowling organized a series of seizures in the south, principally in Limerick and Tipperary. The most noted of these was at Bruree, Co. Limerick, where in August 1921 workers occupied a Cleeves company mill and bakery. The workers continued production until local farmers refused to supply the plant. The Dail Labour ministry established a joint committee to deal with the dispute and suggested the workers could 'negotiate with any parties interested for the purchase of the Company's property and interests'. Not surprisingly, the workers declined this offer.[100]

So alarming was the general situation that Minister for Labour Constance Markievicz submitted a memorandum to the cabinet in October warning of the imminence of social revolution. She pointed to rising unemployment, factory seizures and agrarian violence, as well as to the fact that some sections of the I.R.A. had become involved in farm labour disputes. Madame Markievicz feared a sequence of events, beginning with 'small outbreaks growing more and more frequent and violent, the immediate result of which will be destruction of property and much misery which will tend to disrupt the Republican cause'. The only missing ingredient so far was the emergence of a 'violent popular leader'. To meet the danger she proposed that the government

97 Ibid., pp. 138–39. See also Clarkson, *Labour and nationalism*, pp. 445, 462.

98 Correspondence with Department of Labour, March, April 1921; Dail Eireann, 1919–21, papers, DE 2/5.

99 *Voice of Labour*, 10 December 1921; *Irish Independent*, 25, 26 January 1922; I.L.P. and T.U.C., *1921 report*, p. 9; *1922 report*, p. 8; *Workers Republic*, 28 January, 11 and 18 February 1922; I. O. [C. J. C. Street], *Ireland in 1921* (London 1921), p. 216; *Round Table*, December 1921.

100 *Dail Eireann rep., 1921–22* (26 April 1922), p. 291; statement by John Nolan, T.D. in 1927, *Dail Eireann deb.*, xiv, 1694. See also Street, *Ireland in 1921*, p. 156; *Voice of Labour*, 8 March, 27 May 1922; D. R. O'Connor Lysaght, 'The Bruree Soviet', *The Plough*, January 1972.

investigate farm profits, establish co-operatives and 'commandeer' the Irish Packing Company 'to show the workers that we [have] their interests at heart'. The cabinet rejected her advice, but on at least one occasion, in December 1921, it instructed its police and troops to eject workers who had occupied a plant, It was in that month as well that McGrath, Hedley and Dowling organized a 'Munster Council of Action'.[101]

Standing on the fringe but urging a Bolshevik-style revolution was the newly-formed Communist Party of Ireland. Its leader was Roderic Connolly, son of the 1916 leader, recently returned from the Soviet Union where he attended the second congress of the Communist International. Together with Liam O'Flaherty, Walter Carpenter, George Pollock (pseud. McLay) and Sean McLoughlin, Connolly took control of the moribund Socialist Party of Ireland in September 1921. On 18 October the new group expelled O'Brien and O'Shannon on the grounds of 'reformism, consecutive non-attendance at the Party meetings . . . and their consistent attempts to render futile all efforts to build up a Communist Party in Ireland'. At the beginning of November the party was renamed the C.P.I. It already had a newspaper, which Connolly had established in August. Although the party never exceeded a hundred members, its propagation of revolutionary Marxism was an additional factor in the volatile condition of the country.[102]

The climax in the seizure movement came in May 1922 when the revolutionary trio of Dowling, Hedley and McGrath organized 'soviets' in a dozen Munster factories. The last of the takeovers happened in the dying days of the civil war when, in February 1923, the Cork Flour mills were seized.[103] The Labour leadership apparently decided to overlook the new series of seizures; certainly it said nothing about them. When the Transport Union newspaper reappeared in October 1921 (with Archie Heron as the new editor), it made no attempt to encourage workers to follow the example of the Munster soviets. All the talk about revolution, all the statements and manifestos and demands from the Labour leaders seem to have come from a desire to compensate for lack of political power rather than from a desire for revolutionary action. Although the unions grew rapidly after 1918, the political mortification of that year still rankled.

The 1921 election underlined the party's previous failure. The political impotence of Labour was clearly seen when negotiations began

101 Dail Eireann, 1919–21, papers, DE 2/483, DE 2/5.

102 *Workers Republic*, October-December 1921; interview with Roddy Connolly, 1 October 1965; O'Brien papers, N.L.I., MS 13961(I).

103 In the midst of the civil war a group of workers in a Tipperary town creamery were inside with their 'soviet' while Free State and republican forces battled around the building. Eoin Neeson, *The civil war in Ireland* (Dublin 1967), pp. 105, 107; *Irish Independent*, 1 and 3 August 1922. In a few cases Free State troops were ordered to drive workers from the plants. C. Desmond Greaves, *Liam Mellows and the Irish revolution* (London 1971), pp. 317–18; *Irish Independent*, 3 and 25 August 1923. For the mass seizure of the Cleeve's creameries at this time, see *Irish Times*, 15 May 1922.

between the British government and Dail Eireann. Alexander Stewart, president of the Belfast Trades Council, expressed the feelings of many party members when he told the 1921 Labour conference, 'I feel humiliated that in all we read about this great peace movement we appear nowhere in the negotiations.'[104] Looking back on the period, L. J. Duffy, a leading member of the executive in the 1920s, saw this picture:

> Sinn Fein sought, secured and acknowledged the ready co-operation of the Labour Movement during the Anglo-Irish war. But the Labour Movement entered into the compact as a vassel rather than a co-partner. Let us not blame Sinn Fein for that position. Congress is responsible entirely for the position that grew up around the struggle with England.[105]

104 I.L.P. and T.U.C., *1921 report*, p. 80.

105 I.L.P. and T.U.C., *1924 report*, p. 120.

6

The Treaty, the 1922 Election and the Civil War

The year 1922 is the key to the post-revolutionary period in Ireland. That year the articles of agreement were approved by the Westminster Parliament and Dail Eireann under which the British withdrew from twenty-six counties, but remained in the six northeast counties, thus establishing the fact of partition. A Free State government within the Commonwealth was created, but not without a civil war. The conflict became the basis of the major political division within the new state.

Irish Labour had no significant influence on any of these developments. Although the Irish Labour Party aspired to political power, it did not possess even limited formal political power until June 1922. That the Labour Party failed to act effectively in this period is not due to confusion about its objectives, but rather because of the adoption of inappropriate means to achieve them. Had it been a revolutionary socialist party it could have used the disturbed conditions of the time in an attempt to grasp power and fundamentally alter the social and economic foundations of post-treaty Ireland. However, as a constitutional party, Labour confined itself to the passive role of observer and critic while other groups moulded the future by violence.

THE LABOUR PARTY AND THE TREATY

Negotiations between representatives of the Dail and the British government, which began following the truce on 11 July 1921, culminated in the signing of an agreement on 5 December of that year. During the period of the negotiations the Labour executive put forward three principal demands to be included in any settlement: first, 'the withdrawal of British military and other executive forces'; second, 'that the people of Ireland as a single entity shall be allowed to determine the form of government under which they shall live'; third, 'while granting the fullest freedom to all minorities, the political unity of Ireland must be maintained'. The Labour demands only reinforced the position of the Dail negotiators.

This was Labour's only contribution to the treaty negotiations. The party was never approached or informed by the Irish government on matters pertaining to the agreement. Labour's leaders, while claiming they had no complaints, surely must have experienced humiliation at their exclusion.[1] But brutal reality was dawning on Labour: although the leaders were sought after and consulted when they could be useful to the leaders of the national movement, they were to be excluded

1 William O'Brien, *Forth the banners go*, p. 158, wrote that the Labour leaders 'rather resented the fact that they had not a meeting with Sinn Féin for the purpose of expressing their point of view' during the negotiations. Bart O'Connor, a prominent supporter of the treaty, declared in 1932 that 'certain members of the Labour Party' told Michael Collins before he went to London that there was an over-riding public concern for peace. *Dail Eireann deb*. xli, 769.

from the exercise of political power until they could claim a portion of it in their own right.

The terms of the treaty were revealed on 7 December 1921, and the Dail debated for a month before the vote on ratification was taken. On the issue of approval or disapproval of the treaty, Labour took no official stand. Since the party had had no part in the negotiations and no votes in the Dail, it would not be responsible for the treaty. Instead, the leaders of the labour movement sought to watch the treaty fight from the safety of a defensive trade union foxhold: taking a political stand would split the labour movement. Cathal O'Shannon, editor of the *Voice of Labour*, saw the treaty issue as a political hassle which overlooked the fundamental dangers facing the country:

> These dangers do not arise from the present English occupation or from English 'rights' in Ireland under either the Treaty or the alternative proposition [Document Number Two]. They arise out of the capitalist conception of society prevailing in Ireland. . . . They are dangers and may be disasters which no particular form of government can be a real safe-guard against.[2]

In a series of articles in the Labour newspaper, the republican publicist Aodh de Blacam attempted to rally support in opposition to the treaty. He pointed to the probability of special favours for the Unionists and warned of several obnoxious possibilities: a legislative upper chamber with the power of veto, a government based on mercantilist principles and the domination of Ireland by foreign capital. Liam Mellows and Frank Gallagher appealed for worker support of the anti-treaty stand in *Poblacht na hEireann*.[3]

Apart from the possibilities decried by de Blacam, the treaty contained several provisions which were objectionable to the Labour leadership. The partition provision, which separated the six north-east counties from the proposed Free State, was of crucial importance to the Labour Party. Separation would deprive it of the great potential support of the Belfast industrial area. It would mean that the party would be at a serious disadvantage in the overwhelmingly agricultural twenty-six counties. Partition injured the Labour Party more than it did any other party or institution. Other provisions to which Labour could have objected were the oath of allegiance, the retention by Britain of three naval bases on Irish soil and the commitments given to Unionists: their major representation in the upper house, as well as token representation in the lower chamber, were in opposition to the democratic principles of the Labour Party's constitution.

While practically every other group took a stand on the treaty, the official labour movement seemed to take pride in its neutrality. Both the *Voice of Labour* and the national executive urged the workers to remain neutral:

2 *Voice of Labour*, 14 January 1922.

3 Ibid., 7, 14 January 1922. A reprint of a Mellows article, 'Labour and the Irish republic', appeared in *Irishman*, 4 February 1922.

> We are glad to be able to report that in spite of strong local and national pressure, the campaign of the daily Press and the direct invitation of certain capitalists and some public bodies, the overwhelmingly majority of the Labour organizations refrained from taking part as such in the controversy. . . . Out of upwards of 1,000 branches and councils of unions not more than six were foolish enough and lacking enough in class-consciousness to indulge in resolution passing. These six, representing less than 5,000 workers, declared for the treaty.[4]

Unofficial labour elements, however, did not necessarily follow the congress-party line. From afar came a pronouncement from the man who for years was held to be the voice of the Irish workers. From his American prison cell, James Larkin cabled a characteristically outspoken statement in which he bitterly denounced the treaty:

> We demand the rejection of this foul and destructive bargain. . . . We will not, now or at any time, take the oath of allegiance to any king. . . . We will not, now or at any time, join with any country, government or empire that oppresses or holds in slavery any of the Earth's people. We demand Freedom. We will continue the struggle for Freedom, full and complete freedom, economic and political freedom, for the Irish Working Class.

The *Voice of Labour* (7 January 1922) printed Larkin's statement with the comment that the Transport Union and *Voice* disassociated themselves from his charges of cowardice, treachery and aggrandizement on the part of the Irish delegation. But the editor revealingly admitted, 'We are absolutely and completely opposed to and have always fought, the political and social opinions and many of the actions of most of the Ratificationists.'

From the far left also came opposition to the treaty. The *Workers Republic*, organ of the Communist Party of Ireland and edited by Liam O'Flaherty and Roddy Connolly, stated: 'Those who have accepted the compromise have become afraid of a republic. They fear that the people, glorifying in political freedom, may demand social freedom. They fear that an Irish Republic will be transformed into a Workers Republic.' The paper attacked the officials of both the Transport Union and the Labour Party for their 'weak-kneed, cowardly, yellow attitude' towards the treaty compared to 'Larkin's unmistakeably clear stand with the Communist Party in opposition to the agreement'.[5]

The Dail debate on the acceptance of the treaty demonstrated that the division on the question was not on class or socio-economic lines, but was almost totally political in nature. Of all the speakers, only Joseph McGrath, speaking for ratification, foresaw the possibility of social and economic reform: 'Under this treaty every single thing in

4 *Voice of Labour*, 7 January 1922.

5 *Workers Republic*, 17, 24 December 1921.

the Democratic Programme can be put into force and the democrats in this assembly know that well. Not one of those on the other side have referred to this matter.' Richard Corish, the only Labour Party member in the Dail, declared his reasons for supporting the treaty: firstly, the voters in 1918 had not declared for a republic, but simply had rejected the Irish Parliamentary Party; secondly, 'the people of Wexford want me to vote for it'.[6]

Before Christmas the Dail recessed until 7 January without voting on either the treaty or de Valera's alternative, Document Number Two. In the interval, the Labour executive proposed its own solution, designed to bridge the gap between the requirements of the treaty and the republican insistence that Ireland alone should decide its future. The basic factor in the scheme was that the Dail would continue as the 'supreme governing body'. Although it appeared very likely that a majority in the Dail would favour the treaty, the divisive question of the future government of Ireland would not be dealt with by the Dail itself. Rather, Labour proposed, a 'Southern Ireland Parliament' should be artificially created to accept the treaty, to be followed by the formation of a provisional government which would 'be merely a Committee of the Dail for the purpose of receiving the surrender of powers by the British Government'. It would be in the framing of the constitution that the Dail would make abundantly clear that 'the legislative, executive and judicial authority of Ireland is and shall be derived solely from the people of Ireland'. In regard to the volatile matter of the oath, an emphatically democratic constitution would mean that the necessary oath 'would then imply allegiance to the Constitution of the Irish Free State . . . as by Law established, such Law to be established by Dail Eireann and the Constitution will be governed by this essentially republican clause. This meets the President's point on this question.'[7]

These proposals were, at least, a useful attempt to join the two positions, as was also true of de Valera's external association proposal, which included a modification of the oath of allegiance. Having put forward their ideas, the Labour executive interviewed the principals in the controversy, including Collins, Mulcahy, de Valera, Griffith and McGrath. Collins and Griffith gave the proposals a friendly reception, which led the executive 'to hope that a basis of agreement had been found but this hope was shattered at the interview with Mr. de Valera and the proceedings at the resumed debate in the Dail confirmed our disappointment'.[8] The Labour proposals came to nothing.

There is strong evidence that Thomas Johnson privately urged members of the Dail to approve the treaty. In a letter printed in the *Workers Republic* on 1 April 1922, Patrick Corbett charged Johnson as

6 *Dail Eireann treaty deb.*, pp. 299–300, 306.

7 I.L.P. and T.U.C., *1922 report*, p. 21.

8 Ibid. O'Brien's diary simply lists the dates of the interviews and their participants. O'Brien's diary, 23, 24, 25, 27 December 1921, O'Brien Papers, N.L.I., MS 15705.

the author of Joseph McGrath's Dail speech in favour of the treaty. Certainly McGrath's strongly pro-labour statement was not repeated, even after he broke with the Free State government in 1924. Roderic Connolly and Peadar O'Donnell, both opponents of the treaty and unfriendly towards Johnson, have stated that Johnson urged the acceptance of the treaty.[9] If Johnson actually did become involved in this activity, it was in direct violation of the executive's policy. Johnson's alleged actions at this time were used as a weapon against him throughout his political career. What adds weight to this politically damaging accusation is the fact that, Johnson, so far as is known, never publicly denied it.

It is not surprising that Johnson was inclined towards the treaty. Although he was a home ruler since his Belfast days, he was not committed to the republican ideal.[10] He sought the creation of a democratic structure which could serve as a vehicle to further the workers' cause. He was under no illusions concerning the conditions under which the treaty was concluded; later, in 1924, he voiced agreement with the view that it had been accepted 'under duress and under the threat of greater force'.[11]

According to Peadar O'Donnell, the republican militants looked to the labour movement and especially to the Transport Union to take the side of the republic. 'The Labour movement . . . would take on the role which the Citizen Army played in the period of confusion on the eve of the Rising, it would be the point of rally of the independence movement in the second hour of crisis.' This line of thought, O'Donnell said, was commonly heard around Liberty Hall after 1916. It was assumed that the man who would lead Labour in this effort was William O'Brien, secretary of the Transport Union. O'Brien, some republicans felt, would attempt to carry out Connolly's hope that the Irish working class would be the one class that would not permit the cessation of the national struggle prior to the achievement of full independence. O'Donnell believed O'Brien would be steadfast in the 'hour of crisis' because he was a strict taskmaster whose speeches invariably contained a firm, uncompromising stand on the national question. However, when the time came, O'Brien did not oppose the treaty. O'Donnell believes that O'Brien had become primarily concerned with preserving the gains won by the Transport Union. Later O'Brien said that, although he had been a republican since he was 'sixteen or seventeen', he saw that the republican form of government could not be achieved in 1921–22.[12]

9 Interviews with Connolly, 4 November 1964, and O'Donnell, 21 November 1964. The *Plain People*, 30 April 1922, referred to Johnson's 'assidious Lobby in favour of the "Articles of Agreement" '; *Workers Republic*, 4 February 1922, wrote, 'Bear in mind [Johnson's] actions on behalf of the Free State during the debate and his Executive's manifesto after ratification.' See also J. D. Clarkson, *Labour and nationalism in Ireland*, p. 450.

10 Interview with Cathal O'Shannon, 1 June 1964.

11 *Dail Eireann deb.*, 8, cols. 2429, 2430.

12 Ibid., 1, col. 162, 12 September 1922. Peadar O'Donnell, *There will be another day*, p. 18, and O'Donnell interview. See also *Republican Congress*, 5 January 1935.

Although much was written about the treaty debate during the Dail recess, the only daily paper to mention Labour opinion on the treaty was the *Irish Independent*. The issue of 7 January 1922 reported 'fifteen Labour bodies' in favour of ratification: there were no reports of labour bodies who were opposed. Among the groups mentioned as supporting the treaty were the 'Transport Workers of Midleton and Bandon', 'Trade and Labour—Sligo', the Drogheda Workers Council and the South Wexford executive of the Transport Union.[13]

It would appear that many Labour members of local councils and rural boards voted for resolutions in favour of the treaty. From the results of the elections of January and June 1920, Labour votes were required to pass resolutions in many of the local bodies. The Labour-controlled Wexford County Council unanimously voted for ratification.[14]

It was obvious from the course of the Dail debate, from the tone of the daily press and from the floods of pro-treaty resolutions pouring in from chambers of commerce, farmer organizations and public bodies that the weight of the big farmers, shopkeepers and business interests in general was being thrown on the side of ratification. In the face of this feeling, the *Voice of Labour* retreated to a policy of impartial chastisement of both sides—a hostility apparently engendered by the essentially bourgeois position taken by those opposed to the treaty.

The Dail ratified the treaty on 7 January 1922 by a vote of sixty-four for, fifty-seven against, and the Labour executive made haste to treat the issue as closed. In a statement published four days later, the executive called for the subordination of strictly political issues to the pressing questions of social and economic reform:

> With the vote of Dail Eireann approving the Treaty between Ireland and England, one more chapter of the still uncompleted story of struggle for the freedom of Ireland's men and women begins anew. . . . it is no retrogression on the part of the Labour Party to avail of the machinery of whatever political instrument may be fashioned in pursuance of our objective—i.e., the establishment of a Workers Republic.[15]

As political passions flared in the Dail, a Labour deputation appeared three days after the treaty vote to broach the subjects of relief for the unemployed and the need for socio-economic reform. The deputation, which was the only outside group allowed to address the Dail, consisted of Johnson, O'Shannon, Thomas Foran, J. T. O'Farrell and Denis Cullen. Given the heated atmosphere of the time, it is unlikely that the deputies paid much attention to what the Labour men had to say. (De Valera and his followers had walked out of the Dail earlier in the

13 *Irish Independent*, 3, 5, 6 January 1922.

14 *Freeman's Journal*, 3 January 1922.

15 I.L.P. and T.U.C., *1922 report*, pp. 18–19. The statement appeared in *Irish Independent*, 12 January 1922.

day but returned to hear the Labour address.) Nor were they permitted any illusions of political power. The deputation was introduced by J. J. Walsh with the words 'It is well from many points of view that the country should know the views of Labour from the economic standpoint.'[16]

In his address, Johnson sought reward for Labour's standing down in the parliamentary elections of 1918 and 1921:

> We feel that we are, perhaps, in a somewhat exceptional position in as much as we might have had the right to address the assembly had we considered, at the last election and the previous election, that it was in the interest of Ireland that we should have gone forward as a Labour Party to seek representation in this Dail.

The reward for Labour's alleged sacrifices was a 'hear, hear' from some Dail members. This was the total reward that the Labour Party ever got for its actions, and in politics it was as much as it could expect, but the leaders of the party continued to speak as though they expected the nation to be forever grateful.

Johnson drew attention to the grave economic condition of the country. He estimated that of the 440,000 workers included under the unemployment insurance act, fully 130,000 were jobless. He warned that if the economic crisis was not met promptly, an explosion could follow: 'The people', he told the deputies, 'will rise and sweep you away.' But the Dail was accustomed to threats of violence. Economic problems did wait on political exigencies, and the house quickly returned to their preoccupations with the issue of Free State versus republic.

The newly elected Dail president, Arthur Griffith, did not completely dismiss the Labour plea; he offered to appoint a committee 'to try and deal with this question'. Shortly thereafter the Labour executive met Griffith and some of his ministers and presented Labour's proposals for reducing unemployment. There were the usual ideas for the initiation of public works and housing schemes, but two unique suggestions were also put forward. One of these advocated the nationalization of the Waterford and Drogheda meat factories, which were threatening to close. The other urged the establishment of trade with the Soviet Union in which Ireland would send agricultural machinery and foodstuffs in exchange for raw materials to be used in housing and in manufacturing.[17]

The government response to these proposals bitterly disappointed the Labour executive. At the 1922 Labour conference Johnson revealed that almost all of the suggestions either had been rejected or ignored. Nothing had been done about the importation of flour or a compulsory

16 For the account of this session of the Dail, see *Dail Eireann rep., 1921–22*, pp. 391 ff.

17 The Soviet Union, due to the upheaval of civil war, was in desperate need of foodstuffs and was seeking trade with other European countries. An Anglo-Soviet trade agreement was signed in 1921, to be followed by treaties with other European states. See D. W. Treadgold, *Twentieth-Century Russia* (Chicago 1964), pp. 200–201, 233.

tillage order, and despite the fact that a mission to London by Johnson and a representative of the provisional government to present trade proposals to a Russian envoy had met with a favourable Soviet response, the government concluded that trade with Russia was impractical. It had accepted two minor measures: the use of exclusively trade unionist labour on road work and the provision of seasonal employment by the local government department. Further, it had initiated a housing programme.[18] But these would have little effect on the mounting problem of unemployment. The new government made clear that its immediate concern was not the economic state of the country, but rather the necessity of forestalling its republican opponents.

Both Kevin O'Higgins and de Valera later said that the picture of unemployment and economic suffering presented by the Labour Party delegation to the Dail helped to swing support behind the treaty as a step towards tackling social and economic problems. According to Peadar O'Donnell, however, de Valera at this time 'was incapable of seeing the independence struggle as Tone saw it or Connolly. He was numb, rather than hostile to the working class struggle. He was as scared as Griffith of the gospel of Finton Lalor.'[19]

The narrow approval voted the treaty by the Dail did not end the crisis concerning the future government of Ireland. Final determination was to be by the vote of the people in the election for a constituent assembly—and now the people had to be won.

The solid pro-treaty stand of the daily press made the creation of anti-treaty publications imperative, and partisan weeklies proliferated in the months following. *Poblacht na hEireann*, begun in January 1922, presented the views of the pro-republican elements in the I.R.A.; the *Plain People*, commencing in April 1922, was the organ of the anti-treaty politicians; the nationalist weekly, *New Ireland*, and the extreme leftist *Workers Republic* also supported the republicans. Representing the pro-treaty side were the *Free State* and the *Separatist*, both of which began publication in February.

The *Voice of Labour* initially adopted a passive, self-satisfied attitude towards the treaty, although it clearly recognized the side with which it had most in common: 'When all is said and done the Republican opposition will find that out of the very necessity of the case it will be driven back upon the Workers Republic before the full aims of the Irish Republic are gained' (7 January 1922). *Poblacht na hEireann*, with Liam Mellows as editor, appealed to the workers to support the republican cause in one of its earliest editorials, 'Labour in Ireland', published 17 January:

> Many who served the Republic with all their strength and now remain faithful to it, believed and still believe, that it is only by

18 I.L.P. and T.U.C., *1922 report*, p. 17, also p. 10. For Russo-Irish trade proposals, see confidential report of Diarmaid Fawsitt in Johnson papers, N.L.I. MS 17144.

19 O'Donnell, *There will be another day*, p. 14. The O'Higgins statement is in *Dail Eireann deb.*, 1, col. 1878. For de Valera's statement, see Chapter 7.

> securing the independence of Ireland that the workers can be saved from economic serfdom. . . . It cannot be too widely known that those who strike for national freedom are impelled by as deep a desire for social justice as for liberty.

The *Voice of Labour* replied to Mellows on 28 January: show us the republican social and economic programme instead of giving us generalizations. 'We won't wax indignant even if [the republicans] steal Labour's thunder provided they put Labour's programme into practice.' In February Erskine Childers replaced Mellows as editor of *Poblacht na hEireann*, and henceforth the paper propagated the republic in strictly political terms. The following month (15 March) Aodh de Blacam urged workers to rally to the republic, using an argument that today sounds reminiscent of the de Valera of the 1930s: 'No theory about economics will guide us so surely as the inner light of patriotism.'

Both the pro- and anti-treaty weeklies included excerpts from the writings of Irish patriots, especially Connolly and Pearse, but invariably omitted quoting their social and economic views. In an attempt to counter the neutral stance of the Labour Party, the strongly republican position of James Larkin was prominently proclaimed in the *Plain People*. But the republicans presented no economic or social programme before the June election and the beginning of the civil war. The *Free State* (11 March 1922) pointed out the absence of a republican policy:

> Mr. de Valera has recently told us that the policy of his party is to 'hold on'. . . . We want something a bit more progressive than that. . . . These poor people cry out for work and food and Mr. de Valera's sympathetic answer is to hand them rifles and say 'Fight on, brave soldiers of Ireland; the soul of Ireland is in danger; if the people become prosperous, our cause is lost.'

The supporters of the treaty and the Free State sought backing by offering the prospect of a prosperous economy under the new government. 'The Irish poor will not cease to be true to their love of Ireland', Arthur Griffith advised, 'when the Irish Free State has abolished pauperism and provided them with means of decent livelihood.'[20] Griffith, of course, did not say how his government was going to accomplish this.

Of all the pro-treaty group, Michael Collins provided the most concrete picture of what the Free State might mean to the workers. In his book *The Path to Freedom*, based on a series of articles and published in the autumn of 1922, Collins declared his support for the control of monopolies and capital, full rewards for labour, development of co-operative industry and agriculture and the creation of a self-sufficient economy:

> The development of industry in the new Ireland should be on lines which exclude monopoly profits. The product of industry

20 *Free State*, 25 February 1922.

> would thus be left sufficiently free to supply good wages. . . . The system should be on co-operative lines rather than on the old commercial capitalistic lines . . . At the same time I think we shall safely avoid State Socialism which has nothing to commend it in a country like Ireland and, in any case, is a monopoly of another kind.
>
> The development of mines and minerals will be on national lines and under national direction. This will prevent the monopolizing by private individuals of what are purely national resources. . . . The profits from all these national enterprises . . . will belong to the nation for the advantage of the whole nation.
>
> We shall hope to see in Ireland industrial conciliation and arbitration take the place of strikes and the workers sharing in the ownership and management of business.

Collins also recognized that land must be freely available for economically viable farms, for industry and for housing, but 'land is not freely available in Ireland'. He clearly saw the need to break up large holdings, 'the ranches', which would result in 'plenty of employment and a great increase in the national wealth'. He reminded the homeless that the new government had already begun to tackle the housing problem: 'The Provisional Government grant has been announced to enable a considerable number of houses to be built. This grant . . . is simply a recognition of the existence of the problem.'[21]

The months following the signing of the treaty gave all factions and parties, including Labour, the opportunity to publicize their stands on the economic problems facing Ireland. The Griffith government announced that national elections would be held, and Labour prepared to take the field.

LABOUR AND THE 1922 ELECTION

As required by the treaty, the 1922 election was to be by proportional representation with the single transferable vote. Labour had previously gone on record in support of this system, which would give smaller parties, such as Labour, an excellent chance to win seats. Following the government's announcement of the election, the Labour executive summoned a special two-day conference, beginning on 21 February 1922.

In a memorandum to the conference, the executive argued for acceptance of the treaty and participation in the election.[22] Neither of the two Sinn Fein factions stood for Labour's objective—a republic based on co-operative labour and service. Labour participation in the election, said the executive, would not create dissension among the workers because proportional representation would allow a worker to give his

21 Michael Collins, *The path to freedom* (Dublin 1922), pp. 131–42.

22 For a report of the conference, see I.L.P. and T.U.C., *1922 report*, especially pp. 4, 7, 58–60, 67, 69–76, 84, 87.

first vote to Labour and his second vote to the party he favoured in the treaty dispute. (The argument implies that a worker who voted first on the treaty issue could give his second choice to the Labour candidate.) The memorandum pointed to the unsatisfactory voting record of Sinn Fein and other non-Labour representatives on local bodies, and, finally, urged participation so that Labour could have a hand in shaping the country's constitution.

O'Shannon presided at the special conference, with Johnson presenting the executive's proposals. On the question of participation, there were four opposition groups at the meeting. One group supported the republican cause. Another section wanted Labour to concentrate on the economic, trade-union side of the movement, at least until the treaty issue had been settled by the electorate. This viewpoint was expressed by Louie Bennett, secretary of the Women Workers Union, who said that only a handful of Labour representatives would be returned, and it was better to grip economic power, politics being useless without it. A third group, influenced by P. T. Daly and Delia Larkin, stood opposed because of their hostility to the O'Brien-Foran leadership of the Transport Union.[23] The fourth group were the revolutionaries who favoured 'direct action' by the workers and the unions. Walter Carpenter stated their case: 'Those who worked for a Workers Republic were the men who seized the mills, the creameries and the railways. Russia did not bring the Workers Republic into operation by going to Parliament . . . but through direct action by Lenin and Trotsky.'

Labour's Belfast spokesman, D. R. Campbell, pointed out the consequences if the party did not enter the political arena: 'If the Labour movement were to make any further sacrifices they might as well scrap their constitution. Were they to go back to the days of passing resolutions and sending deputations to the Irish Parliament or to London?' Campbell was supported by the Dublin Workers Council, the Wexford Trades Council, various unions in Wexford and the Clonmel Trades Council.

The only union to explicitly express opposition to participation was the Vehicle Builders Union. The executive of the Transport Union was split on the question, with O'Shannon and O'Brien in favour of political action, and Thomas Foran and Thomas Kennedy opposed. But the Transport Union votes were cast for participation. The issue was met when Helena Moloney, an outspoken republican, proposed 'that the Labour Party do not take part in the forthcoming election'. This was defeated by a vote of 115 to 82, the relatively close margin indicating a sizeable opposition to participation. Shortly afterwards the motion of the executive was carried, 104 to 49. It would appear

23 The Dublin Trades Council, controlled by Daly, later declared against Labour participation (*Voice of Labour*, 6 May 1922). The council had been expelled from the party-congress and replaced by the Transport Union-sponsored Dublin Workers Council as a result of action taken by the 1921 Labour conference. I.L.P. and T.U.C., *1921 report*, pp. 21, 94, 129–30.

that some of the opposition realized they did not have a majority and either left the meeting or did not vote.

By the overwhelming vote of 128 to 12, the conference called for a plebiscite on the question of the treaty before the general election for the constituent assembly. Such a plebiscite would have been very convenient for the Labour Party: by letting the electorate decide on the treaty, the party could preserve its neutrality with advantage; by separating the two voting days, the Labour platform could be considered apart from the diversions of the treaty debate. Although the Sinn Fein ard-fheis had agreed that the election itself was to decide the treaty issue, Johnson urged President Griffith to accept a plebiscite to be held either before or in conjunction with the election. But Griffith rejected the former date as being impractical under the circumstances and the latter as tending to confuse the voters' minds.[24]

The conference voted to allow Labour candidates freedom to state their own positions on the question of the treaty, but it stipulated that, if successful, they were bound to attend the body to which they were elected. Conveniently, no mention was made of the oath of allegiance required by the treaty.

Finally, the meeting approved a party programme for the election. The programme proposed that every man and woman 'willing to work' should be guaranteed employment and a 'living wage'. It urged that before any reduction of taxes on the rich was considered, the taxes on such basic commodities as tea and sugar should be abolished and the tax on tobacco lowered. Pensions were to be provided for the victims of the independence struggle as well as for widowed mothers. The long-standing Labour demand for nationalization of railways and canals was repeated. The party called for the creation of a 'national banking system' and the employment of national credit by the government in order to stimulate industrial growth. Farm labourers would be pleased by the proposal for compulsory tillage of twenty percent of all arable land. The slum dweller and the cotter were offered a national housing authority which would have complete jurisdiction in home building; worker housing would be given priority over all others. And in a nod to the political crisis, the Labour programme firmly recognized the army as the servant of the people.

This was a reform programme plain and simple, not a plan for the socialist transformation of Irish society. The only radical plank was a proposal to suspend payment of land annuities and agricultural rents. During the period of the national struggle annuities and rents had not been paid in various parts of the country, but it had never been the policy of the Dail to encourage the people not to pay them.

Thus, ten years after its establishment as the political arm of the labour movement, the Irish Labour Party prepared to enter its first national election. The party was still largely a paper organization,

24 Letter to national executive, dated 25 March 1922. I.L.P. and T.U.C., *1922 report*, p. 45.

lacking a well-developed system of local backing. Because the trade unions would be relied upon to supply the campaign workers and electoral support, no separate political structure was created at this time.

Beginning in March 1922, local conferences of trade unions and councils were to decide whether to put forward candidates. While there was significant local opposition to Labour participation, the great majority of the conferences favoured nominating candidates; a few were indecisive. Only in Limerick, where the controversy about the Labour executive's actions in the 1919 strike was still remembered, did a conference definitely decide against selecting a candidate: as well, the dissident Dublin Trades Council declared against Labour participation. Thomas Johnson was nominated for County Dublin, Cathal O'Shannon for Louth and Meath, William O'Brien for Dublin South and James Larkin for Dublin North. The day before nominations were due, however, Larkin sent an almost incoherent cable from New York in which he emphatically declined to stand.[25] J. T. O'Farrell, Irish secretary of the Railway Clerks Association, was selected in his place. Richard Corish, the only party member in the Dail was nominated for County Wexford. Twenty-two candidates were originally selected, but in the end there were only eighteen nominees.

Labour Peace Efforts

As the storms of the treaty controversy continued, the Labour executive on 11 April issued a proclamation urging workingmen in the rival armies to refuse to be drawn into violence and calling for all workers to stand ready to take action against militarism.[26] Two days later the republican army executive, led by Rory O'Connor and Liam Mellows, seized and fortified the Four Courts in Dublin.

Once again, Labour leaders held discussions with leading figures in the controversy, and, almost inevitably, discussion again proved fruitless. The Labour executive then called for a strike against 'militarism' set for 24 April. At the same time, it proposed that representatives of the republican army executive be included in the Mansion House conference, at which the principals in the treaty dispute were meeting under the joint chairmanship of the Catholic archbishop of Dublin and the lord mayor.

The general strike took place on the appointed day and was observed throughout the twenty-six counties. 'The stoppage was complete and covered many services not covered by the General Strikes of 1918 and 1920. . . . [The] two most successful were the stoppage in the Post Office and the Great Northern Railway,' the *Voice of Labour* reported on 29 April. The Dublin newspapers heartily approved of the Labour Party's demonstration. Public meetings were held in the larger cities

25 I.T.G.W.U., *The attempt to smash the Irish Transport and General Workers Union*, p. 72. See also Joseph Deasy, *Fiery Cross: the story of Jim Larkin*, p. 29. For the position of the Dublin Trades Council, see its minutes of 25 March 1922.

26 I.L.P. and T.U.C., *1922 report*, p. 24.

although the republican Sunday newspaper called on workers to boycott these gatherings. In Dublin mischief-makers were on the loose: the night before the strike the city was plastered with bogus proclamations of a 'Workers Republic', signed with the names of the Labour executive. At the public meeting Johnson warned, 'While the spirit of militarism [is] abroad, the economic emancipation of the country [cannot] be taken in hand.'[27]

The archbishop of Dublin invited Labour to send representatives to the Mansion House conference. Johnson, O'Shannon and O'Brien attended for the party. Representatives from the Four Courts, however, were not invited because Collins and Griffith refused to meet them. The peace proposals put forward by the Labour group were similar to those proposed before the treaty vote, but now included the idea of a plebiscite. Griffith and Collins offered to hold such a plebiscite before the Dail elections, but de Valera said he would abide by the results of the parliamentary election. The hope that these proposals might bring agreement 'vanished when it was disclosed that the question of an immediate or postponed election was predominant in the minds of the rival parties'. While Griffith insisted on an election in June, de Valera maintained that no election should be held until an adult suffrage register could be compiled.[28]

The conference ended, without agreement, on 29 April. Both parties in the controversy sought to show that they had not rejected Labour's suggestions. For the anti-treaty side, de Valera stated that 'in the proposals of Labour, Cathal Brugha and myself recognized, broadly, in principle, a basis on which immediate peace could be secured, the Army united, and a strong stable Executive set-up . . . The Labour proposals obviously refer to a period during which the question of the Treaty would be left in abeyance.' De Valera also pointed out that there was nothing in the treaty that made it necessary to hold elections before December.[29]

But the edition of the *Irish Times* that reported de Valera's statement also contained the Labour Party's announcement—made with an air of hopelessness—that it would not issue any more statements until it had seen 'what action both parties of Dail Eireann will take on the proposals submitted to the Peace Conference last week'. The Labour leaders, especially Johnson, deserve credit for doing everything in their power to bring the disputants together by means of imaginative compromise proposals. These efforts came to nothing because neither side genuinely was interested in compromise; both were concerned with gaining political advantage in the interim before the election.

The date for the election was set for 16 June 1922. The Labour executive decided against a national appeal for funds; election costs of the Labour candidates were to be met by the local conferences that

27 *Freeman's Journal*, 25 April 1922.

28 I.L.P. and T.U.C., *1922 report*, p. 29.

29 *Irish Times*, 2 May 1922.

had nominated them. Unions which were not sponsoring candidates were asked for contributions—an appeal which received little response. The Transport Union, the largest and richest of the unions, provided a nationwide membership from which election workers could be drawn. The union took complete financial responsibility for two nominees, O'Brien and O'Shannon, and matched local contributions up to £250 for each Transport Union candidate. The only other union to contribute a significant amount of money was the Irish National Teachers Organization which not only gave the party £500 but also nominated in general secretary, T. J. O'Connell, for Galway. The Post Office Workers Union and the Distributive Workers Union each contributed £100. The Labour executive provided for the expenses of Thomas Johnson in County Dublin. In general, the party did not get whole-hearted support from its affiliated unions. Many trade unionists were drawn into the vortex of the treaty dispute and supported either the pro- or anti-treaty candidates. And, despite their nation-wide membership base, the unions were ineffective as electoral organizations.

There were several reasons for the small number of candidates put forward by the Labour Party in the election: a large minority had opposed participation at the special conference; the party feared that if it nominated a large number of candidates, it would lose political prestige if most of them were defeated; the treaty issue had a divisive effect on the workers, and financial support was limited. The Labour effort was a modest claim for representation; less than one seat out of six was contested by the party.

The political situation was altered dramatically when, on 20 May, the Collins—de Valera pact was announced. By its terms, the pro- and anti-treaty groups were to unite to form one slate of nominees in proportion to their present strength in the Dail (sixty-six pro-treaty and fifty-nine anti-treaty). Following the election, a coalition government was to be formed. A minister of defence was to be appointed by a re-united army following a new army conference. It would appear that the two sides decided that one or the other would in the end come out victorious but that the contest was reserved for themselves alone. Once again the call went out for other parties and candidates to stand down in the face of this coalition of leaders of the national struggle. *New Ireland* (27 May) firmly informed the non-pact candidates that until Sinn Fein resolved the treaty controversy 'there is really no scope yet in Irish public life for other groups to intervene.' Johnson had an effective reply to the demand for Labour's withdrawal:

> If it were true, as suggested, that dangers threaten the country, which could only be met by keeping intact the forces which constituted the national resistance, that (is) all the more reason why the organized workers should have representation. . . . Surely, it would not be denied that one of the forces which had constituted

the national resistance . . . had been the organized workers of Ireland.[30]

Had the pact been adhered to by both sides, the public would generally have been denied a chance to voice its opinion on the treaty. It had already been denied a plebiscite on the issue. The pact, however, accomplished nothing because all the pact candidates were listed in the newspapers as either pro- or anti-treaty, and the voters were aware of the position of the candidates in their constituency. Donal O'Sullivan says that the pact was 'partially effective, as out of a total of one hundred and twenty-eight seats not less than thirty-seven were unopposed. . . . By coming forward in sufficient numbers, however, the members of the Labour Party, the Farmers and the Independents vindicated the right of the electors to say whether or not they wanted the treaty.' He adds: 'The Collins-de Valera Pact was known not to have had Griffith's approval.'[31]

Griffith and Collins, busy conferring with the British government about the transfer of administration, spent little time campaigning. De Valera, however, was a most active participant, and it was he who took the lead in urging the withdrawal of non-pact candidates. Organized labour, agriculture, industry and the professions, he declared, were already represented in the Dail. *Poblacht na hEireann* (8 June 1922) made the same point: 'Our two main class interests are not asked to wait for the simple reason that the existing Dail is mainly drawn from these two classes, Labour and Agriculture.'

De Valera had some success. He pressured Patrick Hogan, an able Labour nominee in County Clare, to stand down.[32] But the efforts of other Sinn Fein leaders were not as successful. It was not easy to withstand the influence of popular folk heroes such as Dan Breen, but Labour's candidate in Tipperary, Daniel Morrissey, did so, saying, 'I resent the insinuation that I or any other independent candidate is breaking the spirit of the pact which invites them to stand. . . . The country has nothing to fear from Labour.' Breen later wrote that Morrissey boasted that he was 'not afraid of Dan Breen or of his gun levelled at my temple', but Breen denies threatening him.[33] In Galway T. J. O'Connell successfully resisted pressure designed to force him out.[34] It is significant that it was the anti-treatyites, apparently recognizing their lack of popular support, who were mainly involved in attempts to force the non-pact men to withdraw.

30 Ibid., 6 June 1922.

31 Donal O'Sullivan, *The Irish Free State and its senate* (London 1940), pp. 61, 63. See also F. S. L. Lyons, *Ireland since the famine*, p. 456.

32 O'Brien, *Forth the banners go*, pp. 220–21; Mary Bromage, *De Valera and the march of a nation* (New York 1956), p. 172.

33 *Voice of Labour*, 17 June 1922; Dan Breen, *My fight for Irish freedom* (Tralee 1964), p. 168.

34 Interview with O'Connell, 3 November 1965.

Eighteen Labour candidates refused to budge. Sensing growing public support for the Labour men, who were popularly considered to be pro-treaty, the republicans attempted to discredit them, denouncing the Labour leadership for its tacit support of the treaty and the Free State. The *Plain People* of 4 June exposed a 'Labour Plot', organized by the British government, to replace republicans in the Dail with Labour men: 'Pro-British Capitalists and pro-British "Labour", united and working hand in hand in a common cause . . . are to achieve what the Black and Tans failed to accomplish.'[35] Thomas Johnson's English birth and moderate political position provided grounds for further republican attacks: he was 'a loyal son of the Empire'; at the idea of Johnson 'as an Irish Nationalist one can only shake one's head'. He seemed 'to have the outlook rather of an English Labour Leader rather than of the profound and convinced follower of the policy of James Connolly'. The contributions of Labour in the national struggle were now forgotten. Johnson and O'Brien were accused of attempting to stop the growth of Sinn Fein before 1918 and of having opposed abstention from Westminster. Cathal O'Shannon was labelled an atheist. The republicans reminded workers that their true champion, Jim Larkin, was opposed to the treaty and the Free State.[36]

The campaign concluded with a dramatic statement by Michael Collins in Cork four days before the election:

> You are facing an election here on Friday and I am not hampered now by being on a platform where there are Coalitionists. I can make a straight appeal to you—to the citizens of Cork, to vote for candidates you think best of, whom the electors of Cork think will carry on best in the future the work they want carried on.[37]

Thus Collins no longer urged the people to vote only for pact nominees; his statement was rightfully viewed by republicans as a repudiation of the pact.[38] It lent status to the Labour candidates and doubtlessly helped them at the polls.

President Griffith had promised the Labour executive in March that the draft constitution would be submitted to the people before the election.[39] It was not until the night before the election that the constitution was made public, and it was not published in the press until election day. The Griffith forces probably used this strategy to avoid adverse public reaction at the polls to the many references to England and the monarchy in the document. O'Sullivan states, 'As

35 See also *Poblacht na hEireann*, 30 April 1922, and *Plain People*, 11 June 1922.

36 See *New Ireland*, 10 June 1922; *Plain People*, 4, 11, 18 June 1922; *Voice of Labour*, 24 June 1922; *Workers Republic*, 3, 17 June 1922.

37 Dorothy Macardle, *Irish republic*, p. 656.

38 *Plain People*, 18, 25 June 1922; *Poblacht na hEireann*, 30 June 1922; Breen, *My fight for Irish freedom*, p. 168; see also O'Sullivan, *Irish Free State*, p. 64.

39 Griffith letter to executive, dated 25 March 1922. I.L.P. and T.U.C., *1922 report*, p. 45.

the issue was clearly the acceptance or rejection of the treaty, [the constitution's] belated appearance . . .was of no great importance'.[40] But the people were not clear about what the treaty really meant. The provisions of the draft constitution would have helped the voters to make up their minds on the acceptance or rejection of the treaty, by voting for pro- or anti-treaty candidates. This was the view of the Labour Party.

Both Labour and anti-treaty forces condemned the last-minute publication of the document. They had looked to the constitution as a means whereby the offensive provisions of the treaty might be mitigated. In its 'address to the electors', the Labour executive declared:

> The new assembly is to be a Constituent Assembly, that is to say, a National Authority empowered to devise a Constitution for the future government of the country. The proposals of the Provisional Government can only be considered as the proposals of a political party for the presentation to the Constitutional Assembly. . . . As we understand the position, no issue can arise on this question as between the Irish people and the British Government until the Constitution has passed the Constituent Assembly. The Labour Party stands for the rights of the Irish people to formulate freely the Constitution under which they shall be governed.[41]

A Victory for the Moderates

The election was a victory for the supporters of the treaty: of the sixty-six pro-treaty candidates, fifty-six were elected; of the fifty-nine anti-treaty candidates, only thirty-six were returned. It was also a glorious but small-scale triumph for Labour—seventeen of its eighteen candidates were returned, while the eighteenth nominee, O'Farrell, lost by the narrow margin of thirteen votes. It was believed in Labour Party circles that O'Farrell had been elected but that several blocks of votes had been stolen by anti-treaty poll workers.[42] In five constituencies Labour candidates led the poll, indicating that more Labour nominees might have successfully gone forward. Seven farmer candidates and six independents were also elected, all of them pro-treaty. Four other independents, representing Unionist opinion, were elected on a separate ballot by Trinity College graduates. The inclusion of this group, elected on an undemocratic basis, was to have a decisive effect in the Dail five years later. Several outspoken anti-treaty candidates were defeated. Erskine Childers was at the bottom of the poll in Kildare-Wicklow, and Liam Mellows was defeated in Galway. Of the 128 deputies elected, 92, no matter how reluctantly, were generally in favour of implementing the treaty. This included the pro-treaty panel members, the Labour Party members, the Farmers Union group and

40 O'Sullivan, *Irish Free State*, p. 62.

41 Quoted from election pamphlet of Johnson.

42 Interview with T. J. O'Connell. The returns indicate that Larkin supporters did not vote for O'Farrell.

the independents. The daily press interpreted the results as a victory for the treaty, and the outcome shows that the people had more confidence in the provisional government than they had in the anti-treaty group.

The Labour Party executive, however, denied that the government had received a mandate: 'Despite the efforts made to prevent non-party candidates offering themselves for election, forty-seven were nominated . . . out of the forty-seven . . . no fewer than thirty-four were returned, in most cases with heavy surpluses. If there is one thing that the election decided, it was the electors' want of confidence in the Government.'[43]

The great success of the Labour candidates was partly due to their emphasizing social and economic issues, problems which the other parties hardly touched on at all. More important was that many voters, tired of the wrangling over the treaty and fearful of violent developments, voted for candidates who were obviously peaceful and outside the dispute. T. J. O'Connell believes Labour received many votes from supporters of the defunct Irish Parliamentary Party who were opposed to Sinn Fein and viewed the treaty division simply as a Sinn Fein split; Labour lost these votes at the next election, in 1923, when they went to the pro-treaty government party. Labour received encouraging support from trade unionists, as indicated by the election of Labour deputies from the industrial districts of Dublin and Cork.

Immediately following the election, Labour voiced its dissatisfaction with the draft constitution, but added that it looked forward to modifying the document in the new Dail. Its principal objection was to certain clauses 'which run counter to our own Labour Party Constitution which sets out as one of our objects "the abolition of all powers and privileges, social and political, of institutions or persons, based upon property or ancestry or not granted or confirmed by the freely expressed will of the Irish people" '. The proposed constitution also came under attack from de Valera, who declared: 'As it stands, it will exclude from the public service and practically disfranchise every honest Republican', but he too 'felt confident that Dail Eireann would not pass it as it stood.'[44]

IRISH LABOUR AND THE CIVIL WAR

The Citizen Army and the Labour Leadership

During the six-month period from the signing of the treaty to the national election, the Labour leaders, as we have seen, were involved in finding a compromise solution to the treaty division and preparing the party's electoral machinery. At the same time they engaged in another activity which shows that they foresaw the probability of civil conflict. From the day that the provisional government was created, 14 January, Johnson, O'Brien, O'Shannon and Foran attempted to

43 I.L.P. and T.U.C., *1922 report*, p. 36.

44 Ibid., p. 53; *Dublin Evening Mail*, 21 June 1922.

bring the Citizen Army under their control. This was not an easy task as the army had become increasingly estranged from the Transport Union leadership which had not sought to maintain its former influence in the army. Although the Citizen Army only had about two hundred members at this time, it was an organization with a proud history which could form the nucleus for an expanded body. The motives of the Labour leadership in taking this action, however, are not entirely clear. Were they trying to take hold of an organization which in time of civil war could be used to protect the workers and their unions? Or did they want a force that in a civil conflict could be used to strike for social revolution?

At the very least, the attempt to gain hold of the army shows that the Labour leaders were cognizant of the revolutionary situation and were trying to prepare for eventualities.

Although he does not mention the subject in his published memoirs, William O'Brien's papers provide the best evidence of what followed. After the Dail vote on the treaty the Citizen Army was invited to become part of a new, expanded force to be sponsored by the party-congress—the Workers Army. The leaders of the Citizen Army, apparently in the hope of securing money for its needs, accepted the invitation, and an organizing committee of five members of the Citizen Army and five trade unionists was created. Country branches of the Transport Union were asked if they were prepared to support the new force. By 2 March O'Brien reported that 'very encouraging replies' had been received from the branches; by mid-April an army convention had been held and a number of units formed.[45]

On the night of 13 April republican forces seized the Four Courts, and ten days later the 'anti-militarism' strike took place. These events shattered the fragile agreement on which the Workers Army was established. Michael Kelly, a member of the committee to organize the new force, assigned Citizen Army men to guard speakers at a Labour public meeting held on the day of the strike. According to R. M. Fox, the general feeling in the Citizen Army ranks was that the meeting was directed against the I.R.A. men in the Four Courts. The guards protested to their army council, but Kelly said he acted for a higher authority—the executive of the Workers Army. 'The Citizen Army decided it would not stand for any dual control.'[46]

What followed was a division in the Citizen Army. The strongly republican group led by John Hanratty—probably representing a majority in the army—joined forces with the I.R.A. Hanratty met with one of the Four Courts leaders, Ernie O'Malley, and they agreed that if

45 O'Brien papers, N.L.I., MS 15673(1). In his diary O'Brien noted, without comment, meetings between the Labour and Citizen Army leaders on 14 January (see last page of 1922 diary) and 25 February 1922. O'Brien papers, MS 15705.

46 R. M. Fox, *The history of the Irish Citizen Army*, p. 217. Commandant John Hanratty later charged the Labour leadership with calling the anti-militarism strike in co-operation with the employers in order to give the workers' sanction to the Free State. *Plain People*, 11 June 1922; O'Brien papers, N.L.I., MS 15673(1).

the I.R.A. stronghold was attacked, the Citizen Army would take the field in their support.[47]

Another group, led by Kelly, Frank Robbins and Michael Donnelly, attempted for a time to claim that it was the legitimate leadership of the army. The Transport Union continued to recruit for the Workers Army, and in a letter dated 2 June the Kelly group declared it still favoured the creation of such a force. A later letter (13 June) indicates that the group was still attempting to maintain the appearance of being in control of the Citizen Army.[48] But this effort was without result, and by the time the civil war broke out nothing further was heard of the splinter group.

Frank Robbins believes that the power struggle within the Dublin labour movement was the main reason that the Citizen Army refused to return to its Labour origins. Hanratty and other leaders in the army, he says, were listening to Delia Larkin, P. T. Daly and other opponents of the O'Brien-Johnson leadership; also, resentment of the Transport Union leadership was rife in the Citizen Army at this time.[49] The army's hostility towards the Labour executive continued through the June election. Commandant Hanratty charged the leaders with attempting to crush the army and said that the party was running on a weak, non-revolutionary platform. The workers were urged to stand by Larkin and to reject those Labour leaders who were prepared to accept the Free State.

When the Four Courts was attacked by the Free State Army, the Citizen Army council offered its men to Oscar Traynor, leader of the Dublin brigade of the republican forces. The men (who were joined by the tiny Communist Party contingent) numbered between one hundred fifty and two hundred. The army contributed 3,000 rounds of ammunition but no arms. In the conduct of the struggle the Citizen Army was merely an appendage to the republican force; it had no role in policy-making. When the civil conflict moved to the country shortly thereafter, effective Citizen Army participation ended.[50]

The Brothers' War Begins

The results of the election embittered the republican partisans; they declared the electoral pact had been violated by the pro-treaty side. The breakdown of the pact made the possibility of a coalition government most unlikely, and talk of civil war, which had ceased with the conclusion of the pact, revived again in the republican press:

47 Some Citizen Army militants, including Walter Carpenter, were already in the Four Courts. Fox, *History of the Citizen Army*, p. 217. Peadar O'Donnell described the Citizen Army at this time as even more determined to 'uphold the republic' than was the I.R.A. O'Donnell interview.

48 O'Brien papers, N.L.I., MS 15673(1).

49 Robbins interview.

50 Fox, *History of the Citizen Army*, pp. 218, 222; C. Desmond Greaves, *Liam Mellows and the Irish revolution*, p. 347.

> The pact is broken; everyone realizes that. The pact is gone. . . . with them [the pro-treatyites] as with him [Collins] there can be no Coalition. . . . On now with the work, military and political, of maintaining the Republic and defending it against all who would overthrow it.[51]

On 27 June 1922, the official government publication announced that the Dail would meet on 1 July. The next day, however, the government forces began bombarding the Four Courts. Whether this attack was brought about by British government pressure, as Macardle believes, or by the kidnapping of Gerald O'Connell and the raidings of republican militants, as Collins states, is not a question for this study.[52] But the Labour executive clearly laid the blame on the provisional government for igniting the charge: 'Without giving any satisfactory explanation of their changes in policy they precipitated an attack upon the headquarters of the force with whose leaders they had been in negotiation. . . . ' This sudden onslaught, 'practically drove the whole political Republican Party into giving active support to the Army Executive's policy.'[53]

Once again the Labour leaders attempted to bring about peace, if no more than a truce. Johnson, O'Brien and O'Shannon went to the Four Courts as well as to the government offices, but there was too much ill will and suspicion on both sides for anything to be accomplished. Griffith told the Labour leaders that the cabinet was the government and it was going to govern. As they could do nothing more at this juncture, the Labour men turned their attention to the needs of those who had been driven from their homes during the reduction of the Four Courts. The minister for local government, William Cosgrave, promised to provide temporary shelter for the homeless. Following the capture of the Four Courts garrison, the three Labour leaders went to Mountjoy Prison to talk to the republican leaders. No progress resulted: the Four Courts men decided that the initiative for a truce would have to come from elsewhere in the republican side. Johnson published a letter from the imprisoned leaders in which they denied exploding a mine in the Four Courts. This met with a reply from the Free State army which charged Johnson with 'abusing your privileges at Mountjoy', adding that the Four Courts leaders had admitted setting the mine.[54]

As civil strife spread outside Dublin, the Labour executive called upon organized workers to take no part in the conflict, urging a policy of 'a plague on both your houses'. This met with hostility from both sides. In its issue of 22 July, the *Voice of Labour* commented that the 'most venomous enmity' was being shown by the two protagonists

51 *Plain People*, 25 June 1922. See also *New Ireland*, 24 June 1922.

52 Macardle, *Irish republic* (1951), pp. 739–41; Collins, *Path to freedom*, p. 18.

53 I.L.P. and T.U.C., *1922 report*, p. 39.

54 *Irish Independent*, 5 July 1922. See also I.L.P. and T.U.C., *1922 report*, p. 32.

'because Labour dares to be independent of both armies and parties. . . .' Most of the condemnation of the Labour position came from the republican weeklies. A typical statement was that of *Poblacht na hEireann* (11 August) which declared that the Labour leaders 'forget that if a nation is subject, every class in it is subject; nor do they see that though today Republicans are being shot down, tomorrow it will be Labour's turn.' The article continued:

> Do they think that Mr. Griffith intends to set up their non-existent Workers Republic on the ruins of the existing people's Republic. . . . [The Labour] leadership prefers to encourage the carrying of munitions, the coaling of troop-ships, enlistment in Churchill's army, the hounding down of the I.R.A. and then they pretend they are 'standing aside'. We cannot believe that this pitiful policy is the policy of the rank and file.

Peadar O'Donnell wrote, 'It is England's devilish luck that at a moment when Irish Labour is faced with a situation of tremendous possibilities, the dominant influence on the National Executive should be an Imperialist English mind', referring, of course, to Thomas Johnson.[55] In Mountjoy Jail, Liam Mellows pondered the consequence of Labour's position:

> Labour played a tremendous part in the establishment and maintainance of the Republic. Its leaders had it in their power to fashion that Republic as they wished—to make it a Workers and Peasants Republic. By their acceptance of the treaty and all that it connotes—recognition of the British Monarchy, the British Privy Council and British Imperialism, partition of the country and subserviency to British Capitalism, they have betrayed not alone the Irish Republic but the Labour movement in Ireland and the cause of the workers and peasants throughout the world.[56]

Most skilled and organized workers abstained from the conflict. In Cork a section of Transport Union members joined the republican forces, but this is the only example of a group of trade unionists joining in the fighting.[57]

Two writers who view history as primarily a class struggle see social and economic forces as dominant factors in the civil war. Emil Strauss argues that the poorer classes—the workers of town and farm—supported the republican cause because they saw it as a social revolution:

> The difference between Mr. de Valera's Document No. 2 and the text of the Treaty, though not entirely a matter of terminology, was far too small to explain the violent explosion of the civil war.

55 *Workers Republic*, 26 August 1922.

56 Article by Proinsias Ó Gallchobhair (Frank Gallagher) in *Sinn Fein*, 20 December 1924, quoting Mellows on 3 December 1922, shortly before his execution.

57 *Voice of Labour*, 22 July 1922.

> . . . The social revolution which Sinn Fein had kept within the narrow channels of a national struggle against England was trying to find an outlet now that the English enemy had withdrawn. The paradox that some of the western districts 'which proved so peaceful under the Black and Tan regime became aggressively warlike after the Treaty was signed' throws a glaring light on the crucial implications of Sinn Fein's conservative social policy on political events. If further evidence of the gulf between the under-privileged sections of the Irish people and their national movement were needed, the widespread attacks on the mansions of landlords and ex-landlords, the revolt of the labourers in Wexford and Waterford, the short-lived 'Soviets' in some urban centres and the occupation of creameries by their workpeople amply supply it.[58]

It might be suggested that the reason for prolonged fighting in the western counties was because the republican forces had been driven out of other areas and were forced to take refuge in the rugged terrain there. Yet, there is evidence that the western counties supported the republicans more than did the nation as a whole.

The British Marxist historian T. A. Jackson sees

> an absolute split by a sharp conflict of economic interests, centering upon the Land Hunger. . . . The line-up was between the actually or potentially Land Hungry, supported by Republican intellectuals and urban revolutionaries, on one side and the urban bourgeois, the State functionaries, the land-owners and the upper strata of the peasantry on the other. The skilled-labour element and the Labour Party generally were paralyzed by division.[59]

There were many social and economic cross-currents in Ireland during this period, but in the civil war the sides were not joined to form neat class patterns as Jackson suggests. Darrell Figgis, a man with unusual political insight, believed that seventy-five percent of the 'irregularism' was caused by unemployment, a view shared by Thomas Johnson. The government denied that unemployment was the cause of strife; Cosgrave said the war caused the unemployment, and Blythe thought that farmers' sons simply didn't want to work. To the government, especially to O'Higgins, the civil war was largely the result of sinister plotting and only marginally a product of idealism.[60]

From the very beginning of the civil war the Communist *Workers Republic* urged the republicans to adopt a comprehensive social and economic programme to win the support of the workers; an appeal to patriotism was not enough. As early as 22 July it urged:

> The Republicans must understand that if in the struggle the labouring masses and the small farmers come to their side—then

58 Emil Strauss, *Irish nationalism and British democracy*, p. 271.

59 T. A. Jackson, *Ireland her own* (New York 1970), p. 413.

60 *Dail Eireann deb.*, ii, col. 175; i, cols. 144–47, 1870, 1873.

> the Free State is doomed. . . . Once you show the mass that the Republic of Ireland will bring them definite and concrete advantages in their day to day life . . . then they will consider that the Republic is worth fighting for.

The paper, of course, urged a very radical programme. In a later issue—12 August—it called for a meeting of the republican deputies, to which the Labour members would be invited, and the establishment of a 'republican government', the first duty of which was to be the 'framing of a clearly defined economic programme'.

No such programme was formulated by the republican leadership during the civil war. This omission can be partially explained by the disorganization of the republican forces. But in reading the speeches of the leading republicans and the publications of their spokesmen, it becomes apparent that the sketchy economic and social ideas they possessed at this time had little appeal to the dock worker or small farm tenant. Many young militarists, like Liam Lynch, were fighting for 'pure ideals'.[61]

Among the republicans, only the imprisoned Liam Mellows articulated anything approaching a course of economic action. In August 1922 he wrote a hastily composed programme for the republicans. He urged the immediate creation of a provisional republican government; he also proposed that the democratic programme of 1919 'should be translated into something definite. This is essential if the great body of the workers are to be kept on the side of independence.' Mellows attempted to allay any fears among moderate-minded republicans by assuring them that 'this does not require a change of outlook on the part of Republicans or the adoption of a revolutionary programme as such.' However, his programme (derived from the 22 July edition of the *Workers Republic*) was definitely revolutionary:

> Under the Republic all industry would be controlled by the State for all the workers and farmers benefit. All transport, railways, canals, etc., will be operated by the State. . . . All banks will be operated by the State for the benefit of industry and agriculture. . . . That the lands of the aristocracy (who support the Free State and the British connection) will be seized and divided amongst those who can and will operate them for the national benefit.[62]

He urged the immediate implementation by the I.R.A. executive of a scheme to seize control of large landholdings. This plan, prepared by Patrick Rutledge, Ernie O'Malley and Thomas Deerig, had been

61 Florence O'Donoghue, *No other law*, p. 308. Lynch's opposition to British imperialism is apparent, but this biography gives no indication that he had thought about the non-political problems facing Ireland.

62 *Irish Independent*, 22 September 1922, quoting a letter by Mellows dated 26 August 1922. See also Mellows, *Notes from Mountjoy jail* (London n.d.); Greaves, *Mellows*, pp. 269, 358, 364, 377.

approved by the executive. Divisional units were instructed in May to put it into effect, but little action followed.[63]

Mellow's proposals failed to influence the I.R.A. When a republican government was announced on 28 October 1922, social and economic issues were ignored; there was no mention of the 'democratic programme' in its draft constitution—its message was strictly political. Ironically, Mellows's proposals were used to discredit the republicans. Free State forces captured a copy of his memorandum and the government published its contents. The *Irish Independent* of 22 September gave sensational treatment to the proposals, declaring that 'the policy is to set up a Provisional Republican Government and in effect to establish a Communistic State.' 'The great barrier to Mellows's appeal', O'Donnell believes, 'was not the confusion of the times, nor the late hour of its release but the climate of "innocence" in which the post-1916 independence movement was developed. The economic framework and social relations, which expressed tyrannical aspects of the conquest, were declared outside the scope of the Republican struggle. . . .'[64]

What effect did the civil war have on the political development of Ireland? Sean O'Faolain holds the view that the treaty split and the ensuing civil war allowed the men of property to gain an unjustified influence in the new state:

> The classes which had openly or more commonly secretly opposed or held back from the revolutionary movement of 1913–1921—the cautious, conservative, professional and business classes—realizing towards the end of the Troubles what was about to happen began to insinuate themselves as fast as they could into the movement. . . . Had there been no split in the nationalist movement they would probably have been quickly repressed. Owing to the split they found themselves unexpectedly welcomed. . . . As a result there appeared a sharp division in Irish life, between the conservative and self-seeking and the more democratic and idealistic—the latter represented by the de Valera party.[65]

One would not have to agree completely with O'Faolain's analysis to accept the fact that the business and industrial communities rallied to the side of the Free State in the civil war.

Possibly, also, the civil war made the pro-treaty leaders more cautious and conservative politically than they would otherwise have been; certainly their legislative policy was plainly conservative during the 1920s. Ernest Blythe, who earlier was considered as one who was

63 According to Peadar O'Donnell, the republican forces made no attempt to reveal this scheme either before or during the civil war. O'Donnell, *There will be another day*, p. 10; O'Donnell interview; Greaves, *Mellows*, pp. 313–14.

64 O'Donnell, *There will be another day*, p. 12.

65 Sean O'Faolain, *De Valera* (Dublin 1933, 1964), p. 166.

sympathetic to the aspirations of the labour movement, gave no indication of these leanings as finance minister in the Free State government.[66]

The civil war split the state politically into two large camps, corresponding to the two sides in the struggle. Those who had maintained a generally neutral position in the war, like the Labour Party, were driven to the political sidelines. Political and constitutional issues continued to dominate throughout the decade of the 1920s, much to the disadvantage of the Labour Party, which, of course, was primarily a party of social and economic reform. Donal Nevin has summed it up:

> Loyalties born of the Civil War proved stronger than any class consciousness or any disposition to follow the political promptings of the trade union movement. . . . Because of its attitude to the Treaty and the conservative views on the national question held by some of its leading figures, Labour provided no strong appeal for Republicans.[67]

66 O'Donnell, *There will be another day*, p. 85. Cathal O'Shannon held that the pro-treaty side was forced to a more conservative stance. Interview with O'Shannon.

67 Donal Nevin, Thomas Davis lecture, report in *Irish Times*, 15 December 1964.

7

The Third Dail, the Larkin Split and the 1923 Election

THE CIVIL WAR DAIL

With the outbreak of fighting the government postponed the meeting of the newly elected Dail from 1 July to 15 July. The Labour executive protested the delay: the new Labour members doubtless were anxious to begin participating in the decisions being made, often irresponsibly, by others. But one postponement followed another, with the result that the Free State government fought the civil war in the summer months of 1922 without a vote of confidence from the parliament, and with a president installed in office merely by a vote of the cabinet.

When the meeting of the Dail was further postponed until 15 August, the national executive and the Labour deputies issued an invitation to all Dail members to meet in Dublin on 30 July in order to 'discuss the position of the country in the light of the events of the last three weeks and to consider certain proposals which may, perhaps, lead to peace'.[1] The meeting proved abortive, as only the Labour members and Dublin's Lord Mayor O'Neill attended. The republican deputies took the line that their presence would hinder the work of the conference, but it was known that some of the anti-treaty T.D.s were in favour of attendance. The farmers' group and the independents declined to attend—they were supporters of the government.[2] However, when the annual Labour conference gathered in August, the national executive could honestly declare that it had 'practically exhausted all the avenues that could be explored to find a solution for our present difficulties and the civil war'.[3]

The conference reflected the clash of opinion throughout the country; many delegates were committed to the treaty or to the republicans as well as to their own party. Debate raged over an executive resolution which scored both sides in the civil war and which included the statement, 'Not only do we consider the political claims of the Republican Party to be irrational but their method of warfare is such as must be strongly denounced.' A motion to delete this part of the resolution was defeated by a vote of ninety-one to thirty-five. The question of the Labour deputies taking the oath of allegiance was raised when Walter Carpenter put forward a resolution instructing them not to take the oath. The Carpenter resolution was sidetracked

1 *Irish Independent*, 21 July 1922.

2 For the republican statement, see Sean T. O'Kelly's letter to the conference in O'Brien papers, N.L.I., MS 13961(1). Other information on attitudes toward the meeting is in William O'Brien, *Forth the banners go*, p. 225; *Voice of Labour*, 29 July 1922; *Irish Independent*, 10 August 1922.

3 I.L.P. and T.U.C., *1922 report*, pp. 28–32. For a description of another attempt to bring about peace, see O'Brien's account of the abortive Father Albert conference in *Forth the banners go*, pp. 224–25.

from the floor to the standing orders committee. A meeting of the committee, the national executive and the Labour deputies was called, resulting in a resolution instructing Labour members to resign from the Dail if it did not shortly meet. The issue of taking the oath was quietly dropped, and the meeting was instead presented with this resolution, which it unanimously adopted.[4]

The conference set a deadline for the meeting of the new Dail—26 August—after which the Labour deputies would resign if it had not met. But the tragic deaths of the two leaders of the provisional government, Collins and Griffith, resulted in a further postponement to 9 September. A Labour delegation was given 'definite assurances' by William T. Cosgrave, the new leader of the government, that the Dail would meet on this day. The executive accepted the government's reason as legitimate, and the Labour deputies did not resign.[5]

Cosgrave must have realized that without the Labour deputies the position of the Dail would be further undermined. By August 1922 it was clear that the republicans would not take their seats in the third Dail, even though it was not necessary to take the controversial oath until several months after the session opened. If the Labour Party had resigned there would have been only two tiny groups on the opposition benches—the farmers and the independents—neither of which were organized parties. The government needed the Labour Party as at least a nominal opposition to give the Dail the appearance of being a national assembly rather than a gathering of a political faction. True to his word, Cosgrave convened the Dail on 9 September, and the Labour Party at last assumed its place in the national legislature. But with the country in a shambles there was little time for self-congratulation.

Shortly before the Dail met, Johnson was elected without opposition as the leader of the parliamentary Labour Party. Having been the leading spokesman of organized labour since the re-organization of the movement following the 1916 rising, he was the obvious choice: he had the widest experience and the most coherent political philosophy of any of the Labour deputies. William O'Brien, a man of equal standing both in the labour movement and in national affairs, did not seek the leadership as he was fully occupied with the affairs of the Transport Union.[6] O'Shannon was elected deputy leader while O'Brien and T. J. O'Connell, secretary of the Irish National Teachers' Organization since 1916, were appointed party whips. With the exception of Richard Corish, these four men were the only Labour members with experience in national affairs; the other Labour deputies were generally unknown outside of their home districts.

4 I.L.P. and T.U.C., *1922 report,* pp. 156, 167, 181–82.

5 I.L.P. and T.U.C., *1923 report,* p. 29. The *Workers Republic,* 9 September 1922, accused the Labour Party of 'faking' in its threat.

6 Interviews with T. J. O'Connell, 3 November 1965, and Cathal O'Shannon, 5 June 1964.

Johnson was to remain the uncontested leader of the party through the three Dails which sat during the next five years. He was the leader of the main parliamentary opposition for all but the last month of this period. Johnson had a thoughtful, socialist view of what Ireland needed to do if it was to have a growing, healthy, educated and prosperous population. Based on this, he developed intelligent and clear policies on every issue that came before the Dail. His capacity for work seemed unlimited. No man ever was more devoted to the business of a parliament. It is with justice that Johnson was called a one-man opposition. In his study, *The Irish Free State, 1922–27,* Denis Gwynn paid tribute to Johnson:

> Next to the Speaker, the Dail probably owed most to Mr. Thomas Johnson. . . . He brought to the political development of the Free State that sense of responsibility for popularly elected government, and of immense seriousness in public life, that is characteristic of the English 'moderate' trade union leader. It is hard to imagine that any Irishman could have filled the position in the same way. With an inherited respect for popular assembly, and having been educated in the English constitutional labour agitation, he regarded the position of leader of the Opposition as involving responsibilities scarcely less than those of the Prime Minister.

The Speaker (Ceann Comhairle) referred to, Michael Hayes, has declared that Johnson made an outstanding contribution in the development of the Free State Dail as a viable and respected national instution.[7]

The Labour Party under Johnson's leadership stressed the need for social and economic change, subordinating the issues arising from the Anglo-Irish treaty to this primary concern. By its entrance and continued presence in the Dail, the party was held to support the treaty. But the party took the position that because the treaty had been accepted by a majority of the Irish people, it should be utilized for the maximum benefit of the country. It was Labour's frequent contention that the Cosgrave government failed to do this. At the same time, it held that the people had the right to repudiate the treaty at any time.

Because of the abstention of the anti-treaty deputies, representing one-third of those elected to the Dail, the Free State assembly was unrepresentative during the ensuing five years. The Labour Party assumed the role of parliamentary opposition out of the sheer requirements of the situation. It was the largest non-government party in the house; it was the only opposition party that was an organized, disciplined body, and it was the only party on the opposition benches basically opposed to most government policies. Labour received little or no support from the seven members of the Farmers Party or from the ten independents.

The Cosgrave government's primary concern was the defeat of the anti-treaty forces in the civil war and the implementation of the

7 Interview with Hayes, 19 April 1967.

provisions of the treaty; it viewed social and economic questions as being of completely secondary importance. The life of the third Dail was limited to one year, during which time it had two responsibilities to fulfil: ratification of a Free State constitution and establishment of basic legislation for the new state. At the end of this period the Dail was to be dissolved for a new election.

From its first day in the Dail, the Labour Party, with little ceremony and without a moment's hesitation, plunged into the affairs of government. It immediately launched an assault on the government for failing to call the Dail during the first months of the civil war. This was followed by an attack on the government's policies of secrecy, courts-martial and executions. When Dr Patrick McCartan, on 28 September 1922, proposed a fourteen-day truce between the opposing forces, the Labour Party rushed to his support.[8] These actions did not save Labour from the abuse and threats of the republican forces. Liam Lynch sent a letter to both the Speaker of 'the Provisional Government of Southern Ireland' and Thomas Johnson concerning the executions of republican insurgents:

> Next to the members of your 'Provisional Government', every member of your body who voted for this resolution by which you pretend to make legal the murder of soldiers is equally guilty. We therefore give you and each member of your body due notice that unless your army recognizes the rules of warfare in future, we shall adopt very drastic measures to protect our forces.[9]

Cosgrave told the Labour deputies that they faced the possibility of assassination, and he offered to house them in a guarded hotel near the Dail. This offer was declined. Johnson, of course, was principally endangered, but he courageously continued to commute to his home in Rathmines. Later, when the Labour Party decided to take the oath of allegiance, Johnson was personally attacked in an open letter in the republican *Daily Bulletin* (4 January 1923):

> There are many Englishmen like you, Mr. Johnson, living as you do, in the Rathmines suburbs, and the majority of them, no doubt, share your political opinions. But they are not the opinions of the workers of Ireland. . . . They found their inspiration in James Connolly and not in you who climbed into power as a result of his sacrifice, having sent recent martyrs, workers of Ireland, to share his noble company.

As the civil war dragged into 1923, Johnson became increasingly critical of the republicans continuing what appeared to be a hopeless struggle. Finally, on 9 March 1923, he made this view plain:

> I believe it is time to say that a large section of those who are inspiring the Irregular campaign hold that by a sufficient attack

8 *Dail Eireann deb.*, i, 935.

9 Florence O'Donoghue, *No other law* (Dublin 1954), p. 279.

> upon the national resources the State cannot maintain itself. . . . The present attack is, in reality, an attack upon the social fabric itself. . . . The attack to break up the social fabric, once it is seized upon by the people, will mean that, at any cost and at any sacrifice, the country will rally to the defence of the State . . . even though the private resources of the people are going to be brought to nothing, still for the sake of maintaining society in this country the opposition to society must be resisted and overthrown.[10]

A Constitution for the New Dominion

The Labour Party, among others, had looked forward to the constitution as a means of bridging the sharp division created by the treaty. Arthur Griffith had declared that the third Dail, sitting as a constituent assembly, would be a sovereign body and could freely draw up any constitution it chose. When the Dail began deliberations on the proposed constitution on 18 September 1922 it quickly realized that the Cosgrave government was not prepared to allow the Dail freedom on the form of the constitution. President Cosgrave announced that the government would impose party discipline on all important sections of the proposed constitution which had been previously agreed upon with the British government and Irish Unionists.[11]

Labour contended that the government's proposed constitution was not as favourable to Irish sovereignty as was the treaty. Johnson went so far as to urge the Dail not to draw up a written document at this time, but rather to allow the constitution to grow out of the provisions of the treaty. He got the government to admit that its original draft had been submitted to the British government and had been substantially altered due to British pressure. Labour joined with Patrick McCartan in demanding that Cosgrave submit the original draft to the Dail, but this the government refused to do.

The Labour Party led the unsuccessful opposition to include references to British institutions in the Free State constitution: the mandatory oath of allegiance, the right to appeal Irish court decisions to the British privy council and other references to the British king and commonwealth. Only a few independent deputies supported this position. The government argued that since the Dail had accepted the treaty, it would also have to accept the inclusion of the British powers and institutions in the constitution.

10 *Dail Eireann deb.*, ii, 2279–81.

11 *Dail Eireann deb.*, i, 1006. Documentation for Labour's role in the constitutional debates is found in ibid., 364, 383, 408, 491, 573, 696–99, 707, 735, 750, 777, 1047, 1067, 1118, 1132, 1187–88, 1309, 1404, 1414, 1457, 1534–67, 1619, 1909–10, 1949, 2005. For Labour's attitude toward the governor-generalship, see also *Dail Eireann deb.*, ii, 135; iv, 1154–55. The party's opinions on the senate are further documented in *Dail Eireann deb.*, ii, 2374; xviii, 1155; I.L.P. and T.U.C., *1923 report*, pp. 31, 33, 64–65; *Voice of Labour*, 9 December 1922. On the question of vocational councils and educational provisions, see also *Dail Eireann deb.*, ii, 453; Barra O Briain, *The Irish constitution* (Dublin and Cork 1929), p. 106; Basil Chubb, *The constitution of Ireland* (Dublin 1966), pp. 12–13.

One such institution was the governor-generalship. Johnson claimed that Michael Collins had stated that the representative of the crown would not bear this title. The party centred its criticism on the large expense of the office and the partisan outbursts of its first occupant, the shop-worn Timothy M. Healy. When Healy addressed the Dail in December 1922 the party withdrew, protesting that his appearance was not required by the treaty and that no outsider should address the body without its permission. Labour made repeated attempts to reduce the appropriation for this office.

It was opposed to another Free State institution as well. Both the Dail party and the Labour party-congress were hostile to a second house of the legislature, on the basis that it would be an undemocratic body. Johnson declared that if a senate were necessary, it should represent vocational groups rather than such interests as the Free State Unionists. But later the party did select Labour members for a senate dominated by southern Unionists; it used its share of senate seats to reward trade union leaders and defeated Labour candidates for the Dail. It also participated in the only direct popular election for the senate in 1925. Johnson favoured abolition of the senate in 1923 and continued to be critical of the body's alleged lack of thorough consideration of legislation, but following his defeat for re-election to the Dail, Johnson served in the senate from 1928 until its abolition in 1936.

The party approved of one of the few innovations in the constitution—appointment of ministers who would not be members of the executive council. Johnson, who believed that the 'extern' ministers would be appointed by the Dail rather than the president, probably saw in this a wedge through which his party might gain control of a ministry. But, ultimately, 'extern' ministers were the direct appointees of the president.

Although the constitution provided for the initiative and referendum, the government encumbered these provisions with many restrictions. Whereas the Labour Party wanted them immediately operative, the government feared that the provisions would be used by the anti-treatyites in an attempt to remove the necessity for the oath of allegiance. When the anti-treatyites attempted to operate the initiative in 1927, the government, over the protest of the Labour Party, succeeded in having this provision removed from the constitution.

In one of the few 'free votes' allowed by the government, the Dail voted to admit university representation in the Dail as well as in the senate. Labour opposed this 'undemocratic procedure'. The six university members added nothing to the diversity of opinions presented in the Dail at this time. The three representatives of Trinity College called themselves independents but in all important matters were consistent supporters of the Cosgrave government; the three members from the National University were also pro-treaty—in the 1920s three of them served as ministers. Not until the boundary settlement of 1925 did one of the National University members, William Magennis, break with the government and join the opposition. The Free State parliament had a higher proportion of these special deputies (6 of 153) than did the British House of Commons (12 of 640), where the demand for the abolition of this type of representation was already being voiced. Following the entrance of the anti-treatyites into the Dail in 1927, the university deputies provided the margin whereby the Cosgrave government staved off defeat, and a Labour scheme for a coalition government was wrecked.

The Free State constitution had little socio-economic content. The Labour Party attempted to insert a section of the 1919 'democratic programme' into the preamble; Johnson argued that if the programme had been implemented 'much that has happened within recent months would not have happened'. In opposing Labour's amendment, Kevin O'Higgins declared that Patrick Pearse's words were 'largely poetry'. Labour proposals to extend the government's responsibilities in the fields of education, employment and the development of natural resources were also rejected: O'Higgins said that the Labour proposal on natural resources 'certainly looks very much like a Communistic doctrine'.

One unique provision of the constitution granted the Dail authority to form vocational councils. Johnson saw in this a means towards the establishment of something approaching a co-operative commonwealth, but the government took no steps to implement this provision.

Speaking at the last debate on the constitution, Johnson expressed his belief that the constitution did not 'embody all the liberties for Ireland that were contained or might have been interpreted to have been contained in the Treaty'. Nevertheless, the constitution was a useful and pliable instrument, and, therefore, 'we can . . . make of the constitution what we will'.

Following the passage of the Constitution Bill, members of the Dail were required to take the oath of allegiance to the king and the Free State as a prerequisite of Dail membership. Ernest Blythe, minister for local government, correctly predicted that certain sitting members would refuse to take the oath and would not return to the Dail. After a meeting of the Labour deputies, Johnson announced that all Labour members had agreed to take the oath. In fact, one member, Patrick Gaffney, a strong republican from Carlow, refused. The party said Gaffney believed he would not have to take an oath during the term of the third Dail.[12] The Labour statement described the oath as a formality: 'a condition of Membership of the Legislature, implying no obligation other than the ordinary obligation of every person who accepts the privilege of citizenship'. If the people chose at any time to repudiate the treaty or amend the constitution, 'nothing in our Declaration of Allegiance shall be a barrier to our freedom of action.' The party was following 'the practice of the political parties of the

12 I.L.P. and T.U.C., *1923 report*, p. 40. Gaffney stood as an independent Labour republican in 1923 but was defeated.

workers in all countries where capitalism is the established order'.[13] Five years later the main anti-treatyite party was also to declare that the oath was simply a formality.

Civil War Issues and Legislation

Although it supported the Free State's claim to be the legitimate government of the twenty-six counties, the Labour Party was critical of many of the means the government used to suppress the republican forces. The party's criticism centred on the policies of executions, treatment of political prisoners and security legislation.

Labour stood almost alone in opposing the granting of emergency powers to the army. Among these powers was the right to try prisoners before military courts and, if they were found guilty of such offences as carrying weapons, to execute them. Another was the authority 'to transport overseas any offender against any Regulation that the Army may in its wisdom devise'. Ernest Blythe revealed that the government was negotiating for the lease of an island for this purpose. Johnson warned the Dail that military executions in hot blood, without judicial safeguards and legal defences, were likely to occur. When in November several 'irregulars', including Erskine Childers, were executed for possessing revolvers, Johnson charged the government and the army with adopting the same methods as the rebels. To O'Higgins, Johnson's criticism was 'almost an acquiescence in the armed challenge to democracy'. But Johnson continued to denounce as anarchic the executions, the policy of secret trials and the practice of announcing the trials and sentences only after the executions had taken place.[14]

In December four of the captive leaders of the Four Courts were suddenly executed as a reprisal for the killing of a member of the Dail. The shooting of Liam Mellows, Rory O'Connor, Richard Barrett and Joseph McKelvey, provoked the greatest emotional scene in the third Dail. Johnson rose to denounce the government's action:

> The four men in Mountjoy have been in your charge for five months. You were charged with the care of these men. . . . You thought it well not to try them and not to bring them to the courts, and then because a man is assassinated who is held with honour, the Government of this country . . . announces apparently with pride that they have taken out four men . . . and as a reprisal for that assassination murdered them.[15]

With regard to the 12,000 prisoners arrested during the civil war, the party demanded that they be allowed sanitary accommodations and advocated an early release of the captives in order to enhance the

13 *Dail Eireann deb.*, ii, 3. The *Irish Times*, 7 December 1922, declared that the Labour Party possessed a 'strange attitude' in regard to the oath.

14 *Dail Eireann deb.*, i, 836, 864, 898, 903, 2407, 2529.

15 Ibid., ii, 48. For further Labour opinion on summary execution and army special powers, see ibid., 876, 888, 895, 933. For the treatment of prisoners and the army budget, see ibid., iii, 1450–51, 1455–56, 1458, 1623.

reputation of the state and save a large amount of money which could be used on public works. With the end of the war in April 1923, Labour urged the Dail to cut the army budget by £10 million to the previous year's figure of £7 million, because 'the conditions of to-day do not require the larger amount.' But the minister for defence, Richard Mulcahy, warned that a 'war situation' could easily reoccur.

Before the Dail dissolved for a new election, the Cosgrave government obtained further legislation to assure national security. The 1923 Public Safety Bill allowed the government the power to continue detaining political prisoners and the authority to flog persons guilty of robbery under arms and of arson. The Labour Party brought all its resources to bear in an attempt to defeat this bill, which it labelled the 'Flogging Bill'. Johnson said it was modelled after a Northern Ireland law and, indeed, the northern attorney-general pointed with satisfaction to the fact that the Free State had found it necessary to pass similar legislation. Labour attempted to delay passage of the bill by numerous amendments, long speeches and repeated calls for roll-call votes, probably hoping that delay would result in the release of at least a section of the political prisoners (the courts had ruled that the government's previous authority to hold the prisoners was no longer valid once the civil war was over). However, the Labour Party's opposition to the bill—which resulted in the first all-night sitting of the Dail—was finally overcome when the government allowed almost limitless time for debate.[16] Labour, with only fourteen members and, with the exception of George Gavin Duffy, little support from the independents, did not have the manpower to maintain its protest.[17]

Shortly before the end of the third Dail, the government rushed through a defence forces act, the first legislation to deal in a comprehensive manner with the defence establishment. Although such an act was needed, Johnson nonetheless deplored the haste with which it had been enacted: 'A bill of this kind ought to be before the country for a couple of months rather than a couple of days.'[18]

For its stance on civil war measures, Labour again received abuse from both sides. According to Johnson, Kevin O'Higgins had

> very frequently gone out of his way . . . to charge [Labour] members . . . with acquiescence, hidden or open, with the activities of the Republican Army and with antagonism to the Provisional Government. It has been refuted a dozen times.[19]

When the Labour Party attacked the execution of the four republican leaders, Denis Gorey, the leader of the Farmers Party, charged Labour

16 *Irish Times*, 13 July 1923. Statements on the Public Safety Bill are in *Dail Eireann deb.*, iii, 733, 779, 800, 1980, 1985, 2003, 2501, 2513; iv, 2468. For the collapse of Labour's opposition, see *Irish Times*, 17 July 1923.

17 Of the original seventeen Labour deputies, M. Bradley had died, Patrick Gaffney had declined to take the oath of allegiance, and N. Phelan was expelled from the party for failure to attend Dail sessions. I.L.P. and T.U.C., *1923 report*, pp. 30, 39–40.

18 *Dail Eireann deb.*, iv, 1474.

19 Ibid., i, 2408.

with attempting to incite the people.[20] When Labour took the oath of allegiance, the I.R.A. chief of staff, Liam Lynch, declared:

> The continuing participation of your party in the proceedings of this illegal Parliament can only be construed by us as intentional co-operation with enemy forces in the murder of our soldiers, a great proportion of whom are drawn from the ranks of labour.[21]

The *Workers Republic* called the Labour deputies 'serfs and slaves' of the government and of the 'British-controlled Parliament' and said that Johnson had agreed to the policy of executions.[22] This last charge, together with the claim that the party had kept the Dail up all night in order to force through the 'Flogging Bill', was often repeated in future political campaigns.

Social and Economic Legislation

It was the policy of the Free State government during the civil war crisis to hold social and economic expenditure to the level of the previous year. It also maintained the existing level of taxation. In contrast to the government's 'stand pat' policy, the Labour Party saw the need for urgent change; in Johnson's words:

> The country is in a state somewhat of fluidity, and it is possible today, if we will, to change the habits of thinking, to change the social practices, to change the economic environment during this period of fluidity, whereas if we allow things to stabilize in their present forms, if we allow vested interests to be solidified we are going to find it very difficult indeed, without a new revolution, to make this country what it ought to be . . . a commonwealth where humanity has the first place and property and property relations . . . second.[23]

Although Labour did not demand the immediate establishment of a co-operative commonwealth or the nationalization of industry, it did propose a progressive programme of action on urgent social and economic matters. On the growing unemployment problem the party urged the government to 'set the forces of production in motion' by means of public works projects, increased unemployment payments, the issuance of government notes to be used for Irish products only and the creation of state-sponsored industry, rather than waiting until industry and commerce revived by themselves. But the government's philosophy was that 'irregularism' had caused unemployment and any attempts to 'buy off' irregularism by investing money in public works and other employment schemes would bankrupt the country. According

20 Ibid., ii, 80.

21 *Irish Times*, 9 December 1922.

22 *Workers Republic*, 3 and 16 December 1922.

23 *Dail Eireann deb.*, i, 1911–12.

to O'Higgins, the government wanted 'to restore conditions which will enable commercial enterprise to have free play'. Cosgrave's government satisfied itself with repeated predictions of a rapid revival of business activity once the civil war was ended; in this it was mistaken.[24]

Another Labour proposal was the establishment of a national housing authority, both to provide work for the unemployed and to begin an assault on the mounting housing problem. The proposed authority would draw up a housing programme, standardize housing materials and purchase materials in quantity; the programme would be financed by the issuing of premium bonds. The government rejected the plan, and the housing problem was left in the hands of the largely inactive local authorities.

In the area of education, Labour was fortunate in having T. J. O'Connell of the Irish National Teachers Organization as its spokesman. O'Connell constantly reminded the government that it had not introduced its promised educational reform bill, and, although the Dail had passed a resolution in November 1922 in favour of a compulsory school attendance act, the government had not sponsored legislation to enforce attendance; it was not until 1927 that such a law was passed. While President Cosgrave held that elementary education was costing too much, the government did not move to reduce elementary teachers' salaries at this time. But neither did it propose to do anything to substantially alter the 'wretched status and wretched pay' of the secondary teachers. The minister for education, the well-meaning but inattentive Professor Eoin MacNeill, said that the cost of the civil war, 'when the country was losing £1 million per week', prevented the government from making the improvements in the educational system it undoubtedly would have made.

The government's reliance on indirect taxation quickly became a point of issue with the Labour Party. Johnson pointed out that one-seventh of the Free State's revenue came from taxes on tea and sugar, compared to one-twentieth in Britain. This resulted, he said, in an unfair burden being placed on the aged and the unemployed and urged that the system be replaced by the graduated income tax. The government replied that the income tax (then at a higher rate than in Britain, due to a British reduction) could not be further increased without 'dampening' business.

Labour had two proposals for providing money for socio-economic needs: to withhold for a time the £1 million superannuation payment due to former British officials in the Free State, and to place tariffs on imports. The government rejected the first proposal on the basis that the payment was required by the treaty. To the second suggestion it claimed that duties could not be immediately placed on imports because it was 'not possible to estimate damage to business . . . [and] employment'. The government had put tariffs on a few unimportant products for the purpose of establishing a bargaining position for trade

24 Ibid., 1861, 1873–74, 1881; ii, 172.

negotiations with the British government. The question of protection versus free trade was given over to a special commission.

To Johnson, the government's entire economic policy put the Free State in the position 'that for the present we are an extension of the British Government as far as revenue is concerned, and we will carry on the good work that the British Government placed in our hands.'

Several of the government's legislative proposals won Labour's support. Labour voted for the government's bill to continue rent control. The party also supported the Electoral Reform Bill, but it opposed the provision that deprived policemen of the right to vote and granted businessmen their choice of voting either from their residences or from their business addresses (the government was concerned that businessmen would not be adequately represented). Labour favoured those provisions of the Local Government Act which abolished the work houses and poor law unions, replacing them with county homes for the aged, but it sought in vain to extend the responsibilities of the local authorities to include the prevention of destitution through programmes of public health, family allowances and public works. In general, Labour backed the Land Act, which established a land commission with power to purchase and redistribute farming land, but the party came out against the provision granting landlords twelve percent more than the price paid by the new owners of the land. In the discussion of this bill, Labour voted for several amendments put forward by the Farmers Party. The minister for agriculture, Patrick Hogan, saw this as the beginning of an 'unholy alliance', but the Farmers Party rarely reciprocated in support of Labour.[25]

As the first Dail with full legislative powers in an independent state moved towards dissolution, Johnson pointed to the major achievements of the assembly's year of work. For him, the Dail had 'at least, contributed something to the building up of the idea of Parliamentary institutions'.[26] As the main opposition, the Labour Party shared in this achievement. As its leader, Johnson had done much to elevate the proceedings of the Dail. He had conducted himself in a reasonable and dignified manner, stressing issues and policies rather than personalities and partisanship. His party had devoted great attention to legislation of all kinds, although, recognizing that the government possessed the confidence of a large majority in the Dail, it did not present any bills of its own. As a small band, now shrunk to fourteen and with little support from the other non-government deputies, the Labour Party was in no position to bring about the defeat of any government pro-

25 The Farmers Party opposed Labour amendments to the Land Act as well as amendments to other legislation. *Dail Eireann deb.*, iv, 24–25, 40, 264, 278–79, 1114, 1975–76. For Dail debates on various social and economic legislation, see as follows: housing—ibid., iii, 2362; education—ibid., 1174, 1180, 1192, 1351, 1364, 1366, 1373; taxation—ibid., 327, 331, 334, 386–87; trade and tariffs—ibid., 90, 318–19, 386–87, 1204–05; rent control, electoral reform and local government—ibid., i, 2073–85; ii, 946, 1423, 1951–52; iii, 1535.

26 *Dail Eireann deb.*, iv, 2003.

posals. But it continuously held all of these up to searching examination. Occasionally it succeeded in inserting a helpful amendment or two in some bills.[27] The party played a major role in establishing the rules and procedures of the Dail; it helped to draw up the standing orders for that body. More importantly, it demanded that the Dail be given complete information concerning the government's policies and activities, and insisted that the Dail be allowed adequate time to consider legislation. Finally, the party urged the Dail to retain the power of ultimate responsibility in the state, rather than to grant this power to the government or to the army.

Labour had looked forward to the third Dail for providing a platform for its programme and ideas; it had succeeded in drawing a degree of attention to these. During the one-year term of this Dail, the party established a line of policy it was to follow for the next decade. Firstly, and most importantly, it called attention to the serious social and economic problems of the country, and advocated government action to meet these problems. It was critical of the Cosgrave government's reliance on the revival of private enterprise to alleviate these problems. Secondly, Labour opposed the use of extreme governmental powers to force a peaceful political situation on the country. It sought means to bring about an amicable settlement of the issues behind the civil war, while at the same time it attempted to protect the civil liberties of the people. Although it was prepared to participate in the institutions created, in part, by the Anglo-Irish treaty, it held that the political institutions of the country could be changed if the people so desired.

Labour anticipated that its devoted effort and public position would be rewarded by the voters at the 1923 general election. But other issues were to arise that would largely negate the party's constructive opposition in the third Dail.

DISUNITY IN THE LABOUR MOVEMENT

Any unity the Labour Party and the labour movement in general had achieved prior to 1923 was shattered by the return of James Larkin and the power struggle in the Transport Union. The enmity created in the Labour ranks, like that created among Sinn Feiners over the treaty issue, was to last for decades. For a relatively small movement, as Labour was, the political effect was devastating.

The origin of the conflict was in the O'Brien-Daly split, which has been discussed earlier in these pages. With Larkin away in America, the labour movement in Dublin was divided between the Transport Union and the Dublin Workers Council on the one hand and the Daly-controlled Dublin Trades Council on the other. The Daly group had no official voice in the party-congress after 1921. Both groups claimed to uphold the mantle of the charismatic Larkin. When Big

27 For example, in the case of the 'Flogging Bill', reducing the number of lashes permitted for certain crimes; in the Debt Collection Act, raising the value of property left to debtors. *Dail Eireann deb.*, ii, 1923.

Jim was on trial in New York in 1920 for criminal sedition, the Transport Union stated its willingness to bear the costs; at the same time, the Dublin Trades Council rushed to establish the Larkin Defence Committee.[28]

The Daly group's opposition was not based on the Labour leadership's position in regard to the national struggle. Daly himself was not active in the national struggle and was *persona non grata* with the leaders of that movement because of his actions in the Irish Republican Brotherhood before the world war.[29] Nor was the Daly group critical of the new leadership's position on social and economic questions. The conflict grew out of a clash of personalities and a resulting struggle for power.

During his time in America, Larkin had been active in revolutionary socialist organizations and had been imprisoned from 1920 to 1923. Yet he never lost touch with developments within the labour movement at home. He attempted to 'prevent a cleavage between the two factions fighting for power' within the Transport Union, but his proposals were rejected by the new leadership (consisting of O'Brien, Foran, Farren, Kennedy, O'Shannon and others). During his exile, Larkin retained the title of general secretary of the union. Upon his return, he found the union greatly increased in size and the new leadership firmly in control. It is probable that the new leaders did not desire to oust Larkin from the union (not only had the union paid Larkin's legal expenses in America, but O'Brien had raised the subject of Larkin's qualification for public office in the Dail).[30] What was apparent, however, was that the Labour leaders wanted to limit Larkin's power in the Transport Union. Shortly before Larkin's return, O'Brien warned the union's organizers of Larkin's irresponsibility with money, and new rules were hastily drawn up to limit the power of the general secretary.[31]

Even before his arrival in Ireland, Larkin had the grievances of the Daly group poured into his ears: a delegation from the Trades Council was alone in greeting him in Southampton. But his first activity was to urge the republicans to end any form of armed struggle against the Free State. He noted, however, that some of the union officials were actively supporting the Free State authorities against the republicans; shortly the favour was to be returned.[32] After two

28 An excellent account of the Labour split is found in Emmet Larkin, *James Larkin, Irish Labour leader*, pp. 261–65. See also *Voice of Labour*, 31 May, 28 June, 2 and 23 August 1919; *Daly libel suit*, p. 13; I.L.P. and T.U.C., *1921 report*, pp. 21, 94, 129–30; *Watchword of Labour*, 31 July 1920.

29 *Daly libel suit*, pp. 18–19; proceedings of the National Arbitration Court, 1919, in O'Brien papers, N.L.I., MS 15657.

30 I.T.G.W.U., *The attempt to smash the Irish Transport and General Workers Union*, pp. 135–37; *Dail Eireann deb.*, i, 2096.

31 Interview with Peadar O'Donnell, 21 November 1964 (O'Donnell was an organizer for the union). See also I.T.G.W.U., *Attempt to smash the I.T.G.W.U.*, p. 102.

32 Interview with James Larkin, Jr., 3 February 1966. Roderick Connolly's communist

months of uneasy relations, Larkin launched an onslaught against the executive, directing his attack primarily at personalities, rather than the O'Brien group's ideology or policy. In the ensuing struggle, the O'Brien forces employed their strong legal position to retain control, and Larkin soon set up a rival union, the Workers Union of Ireland.[33]

The split within the country's largest union was bound to effect the political side of the movement, especially as the industrial and political wings were combined in one organization. The party-congress had as one of its responsibilities the resolution of intra-union disputes, but Larkin's impetuous actions precluded assistance from this body. He unsuccessfully appealed to the courts to prevent the Transport Union from paying delegate expenses. With this tactic foiled, a group of Larkin supporters attempted to prevent the delegates from entering the Dublin Mansion House, the site of the conference. When the union dispute was raised from the floor, O'Brien declared that Larkin's actions in seizing control of the union head office made impossible any attempt by the party-congress to bring about a settlement. Larkin's cause received little support at the conference; he was defeated for the chairmanship by the executive's nominee by a vote of 27 to 147.[34] These events proved to be nothing more than episodes in a continuing conflict.

Because the two wings were united in one organization, and because the Transport Union leaders were also leaders in the party-congress, it was inevitable that Larkin would turn his fire on the Labour Party. He centred his attack on Tom Johnson. Johnson, however, stood by O'Brien, as did most other prominent Labour figures. Indeed, Larkin's general onslaught drove men such as Thomas Foran and Thomas MacPartlin into the O'Brien camp. With the exception of Daly, none of them supported Larkin's position.[35]

Larkin had little backing outside Dublin, but in the capital, where the Labour Party was hoping to make gains in the pending election, he mustered a considerable following. The struggle within the Transport Union could only raise questions about the stability and responsibility of the Labour Party. The 23 June issue of the *Voice of Labour* reported, 'The Farmers, the Cumann na nGaedheal, the Republicans are all chuckling at the "Champ" who has queered Labour's pitch in politics.' Labour suffered under other disadvantages. In response to an employers' announcement that wages would be reduced by two shillings a day, the dockers of Dublin, led by Larkin, went on strike in July. The strike soon spread to Cork, and by election day thousands

---

faction also urged Larkin to take action against the moderate leadership of the Transport Union. Interview with Connolly, 1 October 1964. For Trades Council greeting, see its minutes of 5 May 1922.

33 Larkin, *James Larkin*, pp. 267–74, 281–83.

34 *Voice of Labour*, 4, 11 August 1923; *Irish Times, Irish Independent*, 7 August 1923; *Irish Telegraph*, 8 August 1923; I.T.G.W.U., *Attempt to smash the I.T.G.W.U.*, p. 108.

35 Copy of letter from MacPartlin to O'Brien. O'Brien papers, N.L.I., MS 13961(1).

of dockers and other transport workers were idle. Further, a violent farmer—farm labourer conflict (which was to end in defeat for the labourers) raged in County Waterford during the summer months. It was in these unfortunate circumstances that the Labour Party contested the 1923 election.

THE 1923 ELECTION

The Labour Party entered the 1923 parliamentary election confident that it would increase its representation. Party members believed that Labour's constructive role in the Dail and its opposition to repressive legislation would be rewarded by the voters. The *Voice of Labour* (25 August 1923), even after the Larkin split, asserted, 'It is certain that the Labour Party in the new Dail will be considerably stronger.' Other newspapers also predicted Labour advances.[36] Because of the increase in the number of Dail seats from 128 to 153, Labour would have to secure 20 seats merely to retain its existing proportion in the house. Although the party's performance in the third Dail was praised by some of the national press, most of the readers of these papers were not inclined to vote Labour, and working-class voters would not be impressed by praise from these sources.

Labour nominated forty-one candidates. The government party, which adopted the name of Griffith's original party, Cumann na nGaedheal, nominated 109. The republicans, still calling themselves Sinn Fein, put forward eighty-five; the Farmers Party nominated sixty-four, and there were seventy-five independent candidates. Labour contested twenty-six of the thirty constituencies. Local Labour Parties had been formed in Dublin and Cork in the spring of 1923, but the political organization remained inadequate, forcing the party to rely once again on the unions and the trade councils for its campaign workers, organization and money. The party published a series of well-written campaign pamphlets: *How to get houses, The betrayal of the unemployed, If you want your child to get a fair start in life* and *How to reduce the cost of living*. As in 1922, the nominees were drawn exclusively from the trade unions, and the Transport Union, as before, sponsored the largest number of candidates. Other nominees were members of unions of printers, shop assistants and clerks, bakers, railway clerks, building trades workers and teachers.

Independently from the Labour Party, the Dublin Trades Council, with Larkin's support, nominated four candidates—including P. T. Daly—for the Dublin constituencies. Larkin himself did not stand, probably because he was disqualified from sitting in the Dail, having earlier been declared a bankrupt. Outside of Dublin, Larkin endorsed a fifth candidate, J. Gleeson, for County Tipperary.

36 A commentator in the *Irish Telegraph* (10 August 1923) estimated that Labour would win thirty-five seats; the pro-treatyites, fifty; the farmers, thirty-five; the republicans, twenty-three, and the independents, ten. *Irish Independent*, 10 August 1923. The Irish correspondent of the *Manchester Guardian*, 20 August 1923, saw Labour doubling its representation.

Through the pages of the revived *Irish Worker* Larkin conducted an abusive campaign against the Labour Party. In the 16 June issue he modestly wrote:

> We had the honour of initiating the Irish Labour movement. We returned to find a Labour Party lost to all sense of dignity, manipulated by ambitious self-seekers . . . a feeble imitation of the English Labour Party.

Larkin did not restrict his fight to the newspapers. O'Brien denounced a 'lying' handbill distributed by the Larkin forces in his constituency, South Dublin. A band for an O'Brien parade was prevented from leaving Liberty Hall by a hostile crowd and a meeting of the Labour candidates in North Dublin was broken up by the Larkinites. Larkin followed party leader Johnson from meeting to meeting in County Dublin.

There were reports of voting agreements between local Labour groups and republicans. The *Irish Times* said a 'tacit agreement' had been reached in Waterford in which some Labour supporters agreed to cast their third preference votes for the republican candidate. The *Freeman's Journal* reported 'several instances' of inter-changing preferences between republican and Labour voters. In Dublin Sinn Fein sent out sample ballots marked with lower preferences for the Labour candidates.[37] However, no national agreement was made between Labour and Sinn Fein to exchange lower preference votes; agreements at the local level were few and generally ineffective.

For its part, Cumann na nGaedheal came to an arrangement with the business candidates of the 'Progressive Association' in Cork city. For a district with five seats, Cumann na nGaedheal nominated only one candidate, while the business group put forward three; there also was one independent business candidate. In North Cork, where there was three seats, the sole Cumann na nGaedheal candidate also stood as a 'Commercial' candidate. The government party did little to oppose the business candidates in County Dublin, although there apparently was no formal arrangement between the two groups. The agreements made by Cosgrave's party show that it was seeking to broaden its base by building alliances with conservative elements in the country. Cosgrave also sought support from quasi-labour candidates where possible. He spoke from the same platform as Sean Lyons, T.D., independent labour candidate in Westmeath-Longford. Lyons had been refused a Labour Party nomination because of his lack of party loyalty in the Dail. Cosgrave also successfully appealed to Joseph McGrath, minister for industry and commerce, to stand again for the Dail. Having been accountant for the Transport Union for several years, McGrath had many friends in the labour movement and was considered to be friendly to the Labour Party.[38]

37 *Irish Times*, 10 August 1923; see also 31 August. *Freeman's Journal*, 30 August 1923.

38 *Irish Times*, 31 July, 25 August 1923; *Freeman's Journal*, 3 September 1923; *Cork Examiner*, 22 August 1923; *Irish Independent*, 10 August 1923.

Election Issues

The Labour Party campaigned on the need for productive work for the unemployed and criticized the government's lack of action in the fields of education, housing, health and tax reform. On political issues, the party called for abolition of the oath of allegiance, release of the political prisoners and the end to executions and military courts. Apparently in an effort to blunt republican criticism, Johnson declared that he would vote for the immediate establishment of a republic if his vote would decide the issue. At the same time, he attacked the parliamentary abstention of the republicans.

The republicans presented a programme to tackle the unemployment problem by means of public works projects and protection for home industry, but there was an unconvincing vagueness to many of their proposals. For example, the programme stated that a republican government 'will administer the public services for the nation and in this work will see that no man or woman is unjustly treated.'[39] A major drawback to the republican appeal, however, was the Sinn Fein policy of abstention from the Dail.

The Cumann na nGaedheal election appeal had two themes. On the one hand, it pointed with pride to the achievements of the government in the past year, and stressed the need for its continuation; on the other, it warned the electorate of the dire consequences of voting for the republicans. Its manifesto declared that anarchy and revolution could only be avoided by voting Cumann na nGaedheal. Even the Labour Party presented a threat because it could not secure a majority in the Dail, and it might upset the present stable government. Cumann na nGaedheal attempted to overlook the existence of substantial unemployment, concentrating instead on the need for strong government, capable of dealing firmly with Britain. Neither the Farmers Party nor the independent candidates presented coherent election programmes, but candidates from both groups supported the Free State constitution.

Two events brought to a conclusion the unexpectedly peaceful campaign. On 11 August 1923 Cardinal Logue issued a statement which supported the Cosgrave government and warned of the danger of voting for independent candidates. Although the Labour Party was not mentioned, the cardinal's statement probably cost Labour some votes. Four days later de Valera emerged from hiding and was arrested while addressing a meeting at Ennis, County Clare. His supporters immediately called upon the Labour and Farmer parties to withdraw from the election as a protest.[40] The Labour Party ignored the appeal.

39 *Manchester Guardian,* 25 August 1923; Donal O'Sullivan, *The Irish Free State and its senate,* p. 131.

40 This political stratagem had been used in two of the last three general elections. In 1921 it was unnecessary as only Sinn Fein contested the election.

Election Results

Labour received a serious set-back in the 1923 election, returning only fourteen deputies as compared to seventeen the year before. More significantly, it lost all its seats in the cities; the parliamentary party would now consist of members from predominantly rural district only. In returning sixty-three members, the government party did not achieve its expected overall majority. The republicans demonstrated considerable political strength in electing forty-four deputies under difficult circumstances. The Farmers Party won fifteen seats, and there were sixteen independents returned.[41]

In Dublin the opposing forces in the Larkin split fought themselves to a standstill—neither side elected any candidates. In South Dublin O'Brien received only 933 votes (thereafter he abandoned the Dublin political field to stand in County Tipperary). In North Dublin the Labour Party candidate, E. O'Carroll, got 900 fewer votes than P. T. Daly's total of 2,100 votes. Indeed, in the Dublin area where there were twenty-one seats, Labour elected only Thomas Johnson, who held his seat in County Dublin with some difficulty. The situation in other urban areas was equally as bad. Cathal O'Shannon, who had led the poll in County Louth the year before, found himself in the opposite position in this election. The three Labour candidates in Cork city failed to receive enough votes to elect one candidate: they polled a total of 5,300 votes, and the quota for the election of one candidate was 7,000. The apathetic attitude of the Cork workers towards the election and the Labour Party is evidenced by the fact that 10,000 workers were on strike in the city at this time. On the other hand, two prominent employers, nominees of the Progressive Association, were elected. The leader of the Farmers Party, Denis Gorey, later declared:

> The strike in Cork was a live question at the recent election. There were more people on strike in Cork than would have returned two deputies. . . . There were sufficient men idle about the docks in Dublin to elect three or four deputies, if you take into account the votes of their families.[42]

The *Voice of Labour* (8 September 1823) attributed the Labour debacle in the cities principally to the efforts of the Larkin forces: 'The . . . reverses . . . , particularly in Dublin, were not unexpected. Lying tongues, insidious propaganda, baseless innuendo, assisted by downright ruffianism, made success impossible.'

George Russell's *Irish Statesman* (15 September 1923) believed that disunity in the labour ranks was only one factor in the reversal throughout the country:

41 Total first preference votes were: Cumann na nGaedheal—406,000 (38.6%); Sinn Fein—284,000 (27%); Labour—119,000 (11.4%); Farmers Party—135,000 (12.9%); independent Labour—12,000 (1%); Larkin nominees—4,500 (0.4%); I.L.P. and T.U.C., *1924 report*, pp. 88–89; *Voice of Labour*, 8 September 1923; *Irish Times*, 1 September 1923.

42 *Dail Eireann deb.*, v, 125.

> Labour went down also because of its failure to square its nominal policy with actual facts. The strong card of the dissidents is that they hold by the rigid Marxite doctrine of class war. The official heads realize that the special conditions of Ireland make the application of undiluted Marxism impossible, but while they have no hesitation in varying it in practice, in theory they still cling to the empty formula, thus laying themselves open to the shrewd thrusts from the neck or nothing devotees.

In its edition of 1 September, the *Manchester Guardian,* which devoted considerable attention to the election, identified two main causes for Labour's set-back: 'a diffused crossness aroused among Irishmen and Irishwomen by the vexations of recent strikes' and the domination of nationalism on the Irish electorate. The *Voice of Labour* agreed that the election had shown the predominance of political issues over socio-economic questions.

The most important factor in the 'green election' of 1923 was the civil war, which had ended only four months before. Most voters cast their ballots for the side they had favoured in that conflict. The election marked the first political encounter of the two sides since the conclusion of the conflict. Related to this, according to T. J. O'Connell, was the possibility that many voters who had supported Labour as the party of peace in 1922, now supported the government party as the upholder of peace and stability.[43]

The Labour Party's role as a serious and constructive opposition in the Dail was of little import to working-class voters whose lives it did not directly effect. The workers and the general public were apathetic about the election; only sixty percent of the voters went to the polls. Undoubtedly a smaller percentage of workers voted than did the general public.

Not only did the Larkin split cost the party thousands of votes in Dublin, but this bitter and sensational struggle, along with the resulting strikes, surely cost Labour many thousands of votes outside the capital as well. The disunity of the labour movement must have shaken the confidence of many; the minor reputation for restraint and level-headness that Labour had built over a year was destroyed in a few weeks of dissension and controversy.

A final but not unimportant factor in the failure of the party in this election was that Labour had little money to spend on the campaign, while, based on the amount of newspaper space purchased, its principal opponents had a great deal. A £20,000 campaign contribution to Sinn Fein from supporting Irish organizations in America was partly responsible for the surprisingly good showing the republicans made in this election.[44] Throughout the 1920s, parties led by de Valera—

43 Interview with T. J. O'Connell.

44 Peter Pyne, 'The third Sinn Fein: 1923–1926', *Economic and Social Review,* I, no. 1 (Oct. 1969), p. 33; see also pp. 39, 41.

first Sinn Fein and then Fianna Fail—were dependent on funds from the United States, while the pro-treaty party received ample financial backing from well-to-do supporters in business and the professions. The financial poverty of Labour compared to its chief rivals continued to be an important element in succeeding elections.

As a result of the 1923 election the Labour Party's position in the Dail was made more difficult. In the new Dail it could no longer give the appearance of a growing political force, as a party capable of forming a government in the near future. But because the Farmers Party, which held one more seat than Labour, was not fundamentally opposed to the Cosgrave government, and the anti-treatyites continued to abstain, Labour was forced to continue as the principal opposition in the Dail.

8

The Labour Party and the Fourth Dail, 1923–27

A situation injurious to the proper working of parliamentary democracy existed during the four-year period of the fourth Dail. The government party had been returned with a few additional seats, but without a total majority. Its position in the Dail, however, was made inviolable by the continued abstention of the anti-treaty deputies. The overall strength of the non-government parties in the Dail had been reduced, and this, combined with abstention, afforded the government an artificial but overwhelming majority.

The Labour Party returned to the Dail in chastened spirits. It could not claim to have secured public approval of its role as the principal constitutional opposition, nor could it give the appearance that it was likely to develop into the real opposition to the Cosgrave government. In a curious statement at the opening of the new Dail, Thomas Johnson implied that his party would not continue as the main parliamentary opposition, that it would restrict itself solely to socio-economic questions:

> It has been intimated fairly and clearly by the electorate that they do not desire we of the Labour Party should take the responsibility of criticizing Government action. Questions of this kind have . . . been relegated rather to the Deputies of the Government Party and to the Deputies of what is known as the Republican Party.[1]

Kevin O'Higgins later paraphrased Johnson's statement:

> Very good. You have brought it on yourselves. I interpret these results as an instruction to me and to my party to refrain from commenting, from criticizing on the broad matters of policy, to confine myself strictly to what might be regarded as industrial matters, strictly labour matters.[2]

Had the Labour Party restricted itself to social and economic matters, an almost impossible situation would have been created for both the party and the Dail. The party would have exposed itself to the criticism that it was simply a special interest group, a delegation from the trade unions. The Dail, without an active opposition, would have been reduced practically to a one-party assembly. No other group in the Dail could have formed a meaningful opposition. The Farmers Party, a loosely bound group with little party discipline, was basically in agreement with the economic and political policies of the government. The independent deputies, by their very nature, could not form a real opposition, and in fact most of them supported the government.

1 *Dail Eireann deb.*, v, 35–36.

2 Ibid., vii, 2431.

Johnson later denied stating that the Labour Party would discontinue to be the main parliamentary opposition. In fact, during the ensuing four years, the party vigorously upheld this responsibility thrust on it. Being the official opposition from 1922 to 1927 was both an opportunity and a handicap to the party. On the one hand its speeches and policy positions received considerable attention in the newspapers, and its leadership became known to the public. On the other hand, the Labour membership was too small to be really effective as an opposition group, although on economic and social questions it was the only party in Irish politics fundamentally opposed to the policy of the government.

Thomas Johnson remained the undisputed leader of the party until he was defeated for the Dail in the September 1927 election. His leadership was characterized by carefully argued speeches on every major question before the Dail; he did not miss a single division until the spring of 1927. According to the *Irish Statesman*, the Labour Party's 'general weakness in personnel is camouflaged by the real ability of its leader'. But it also said of Johnson:

> He is not content to do one man's work but insists upon tackling tasks that would be more than enough for half a dozen ordinary members. . . . He ought to remember that a general who is always in the firing line rarely sees the battle as a whole. There is no necessity why he should speak, as is now his custom, on practically every issue raised in debate, whether great or small. . . . It is not in Mr. Johnson's nature to spare himself.[3]

Johnson did much of the speaking for the Labour Party, but the other members were not dissatisfied with this arrangement.[4] In the spring of 1927, overworked and near to breakdown, Johnson rested from his legislative responsibilities for two weeks.

For the fourth Dail T. J. O'Connell replaced O'Shannon, who was defeated in the 1923 election, as deputy party leader. Daniel Morrissey and Thomas Nagle replaced William O'Brien, also defeated, and O'Connell as whips. Party discipline remained very good; rarely did a Labour deputy vote against the party's position, and only one member resigned from the party.[5] 'The Labour Party is a splendidly united Party', the minister for agriculture, Patrick Hogan, observed at this time, 'They keep their differences well within themselves and they are very well regimented'.[6] The party probably had the best attendance

3 *Irish Statesman,* 5, 19 March 1927.

4 Interview with T. J. O'Connell, 4 November 1965.

5 Richard Corish very occasionally did not vote with the party. J. Butler resigned from the party early in 1927 for unstated reasons. I.L.P. and T.U.C., *1927 report,* p. 12.

6 *Dail Eireann deb.,* xvii, 263. Warner Moss, *Political parties in the Irish Free State,* p. 73, says that Johnson's all-embracing leadership 'was not welcome by all parts of the Labour movement or by all the deputies'. But for evidence Moss cites only a minor matter raised by Deputy William Davin in 1925—his call for an inquiry into the relationship between the party-congress executive and the Dail party. I.L.P. and T.U.C., *1926 report,* p. 89.

record of any group in the Dail. Both the contemporary and later statements of his party colleagues agree to Johnson's dedication and resourcefulness as spokesman and leader. It is very probable, however, that his willingness to assume every task had the effect of preventing the development of initiative among both the other members of the Dail party and the Labour executive.

The fourth Dail can be termed the first 'normal' Dail; the third Dail, of 1922–23, sat during a period of transition and civil war. Generally speaking, the government had made no new departures but had carried forward existing legislation. In the fourth Dail, however, the government began to abandon the status quo. With a mass of legislation to be considered, Labour proposed, without success, the establishment of a committee system to conduct this business efficiently.

The parliamentary Labour Party took the position that the Cosgrave government pursued generally regressive social and economic policies. Labour also charged the government with failure to secure maximum constitutional benefits from the provisions of the Anglo-Irish treaty. The party produced four legislative proposals—a transportation and communications bill, the first non-government bill presented, an education bill and proposals for agriculture and fisheries. As in the previous Dail, Labour's opposition to the government, as well as the party's proposals, received little support from the other non-government groups.

SOCIAL AND ECONOMIC POLICY AND LEGISLATION

The socio-economic policy of the Cosgrave government following the 1923 election could be described as one of general retrenchment and deflation. The government argued that wages and profits should be reduced to correspond with what it claimed was a lowered cost of living. As its first measure it reduced old age and blind persons' pensions and teachers' salaries. Then it cut the wages of government employees and stopped the payment of unemployment money not covered by insurance; to meet the continuing unemployment situation it began a small-scale public works programme. It did little to meet the housing and educational needs of the country.

The government claimed that reduction in government expenditure was necessary because current expenditure exceeded tax receipts. But, as Nicholas Mansergh notes, the revenue of the government not only met the normal expenses but also met part of the extraordinary expenditure caused by the civil war and treaty obligations.[7] Fearful of the possibilities of rampant inflation such as was affecting some European nations, the government opposed large-scale borrowing. The Free State adhered to the generally accepted economic doctrines of the pre-Keynesian period.

The government gradually developed a selective tariff policy. Its tax policy involved the reduction of taxes, starting with the income

7 *The Irish Free State: its government and politics*, p. 256.

tax and then progressing to the indirect taxes if possible. The only major development schemes put forward by the government were the Shannon electrification project and the sugar beet scheme. These, however, represented a major departure from the Cosgrave government's position that the state had no business directing or controlling industries.

At the beginning of the new Dail, Johnson warned the government that social and economic problems would

> prevent the re-establishment of peace and stability of the State unless they are dealt with on lines very different from those hinted at and suggested by the government. The mind of the government is running in the direction of allowing the development of economic affairs to follow the beaten path and to trust to the ordinary operations of commerce and exchange to bring about prosperity in this country.

He advised against relying on the British export market and the British example of wage-cutting as the road to prosperity, urging rather that existing wages be maintained and that the economic system be adjusted 'to ensure those wages will be spent in the purchase of Irish goods'.[8]

The Labour Party alone opposed the reductions in pensions and teachers' salaries imposed in 1923. It rejected the government's contention that the civil war made these reductions necessary; according to Labour, the money for these important items was part of the recurrent expenditure and was not part of the extraordinary expenses caused by the civil war. Labour spokesmen scornfully recalled that Cosgrave had told the last Dail, 'It is not intended by the Dail to make any alteration' in old age pensions, and the government party's electoral programme supported 'adequate remuneration' for teachers without mentioning salary reductions. If the government's electoral programme was to be put into effect, argued Johnson, there could be no real reduction in government spending. The Labour Party warned that the pension reductions might injure the cause of national unity. (As a result of Westminster legislation, pensions were then the same in both parts of Ireland. The gap in social services between the twenty-six counties and the six counties was originally created, not by any advances in British or Northern Ireland legislation, but by the reductions undertaken by the Free State in 1923.) The government promised to restore pensions to their former levels when the financial condition improved and before it reduced income taxes. But twice, in 1925 and 1927, it lowered income taxes without restoring any part of the pension reductions. It was not until 1928 that pensions were restored to near their 1923 levels.[9]

8 *Dail Eireann deb.*, v, 36–38.

9 Statements on the issues of pensions and teachers' salaries can be found in ibid., i, 2127; iii, 111; v, 769, 772, 774; vi, 276, 809, 1319–20; xi, 25–31; xv, 173–74; xvi, 1455; xviii, 1242. See also Desmond Farley, *Social insurance and social assistance in Ireland*, p. 20.

At the beginning of the fourth Dail the government, believing that wages, profits and prices should be reduced, established a committee to investigate profiteering. But since the business community generally refused to co-operate, the committee accomplished little. The government did have some success in reducing wages. Acting as arbitrator, Cosgrave recommended a one shilling per day reduction for Dublin dockers. The Labour Party in opposition cited the wage rates in legislation dealing with local government, relief work and road work, as well as the wages paid on the Shannon electrification scheme. But Vice-President O'Higgins claimed, 'It is not the duty and it is not the practice of governments to create wage rates.' Johnson charged that the government had only one wage policy, the objective of which 'is to get down wages at any cost, and with any argument, and for any purpose'.[10]

The major wage dispute between the government and the Labour Party arose from the wages paid on the Shannon electrification scheme. Labour had supported this scheme, as well as the other major development project of the government—the sugar beet scheme. However, when the contractor on the Shannon project set the wages for labourers at thirty-two shillings per week, the party and the trade unions protested that this was less than a decent living wage and a violation of the 'fair wages' clause for government contracts to which the government had agreed in 1923. The government maintained that it had no responsibility for setting wages; a living wage was a case of supply and demand. And by comparing the job of a Shannon worker to that of an agricultural labourer in the surrounding counties, the government denied violating the fair wages clause.

Johnson was prepared to define a 'decent' standard of living in terms of Pope Leo XIII's 'frugal comfort'. The Labour Party argued that a Shannon labourer's job was not similar to that of an agricultural worker, but more comparable with that of a navvy who received a much higher wage. Labour declared it would urge the workers to impede the scheme until decent wages were established. The trade unions, led by the Transport Union, joined the party in opposition. O'Higgins denounced the Labour stand as part of a pro-British plot to sabotage the scheme and 'ruin the good name of the Free State'. There is no evidence that this was the case, but the I.R.A., taking advantage of an opportunity to strike a blow at the Free Staters, supported the unions in their opposition.[11]

The boycott of the scheme, sustained from November 1925 to January 1926, was unsuccessful. The government refused to intervene on the question of wages; unemployed men poured in, and the unions

10 *Dail Eireann deb.*, v, 4, 108, 223; xiii, 38–39, 63, 72–73.

11 For Labour's initial praise of the scheme, see Johnson's statement in *Dail Eireann deb.*, xi, 2215, and *Voice of Labour*, 2 October 1926. Further statements and discussions on the wage disputes are in I.T.G.W.U., *1923 report*, p. 13; *1926 report*, pp. 5–7; *Dail Eireann deb.*, xiii, 39–70; *Voice of Labour*, 10 October 1925; *Irish Times*, 1 December 1925; I.L.P. and T.U.C., *1926 report*, pp. 13, 18; T. P. Coogan, *Ireland since the rising*, p. 55.

had little success in organizing the workers on the scheme. In 1927 the Transport Union declared:

> Wages and conditions on this great undertaking still remain the blackest feature in the recent industrial history of this country and this reproach is not likely to be removed until Labour has become much stronger, both in the political and industrial fields.[12]

The third Dail had passed a resolution recommending the arrangement of a general conference of employers and labour. Differences as to the objectives to be discussed prevented the conference from materializing, although the project continued to be debated by business leaders and the Labour Party for the next four years. President Cosgrave declined to act as the agent in bringing the two sides together because he did not believe it was the function of the state to intervene in capital-labour relations. Johnson agreed to participate in such a conference without preconditions. He believed, however, that an effective solution would only be found in a national economic council. He suggested that the following principles might be supported by such a council: first, that no strikes or lock-outs take place without notification of the other party and that all disputes be presented to a conciliation board; second, that both sides agree to strive for greater productivity; third, that there be no reduction in wages, but that wages be increased as production increases.[13]

As the Irish economy was generally depressed in the 1920s, unemployment remained a serious problem. In 1923–24 the Cosgrave government repeatedly predicted an imminent general revival of the economy. The government attempted to meet the unemployment problem by the extension of uncovenanted unemployment payments and a programme of public works.[14] In December 1924, however, the minister for industry and commerce announced that uncovenanted payments would cease. Patrick McGilligan declared that the government had no responsibility to provide work: 'There are certain limited funds at our disposal. People may have to die in this country and may have to die through starvation.'[15] This statement provided the opponents of Cumann na nGaedheal with ammunition for years to come.

The Labour Party had often protested that the government had not taken adequate measures to meet the unemployment problem and that

12 I.T.G.W.U., *1926 report*, pp. 5–7; *Voice of Labour*, 24 July 1926. See also edition of 31 October 1925.

13 *Dail Eireann deb.*, xiv, 1387; xiii, 2144; *Dublin Evening Mail*, 18 December 1925; *Irish Times*, 15 March 1926.

14 Uncovenanted unemployment payments were monies given to workers who had exhausted their rights, through contributions, to such payments. *Dail Eireann deb.*, v, 109; vii, 2216, 2221; ix, 501–503.

15 Ibid., xii, 1770; ix, 562.

it had suppressed the unemployment figures.[16] Johnson saw the government as the agent of society responsible for social welfare, with a duty to uphold 'when private industry fails to feed, clothe and house the citizens of a country'. He said his party was 'hungering for an opportunity to go out and preach the gospel of reconstruction and national development', but this could not be done if the workers had no prospects of steady employment. Johnson warned that the government's lack of action on the unemployment problem and the cutting off of uncovenanted compensation would force the unemployed 'into aggressive industrial and social activities'; the jobless would 'lose faith in parliamentary institutions' and resort to violence. One Labour deputy accredited Johnson with keeping the jobless from violent action in the past. Cosgrave termed Johnson's denunciation of the government's policy 'a condemnation such as . . . I have not listened to in this House before'. When the government ended the payments, Labour threatened to obstruct the proceedings of the Dail. Johnson resigned his party leadership for a time and contemplated withdrawing from the Dail to lead an 'aroused labour movement'.[17]

In June 1926 the minister for industry and commerce promised that if measures taken by the government did not reduce unemployment, the uncovenanted benefit would be restored. In the autumn of that year the Labour Party demanded the fulfillment of the pledge, contending that unemployment had risen. McGilligan, brushing aside the party's unemployment figures as 'exaggerated', declared that if the uncovenanted benefit were restored, both the employers and employed workers would protest that the unemployment fund would not be solvent for the next generation.[18]

The Labour Party did not concentrate all its energy on the problem of unemployment. In its transportation and communications bill of 1923, it proposed the nationalization of Irish railways and the co-ordination of all transportation services. Although the government congratulated Labour for its 'remarkable contribution to constructive legislation,' it preferred to keep the railways in private hands, forcing consolidation of the lines through a system of subsidies. Johnson termed the subsidies 'a sop to make quite sure that private enterprise or rather private unenterprise is going to be paid well for its lack of enterprise.' The Labour Party further charged that the terms of compensation proposed by the government to workers who lost their positions in

16 After October 1924 the government declined to publish its unemployment figures, which only included workers in insured occupations, because it claimed that they were being 'misconstrued'. Ibid., ix. 549.

17 *Voice of Labour,* 11 July, 15 August 1925. The *Irish Independent* commented, 'If Mr. Johnson left the Dail he would be followed by the whole band of Labour representatives.' For the debate, see *Dail Eireann deb.,* xii, 1806, 1813, 1818, 1836.

18 Johnson quoted figures to prove that industrial disputes were not a major cause of unemployment, as charged by the government and many businessmen. In 1922, 31,780 workers were involved in strikes; in 1925 only 6,200 were so involved. *Dail Eireann deb.,* xvii, 185–90, 292. See also ibid., 237–39.

the consolidation 'invites workmen . . . to impede improvements in organization because the cost of these improvements is, in the first case, going to be borne by the workmen themselves'.[19]

According to the 1926 census, almost half the population was living in houses or apartments of three rooms or less. Labour was convinced that the problem could best be attacked through the organization of a national housing authority with powers to plan large-scale projects and purchase building materials in bulk. The government declined to commit itself to a 'big bold housing effort' and passed legislation which simply allowed the payment of subsidies to housing built by local authorities. On a related issue—rent control—the Labour Party, because of its weak parliamentary position, was forced in 1926 to compromise and support the government's bill gradually ending rent control. Labour also supported William Redmond's Town Tenant Bill, whose purpose was to provide fixity of tenure for urban rent-payers.[20]

It was the often-reiterated charge of the Labour Party that the Cosgrave government had done little for Irish education. The party pointed to the facts that the promised inclusive education bill had not been introduced, that almost nothing had been done to improve the poor conditions of many school buildings, that primary teachers' salaries had been reduced and the salaries and status of the secondary teachers showed little improvement. Although the Dail had passed a resolution in 1922 supporting the principle of compulsory school attendance, the government had not acted; it was estimated that about forty percent of the children attended school in an irregular and sporadic fashion. Labour criticism centred on Eoin MacNeill, the minister for education until 1925, who was frequently absent from the Dail while serving as a member of the Army Inquiry Committee and as the Free State representative on the Boundary Commission. The party charged MacNeill and his ministry with inactivity and lack of progress in educational reform and development. Some independent deputies joined the Labour Party in criticizing the government on educational matters. The Farmers Party, however, believed that education was costing the state too much money, and it generally opposed any compulsory school attendance legislation because it feared that the farmers would be deprived of child labour.[21]

As a result of a study by a committee of teachers and trade unionists, a Labour Party programme for education was produced in 1925. Its guiding principle was that no child should be prevented from taking advantage of education because of social standing or lack of money.

19 Ibid., v, 1098, 1454–1787, 1872–76, 1906; vi, 302, 3235–37; xv, 1467–69.

20 For housing, see ibid., vi, 1836–39, 1844, 1846, 1854; x, 1136–43, 1679. For rent control, ibid., vii, 1287, 1296; xv, 1421–42, 2384; xviii, 280, 289–90.

21 For attitudes toward education, see ibid., ii, 2244–45; iii, 1174, 1180, 1351, 1366, 1373; viii, 411–13, 428–29, 575; xii, 822–25; xiii, 199, 203–204, 244, 478–79, 490–97; xvi, 401.

The programme proposed raising the school leaving age from fourteen to sixteen, reducing the teacher-pupil ratios, consolidating small schools, modernizing teacher training, providing modern plumbing in schools and establishing a council on education. It particularly stressed the need for adult and technical education. Under this scheme the state would assume responsibility for books, transportation, meals and medical-dental treatment. Its overall effect would lessen clerical control over education. Although the programme was given a friendly reception by the government, it considered the plan beyond the means of the state at that time.[22]

In spite of MacNeill's absences, some progress was made by the ministry for education in the years 1922–27. The primary and secondary curricula were revised, new teacher training colleges established and secondary teachers given some pay increases, but the problem of tenure remained untouched. A school attendance act finally came into effect in 1927. The government claimed that the cost of the civil war and lack of money made further progress impossible. The Labour spokesman for education, T. J. O'Connell, estimated that ninety percent of the children did not go further than national school, that ten to fifteen percent never got any formal education and that only fifty-two to sixty percent attended school regularly. Johnson considered the government's education policy to be consistent with its overall socio-economic policy:

> There is little use educating the children of the poor if it is the business of the Ministry . . . to leave the children of the workingman . . . to be merely the recipient of the lowest possible standard of life that the competitive [system] will allow him to obtain.[23]

On taxes, Labour's policy called for the reduction of indirect taxes on food and other commodities before any reduction in income tax. The government, taking the opposite view, claimed that reducing income taxes would stimulate the economy; in the years 1922–27 the government cut this tax by forty percent. Some indirect taxes were also reduced, but the revenue from this source continued to grow as a percentage of government income.[24]

Until 1924 the party-congress took no position on the question of tariff protection for Irish industry. It had been argued in the labour movement that tariffs protected only the capitalist—and this at the expense of higher living costs for the worker—and that such protection

22 Ibid., xiii, 188; *Voice of Labour,* 8, 22, 29 August 1925.

23 *Dail Eireann deb.,* xiii, 306–307. See also ibid., iii, 1192, 1364; xiv, 914, 973, 526–27; xvi, 401. The percentage of the budget spent on education rose from 11.66% for 1923–24 to 14.66% for 1927–28. Mansergh, *Irish Free State,* p. 257. The 1926–27 budget provided £2 10s annually per school for maintenance.

24 Labour advocated the granting of income tax exemptions for educational expenses. *Dail Eireann deb.,* xi, 41. The government's income tax cuts reduced the rate from 5s per pound in 1922 (6d above the British rate) to 3s by 1927 (1s below the British rate). See also Mansergh, *Irish Free State,* p. 257.

would create a barrier between the Free State and the North. In 1924 a special party-congress meeting, by a narrow margin, gave approval to the imposition of tariffs providing that the benefits from protection were transmitted to the workers in the affected industries.[25] The *Irish Times* (17 March 1924) asked the party an obvious question: Why should a capitalist invest in the Free State if the benefits were to be given to the workers?

Although it had imposed no tariffs in 1922–23, the Cosgrave government in 1924 decided to impose tariffs on a few goods as an 'experiment'. The Labour Party, with some misgivings, voted with the government.

Both parties opposed the creation of a general tariff wall, but Labour particularly favoured a tariff on imported food. Johnson estimated that forty-five percent of all the goods imported were foodstuffs. A large home market for agricultural goods would be created if the wages of the many town dwellers were raised; thus the raising of the wages and living standards of the town workers would help to raise the incomes of Irish farmers. In 1927 the party proposed the establishment of an industrial development commission. This body would be empowered to employ various devices—tariffs, bounties, export bonuses and other means—in an effort to develop Irish industry.[26]

In early 1927, Labour produced its policies dealing with agriculture and fisheries. The agricultural programme advocated the division of large farms into small holdings, fixing of minimum farm prices and minimum wages for farm labourers, encouragement of tillage and the imposition of duties on imported foods. The Irish correspondent of the *Round Table* said of the programme: 'It is difficult to envisage such a revolutionary proposal commanding extensive support in a conservative country like Ireland. But it has certainly the merit of being definite, and should, no doubt be popular among the sons of small farmers and other landless men.'[27] The fisheries programme, published by the party-congress the same year, called for the organization of fishermen's co-operatives and state aid for the industry.

George Russell's *Irish Statesman* declared that the Labour Party was the only party, other than the government party, which had 'formulated its policies with any precision', but Labour was 'hampered by its theoretical adhesion to Marxian economics and to policies of nationalization which we fancy the leaders would admit are impractical and which would arouse against this party the whole agricultural interests in Ireland.'[28] Actually, while the party favoured govern-

25 I.L.P. and T.U.C., *1924 report,* pp. 12–18.

26 On matters of protection and Labour's proposals for industrial development, see *Dail Eireann deb.,* xii, 40–45; xi, 19–22, 108–205, 212–16; xv, 992; xix, 1462; I.L.P. and T.U.C., *1927 report,* p. 72.

27 *Round Table,* June 1926. See also M. P. Linehan, 'Labour and the Farmer', *Irishman,* 28 May 1927; *Irish Statesman,* 21 May 1927.

28 *Irish Statesman,* 5 March 1927. Johnson claimed that the party also drew inspiration from Lalor, Pearse and George Russell. See *Irish Statesman,* 12, 19, 26 March 1927, for discussion.

ment participation in production, the only nationalization proposal Labour put forward in this period had to do with the railways, and other groups also saw the necessity of railway nationalization.

The Cosgrave government claimed that it shared the social objectives of the Labour Party, but it said the money necessary for their attainment was not available. The government held that Labour was making unrealistic demands; it was not taking into consideration either the problems of establishing a new state or the fact of the depressed economic conditions. Yet the government made little attempt even to maintain existing levels for the social services and education. In economic matters it followed a policy of non-interference and fiscal conservatism; it borrowed very little, even for non-recurrent expenditures such as civil war compensation. It made no serious attempt to raise money for social purposes. For example, the government could have both imposed tariffs earlier and imposed additional tariffs for revenue. When there was a surplus in revenue, the government reduced income taxes rather than restore reductions in the social services.

Many Labour proposals, especially in the fields of education, transportation, agriculture, fisheries and the social services were adopted by future governments. The primacy of socio-economic matters in the party's outlook is signified by Johnson's conditions for a Labour Party alliance with any other party. He said that both parties would have to agree to three requirements; first, work or unemployment pay for the jobless; second, guaranteed prices for working farmers; third, maximum production of useful things for the widespread benefit of the whole people. No political requirement was included.[29]

CONSTITUTIONAL ISSUES

All purely political issues arising in Irish politics after 1922 had their origins in the Anglo-Irish treaty and the ensuing civil war. The pro-treaty Cosgrave government chose to work for greater political freedom through the machinery of the evolving British Commonwealth. The anti-treaty group, led by Eamon de Valera, sought repudiation of the treaty. The Labour position was mid-way between: full advantage should be taken of the provisions of the treaty to secure maximum benefit to the country, while sections of the constitution repugnant to Irish sovereignty and national sentiment should be removed.

Though Labour had a clearly defined policy on constitutional questions, it approached political issues with apparent distaste. As party leader, Johnson sought to emphasize the social and economic problems of the country. His attitude towards political issues is typified by his response to the report of the 1926 Imperial Conference. It would have been better, he said, to have 'left this rather big constitutional question somewhat aside for a little while, because I would like not to be an agent in forcing an issue of this kind upon the public

29 *Irish Times*, 1 November 1926.

mind to the exclusion, even partial exclusion, of economic and industrial questions.'[30]

But whether they liked it or not, Johnson and the Labour Party were required to devote a great deal of attention to constitutional issues. They were, after all, the official opposition in the Dail; they were generally critical of the government's policies on constitutional matters, and, with the exception of a few independents, no one else in the Dail opposed the government on these issues. But Labour did not attempt to exploit strictly political issues for party advantage.

The party had consistently opposed the mandatory oath of allegiance to the British Crown and the Free State constitution because the oath would deprive the country of the services of many capable men and women. Not only were all members of the Dail and senate required to take the oath but also many state employees such as teachers, doctors and nurses. Labour's election programmes in 1923 and 1927 supported the removal of the oath from the constitution. However, when a resolution was put forward at the 1926 party-congress meeting urging the executive to make a 'more determined effort' to remove the oath, Johnson objected on the grounds that the executive should not be asked to make this question a major part of its programme—social and economic issues should come first. The resolution was defeated.[31]

Only once in this period was there an attempt made in the Dail to remove the oath. In April 1927 Daniel Breen, a hero of the national struggle and a republican victor in the 1923 election, took the oath and entered the Dail. He immediately put forward a bill to remove the oath. The Ceann Comhairle imposed the strictest parliamentary rules: only two speakers, Breen and David Hall, a little-known member of the Labour Party, were allowed to speak in favour of the bill: only President Cosgrave spoke in opposition. Hall stated that he was acting as an individual—'that it has no connection with the party to which I belong'. However, on the vote (seventeen for, forty-seven against) ten Labour deputies voted for the proposal, none were against, and three were not recorded.[32] Based on this record, the party could claim to have made a reasonable effort to remove the oath, bearing in mind that this was not an essential issue for Labour.

Another constitutional issue that arose out of the treaty concerned the right to appeal Irish court decisions to the British privy council. The first appeal was accepted by the council in 1925. In reaction, the Cosgrave government introduced legislation in January 1926 which declared the Irish courts to be the final court of appeal. The Labour Party supported the government's contention, but disagreed with its

30 *Dail Eireann deb.*, xvii, 728–29.

31 I.L.P. and T.U.C., *1926 report*, pp. 166–68.

32 Following the defeat of his bill, Breen apparently left the Dail. He is not mentioned again in the debates of this period. It is not known if the three Labour deputies who did not vote—Corish, Everett and Bradley—were present, as no other vote was taken that day. *Dail Eireann deb.*, xix, 990–94.

action in negating a provision of the constitution which it earlier insisted must be included. Recalling Labour's opposition to this provision at the time of the constituent assembly, Johnson felt the government ought to amend the constitution. The government, however, content that it had warned off further attempts to use the right of appeal, declined to take that action.[33] This did not mean that the government believed in the unalterability of the constitution. When it served partisan advantage, Cosgrave's party hastily stripped the constitution of the provisions which provided for initiative and referendum.

The ministry for external affairs, under Desmond FitzGerald, was the frequent object of Labour Party criticism, which centred on the ministry's alleged lack of vigour in demonstrating the Free State's political independence. The party urged the ministry to demonstrate continually that the Free State, although a member of the British Commonwealth, set its own course and made its own foreign policy. Pointing to British government statements which gave the impression that the dominions together comprised one political unit, Johnson declared: 'We must not allow this view of what is called the diplomatic unity of the Empire to prevail.' The party attacked the ministry's report of the 1926 Imperial Conference on the grounds 'that so far from having achieved an advance in the constitutional position of the Free State, there has been, in fact, a retrogression' because the report 'fixes in the mind of the Conference participants and the world the idea of the diplomatic unity of the British Empire'. Raising a question that was to be of crucial importance a dozen years later, Johnson urged the government to state clearly that a declaration of war by the British government would in no way commit the Free State.[34]

THE 1924 ARMY MUTINY

Both during and after the civil war, the Labour Party was alive to the danger of granting unlimited power to the military; it constantly urged the government to make certain that civilian control of the military was maintained. In April 1923 there were reports of unrest in the Free State army; the matter was raised in the Dail by Patrick McCartan. Cosgrave promptly denied the reports; Labour accepted the president's denial and expressed confidence in the department of defence and its minister, Richard Mulcahy. Two months later, shortly before the national election, a serious case of army indiscipline occurred, but the situation did not come to public attention until a year later; a secret inquiry into the occurrence was not begun until after the election.[35]

During consideration of the Ministers and Secretaries Bill in November 1923, the Labour Party protested against granting the

33 Ibid., xiv, 342–50. Mansergh (*Irish Free State,* pp. 322–23) declares that the right of appeal remained ineffective in this period.

34 *Dail Eireann deb.,* xiv, 543, 573, 729, 751; xvii, 734. For criticism of Labour's attack on the conference report, see *Irish Independent,* 16 December 1926.

35 *Dail Eireann deb.,* iii, 58–68; vii, 1981–82; Terence deVere White, *Kevin O'Higgins,* pp. 154, 156.

army council permanent status. The legislation, it argued, would place the council in a position of exceptional strength in relation to the Dail, since it would be comprised of non-civilians who were not in the Dail and would not be responsible to it. Indeed, the council appeared to be free from any governmental control. One provision of the bill stated that the council should 'act as a collective body and shall be collectively responsible for all matters entrusted to it . . . whether by act of the Oireachtas or otherwise'. Johnson wondered what situation this provision foreshadowed, and Labour's fear of granting the army great power was to be justified by the events of 1924.

Despite the denials of the government, tensions within the army were increasing. In the aftermath of the civil war, and with the government's knowledge two groups had been secretly formed within the army. One group, known as the Irish Republican Army Organization, had as its objective the transformation of the Free State into a republic; they claimed to hold to the policy of Michael Collins. As a counterforce to this organization, Richard Mulcahy had revived the Irish Republican Brotherhood.

In March 1924 the government announced plans to reduce the size of the army, then at near civil war strength, from 55,000 to 18,000.[36] Because of the depressed economy, thousands of soldiers faced the prospect of unemployment. The announcement was followed by outbreaks of desertion and seizure of arms. The I.R.A.O. (not to be confused with I.R.A., which fought the Free State in the civil war and still existed) sent a letter, signed by some high officers, demanding a withdrawal of the government plans for reducing the arms and government action to move the Free State towards an independent republic. In the face of this threat to constitutional authority, the Labour Party immediately supported the government. Within a few days, Joseph McGrath, the minister for industry and commerce and sympathetic to the pro-republican group, resigned, to be followed shortly by Mulcahy. All the members of the army council were removed.

At the next meeting of the Dail, President Cosgrave gave only the briefest description of the causes of the mutiny, declaring that a cabinet committee would be appointed to investigate the matter. Johnson branded Cosgrave's statement as grossly inadequate and demanded that the Dail be fully informed. He ridiculed the idea of a cabinet committee investigating the upheaval: it would be a case of the government investigating itself. Johnson laid responsibility for the mutiny on the policy of the government and on the Dail itself. He said a feeling had been created in the minds of many who had participated in the national struggle that 'the full interpretation of the treaty has not been given to it by the government'. The government had made no provision for employment of the thousands of soldiers to be demobilized, and

36 *Irish Times*, 8, 10 March 1924. Compare these figures with those for the Irish Army in 1965: 7,148 men, 1,098 officers. John Murdoch in *Sunday Press*, 31 October 1965.

there was a lack of belief in using democratic, parliamentary processes to effect political change. The Dail itself, he said, was partly responsible for this frame of mind:

> If there had been adequate criticism from all sides of the Dail of the acts of the government there would have been more confidence in parliamentary representation. . . . The policy of abstention is only a little further removed from the policy of silence in the Dail.

The Labour leader called for a Dail committee to probe into the army situation and requested that the government allow a 'free vote' on his proposal; this request was refused. The next month, however, the government gave ground. It announced that the inquiry membership would be expanded to include representatives of each of the constitutional parties as well as a representative of the judiciary. The Labour Party, objecting to the inclusion of a non-legislator on the grounds that he would not be responsible to the Dail, refused to participate. The report of the inquiry was submitted to the cabinet in June 1924, but the government refused to present the full report to the Dail. Labour attacked the government's action, and termed the portion of the report which was revealed to the Dail 'an emasculated and partial report'. The party refused to take sides in the debate between the supporters of the two army factions.[37]

The government had succeeded in preventing the Dail from getting all but the barest information, but the ministers had addressed the government party at which time they supposedly told the whole story. Johnson angrily declared that the government's action had placed the Dail in a subordinate position to the Cumann na nGaedheal party, that 'this is an undignified position to put the Dail in, and it is not carrying out the spirit of the constitution.' If the Dail is not to be given information of public importance, he warned 'then we had better dissolve the Dail and set up what you want to set up—a dictatorship'.[38] The Labour Party itself was partly to blame for these developments. By its diffident refusal to take part in the inquiry, the party showed a concern for the role of parliament which was almost too proper to be practical. It is likely that Johnson's devotion to parliamentary methods was responsible for this position. The refusal of Labour to participate undermined its position as the opposition party in the Dail and allowed the government near free rein in the inquiry.

The controversy surrounding the mutiny caused the first serious split in the government party. Nine Cumann na nGaedheal deputies left the party, and several of them indicated that they would resign from the Dail. Labour, naturally eager to build up the strength of

37 *Dail Eireann deb.*, vi, 1896–97, 1971, 1989–90; vii, 2502, 3196; viii, 1977–78. An *Irish Times* editorial (4 April 1924) criticized the Labour Party for not participating in the inquiry.

38 *Dail Eireann deb.*, vi, 2354–55.

the Dail opposition, urged these members to remain. The dissident deputies at last decided to stay in the Dail where they formed a faction called the 'National Group' under the leadership of McGrath. This development was heralded by the *Irish Times* as the beginning of a real opposition because the group 'was divided from the government by political issues of a vital character', while the other non-government parties in the Dail, including Labour, were 'at one with the government on the main issues of the treaty and the constitution'.[39]

After several weeks of silence, the National Group in July 1924 challenged the government on the minor but symbolic matter of the appropriation for the executive council. The government took the challenge quite seriously, mentioning the possibility of a change in government and a new election, probably because it feared further defections. Although McGrath's speech simply raked over the mutiny and surrounding events, some of the National Group criticized the government's conservative economic policies. This led to an attack by several Labour deputies for the group's past support of the economic policies they now criticized. Johnson said, 'They [the National Group] have come today with a motion of no confidence but for quite a considerable number of weeks they have missed occasion after occasion and opportunity after opportunity to express that lack of confidence.' Although it was supported by the Labour Party, the amendment put forward by the National Group secured only eighteen votes to the government's fifty.[40]

The National Group failed to develop a clear political position, much less social and economic policies. Despite his long association with the labour movement and his sympathy with Labour's programme during his tenure as minister for industry and commerce, McGrath, as leader of the National Group, showed no real concern for social and economic problems. Even before his resignation, Cosgrave and the government had adopted a policy of economy and retrenchment. McGrath had become deeply involved in Free State army politics and appears to have moved away from his earlier labour outlook. The National Group gave up the pretence of being a political party in the autumn of 1924 when the nine members resigned their seats; only one of them, Sean Milroy, stood for re-election and he was defeated. The government party won seven of the seats and the republicans won two. Thus the political balance was restored to what it had been before the mutiny; the parliamentary opposition was no stronger than before.

THE BOUNDARY ISSUE

The army mutiny was followed by the mounting problem of the boundary which was to culminate in disaster at the end of 1925. The Anglo-

39 The group first thought of calling itself the 'Constitutional Republicans'. *Irish Times*, 28, 31 March, 3 April 1924.

40 *Dail Eireann deb.*, viii, 1284–1300, 1303–30, 1437–39. With the exception of Corish, Labour supported the group's amendment, but voted with the government on the motion,

Irish treaty provided for the establishment of a boundary commission to delimit the territory of the Free State and Northern Ireland. The Labour Party urged the Cosgrave government to strive for the early organization of the body. The Labour party-congress, as a thirty-two county organization, had repeatedly supported Irish unification, although the bulk of northern opinion favoured the British connection. Frustrated by government inaction in setting up the commission, Labour supported a Dail motion in June 1924 which would set a time limit for the accomplishment of this task.

The party took special interest in another provision of the treaty that could be used to further Irish unification—the Council of Ireland. The Collins-Craig agreement of 1922 had postponed establishing of the council for five years, but Labour felt this was not binding on the present government. To Johnson the council was of crucial importance: it was

> infinitely more important than fixing the Boundary. If you have secured unification of control, or rather, if you have secured for the Free State such authority in respect to railways in the Northern area you have ensured ultimate unity.[41]

The government and the Labour Party had different interpretations of the powers of the council. Labour held that the treaty granted the Free State equal powers in the control of railways, fisheries and some minor services in Northern Ireland, but that in the twenty-six counties these services were under the exclusive control of the Free State government. The government opposed the establishment because it said that the northern government would gain partial control of the Free State's railways and fisheries. The government made it plain that it did not consider the council to be an important device in the attainment of national unification, even though in the treaty debate in 1921 it was repeatedly stated that the council would ensure ultimate unity. On the other side, the northern government remained greatly concerned about the powers granted to the Free State in the council.[42]

The central issue remained the Boundary Commission. President Cosgrave won the support of the Labour Party when he asserted that if the northern government refused to appoint a member to the Boundary Commission, it would have failed to comply with the conditions which allowed the six counties to secede from the Free State in 1922; the northern parliament therefore would be a subordinate parliament within the Free State. When the northern government did refuse,

---

leaving the National Group in isolated opposition. For the government's defeat on a minor amendment, see *Irish Independent*, 18 July 1924.

41 *Dail Eireann deb.*, vii, 2379. See also ibid., 2354, 2368, 2374.

42 Ibid., 2369–70. For northern opinion, see Henry Harrison, *Ireland and the British empire*, pp. 234–35.

Cosgrave backed down from his position and agreed to allow the British government to make this appointment.[43]

The Labour Party resolutely opposed any tampering with the structure of the commission. The long delay in setting up the body had destroyed its value, according to Johnson, who concluded that the treaty had been violated and should be renounced, and that the Dail should proceed to rewrite the constitution, removing its 'obnoxious sections', including the oath of allegiance. The party warned the government that it was committing itself to accept the commission's report, while neither the British nor the northern government were so committed. Cosgrave argued that the treaty had not been violated—only an article dealing with the commission was being altered. O'Higgins warned the Dail of the economic and military consequences of renunciations of the treaty.[44]

The commission finally was organized in the spring of 1925, with the British government appointing two members and the Free State appointing one—Eoin MacNeill. The Dail avoided discussing the subject in order to allow the commission to proceed without outside debate. By November 1925, however, as the commission neared completion of its report, the Labour Party became apprehensive. Johnson's scepticism was reinforced when he drew from Cosgrave the admission that the commission had not requested facilities for a plebiscite from either the Free State or the Belfast government. It was Johnson's view that if the wishes of the border population were not ascertained, the article in the treaty providing for a boundary commission would not have been fulfilled. In this obviously deteriorating situation, he urged the government to insist on a plebiscite and the immediate establishment of the council of Ireland.[45]

The only explanation given by the government as to why a plebiscite had not been held was later offered by O'Higgins: it had not been done because the commission lacked the machinery and the legislative authority to arrange it; further legislation would have meant more delay, and there was the problem of the House of Lords. The Lords, in approving the bill altering the commission, had stipulated that the boundary must be drawn 'in the sense indicated by the British signatories to the treaty'. Some of the signatories insisted that the commission had no right to take any territory away from the northern government.[46]

On 19 November 1925 MacNeill resigned from the commission, because, he said, the chairman, Chief Justice Feetham of South Africa, had subordinated the wishes of the border population to political considerations. Cosgrave and the leading ministers went to London in

43 Legislation to this effect, the Treaty (Confirmation of Supplemental Agreement) Bill, was introduced in the Dail on 1 August 1924. White, *O'Higgins*, p. 201; *Dail Eireann deb.*, viii, 2503.

44 *Dail Eireann deb.*, viii, 2364–65, 2374, 2414, 2423, 2429, 2433–35, 2506.

45 Ibid., 626–33.

46 *Round Table*, March 1926.

an attempt to salvage something from the wreckage of the Boundary Commission. For its part, the Labour Party demanded that before any agreement was signed in London 'there should be consultations and discussion in the Free State'. Until MacNeill's resignation, Johnson pointed out, public discussion had been held down by the argument that ' we must trust the government'. Now Johnson insisted that the border must be drawn according to the wishes of the population along the border and that 'this view must be upheld regardless of any British legal interpretation of the Irish treaty and regardless of whatever the Boundary Commission may decide.' At no time did Cosgrave present a public case that nationalist areas presently in Northern Ireland should be allowed to join the Free State. His strongest statement was, 'If the commission doesn't fulfil its terms of reference . . . they will have done a bad day's work not only for Ireland alone but for the whole Commonwealth.' The Labour Party strenuously opposed the government's motion to adjourn the Dail during the time when negotiations were proceeding in London. The government obviously did not want the Dail available and, as predicted by Labour, Cosgrave, upon his return from London on 4 December, rushed to a meeting of his party and revealed the agreement which had been reached.[47]

The agreement stated that the report of the commission would not be published or implemented; the boundary was to remain as it was. The Free State was released from assuming a share in the cost of the British public debt. It was, however, to assume the total cost for all damages during the 1919–22 period and was to pay an additional ten percent compensation for damage to property. It was later revealed that the Free State would continue to pay land annuities to the British government. The British government's share in the power in the Council of Ireland was transferred to the northern government, thus effectively killing the council. In return, the Belfast government offered the vague promise to meet with the Free State cabinet when it felt this was necessary.

On the afternoon of the day the agreement was published, the Labour Party issued a statement labelling it an 'unmitigated betrayal'. The agreement, according to Labour, reversed the underlying principle of the treaty and the constitution: that Ireland was one and indivisable. The nationalist people in the six counties were offered 'absolutely nothing', and, 'The assumption by the Free State of responsibility for the whole cost of the Anglo-Irish war is a tacit admission that Ireland was not entitled to wage that war, had no right to be a belligerent and had not the status of a treaty-making power.'[48] All the national newspapers, however, hailed the agreement, stressing its financial aspects and the fact that it was too late to redress the Boundary Commission

47 See *Dail Eireann deb.*, viii, 634–39; xiii, 801, 805–12, 1172, 1183–86. Also *Irish Times*, 2 December 1925; *Dublin Evening Mail*, 4 December 1925.

48 *Irish Independent*, 5 December 1925; *Cork Examiner*, 5 December 1925.

fiasco. Labour's opposition came in for sweeping criticism.[49]

The failure of the Boundary Commission to re-draw the border produced the greatest political shock in the country since the civil war. Even some sections of the government party were decidedly disappointed with the agreement and the failure of the commission. The government declared, defensively, that if there was a considerable body of opinion against the agreement 'in the Dail' it would not have 'the slightest hesitation' in calling a national election—a statement apparently designed to warn wavering back-benchers that the price of voting against the agreement would be the defence of their newly won seats.[50] One deputy who broke with the government was Professor William Magennis of University College, Dublin, who later organized his own party.

Those deputies opposed to the agreement turned to the only force with which they could combine to defeat it—the abstentionist anti-treaty deputies. Johnson, together with Patrick O'Maille of the National Group and Patrick Baxter of the Farmers Party, called for a meeting 'of all deputies elected to the Dail' to be held in the Shelbourne Hotel. Eamon de Valera urged all anti-treaty deputies to attend.

No united course of action resulted from the meeting, which followed another meeting of a different group of deputies opposed to the agreement. It is obvious that the deputies in the Dail attempted to convince the anti-treatyites that this was the time for them to enter parliament. Although there were reports that a majority of the anti-treaty deputies were prepared to drop abstention, and their arrival in the Dail was indeed anticipated, they failed to appear. Both Johnson and de Valera, as well as Professor Magennis (chairman of the earlier meeting), called for a referendum on the agreement, but this was a futile gesture as the government could easily avoid a referendum by attaching an emergency resolution to the bill—which is exactly what it did. The Labour executive blamed both the government and the republicans, who 'were not prepared to take any practical, effective steps to prevent the passage of the bill. The responsibility of the Ministry and the Republican party in this vital matter is for history to judge.'[51] The anti-treatyites contented themselves with the pathetic gesture of passing a resolution denouncing the agreement at a meeting held at the Rotunda theatre, the site of the founding of the Volunteers.

When the agreement was presented to the Dail the Labour Party used every parliamentary device to impede its passage. Due to this obstructionist activity, the government was obliged to move the

49 See, e.g., *Irish Independent,* 5 December 1925; *Irish Times,* 5, 7, 11, 17 December 1925; *Cork Examiner,* 5 December 1925; *Dublin Evening Mail,* 4 December 1925.

50 *Irish Times, Dublin Evening Mail,* 5 December 1925.

51 I.L.P. and T.U.C., *1925 report,* p. 57. For the efforts of the anti-government group, see also *Irish Independent* and *Dublin Evening Mail,* 8 December 1925; *Irish Times,* 9 December 1925.

suspension of the standing orders. Opponents of the agreement were warned that the Boundary Commission remained in existence until legislation was passed by the Dublin and London parliaments, implying that the commission's report would deprive the Free State of some territory. Johnson later declared that the government's method of making an agreement in London and then presenting it to the Dail on 'a take it or leave it basis' was 'calculated to lead to the overthrow of Parliamentary Government and the removal of democratic control of Ministries'.[52]

In his presentation, Cosgrave spoke glowingly of the 'new spirit of cordial co-operation and friendship' which was emerging between the Free State and Northern Ireland as a result of the agreement.[53] Although the northern nationalists were not protected by any provision of the agreement, he said, 'Those present at the negotiations were resolved that the minority should have the only real security, which is . . . to be sought only in neighbourly feeling'. In keeping with this approach, he refused to allow a delegation of northern nationalists to present a petition opposing the agreement. O'Higgins went so far as to claim that most northern nationalists were satisfied with leaving the border as it was—a statement vigorously denied by both Johnson and Baxter of the Farmers Party.

Cosgrave claimed that he got a 'huge nought' for the Free State when it was released from the obligation of sharing in the payment of the British national debt. (But Sir Edward Carson, now Lord Carson, had earlier said that the British government had always considered the Free State's share of the debt a 'bad debt', and not recoverable. Further, in another section of the agreement, the Free State assumed new and additional financial burdens, and at the same time the Free State was to continue to pay land annuity payments to the British government.) Finally, Cosgrave declared that 'in abandoning the Council of Ireland the Free State will lose nothing. It will gain goodwill.'

The Labour Party launched a general attack on the agreement, lashing the government for not presenting a counter-claim to the British financial demands. The proposed joint meetings of the Dublin and Belfast governments were, in the words of Labour deputy O'Connell, 'only a pious aspiration put into this treaty, and it could never be anything more because it cannot be made effective'. The party questioned the genuineness of the 'new atmosphere of friendship and brotherhood' both in the six counties and between the two governments. Johnson, who had lived in Belfast from 1902 to 1918, pointed out that persecution of the northern nationalists had increased. Labour doubted the need to continue paying annuities to the British government now that the Free State had been released from paying a share of the British national debt.

52 Johnson's motion for immediate adjournment was supported by twenty-six deputies. *Dail Eireann deb.*, xiii, 1265, 1313; xiv, 1243; *Irish Independent,* 8 December 1925.

53 For the debate over the agreement, see *Dail Eireann deb.*, xiii, 1307, 1309, 1312–13, 1347, 1356, 1391, 1458, 1468, 1473–74, 1479–90, 1542–43, 1547, 1562, 1856–60.

In decrying the loss of the Council of Ireland—a factor which for years he had stressed as a unifying mechanism—Johnson quoted Michael Collins's argument that the council would be a means to preserve essential unity and prevent the absolute break demanded by the northern Unionists. The treaty would not have been accepted by the Dail if permanent, 'complete and absolute' severance of the six counties had been known to be a consequence. Johnson's statement was strongly supported by Richard Corish, who had voted for the treaty.

In a bitter and acrimonious debate on the committee stage of the bill, ministers heaped personal abuse on Johnson and other Labour deputies. Cosgrave charged him with inactivity during the national struggle. Patrick McGilligan, now minister for industry and commerce, said Labour opposition to the agreement was to chastise the government for its Shannon scheme wage policy, a charge repeated by Cosgrave in the senate and echoed by the *Irish Times*.

The agreement was approved by a vote of fifty-five for, fourteen against. The small vote against the agreement does not give an accurate picture of the actual opposition. Twenty deputies voted against the bill on its second reading; several of these did not vote on the final stage of the bill. Further, twenty-six deputies had supported the Labour Party's motion for immediate adjournment upon the bill's introduction. It is quite probable that had the bulk of the abstentionist deputies entered the Dail and voted against the agreement, a considerable number of wavering deputies, including some in the government party, would have joined the opposition. In these circumstances, there was the clear possibility that the agreement would have been rejected. Even had it not been, a strong vote against the agreement might have forced the government to call an election, as it had threatened to do, and defend the agreement from the public platform.[54]

THE ANNUITIES ISSUE

The extended debate on the boundary agreement brought out the fact that the Free State would continue to pay the land purchase annuities to the British government. When de Valera returned to power in 1932 the question of continuing these payments to Britain became a major issue between the two countries and led to a lengthy diplomatic and economic struggle. The annuities were payments made by Irish farmers for land which had been given by the British government before 1922. The British considered annuities as re-payments on the money expended to buy out the former owners. Under the 1920 Government of Ireland Act, the annuities in both the twenty-six counties and the six counties were to be retained by the home rule parliaments. The government of Northern Ireland did in fact retain the payments. But the act did not come into force in the twenty-six counties due to opposition from the Sinn Fein movement and its supporters. During

54 Ibid., xiii, 1955–56, 1767–68, 1256–66. A majority in the 153-member Dail was 77; the highest vote for the agreement was 71.

the Anglo-Irish war many farmers in the twenty-six counties failed to make these payments, although the rebel government of Dail Eireann had not urged them to this course. The 1921 treaty made no mention of annuity payments but did say that Ireland was to assume a share of the United Kingdom public debt. Later the Free State government willingly agreed to continue to pay the annuities to the British government: under the secret Hills-Cosgrave agreement of 1922 the Free State consented to act as collector of the payments.[55]

The Labour Party took no consistent position on the necessity to continue annuity payments. The party's concern with annuities dates to at least 1921, when its Easter manifesto proposed temporary suspension of the payments. In the 1922 election platform Labour again advocated suspension 'pending a Government inquiry into the whole question of agricultural conditions'.[56] Labour's 1923 platform, however, made no mention of annuities.

Under the Free State, legal authority to continue the payments to Britain was contained in the 1923 Land Act which established an annuities fund 'under the control of the Minister for Finance to the appropriate authority for the credit of the Land Purchase Account'. The government did not say who the 'appropriate authority' was, and no deputy asked. In the same year, for the first and only time, an annuities estimate was presented to the Dail. The government put forward the estimate without due notice and encumbered it in financial terminology; Cosgrave said of it that 'this estimate is one which is concerned solely with accounting transactions, as to which no controversy can arise'. It is difficult to resist the idea that the government was attempting to disguise what was involved in this estimate.[57]

The Labour Party realized that the government was continuing to hand over the annuities to Britain, and in 1924 Johnson proposed that the payments be suspended and this money used to avoid reducing old age pensions. A year later the party position was that the payments would cease to be paid to Britain when the settlement regarding the Free State's share in the British public debt had been reached. Johnson said, 'The re-arrangement, whatever it may be, will not, we contend, mean henceforth annual payments to the British Government.' No government spokesman rose to dispute this statement. The Labour Party alone objected to allowing the British government to guarantee payment of the annuities based on Free State legislation. One member of the Farmers Party, Conor Hogan, demanded the immediate suspension of the payments, but the Farmers Party itself neither opposed this legislation nor the continuation of the payments.

55 For background to the annuities issue, see Peadar O'Donnell, *There will be another day*.

56 Originally the party had proposed suspension of the payments 'pending the recovery of normal economic conditions'. *Voice of Labour*, 25 February, 6 May 1922.

57 The amount due that year was £3,133,577, equal to one-third of the government's income. Johnson's only comment at that time was to inquire as to the government's success in collecting the annuities. *Dail Eireann deb.*, iv, 1014, 2468–99.

The 1925 boundary agreement released the Free State from the obligation of paying a portion of the British public debt. Pressed by the Labour Party, the government admitted that annuity payments would still be handed over to the British; the annuities were not to be considered part of the public debt section of the treaty, but rather were 'contingent' to the public debt. Labour held that the payments were a public charge; therefore, they were part of the public debt.

On 1 December 1926 the government published an 'ultimate financial settlement' agreed to by the Free State minister for finance, Ernest Blythe, and the British government the previous March. Earlier, in February 1926, Professor Magennis (with Labour support) had put forward a motion condemning 'secret negotiations with external governments', to which the government denied that secret dealings were under way. Yet the 'ultimate' settlement was dated 19 March 1926. It had not been submitted to the Dail for approval (nor had the Hills-Cosgrave agreement of 1922, which remained secret until 1932). It revealed that the Free State had agreed to continue to pay the annuities to the British government. Again Labour argued that the annuities were part of the public debt and the payments need not be continued. Despite the prodding of Senator Maurice Moore, who had developed a strong interest in this question, the party did not demand stoppage of the payments. Johnson merely said, 'On the information that is before me at present it seems to me that we are not liable to pay.'[58]

Despite Johnson's serious doubts, Labour made no attempt to develop this question into a major political issue and thereby achieve much-needed agricultural support. The party ignored at least one republican invitation to oppose the annuity payments, and it did not support Peadar O'Donnell's anti-payment campaign in the mid-1920s.[59] Annuities were not mentioned in Labour's 1927 election platform. Here was an issue which could have gained the party support from small farmers, an issue which would have broken the party out of its trade unionist mould. De Valera's new party, Fianna Fail, seized upon this issue and the ending of annuity payments to Britain became an important and popular part of its programme.

Perhaps the Labour Party considered that this question was somewhat out of its line. It must be remembered that Johnson was a cautious leader with a predilection for strict legality, and the annuities issue—from the legal side—was an explosive one. In a series of articles written in 1928, Johnson concluded that the only way the Free State could end the payments, short of repudiation, was by re-opening the 1926 financial agreement with the British government.[60] His successor as

58 For the annuities issue, see ibid., vi, 1278; x, 1531–33, 1536, 1565–66; xiii, 1910–11; xvii, 649, 659–63; memorandum from Moore to Johnson, 12 December 1925, Johnson papers, N.L.I., MS 17242.

59 Letters by Frank Mitchel, *An Phoblacht*, 13, 20 August 1926; interview with Peadar O'Donnell, 21 November 1964.

60 *Irishman*, 4, 18, 25 August 1928. Other Labour men urged the party to make an issue of the annuities payments. Interview with James Everett, 24 June 1964.

party leader, T. J. O'Connell, held the same view. O'Connell's position was based not only on legal considerations, but also on the view that an issue of this type was beyond the scope of the party.[61] It was not until William Norton became the party leader that Labour supported the Fianna Fail government in refusing to continue the payments to Britain.

61 Interview with T. J. O'Connell, 4 November 1965.

9

Politics outside the Dail

During the term of the fourth Dail, from 1923 to 1927, the Labour Party dealt with a wide range of non-parliamentary matters, including party organization, industrial versus political interests in the party-congress, the question of co-operativism, political activity in Northern Ireland, relations with international labour organizations, the British general strike, the continuing Larkin split and relations with the republican movement. Of all the problems that faced the Labour Party after the 1923 election the most obvious and pressing was the need to create the foundations of a political party.

LABOUR PARTY ORGANIZATION

The Irish Labour Party and Trade Union Congress was a very imposing organization on paper. It consisted of a large number of unions and trade councils, representing over 200,000 workers, with branches throughout the whole of Ireland. But for electoral purposes, as shown in the 1923 election, the organization had proved to be a paper tiger. As a consequence of this reversal, the Labour executive recognized the need for a new political apparatus. As far back as 1918 the party-congress had provided for individual subscribing members to be drawn from the ranks of the trade-union activists and for the formation of local Labour Parties in areas where the trade councils were not prepared to undertake electoral activity. But very few individual members were subscribed, and the two local Labour Parties established—those in Dublin and Cork—proved to be ineffective, as the party lost in 1923 the single seats it had in both cities. The major weakness, however, proved to be the inability of the trade councils and the unions to organize electoral activity.

Following the 1923 election the Labour executive drew up a new scheme for political organization. Labour clubs were to be organized in each parish and chapel district, divisional Labour Parties in each electoral district and joint constituency parties in each parliamentary district. The plan had as its objectives the attraction of political activists through individual party memberships, the creation of grass-roots party organization and the raising of funds. During the first six months party leaders addressed meetings in different parts of the state to stimulate the formation of Labour clubs. Thirty clubs were created during this time.[1]

The 1924 Labour conference was largely concerned with the posture and position of the party. As in 1918, the conference rejected a proposal to widen the party base by allowing the affiliation of 'Independent Labour and Workers Parties, co-operative Societies and other working

1 I.L.P. & T.U.C., *1924 report*, p. 102.

class organizations'. Speaking for the executive, Thomas Farren declared that the constitution already allowed for the affiliation of local groups and individual members. In an apparent reference to Larkin's new union, he said that to widen affiliation might invite 'opportunist local associations purporting to be trade unions'. Another executive member, J. T. O'Farrell, admitted that the organization's base previously had been too narrow, that 'there had been an unreasoning fear . . . to accept anyone who was not a trade unionist'. Labour, he said, 'was the one Party that had so far denied the right to the general body of the electorate', but held that the new Labour clubs removed this bar.[2]

The conference also agreed to raise the affiliation fees of all components of the organization. Trade union fees were raised from two pence to three pence per member annually, and the fees for trade councils were raised to six pence per member annually.[3] The increase was to finance the broadening political activity of the organization and to provide additional headquarters staff. Thomas Johnson continued to serve as both secretary of the party-congress and the leader of the Dail Labour Party through 1927. It was decided at this time to relieve him of some headquarters responsibility by the appointment of an assistant secretary. This post was given to the able and well-informed R. J. P. Mortished. London-born, he was an adherent of the parliamentary, moderate approach to socialism and undoubtedly reinforced Johnson's commitment to this method. Involved in the affairs of the Irish labour movement since 1909, Mortished did valuable work in preparing bills and amendments for the Dail party; he was Johnson's aide from 1922 (years later he was to be the first chairman of the Labour Court).[4]

The emphasis on party organization brought forward the complaint from the small Irish Women Workers Union that the Labour executive was not giving proper attention to the industrial side of the movement. The union's secretary, Louie Bennett, strongly advocated the creation of a powerful trade-union movement as an essential prerequisite to the fostering of an effective political party. Tom Farren responded that the women's union was proposing to divide the political and industrial arms of the organization, but that the party-congress constitution 'was based throughout on the principle advocated by Connolly that political and industrial organization should go hand in hand. Miss Bennett wanted organization on the English model' Johnson pointed out that almost all the resolutions submitted by the unions at the last conference dealt with social and political matters; not one was entirely industrial in nature. The women's union was appeased when the

2 Ibid., pp. 182–83, 163.

3 In 1970 the Irish Congress of Trade Unions received one shilling per member annually; the Labour Party received an average of two shillings per month from each member.

4 I.L.P. & T.U.C., *1924 report*, p. 183. O'Brien papers, Ms. 15672(2); article by Milo MacGarry, *The Star*, 16 February 1929.

conference voted to set up separate subcommittees for political and industrial affairs.[5]

The next year's conference instructed the executive to take further steps to improve the party organization. A committee appointed to study the problem recommended that the trades councils be relieved of all responsibility for political work, that a system of local Labour Parties, replacing the Labour clubs, be created to assume this task and that a political organizer be employed to inaugurate the scheme. This appointment went to Archie Heron, a native of Portadown, County Armagh, and a man of wide experience, having been an officer in the I.R.A., a Transport Union organizer, editor of the Labour newspaper and a Labour candidate in several by-elections. To finance the organizational campaign the executive decided to set up a voluntary '100,000 shillings' (£5,000) fund rather than again raise affiliation fees. It also created a panel of candidates for the Dail in order to make the selection of parliamentary candidates more systematic. Previously, nominations had been made shortly before national elections by the unions and the trades councils, with the approval of the executive (the executive itself had nominated candidates as well). This method often led to hasty action, poor preparation and occasional failure to nominate candidates in some areas.[6]

The 1926 conference, with only the Women Workers Union opposed, approved the scheme for expanded political organization. The executive sought to allay the fears of some trade unionists that the party-congress would be swamped by delegates from the newly constituted local parties. It admitted that 'the presence . . . of delegates directly representing the political side of the organization will naturally have some effect on the subject and nature of the discussion which takes place' as well as on policy votes and the composition of the executive. But it also held that there would be little effect in the short term. The unity of the political and industrial sides of the movement in one body was a 'decided strength', and it would be 'fatal to separate the two sides and establish distinct organizations'. The new scheme, declared Heron, simply proposed to enlist the support of the 'many people who were not eligible to join a trade union', yet 'had everything in common with the working class'.[7]

Heron felt that the trade union branches were ineffective political organizations because the unions had many members who did not subscribe to the Labour Party. The new political groups, he argued, would take their instructions from the party-congress and the executive, and would be in close touch with the unions. He correctly forecast that

5 *1924 report*, pp. 46, 51, 50, 49.

6 *1926 report*, pp. 91–94. In the British labour movement trades councils from an early date had not functioned as political or electoral organizations. Bodies to elect labour representatives, although often sponsored by trades councils, were separate organizations. In 1895 trades councils were excluded from the British T.U.C. G. D. H. Cole, *British working class politics*, pp. 113–14, 156.

7 *1926 report*, pp. 143, 95, 91, 140.

the unions, being mass bodies with memberships larger than the local parties were ever likely to achieve, would continue to have the largest voice in the party-congress. Thus, the affiliation of the local Labour Parties to the organization would be a guarantee that the political side of the movement would never 'get into the hands of non-union people'.[8] As a further precaution, the conference decided that only constituency federations of local parties would be allowed to send delegates to the annual meeting. By 1927 only four federations had been formed, sending a total of three delegates; three delegates also attended from the Northern Ireland Labour Party. These developments belied the fears of some trade unionists that the party-congress would be swamped by non-trade union political activists.[9]

Even before the local parties scheme had been approved, the energetic Heron had set to work. Supported by speakers from the executive, he succeeded in organizing forty-one local parties by July 1926. Five months later there were between 130 and 150 local parties, most of which were in the south-east. Heron continued to act as political organizer up to the eve of the next parliamentary election, resigning his post in April 1927. The party was able to face the coming election with a measure of confidence about its basic organization. It also began early to select candidates for the parliamentary panel. On 13 December 1926 the *Irish Times* noted, 'For the Labour Party the last six months have been a period of the most intensive electoral effort. . . . The machinery of organization is to be extended and perfected in every possible way, and it is proposed to nominate over fifty candidates.' There was one area in which the party had not significantly improved its position. Despite all its efforts, the party remained in a poor financial condition to launch a major political campaign. The '100,000 shillings' fund did not attain its goal of £5,000. Furthermore, the raising of affiliation fees in 1924 did not secure the party-congress a higher income because union membership began a gradual decline in the mid-1920s.

Northern Ireland Labour

Not only was the party-congress an organization that combined in itself both political and trade union activity, but it also was a thirty-two county organization with a twenty-six county political party. The northern delegates consistently refrained from involving themselves in political questions solely relating to the Free State. They felt it necessary, however, to warn that Free State tariffs and reductions in social services would hinder the cause of national unification.[10]

8 Ibid., pp. 140–41. For criticism of the expanded political base by a trade unionist and Heron's reply, see *Irish Independent*, 11, 12 May 1926.

9 The four federations were in Dublin, Kildare, Limerick and Tipperary. The great majority of the local parties were in Leinster and Munster. Only one delegate from the federations attended the 1928 meeting. *1927 report*, pp. 100–01; *1928 report*, pp. 132–34.

10 Warner Moss, *Political parties in the Irish Free State*, p. 74; *1924 report*, pp. 166–68. Moss said the northern trade unionists were concerned about the relationship of the Dail party to the party-congress. This may have existed, but no northern delegate raised the question at a Labour conference in the 1920s.

In the immediate aftermath of the civil war, the Labour Party leadership was so preoccupied with its responsibilities in the Free State that it did nothing to develop the Labour political forces in Northern Ireland. The executive took the position that 'they had no means of attempting organization in the North until they had a volume of success in the South.' But the Labour political activists of the north were not prepared to wait for this eventuality. In March 1924 the Belfast Labour Party, without informing the party-congress executive, called a conference of its two divisional parties and its twenty affiliated unions which resulted in the formation of the Labour Party (Northern Ireland). The constitution of new body, which was to come into operation on 1 February 1926, skirted the issue of partition; it addressed itself to the need for worker representation and for immediate socio-economic reforms. It elected as president the veteran trade unionist Alexander Stewart and as secretary Harry Midgley, who had stood as a Labour candidate in the 1921 election and who was to become the leading figure in the party.[11]

Responding to this development, the party-congress executive warned the new party that it must associate itself with and conform to the policies of the Irish Labour Party or the latter would challenge the northern organization on its home ground. The breach was healed in 1927 when the northern party became affiliated with the party-congress. Although there were no formal arrangements for joint meetings of the two party executives, informal contact was maintained through northern membership on the party-congress executive. The Transport Union had a considerable Belfast membership and it supported Labour candidates on both sides of the border. Based on these factors the party-congress asserted its claim not only to be an all-Ireland industrial organization, but the only all-Ireland political party.

Despite the existence of a mass labour force in Belfast and the high proportion of trade union membership, the northern party found that the profound sectarian divisions in the area prevented permanent growth. It failed to attract nationalist workers because it took no position on Irish political unity, while it repulsed Unionist workers when it decried the virtual abolition of the Council of Ireland. But the party did have some early successes. In the 1924 Stormont election, held under proportional representation, it elected three members, including William McMullen, northern secretary of the Transport Union and member of the party-congress executive. In the local elections of the following year it returned several candidates. When the Unionist government abolished proportional representation, the three Labour M.P.s were defeated in 1929.[12] Although the party remained alive,

11 *1924 report*, p. 171; John F. Harbinson, 'A history of the Northern Ireland Labour Party, 1891–1949' (unpublished MS of Econ. thesis, Queen's University of Belfast, 1966), pp. 44–46.

12 Interview with William McMullen, 30 Nov. 1965. McMullen served as northern secretary of the Transport Union in the 1920s, and later as union general president.

achieving a short period of growth in the early 1930s, it had an even less significant role in northern politics than did the Irish Labour Party in the Free State.

LOCAL GOVERNMENT ELECTIONS AND BY-ELECTIONS

The testing time for the new party organization came in the local government elections of 1925 and in a series of parliamentary by-elections. The only local government elections held in the period 1923–27 took place, after repeated delays, in June 1925. Before the elections were held the Cosgrave government abolished the lowest local bodies—the rural district councils. Labour opposed abolition on the grounds that this move would result in the county councils becoming over-burdened and that the people would be deprived of democratic control of local affairs.

The ministry of local government made extensive use of its power to dissolve hostile local bodies during this period. Among the bodies disbanded were the Dublin and Cork corporations, the county councils of Kerry, Leitrim and Offaly, the urban district councils of Cobh and Tipperary and the Dublin board of guardians. What was needed, said Johnson, was not suppression but new elections. Labour claimed that one of the principal reasons for dissolving the Dublin corporation was that the corporation had refused to lower wages and pensions when ordered to do so by the ministry.[13] Because of the government's actions, there were no local elections in the two largest cities in the state. This was a blow to Labour, which was eager to establish itself in the city working-class districts.

When Cumann na nGaedheal decided not to contest the local elections, the field was left to the Labour Party, the Farmers Party, republicans, ratepayers, independents and a few Larkinites. The Transport Union, which put forward a large number of candidates and a high proportion of campaign funds, was the spearhead of the Labour campaign. In a low poll (no constituency had a turn-out of more than fifty percent), the Labour Party achieved considerable success. The Larkinites, deprived of the opportunity to stand in their core area of Dublin city, polled poorly, while the republicans did not achieve any major successes. The efforts of the Transport Union were rewarded, as the great majority of the Labour candidates elected were members of the union. The *Voice of Labour* (4 July 1925) enthusiastically proclaimed a new era in Irish politics: 'Everywhere the decks have been cleared for straight fighting on economic issues.' But the Labour victories were concentrated in the eastern counties, with notable successes in Counties Wexford, Kildare and Wicklow, as well as in some Dublin suburbs, the latter being something of a breakthrough for the party. Although the weak Labour showing in the west was not unexpected, the failure of Labour in the south, especially in Cork, was a serious reverse.

13 *Dail Eireann deb.*, vii, 1867–72; *Irish Times*, 23 June 1925.

The numerous by-elections, especially those in Dublin and Cork, provided the party with further opportunities for political combat. Due to limited resources, Labour contested only five of the twenty-one by-elections held between the general elections of 1923 and June 1927. Most of the contests that the party entered were in the Dublin area, where Labour had made a miserable showing in 1923, but which contained the greatest potential Labour support in the country. In all five by-elections the party polled well above its 1923 vote; if it had done as well in that election it very likely would have won seats in these constituencies. The party presented the same programme as it had in 1923, which indicates that factors other than the party's platform were responsible for its reverse in that election.

Labour continued to stress social and economic issues, boring away at the government's lack of progress in dealing with unemployment and at its reductions in social services. The other two parties concentrated on political aspects, particularly the treaty. Other factors which aided Labour, as well as the anti-treatyites, were the army mutiny, the Boundary Commission disaster and the government's conservative economic policies. Certainly the pension cuts, the Shannon wages, the public safety laws and arrests, combined with the government's inadequate measures for education, housing and social welfare, swelled the opposition's strength.

The first seat contested was in County Dublin in March 1924 where Archie Heron, the party organizer, increased the Labour poll from eight percent first preference votes (polled by Johnson in 1923) to fifteen percent. A minor scandal occurred in Cork city later in 1924 when the labour organization there failed to nominate a candidate to oppose the government party nominee, a former party-congress president. In the 'little general election' of 1925, caused by the resignation of nine National Group deputies, Labour stood only in the two Dublin constituencies. The two candidates, Denis Cullen and Thomas Lawlor, both of whom were union officials and members of local public boards, polled a total of thirteen percent, enough to elect them in a general election. The last round of by-elections for the party occurred in June 1926, when Labour contested seats in Leix-Offaly and County Dublin. The Labour candidate in Leix-Offaly won an impressive twenty-two percent of the vote. This performance was as nothing compared to Labour's result in County Dublin where William Norton, the general secretary to the Irish Post Office Workers Union and a local public official, won the seat. Norton's success was principally due to the absence of a republican candidate and the failure of many middle-class voters to go to the polls. The Irish correspondent of *Round Table* (June 1926) believed the government supporters had lost the seat 'largely because they chose a publican for their candidate'. The rise of William Norton had begun, and Labour had won its first by-election.

The greatly increased percentage of votes won by the Labour candidates in the by-elections, combined with the improved party organization and its victories in the 1925 local elections, caused Labour to face the oncoming general election with confidence.

THE CO-OPERATIVE IDEAL

The ideological position of the Labour Party remained firmly tied to the objectives stated in the 1918 party-congress constitution. These objectives were collectivist, but only mildly socialist. While the party sought for the workers collectively the 'ownership and control of the whole product of their labour', it did not advocate simple workers' control of industry. Nor did it assert the conventional social democratic demand for 'the common ownership of the means of production'; rather, it proposed to secure only 'the democratic management and control of all industries and services by the whole body of workers, manual and mental, engaged therein, in the interest of the Nation, and subject to the supreme authority of the National Government.' The party claimed that it had avoided more plainly socialist terminology because it recognized that in Ireland the working class comprised only half the population. Therefore, the adoption of the socialist postulates of the British Labour Party would be wholely inappropriate; in Tom Johnson's words, Irish Labour drew its inspiration from James Connolly and George Russell.

Regardless of the fact that Labour's objectives were vaguely stated, had the party been given the opportunity to implement them fully the result would have been the creation of a socialist society, with all enterprise, in fact, nationalized. The only Labour demand for nationalization put forward in the election campaigns of the 1920s was the call for government control of railways and canals, first included in the party programme in 1922, but advocated by the party-congress as early as ten years before. The first bill Labour introduced in the Dail was for this purpose. The advocacy of state ownership of public transportation was not an exclusively socialist proposal; it was widely held in many European countries simply to be of utilitarian value. Nationalization of Irish railways had been proposed by the majority report of a viceregal commission in 1910. A Labour scheme for a national housing authority included an element of nationalization; the state would assume all responsibility for the construction of the necessary buildings. A similar proposal was for a 'national banking system', but again, the precise role of and the amount of control by the state in the scheme was not clearly spelled out. The basic Labour appeal was for greater public investment in education and social services and for employment of national credit and finance in industrial development.

The methods to be used to attain these objectives were to be expansion of trade-union membership, development of the Labour Party and promotion of 'Co-operative Societies (both of producers and consumers)'. Although the Labour executive gave great attention to the organization of both the unions and the party, it did not attempt to foster co-operatives. Certainly the small group who comprised the leadership of the Irish labour movement had their hands full with the first two tasks, and the leaders apparently assumed that the creation of co-operatives would be undertaken by an outside body. The co-operative movement—which had grown rapidly in the first two decades of the century—was based almost entirely in agricultural areas, where groups of farmers established co-ops, principally for the processing of dairy products. The leader of this movement was Horace Plunkett, who had founded the Irish Agricultural Organization Society in 1894. Plunkett's movement met with hostility from many of the Catholic clergy and from various nationalist politicians.[14] This may help to explain why so little was done to spread the co-operative idea in urban areas, either by the labour movement or by others. In any case, when in 1914 the party-congress was determining who should be eligible for inclusion in that body, it decided to exclude co-operative societies. The only co-operatives sponsored by trade unions were found in Belfast, where an active wholesale and consumer body had existed from the early years of the century, and in Dublin, where the Transport Union organized a co-operative clothing factory in the early 1920s. Yet the unofficial but explicit objective of the labour movement, proclaimed by both Larkin and Connolly, was the attainment of a co-operative commonwealth; in the case of the Transport Union, it was the official goal.[15]

The most important individual advocating the co-operative ideal was George Russell (AE), whose examination of rural Ireland, *The national being* (1918), has already been discussed in these pages. Russell saw co-operatives as eliminating the middle man and avoiding state control in a situation where the state was run by the same class that comprised the middle men.

AE held that the co-operative movement would also be the means of economic liberation of the town workers. 'The wages of the workers, little to the individual, yet a large part of the national income if taken for the mass', he declared, 'goes back to strengthen the system they protest against through purchases of domestic requirements.' The creation of co-operative stores should be the first constructive policy adopted by Irish labour: these stores would not only provide a 'labour commissariat' during strikes, but they would also bring about a democratization of the distribution trade, which would mean 'a large measure of control over production'. Further, the stores would create a 'tied trade' for co-operative workshops. Both of these forms of organization would 'assist trade unions gradually to transform themselves into co-operative guilds of producers, which should be their ultimate ideal'. These producer and consumer co-ops would enable 'the urban worker to enter into intimate alliance with the rural producer. Their interests are really identical.'[16]

14 Giovanni Costigan, *A history of modern Ireland*, pp. 266–67.

15 I.T.U.C. & L.P., *1914 report*, pp. 44–48; I.T.G.W.U., *Rule book*, 1909, preface.

16 *The national being* (Dublin, 1920 ed.), pp. 61–81, 92–97.

Over the next decade, Russell urged the labour movement to turn at least part of its energies to the development of co-operatives. Since 'it is certain there can never be a proletarian majority in the political sphere of things' in Ireland, he argued, 'we believe Irish Labour would do a thousand times more for itself if it concentrated more on co-operative action and acquired experience in the management of business.'[17] In 1927 he returned to this theme, pointing to 'extra-political lines of advance' employed by other labour movements. But in Ireland, 'The only tradition of direct action . . . is the tradition of the strike. The possibility of an economic revolution by the enterprise of labour until it becomes as securely integrated into the national being as capitalism has not been considered as it ought to be.'[18]

Both AE and Thomas Johnson hailed the provision in the Free State constitution which provided for the creation of vocational councils. The Free State government, however, made no move to establish the councils. Moreover, whereas the British government for many years had given a grant to the Irish Agricultural Organization Society, the grant was discontinued under the Free State. Although prior to 1922 Sinn Féin had many kind words for the methods and objectives of co-operativism, after independence neither the government party nor the republicans did anything to encourage the movement. The Free State government did, however, declare that there were too many non-producers and middlemen in the country, and Kevin O'Higgins, somewhat surprisingly, proposed that the Transport Union should sponsor a co-operative organization which would bring the consumer into direct relations with the producer.[19]

The Irish labour movement's lack of commitment to the development of co-operatives in the 1920s may be partially explained by the conditions of the time. The trade unions were on the defensive; wages had fallen and union membership had declined. The Labour Party, with few resources, was struggling to establish itself, and no Horace Plunkett arose in the labour movement to lead it on to the co-operative road.

INTERNATIONAL AFFILIATION

As has been mentioned in an earlier chapter, Irish labour severed itself from contact with European labour organizations in the 1920s. The party-congress was alone among representative labour bodies in Europe in not affiliating with either of the labour internationals. When an open conflict developed between the 'red' international in Moscow and the social democratic body, the executive decided against affiliation with either organization until the controversy was resolved. At the 1920 labour conference a group supporting affiliation with the communist

17 *Irish Homestead,* 11 Aug. 1923.

18 *Irish Statesman,* 28 May 1927.

19 T. deV. White, *Kevin O'Higgins* (1948 ed.), pp. 184–85. See also G. D. H. Cole on Irish co-operation. *Irish Economist,* May 1922.

international received considerable support, although the majority accepted the executive's position of temporary non-membership in either organization.[20] In 1923 and 1925, the executive declined invitations to join the re-organized socialist International Federation of Trade Unions or the Labour and Socialist International because the controversy concerning the proper organization of the international labour movement still existed.

With the party-congress opting out of the communist international, the Communist Party of Ireland, formerly the Socialist Party of Ireland, became the Irish affiliate. Following the C.P.I.'s collapse in the wake of the civil war, James Larkin's Irish Workers League assumed this position, and Larkin attended meetings in Moscow in 1924 and 1928.[21] The split in the Irish labour movement affected co-operation with other international labour bodies: an attempt to establish an Irish branch of the Workers International Relief Organization came to grief when the party-congress leadership refused to participate because it declined to share control with the Larkin group.

Although it had rejected invitations to join either the communist or the socialist international, the party-congress accepted an invitation to the 'British Commonwealth of Nations Labour Conference' in 1924. There was no question of affiliation, as the conference was an informal body, but the executive's participation was attacked by militantly nationalist delegates at the 1925 labour conference. The executive argued that the conference offered it the opportunity to explore relations between the states of the commonwealth, and that English labour legislation would have considerable effect on Irish labour 'whether they liked it or not'. It sent delegations to the 1928 and 1930 meetings of the conference.[22]

In 1927, in a rare commentary on labour affairs by a Catholic clergyman, an Irish Dominican proposed that the party-congress affiliate with the Christian International of Trade Unions, an organization of Catholic unions established in 1922. In an article in the *Irish Rosary* (June 1927), Rev. Ambrose M. Crofts, O.P., declared that both the socialist and the communist internationals were 'distinctly un-Christian and anti-Catholic in tendency', while 'Labour in Ireland is essentially Catholic; should it not openly show itself proudly in its true colours?' He urged this course on the party-congress as a means of overcoming the 'disrepute' into which Irish Labour had fallen due to anti-Catholic leaders', an apparent reference to Larkin. What Father Crofts obviously overlooked in his analysis of the labour movement was the large number of Protestant workers in the north. The party-

20 A resolution proposed by Eamonn Rooney, Walter Carpenter and the Dublin Trades Council criticizing the executive for its non-affiliation policy was defeated by a vote of 54 for, 97 against. I.L.P. & T.U.C., *1920 report*, pp. 97, 106–08.

21 Larkin, *James Larkin*, p. 275; *Irish Worker*, 27 Sept. 1924; *Irishman*, 19 May 1928.

22 *1924 report*, pp. 84, 150–51; *1925 report*, pp. 21. John Price, *The international labour movement*, p. 209.

congress was striving to maintain an all-Ireland organization, and affiliation with the Catholic international surely would have fractured this unity.

Throughout the decade the Labour executive appointed worker representatives to the Free State delegations which attended conferences of the International Labour Organization. The Free State was an active participant in the affairs of this body.[23] Apart from this affiliation, however, Irish labour stood outside the general international labour movement. The leadership's inability to decide which organization the Irish movement should join can only be characterized as sheer indecisiveness.

THE CATHOLIC CHURCH AND THE LABOUR MOVEMENT

That the Catholic clergy almost totally ignored the labour movement in the 1920s is not surprising: the church as a whole showed little interest in social questions at this time, and the labour movement had become less controversial. Connolly, who had carried on an extended debate with a priest concerning the mutuality of religion and socialism, was gone. Larkin was no longer Labour's champion; the danger that he might convert masses of good Catholic workmen to Marxism had passed. Further, labour organizations had given up saluting the Russian revolution around 1921. The 1918 Labour constitution was constructed in such a way as to avoid clerical censure. The actions and the policies of the labour movement had avoided church condemnation, but where was the support and the encouragement for Labour's struggle for social justice?

A small group of priests attempted to come to grips with the country's many social problems. In a letter to William O'Brien in 1921, Rev. Dr Peter Coffey, a Maynooth professor, declared, 'We all realize the wrongs and evils of the Capitalist system. . . . Personally I'm not in the least disposed to quarrel at such words and phrases as "class-war" and "revolution" and "Socialism", as long as the head and heart of the Irish labour movement keeps sound and Christian.' Father Coffey believed the best means to deal with social problems was not nationalization or common ownership, but 'diffusion of ownership, co-operation and share ownership'. The controversial Dr Walter McDonald discussed the labour question in a manner most sympathetic to the workers' position in his small book, *Some ethical aspects of the social question,* published in 1920. Among other priests who gave attention to this area, usually employing Catholic journals for their platform, were Father Thomas Finlay, Dr Patrick Moran, Father John Kelleher and the aforementioned Father Crofts.[24]

The Catholic bishops occasionally decried the fact that strong and willing men could not find work, but no serious attempt was made to

23 It has been claimed that it was through the I.L.O., rather than the League of Nations, that Ireland developed her international position. *Studies,* 25 Sept. 1926; *Irish Statesman,* 26 Oct. 1926.

24 Coffey to O'Brien, 23 April 1921, O'Brien papers, MS 13961(1).

apply the encyclicals of Leo XIII before the early 1930s. Writing in 1930, Father Edward Cahill asserted, 'In Ireland a Catholic social movement in the ordinary sense was practically impossible' because of the dominating issues of land, nationality and religion. Another view is that of Father James Good who stated in 1971 that the bishops had possession of Catholic social teaching in the 1920s but they misused this instrument: 'They might have used it to attack the massive social problems of Irish society—unemployment, bad housing, injustice and a dozen more. Instead, they kept it as a weapon to be used in an emergency—as the ultimate sanction to be hurled at the head of any politician who sought to change the status quo.'[25]

THE BRITISH GENERAL STRIKE

During the decade of the 1920s, indeed since 1894, the party-congress maintained no formal contact with either the British Labour Party or the British Trade Union Congress. Although it exchanged fraternal delegations with the Scottish Trade Union Congress, it did not do so with the English bodies, probably in order to avoid nationalist objections. Because of the close economic ties between the two islands, the British general strike of 1926 had a considerable effect on the Irish economy. Shipping between the two islands was held up for a week and Irish exporters claimed substantial damage through lost orders.

Confusion and lack of co-ordination characterized the relationship between the British and Irish leaderships during the strike. The British Trade Union Congress did not notify the Irish executive that it was calling the strike; the latter expressed 'surprise and regret' at this omission. At the beginning of the conflict Thomas Johnson sent a telegram offering the support of Irish Labour. This action, apparently made without the authority of the executive, was to become an issue during the political crisis of the following year. The Irish leadership adopted the policy of aiding the British strikers as far as it could, while at the same time it sought to prevent the strike from spreading to Ireland.

When Irish railwaymen and dockers refused to handle goods being shipped to England, the party-congress executive told exporters that until the British strike council 'notifies us that shipments from Ireland can with safety be resumed, shippers on this side would not be wise to send any goods forward'.[26] At this stage the executive unsuccessfully sought British Labour's permission to direct the activities of all unions in Ireland, including British-based unions, that might become involved in the strike. This action brought a torrent of criticism from the Irish press. The *Irish Times* thundered, 'Labour in this country has no quarrel with His Majesty's Government', adding that to hamper shipments to Britain would injure Irish industry. The *Dublin Evening*

25 James Good, review of John Whyte, *Church and state in modern Ireland*, 1923–70 (Dublin 1971), *Irish Times*, 23 April 1971. See pp. 62–67 of Whyte's book.

26 *Irish Times*, 10 May 1926.

Mail observed that the Irish Labour leaders were watching the progress of the strike 'with a good deal more interest than bodes well for this country'. Both the *Irish Independent* and the *Irish Times* published a letter from Henry Harrison, former Nationalist M.P. and Parnellite, in which he asked: 'Is Irish Labour patriotic or is it unpatriotic? . . . Does Irish Labour prefer British Labour interests to Irish interests, economic as well as national?' He added that some Irish unions were led by Englishmen.[27] When the strike was over, however, the *Irish Times* (13 May 1926) congratulated the Labour leadership for its 'restraint and caution' during the struggle. But the political opponents of the Labour Party pointed to the economic dislocation caused by the strike and attempted to maintain a public memory of the party's involvement in the affair.

In Ireland the principal consequence of the strike was the introduction of emergency legislation in both the Dublin and the Belfast parliaments. On the day the strike ended the Cosgrave government initiated a bill which would allow the state to take control of distribution of commodities in an emergency. In opposing the bill, the Labour Party claimed that it could be used to break legal strikes and threaten strikers with military conscription. The government, of course, denied that this was the intention of the legislation.[28] Labour's political organizer, Archie Heron, drew this lesson from the strike:

> The minority in the Irish labour movement which is opposed to political activity would be well advised to study the present situation in Britain, as an example of a big industrial struggle which has taken on a political complexion—viz., the workers' demand for nationalization and the employers utilization of the power of the State to crush the workers.[29]

It is noteworthy that Ireland, where strikes often occur, has never had a nation-wide general strike whose objective was economic. There were several national general strikes during the independence struggle, but all of these had political objectives. The nearest thing to an economically motivated national strike was the 1913 struggle in Dublin. Certainly the failure of the British effort in 1926 was a discouraging example.

THE CONTINUING LARKIN SPLIT

A constant factor in Labour's activities in the 1920s, from participation in the local elections to its role in the Dail, was the Larkin split. When Larkin failed to regain control of the Transport Union in 1923, he organized a rival union, the Workers Union of Ireland, the following year. Two-thirds of the Dublin members of the Transport Union went

27 *Irish Times, Dublin Evening Mail,* 10 May 1926. Harrison's letter appeared on 11 May 1926.

28 *Dail Eireann deb.,* xv, 1510–18; I.L.P. and T.U.C., *1926 report,* p. 65.

29 *Voice of Labour,* 8 May 1926.

over to the new union, but outside Dublin it had almost no success. Larkin's support was almost exclusively in the capital, just the area that the Labour Party desperately needed to build its strength. When the party attempted to develop a political organization in Dublin, it was constantly assaulted by the Larkinites. The Transport Union leadership under O'Brien fought back with a barrage of articles condemning Larkin, and all his works, in the Labour newspaper which it controlled, as well as publishing acrimonious handbills, several pamphlets filled with copies of letters, excerpts from speeches and courtroom testimony; the most important of these publications was *The attempt to smash the Irish Transport and General Workers Union,* which was printed in 1924. Larkin countered by distributing his own abusive handbills and by publishing a weekly newspaper, the *Irish Worker,* which achieved nothing like the circulation of its pre-war namesake. Larkin also had his great gift of public oratory, but by the mid-twenties the public had become satiated with inflammatory speeches. There was a wider effect to this lingering dispute. At the same time he was denouncing both the leaders of the trade unions and the Labour Party, Larkin continued to present himself as a spokesman of the Irish working class. The general public could only assume that the labour movement was divided against itself, incapable of either political or industrial responsibility.

Conflict between Larkin's union and the Transport Union continued unabated throughout the 1920s. The party-congress normally would have been the body to attempt to bring about a resolution of inter-union disputes. From the very beginning of this conflict, however, the Transport Union executive, led by William O'Brien, opposed any move in this direction because it held that Larkin's violent actions had made any settlement impossible. It was in a strong position to secure party-congress support in the Larkin split as it had a larger membership than all other unions combined in the Free State.[30] Further, the union had the confidence of the party-congress executive; indeed, O'Brien was a leading member of the Labour executive throughout this period, and for long after. Thus, the influence and strength of the Transport Union made certain that Larkin and his supporters would be kept out of the Labour conference.

At the 1924 meeting, O'Brien made this position plain: 'If any workers had been led astray by vilification and abuse, they would have to be given their heads, but by suffering and education they would learn their mistake and would come back to the true fold again.' Helena Molony warned the conference, however, of the danger of 'sinking into the conviction that they themselves were right and all the others wrong. They did not want Irish Labour to adopt a stick-in-the-mud

30 I.T.G.W.U., *The attempt to smash the Irish Transport and General Workers Union,* p. 108. In 1924 50,000 of the 100,000 workers in the Free State affiliated to the party-congress were Transport Union members. Larkin's union had about 15,000 members at this time.

policy while the free-lancers outside urged the workers to forge ahead.' But when her union, the Irish Women Workers Union, attempted to present a resolution urging that the meeting discuss the 'sharp points of difference' in the Larkin dispute, the Labour executive succeeded in squelching the move.[31]

In September of that year the party-congress executive went on record as supporting O'Brien and the Transport Union and condemning Larkin and his supporters. In a manifesto, *A call for unity,* it declared that the labour movement should be taking a dominant role in the reconstruction of the nation:

> This cannot be done if unions are to be weakened by internal dissension, where jealousy and envy take the place of goodwill and helpful criticism. Nor can it be accomplished by organizations which emanate from a craving for notoriety in any individual, whether he has attained international renown as a disruptionist or merely enjoys local fame as a shallow but shrewd 'chancer', lacking any knowledge of what is meant by trade unionism.[32]

The man of 1913 had shrunk, partly of his own doing, to the status of a spiteful troublemaker in the eyes of his former colleagues and subordinates. And his supporter, P. T. Daly, who had been prominent in the labour movement years before any of the present leaders, was dismissed as a mere opportunist.

This dispute sprang, in part, from a power struggle between two strong men, both of whom wanted to control the country's largest union. It also arose from a personality conflict between the careful, frugal, largely unimaginative trade union *apparatchik* and the dynamic but domineering and undisciplined workers' advocate. The conflict reflected differing philosophies: should the labour movement be pursuing a moderate, practical policy or should it be militant and activist? The split was Ireland's version of the division that occurred between social democrats and communists in almost every western country. During his years in America Larkin was active in various revolutionary socialist organizations, and shortly before his return home he was elected a member of the Moscow Soviet. In 1924 his Irish Workers League became the Irish affiliate of the 'red' international, and that same year Larkin attended a meeting of the organization in Moscow. There he supported a proposal to allow British communists to work within the official labour movement in Britain, at the same time that he was unable to do this in Ireland. He also attended the 1928 meeting, but his public stance as a communist was clearly a disadvantage in Ireland. Ever the individualist, he became disillusioned with international communism and severed his connection with that movement in the early 1930s.[33]

31 I.L.P. & T.U.C., *1924 report,* pp. 174, 179, 206. See also *1925 report,* p. 79.

32 I.L.P. & T.U.C., *1925 report,* pp. 32–33 and pamphlet dated 26 Sept. 1924.

33 Larkin, *James Larkin,* pp. 275–78, 290–92, 297.

Now an outcast from the 'official' labour movement, Larkin spent part of his enormous energy denouncing both the policy and leadership of the Labour Party. Through the pages of his weekly paper, the *Irish Worker,* he condemned the party as an imperialist appendage to the pro-British Free State government and, therefore, valueless to the workers. Larkin was especially hard on Thomas Johnson. In article after article ('The God save the king Labour Party', 'Johnsonian fudge', 'Johnson says to workers, love the boss; he's a good fellow') he poured on abuse. The English-born Larkin did not overlook Johnson's English birth. Finally Larkin went too far. In 1925 he accused Johnson of declaring in the Dail that workers who were unemployed must be shot down and that the government should use a scab army to break strikes. Johnson successfully sued Larkin and his paper for libel.[34]

The Larkin-Daly group did not enter candidates in the Dublin by-elections, but Larkin bitterly opposed the Labour Party nominees. He was again convicted of libel after he accused one of the Labour candidates of 'scabbing' in an earlier labour dispute.[35] In 1924 Daly had brought libel charges against William O'Brien and the Transport Union leadership. At issue was the union leaders' declarations that Daly had been expelled and condemned by the Irish Republican Brotherhood for misappropriation of funds before the war and that as secretary of the union's insurance section he had been guilty of 'gross mismanagement and neglect of duty'. Daly declared that these assertions had cost him a seat in the Dail. His libel action failed; as a result his reputation further suffered.[36]

Despite several beginnings, Larkin made no sustained effort to create a rival to the Labour Party. In the autumn of 1923 he established the Irish Workers League as a social and political body. At a Mansion House meeting the following March, Larkin announced the formation of a 'true Labour Party' and declared that a financial fund was to be opened. There the matter rested. In February 1925, however, the *Irish Worker* said that the workers' league was to be transformed into a 'revolutionary Workers' Party in Ireland'. The proposed programme for the party, far from being revolutionary, merely offered long-standing proposals for social and economic reform.[37] The following Easter Larkin's ally, the Dublin Trades Council, joined with the dissident Dundalk Trades Council in calling an 'All Ireland Labour Conference' to protest the official labour movement's lack of militancy concerning unemployment. All of these efforts by Larkin and his supporters proved to be ephemeral.

34 The libelous article appeared in *Irish Worker,* 18 Jan. 1925; for libel suit see *Voice of Labour,* 18 April 1925, and Johnson papers, N.L.I. MS 17149.

35 *Irish Worker,* 24 Jan. 1925; Larkin's 'elections bulletins', dated 24, 28 Feb. 1925 in National Library of Ireland; *Voice of Labour,* 14 Nov. 1925.

36 I.T.G.W.U., *P. T. Daly's libel suit,* pp. 2, 11–20, 30.

37 *Irish Worker,* 14 Feb. 14 March, 18 April 1925.

One reason that Larkin did not establish some sort of rival political organization at this time was that the pending local elections for the Dublin corporation were cancelled and the corporation dissolved. The Dublin Trades Council, stung by defeat in 1923, was no longer interested in this activity, Larkin's first commitment was to his struggling union, and at a time when a new national election was imminent, and all parties were busy organizing. Larkin ignored political activity. It is true to say, that organization was not his strongest point, and that a man of his impetuous nature could respond to a situation in an unpredictable manner.[38] Although Larkin was completely opposed to the Labour Party, there is no evidence that he directly supported the candidatures of any republicans or that he had any arrangement or connection with the anti-treaty forces in the mid-1920s. Larkin's assaults on the Labour candidates in the by-elections, of course, could not but have helped the republican standard-bearers. He maintained a sturdy, if lonely, independence of all organizations but his own at this time. He was strangely inactive when the next national election occurred in June 1927. Then, during the summer, the political crisis stirred his volcanic energies to action.

By this time his long-standing ally, P. T. Daly, and the Dublin Trades Council had wandered from allegiance. Disputes between Larkin and the council had occurred (beginning in 1925), and, his union, in poor financial condition, had not affiliated with the council. In 1926 the council sought to return to affiliation with the party-congress. Although it did not merge with the Dublin Workers' Council until 1929, good relations had been established between the two councils before the first general election of 1927. Thus the Labour Party entered the political campaign unhampered by its familiar scourges, Jim Larkin and the Dublin Trades Council.

The socialist left in the mid- and late 1920s was a desolate place. In addition to Larkin there was only the short-lived Workers Party of Ireland, launched in the spring of 1926 by Roddy Connolly and his sister Nora, Tom Lyng, a member of their father's original party, Capt. Jack White of Citizen Army fame and P. T. Daly, who was then seeking new allies. The party announced that its objective was a 'Workers' State', with sweeping nationalization and workers' control of industry. The initial span of the party paralleled that of its mimiographed weekly, the *Irish Hammer and Plough,* which was published from 22 May until 16 October 1926. When the party failed in its bid to replace Larkin's Irish Workers League as the Irish affiliate to the Communist International, the founding leaders abandoned the tiny body. But at a meeting held in February 1927, other members, led by George Pollock ('George McLay') and John Nolan, rejected the order of the Comintern that the party dissolve itself and decided to continue its operation. The result was another short-lived paper, the *Workers Republic* (26 March–

38 Interview with James Larkin, Jr., 3 Feb. 1966, Dublin Trades Council minutes, 11 June 1925.

December 1927). In the two general elections of 1927 the party offered not candidates but condemnation of the Free State.

In early 1928 the W.P.I. transformed itself into the James Connolly Workers Education Club, which led in turn to the establishment in late 1929 of Revolutionary Workers Groups in Dublin and Belfast (the chain ending with the birth of a new Communist Party of Ireland in June 1933). The party's sole achievement was the creation of a body called the Irish National Unemployed Movement, which continued as a pressure group until the early 1930s.[39] In the context of Irish politics, however, the left or the radical position was held by those who stood for basic constitutional change—the republicans.

LABOUR AND THE REPUBLICAN MOVEMENT

At the same time that the Labour Party was fighting off attacks from the Larkinites and developing its organizational base it was involved in a curious relationship with the republican movement. The battered anti-treaty forces had contested the 1923 election under the label of Sinn Fein and with the programme of the pre-treaty Sinn Fein body. With the election following so closely after the end of the civil war, the republicans received an encouraging and surprising one-third of the vote. A year later, following the release of Eamon de Valera from prison, the anti-treatyites revived their political organization, still called Sinn Fein, and drew up a revised party programme.

The party programme, as well as policy statements, revealed that the anti-treaty party would pursue a progressive policy in social and economic matters. The programme of March 1924 advocated improvements in social and working conditions, expanded technical education, imposition of tariffs, establishment of industrial councils, division of large land-holdings and creation of a national housing authority. Almost all of these proposals had already been put forward by the Labour Party. The Sinn Fein programme for local government also contained many progressive proposals, again items that Labour had sponsored previously.[40] De Valera presented himself as a friend of the workers. In September 1924 he declared that it was the 'essential duty' of the state to see that work was supplied for its citizens. The following January he declared his allegiance to the democratic programme. Now two major parties were committed to the objectives of the 1919 Dail document. Yet there remained fundamental differences. Sinn Fein was firmly abstentionist, while Labour actively participated in the Free State Dail. Labour sought a socialist Ireland, while Sinn Fein did not—this despite Constance de Markievicz's pamphleteering activities in which she proposed that the republicans should adopt the co-operative

39 Interview with John Nolan, 1 Dec. 1963; D. R. O'Connor Lysaght, *Republic of Ireland*, pp. 135–36.

40 Sinn Fein Re-organization Committee, *Sinn Fein's economic programme*. For the local government programme see *An Phoblacht*, 24 July 1925. For a study of Sinn Fein in this period see thesis of Peter Pine, 'Sinn Fein, 1923–26', University College, Dublin.

movement as the model for the new Ireland.[41] Sinn Fein stood for an independent Irish republic, while Labour was prepared to accept the Free State as a means towards total national self-determination.

When de Valera broke with Sinn Fein and established Fianna Fail in 1926, the new party's constitution contained a largely progressive social and economic policy. It advocated the development of a 'social system equal in opportunity as far as possible', wide-spread distribution of land and the creation of a self-sufficient economy by means of a protective tariff policy. It further declared that the 'resources and wealth of Ireland are subservient to the needs and welfare of all the people . . .'.[42] There is a view that the anti-treaty political forces did not develop a progressive socio-economic programme until the late 1920s or early 1930s, but the fact is that this policy dates to 1924. This is not to say, however, that the anti-treatyites placed primary emphasis on this programme—political issues always were to the forefront. But the combination of a progressive socio-economic policy and militant nationalism proved to be most attractive to the electorate.

There was an uneven relationship between the Labour Party and the anti-treatyites. Labour criticized the republicans for abstaining from the Dail and urged them to enter the parliament, thereby greatly strengthening the opposition to the Cosgrave government. Statements of the party leadership were generally moderate in tone in reference to the republican leaders, but Labour backbenchers occasionally cast bitter words in their direction. For example, Richard Corish in 1925 declared that he would prefer to see the government party candidates win by-elections 'anytime they are up against people who do not want any Government in the country'.[43]

On the other side, Labour was attacked continually in the pages of the anti-treaty publications. The republican papers were *Eire* (1923–24), *Sinn Fein* (1923–25) and *The Nation* (1925–31), all of which reflected the views of the de Valera leadership, and *An Phoblacht* (1925–26, 1927–28), an Irish Republican Army newspaper edited by Peadar O'Donnell. These papers attacked Labour for accepting the treaty and for harbouring 'anti-national' opinion. Some of the charges—for example, that the party had attempted to split national unity in 1918 and that it had supported executions during the civil war—were blatant distortions. Johnson, by fact of his English birth, offered these organs a convenient target for abuse. When the Cosgrave regime pursued a conservative social and economic policy, the republicans declared that the Labour Party was to suffer the consequences for its acceptance of the treaty.

41 Jacqueline Van Voris, *Constance de Markievicz: in the cause of Ireland*, pp. 330–31; see also pp. 336–37.

42 *An Phoblacht*, 23 April, 17 Dec. 1926.

43 On another occasion, Corish charged that the republicans had made 'the greatest contribution of any party . . . to unemployment'. Another severe critic was T. J. Murphy. *Dail Eireann deb.*, xi, 711; ix, 2036; *Irish Independent*, 10 Dec. 1925.

At first *An Phoblacht* declared there was a need for a strong, nationally minded Labour Party, but that the present 'opportunist' leadership would have to be removed. Later, as the anti-treatyite political machinery was developed, it held that the Labour Party was paying too much attention to political matters while ignoring the growing problems of the industrial side of the labour movement. *Eire* saw a 'clear distinction between the Trade Union movement in Ireland and the Labour Party' whose record in the national struggle 'is a funny one'. The anti-treaty press further attempted to undermine Labour by occasional laudation of James Larkin for his appreciation of Irish national aspirations.[44]

The anti-treaty fire was not unrelenting. On 23 February 1924, *Eire*, in the wake of Labour and republican co-operation in the Dublin corporation to defeat the wage-cutting proposals of the Cosgrave government, raised the question of a Labour-republican 'working agreement'. Since the enemies of both parties were the same and 'the objectives they have at heart are really the same', it asked, 'what is the objection?' Replying for the Labour Party in the *Voice of Labour* (28 February 1924), Archie Heron declared that there could be no Labour-republican co-operation as long as the republicans refused to enter the Dail and join in Labour's fight against the regressive socio-economic policy of the government. The question of Labour-republican co-operation was next broached by de Valera shortly before the next general election.

Declaring his support of the 'democratic programme' in January 1925, de Valera recalled that the Labour leaders had said they would accept the treaty because it provided the means to put the programme into effect. He said this had not happened; Labour should have foreseen that 'it was a backward and not a forward movement from the economic point of view to accept the treaty'.[45] Labour replied in an 'open letter', arguing that if de Valera accepted the programme's statement that it was the 'first duty' of the government to assure that no child went hungry, 'then disputes and contentions about forms of government would give place to an endeavour to find the best means of fulfilling that first duty'. It questioned the republicans' ability to implement the programme if they won a majority of Dail seats yet refused to use the constitutional machinery of the Free State.[46] *Sinn Fein* (24 January) could only reply by declaring that the anti-treatyites would not enter the Dail because this would entail a violation of what it called the 'anti-imperialist clauses' in the programme.

Labour and the anti-treaty parties also clashed in the by-elections. The anti-treatyites claimed that Labour participation split the opposition vote. The Labour Party held that when a republican candidate went forward political issues dominated the campaign, and

44 See *Eire*, 23 Feb., 15 March 1924; *An Phoblacht*, 21 Aug., 23 Oct. 1925, 22 Jan., 29 July, 13, 20 Aug. 1926.

45 *Irish Times*, 5 Jan. 1925.

46 Broadsheet dated 10 Jan. 1925 and *Voice of Labour*, 17 Jan. 1925.

social and economic questions were submerged. When Labour won its only by-election, without a republican in the field, the *Voice of Labour* (7 February 1926) stated, 'The result is proof positive that it is only the opposition of abstentionist Republicans that keeps the Government in power and enables them to return candidates.' Labour's transfer votes generally did not go to the anti-treaty candidates.[47]

The one attempt of Labour and the republicans to form a common policy ended in failure. The event that drew the two parties, as well as other political groups, together to create a united front was the Boundary Settlement Bill of 1925. It is apparent that the Labour Party urged the anti-treaty deputies to enter the Dail as the only means of defeating the agreement. This they did not do. The anti-treatyites urged the labour deputies to leave the Dail as a protest; this Labour refused to do. To conceal their failure to agree on a common policy, the two parties made the gesture of appointing a committee to oppose the legislation; nothing further was heard of it.[48]

This attempt at co-operative action had the effect of worsening relations between Labour and republicanism. At this juncture there could be no meaningful collaboration between a party participating in the parliamentary system and a party which refused to accept the legitimacy of the governing body. Neither party, however, closed the door on future co-operation. De Valera had said that he could not work with a small group in the Dail under the leadership of Professor Magennis because its members had taken the oath. Despite the prompting of the I.R.A. newspaper, he did not take the same position in regard to the Labour party. On Labour's side, the conditions laid down by Johnson in 1926 under which his party would form a parliamentary alliance with any other party did not include political or constitutional considerations, and, thus, did not bar the possibility of a Labour-republican arrangement.[49]

There were good reasons why Labour might not have wanted to join forces with the republicans at this time. The party was struggling to become the second largest in the country, to fulfill its role of official opposition. It could do this only by maintaining an independent policy and image; close co-operation with the anti-treatyites would have blurred this appearance. Further, the republicans were believed to be in general disfavour not only for their part in the civil war but also for their refusal to enter the Dail. There were some political observers who saw the anti-treatyites declining in political influence and support. The Irish correspondent of *Round Table* was one of these. In 1926 he

47 *Irish Independent,* 19 Jan. 1925; *Voice of Labour,* 25 Oct., 1, 8, Nov. 1924; *An Phoblacht,* 7 March 1926; *Voice of Labour,* 20 March 1926.

48 Johnson and de Valera were appointed joint-chairmen of the committee. *Dublin Evening Mail,* 8 Dec. 1925. See also statement of T. J. Murphy, *Irish Independent,* 10 Dec. 1925.

49 The three conditions put forward by Johnson proposed action to stimulate the economy and employment. *Irish Times,* 1 Nov. 1926.

declared his conviction that republicanism had ceased to be a serious political force because it was split into two 'irreconcilable factions'; he doubted if both together would elect ten deputies at the next election. Shortly before the election, however, he revised his prediction, estimating that half the republican deputies would be defeated as a result of their abstentionist policy. He had earlier pointed out in regard to Labour that 'no party stands to gain more by the Republican debacle'; had Labour the financial support and a strong rural organization, 'it might easily become the centre of a real and effective opposition'.[50] To both Labour and the republicans the pending general election began to take on the appearance of a scramble for the succession.

50 *Round Table,* Sept. 1926, June 1927, June 1926.

10
On the Edge of Power

THE JUNE 1927 ELECTION

As the time for the general election approached, the Labour Party devoted late 1926 and early 1927 to political organization. Local party groups were established, funds collected and candidates selected. As membership in the trade unions had begun to decline in the mid-1920s, the party chose to organize a voluntary political activity fund, rather than raise the party-congress affiliation fees. The 'hundred thousand shillings' fund succeeded in raising a 'substantial' amount, but William O'Brien, the party's treasurer, estimated that £60,000 would be necessary to run candidates for every seat. As is the case to-day, a deposit of a £100 was required from each candidate, and individual election expenses were estimated at £300 to £500. The party executive spent only about £3,600 on the campaign, but individual Labour candidates received funds from their unions and from personal contributions.[1]

Compared to its rivals, Labour was gravely underfinanced. Both Cumann na nGaedheal and Fianna Fail purchased huge amounts of space in the national press, whereas the Labour Party only placed one small advertisement, entitled 'The big guns boom'. Cumann na nGaedheal received contributions from businessmen while Fianna Fail was largely dependent on funds from America; de Valera spent the spring of 1927 there collecting.[2]

Labour, nevertheless, viewed the coming election with considerable confidence. The party felt that its socio-economic message had been drowned out by political issues in the 1923 election. Since that time the Cosgrave government had revealed a relatively conservative attitude towards social welfare and economic development. Further, the country was far from prosperous. The anti-treatyites, Labour felt, had lost public favour by their continued abstention from the Dail. Meanwhile, the Labour Party had established some reputation for responsibility and seriousness through its role of official opposition.

No fewer than seven parties, plus a large number of independent candidates, contested the election, which was set for 9 June. Cumann na nGaedheal nominated ninety-six candidates. There was a total of 104 anti-treaty candidates—87 for Fianna Fail, 15 for Sinn Féin, plus 2 independent republicans. The Farmers Party, rent by the accession of its leaders to Cumann na nGaedheal, nominated only thirty-eight. Professor Magennis's Clan Eireann put forward eight candidates, while the recently organized National League nominated thirty, including a dozen former Nationalist M.P.s; an event which marked

1 Irish Labour Party and Trade Union Congress, *1927 report*, pp. 11,15; *Irish Statesman*, 2 April 1927; *An Dion* (the journal of the Post Office Workers Union), April 1927.

2 During the first eighteen months of its existence, Fianna Fail had receipts of £30,407 with £29,762 coming from America and Australia. *Irish Times*, 26 Nov. 1926.

the return of the Nationalist politicians to Irish public life. There were fifty-seven independent candidates including five independent labour candidates in Munster.[3]

The Labour Party nominated forty-four candidates, three less than in 1923. The party executive 'desired' that Labour candidates be nominated in every constituency, but Cavan and Monaghan went uncontested. The executive was further disappointed that the new machinery for nomination—the panel of candidates nominated by the affiliated organizations—did not result in a larger number of candidates. British-based unions 'found it impossible or difficult' to submit nominations because their rules were not designed to support candidates for the Irish parliament. The Amalgamated Society of Woodworkers, with 7,000 Irish members, said it could not nominate Labour candidates in Ireland because its political fund was only for British parliamentary elections. R. J. P. Mortished, the party-congress assistant secretary, declared that it was 'absurd' that Irish members should pay funds to British elections and demanded that a separate political fund for Irish elections should be established in British-based unions. 'Quite a number' of Irish unions failed to respond to the invitation to nominate candidates. This situation is partially explained by the fact that the unions were experiencing declining memberships and revenue.[4]

The party's failure to nominate enough candidates to form a possible alternative government was widely noted by the press and criticized by rival parties. Johnson's response was that 'the Labour Party had a sense of realities and could not afford to hand over to the Government three or four thousand pounds in forfeited deposits.' He also put forward the rather unimpressive argument that if forty of the forty-four Labour candidates were elected, 'they would have in the Dail a Labour Party proportionally as strong as the Labour Party in Denmark, Finland, Sweden or Germany, and stronger than the Labour Party in Britain, Switzerland, Norway and France.' Although the party could not form an alternative government, Johnson held that 'the larger the minority in the Dail, the greater is the check upon reaction and rushed legislation.'[5] Neveretheless, the relatively small number of candidates put forward by Labour was an admission that, after five years in the

3 *Irish Independent*, 2 June 1927. 'Independent Labour' candidates stood in Munster throughout this period. They differed from the Labour Party's nominees in that they were generally neither workers nor trade unionists; rather they usually were grocers or publicans. There were two independent labour deputies in the 1923–27 Dail—John Daly of Cork and Sean Lyons, a former Labour Party deputy. The Labour Party received considerable support in rural Munster. Both Johnson and T. J. Murphy attribute Labour's strength in Munster to the effect of the Land and Labour Associations established under the inspiration of Michael Davitt in the 1890s. Interview with Donal Nevin, 10 Nov. 1964; *Irish Times*, 18 Nov. 1965.

4 *1927 report*, pp. 9, 11–12. The party originally had expected to nominate fifty candidates. *Irish Times*, 13 Dec. 1926. The British-based Amalgamated Transport and General Workers Union offered to support any of its members that were nominated, but none were. *Irishman*, 30 July 1927; *1927 report*, pp. 9, 57–58.

5 *Irish Independent*, 8 June 1927.

political arena, the party had not accumulated enough support to present itself as a party capable of forming an alternative government.

The list of Labour candidates included no new figures of national importance. Although the party had broadened its political philosophy (for example, in its agricultural policy), its candidates were again overwhelmingly trade unionists; none of them were farmers or professional men, (other than teachers). Of the forty-four Labour candidates, twenty-seven were trade union officials; eighteen of the forty-four belonged to the Irish Transport Union, twenty-three to other unions and only four were not known to be trade union members. In contrast, the Cumann na nGaedheal candidates were overwhelmingly from the business and professional classes—merchants, doctors, lawyers, farmers, and auctioneers.[6] However, Cumann na nGaedheal did include a couple of trade unionists among its nominees. The National League also nominated two men with trade union connections—J. Coburn for Louth and D. Hinchin, former member of the Cork Trades Council. Although Fianna Fail claimed it was representative of the workers as well as of everybody else, most of its nominees were from the lower middle-class—generally teachers, farmers and small businessmen; there was no trade unionist prominent amongst its candidates.[7]

William O'Brien, who had formerly stood for Dublin south, was nominated for County Tipperary. This move, together with the unexplained inactivity of James Larkin, secured a peaceful Dublin Labour scene during the campaign.[8] A further factor was that the formerly pro-Larkin Dublin Trades Council, moving towards amalgamation with the 'official' Dublin Workers Council, did not nominate candidates. The Labour Party made a determined effort to establish itself in Dublin in this election; it nominated three candidates for Dublin north and three for Dublin south, as well as two for County Dublin. The party also conducted a vigorous campaign in Cork city, where it also had failed to elect any candidates in the previous election.

The party employed one novel campaign technique: several of its speakers were six-county Labour leaders, including two Labour M.P.s. The northerners proclaimed the Labour Party as the only all-Ireland party and warned that the Cosgrave government was damaging the possibility of national unity by its reactionary social and economic policy. Another feature of the Labour campaign was the use of electioneering newspapers in agricultural areas where the party was attempting to gain the support of small farmers and farm labourers;

6 Of the Labour nominees who were not union officials, two were agricultural workers, two were teachers, four were railway workers and one was a coal dealer. *Irish Times*, 8 June 1927.

7 Sean MacEntee, candidate in County Dublin, had been active in the labour movement in Belfast, but he does not appear to have stressed this background in his campaign. Interview with William McMullen, 30 Nov. 1965.

8 James Larkin, Jr. had no explanation of his father's inactivity in this election, but simply laid it to the unpredictable nature of the man. Interview, 3 February 1966.

in the Sligo-Leitrim constituency the Labour paper was entitled *The Farmer—Labour Liberator*.[9]

Social and Economic Programmes and Issues

Labour's 1927 election programme was very similar to its 1922 and 1923 programmes. Although the party still upheld the goal of a co-operative commonwealth, its programme laid stress on the need for social and economic reform. Labour declared that it did not propose to nationalize land or industry; rather, it proposed that employment be created for all by means of large-scale housing and public work schemes, enforced domestic spending of incomes and investment, guaranteed prices for farmers, and increased welfare and educational expenditure. Industrial development would be fostered by a national system of technical education, industrial research and the use of loans, credits and tariffs. Its agricultural proposals stressed the need to encourage tillage and farm improvements; this was to be accomplished through tax allowances, marketing boards and extension of credit facilities.[10]

This programme, Labour declared, was 'constructive', a 'practical, almost humdrum affair', with its dominating principle being 'that the powers of the State ought to be used for the common welfare. . . . It is the immediacy and coherence of the Labour Party's programme that stands out in contrast with the "high-falutin" promises offered by the other parties.' Further, the party saw itself as being 'responsible' and restrained; it felt that it was not guilty of excessive promises, although it recognized that this policy would cost it votes.

Labour warned the voters to beware of 'fake politics' that it said were perpetrated by the other two major parties:

> The electorate has had enough of playboy politics . . . to mask, on the one side, a lazy-minded refusal to face facts, and, on the other, a fear of progress. . . . The electorate are being asked to believe that the real contest is between the two parties and that they must vote for one or the other of them. And both use the poverty of the Labour Party as an argument against it, lacking any other argument.[11]

The Cumann na nGaedheal programme dealt mostly with the need to preserve stable, constitutional government and the necessity of continuing the process of 'nation building'. On social and economic matters the government party pointed with pride to its accomplishments but made no significant promises of improvements in these

9 *Irish Independent*, 9, 30 May, 7 June 1927; interview with Archie Heron, 30 Nov. 1964.

10 *Irishman*, 14 May, 4 July 1927. *Irishman*, a weekly newspaper controlled by the party-congress, succeeded the *Voice of Labour* in May 1927. The *Voice* had followed the party line but was the organ of the Transport Union. 1927 saw the re-appearance of a number of party newspapers, for the first time since 1922.

11 *Irishman*, 21 May, 4 June 1927 statement by Johnson, *Dail Eireann deb.*, xx, 177–78.

matters in future. Labour attacked the government's lack of progress in social and educational reform, but at the same time devoted considerable attention to Fianna Fail's policy of abstention, which it declared could not possibly do the workers any good.

A key struggle in this election was the battle between the Labour Party and Fianna Fail for the votes of the workers, both agricultural and industrial. As has been seen, Fianna Fail had developed a programme which was decidedly attractive to the workers. To Thomas Johnson de Valera's party had stolen Labour's clothes: 'The Fianna Fail programme contains fifteen items of which twelve were identical with the Labour programme at the last elections'. However, the Fianna Fail programme differed from the Labour programme on at least two important points. Firstly, Fianna Fail advocated the establishment of a total tariff wall to encourage Irish industry, while Labour continued to urge the adoption of a variety of measures, including tariffs, to stimulate economic growth. Secondly, Fianna Fail said it would withhold payment of land purchase annuities to Britain, while the Labour Party did not mention this issue.

There was another difference between the two parties, one observed many times by Johnson: his party was in the Dail where its programme could be implemented, and Fianna Fail was not. In reply, Fianna Fail said that the Labour Party could not carry out its programme because it had not nominated enough candidates to form a government and would continue to be a helpless minority in the Dail; 'The workers' true hope is in Fianna Fail, which is putting forward 115 candidates for election.' It charged Labour with doing everything in its power to prevent the return of the 'only possible alternative government.'[12]

Sean Lemass, already a leading figure in Fianna Fail, attacked Labour's policy on unemployment. He said this policy was defective because it relied too much on the 'dole'. Dismissing Labour's proposals for stimulation of industry, he declared that only Fianna Fail acknowledged the right of every man to work and was prepared to use the credit of the state for national schemes.[13] The Labour retort was that 'if it were not for the destructive tendencies of Mr. Lemass and his party, thousands of workers now idle would be usefully employed.'[14]

Although the subject was never mentioned by Labour Party speakers during the campaign, de Valera indicated that his party was prepared to work with the Labour Party, since their positions on social and economic issues were roughly similar. Speaking in Tipperary, where Labour was conducting a vigorous campaign, de Valera expressed 'regret' that there should be any differences between Labour and 'Republicanism' because the differences 'were due almost entirely to

12 *Nation*, 14 May 1927. See also ibid., 21, 28 May 1927 and *Irish Independent*, 23 May 1927.

13 *Irish Independent*, 14, 19 May 1927. An article in the *Irish Rosary* (May 1927) was sharply critical of the use of 'doles'; it did not mention the Labour Party.

14 Statement by Sen. J. T. O'Farrell, *Irish Independent*, 17 May 1927.

misunderstanding of each other's policy'. He declared that every effort he had made to work 'hand in hand' with Labour 'had been spurned'.[15] Labour interpreted de Valera's statement as an attempt to lure away Labour votes.

The other parties made little attempt to appeal directly for workers' support. The National League offered only a town tenants bill for the protection of tenants, while it declared that something should be done for the unemployed. Professor Magennis's Clan Eireann stressed the need for the reduction in taxation, especially income tax, and a policy of protection. Sinn Fein, which put forward but fifteen candidates, presented the vague declaration that it was 'for labour'.[16]

Political and Constitutional Issues

Despite the exertions of the Labour Party, political rather than social and economic issues dominated the campaign. The government party declared that the principal issue was the maintenance of the treaty and the constitution. Fianna Fail demanded that the oath of allegiance must be removed. It stated that after the elections its victorious candidates would enter the Dail without taking the oath. Huge advertisements proclaimed that 'Fianna Fail is going in' and the readers were left to interpret the exact meaning of the words.

Although the Labour Party had consistently opposed the oath and had stated that socio-economic issues should predominate in the campaign, Johnson felt constrained to challenge the republicans to clarify their position concerning the oath and entrance into the Dail. He foresaw violence if a majority was returned which refused to take the oath, but yet attempted to take control of the government. Johnson queried de Valera: 'If the oath were removed by agreement or otherwise . . . is the Fianna Fail party willing to go into the Dail and work the Constitution for ten years and make the most of it without any further changes?'. De Valera replied to the question with a question:

> Mr. Johnson had said that the Constitution had been accepted by the majority of the people, but he asked if Mr. Johnson would admit a majority vote given now for the first time against the oath as a vote of the people.[17]

Johnson's caution is clearly seen in his assertion that alteration of the oath 'probably' would not result in war with England. 'but . . . it would provoke such an upheaval in commerce and industry, and such a destruction of the still growing sense of stability that the consequences to the country would be very grave indeed.' He added, 'We have had one revolution and one revolution in a generation is enough.'[18]

15 'De Valera and Miss Labour', editorial, *Dublin Evening Mail*, 4 June 1927.

16 *Irish Independent*, 17 May 1927; *Cork Examiner*, 28 May 1927.

17 *Irish Independent*, 18 May, 6 June 1927.

18 Ibid., 31 May; *Sunday Independent*, 5 June 1927.

Johnson's challenge to Fianna Fail received high praise and prominent display in the *Irish Times* and the *Irish Independent*, both of which opposed any constitutional changes. As well, government ministers lauded Johnson and his party for providing a constructive opposition in the Dail. To Johnson, this 'fulsome patronizing praise' was designed to damage his chances of re-election. These accolades for Johnson set off a wave of anger in the ranks of the warriors of Ir. The Fianna Fail weekly the *Nation* reverted to 1916:

> The *Independent* demanded the execution of Connolly because, with Larkin, they smashed the tyranny of the sweating employers and are still hounding Larkin. . . . They have now however discovered a Labour leader after their own heart. . . . He will never smash any tyranny—native or foreign. He is entirely 'safe' and entirely respectable.

The I.R.A. publication, *An Phoblacht* viewed Johnson as an English imperialist who could not understand Irish nationalism.[19]

Cumann na nGaedheal concentrated on warning about the dangers of coalition government. The electoral system, the large number of candidates and widespread discontent with the Cosgrave ministry made this a distinct possibility. The government party argued that a republican government would mean chaos and a coalition government weakness and instability; in Cosgrave's words, 'There is only one possible ministry'. Only the National League leader William Redmond supported the idea of a coalition government. The Labour Party avoided the subject, except to deny a report that it had been approached by Cumann na nGaedheal on the matter.

As in the other elections in the 1920s, priests of all ranks presided and spoke at Cumann na nGaedheal meetings, as well as acting as nominators of government party candidates. At least one priest presided at a Fianna Fail meeting in this election; in other elections the anti-treatyites always had a few priests as speakers. On the other hand, there is no example of a clergyman of any denomination appearing at a Labour Party meeting or indicating in any way support for the party. During the time of the Larkin and Connolly leadership the clergy often denounced the labour movement for adopting socialism and syndicalism. After 1916, on the rare occasion when a priest addressed himself to the labour movement, it was to warn the Labour leaders to avoid the anti-Catholic social and economic teachings of their predecessors.[20]

Election Results

Cumann na nGaedheal was reduced to forty-seven seats, a loss of thirteen. This meant that the Cosgrave government would not have a

19 *Nation*, 11 June 1927; *An Phoblacht*, 10 June 1927.

20 Rev. L. Kelliher, S.T.L., in *Dublin Saturday Post*, 20 Jan. 1917; Fr. Delahunty in *New Ireland*, 9 Nov. 1918; Rev. Lambert McKenna, S.J., *Social teachings of James Connolly*; Rev. Ambrose Crofts, O.P., in *Irish Rosary*, June 1927; *Voice of Labour*, 20 October 1923.

majority of sitting deputies in the new Dail. Fianna Fail captured a surprising forty-four seats and Sinn Fein won seven, raising the combined anti-treaty number from forty-seven to fifty-one. The National League elected eight and the Farmers Party was reduced from thirteen to eleven. The number of successful independents remained at fourteen. The most significant advance in the number of seats won was made by the Labour Party, which elected twenty-two; it had held fourteen seats in the previous Dail.

In the number of first preference votes won, however, Labour's advance was much less impressive. In this election it received 143,000 first votes, which was only 18,000 more than it had received in 1923. At the same time, the combined anti-treaty vote soared from 288,000 to 340,000, while the Cumann na nGaedheal vote plunged from 409,000 to 312,000.[21] Labour maximized the value of its first preferences by putting forward more than one candidate in areas where it already had considerable strength; the result was that the party elected two members each in four districts—Tipperary, Leix-Offaly, Wexford and Limerick. An embarrassing interlude was ended when Labour regained representation in the two major cities, with two seats in Dublin and one in Cork.[22]

Rivalling Labour's advance as the most significant outcome of the election was the impressive showing of the anti-treaty parties. Despite some dire predictions, Fianna Fail and Sinn Fein together elected more deputies than did the government party. The continued and growing appeal of the anti-treaty parties, especially Fianna Fail, was due to two principal factors. First, Fianna Fail blunted criticism of its abstentionist past by declaring that it would enter the next Dail without taking the oath. Second, both Fianna Fail and Sinn Fein presented socio-economic programmes attractive to wage-earners and the unemployed. Johnson believed that this factor was the principal cause of Fianna Fail's success. Other and probably equally important factors were the public disenchantment with the Cosgrave regime and the fact that Fianna Fail had put forward enough candidates to form an alternative government.

21 First preference votes

	1923	*1927*	dissolution seats at	seats won
Labour Party	125,000	143,000	14	27
Cummann na nGaedheal	409,000	312,000	60	47
Fianna Fail	———	299,000	—	44
Sinn Fein	288,000	41,000	47	7
Farmers Party	124,000	101,000	11	13
National League	———	83,000	2	8
Clann Eireann	———	5,000	2	0
Independents	106,000	154,000	14	14

22 Labour also gained seats in Longford-Westmeath, Mayo south; it had a near miss in Donegal. The only Labour candidate to lose the seat he held at dissolution was William Norton who was narrowly defeated in County Dublin, where Johnson retained his seat with difficulty. I.L.P. & T.U.C., *1927 report*, p. 12; *Irish Independent*, 13 June 1927.

Judging by the type of candidate elected to the Dail, this election gives no indication of any marked shift to the left, towards radical solutions of social and economic problems by the Irish public. Only one of the independent labour candidates was elected; several lost their deposits.[23] However, the election of a large number of anti-treaty candidates demonstrated that militant nationalism still had great appeal.

Although Labour had calculated that it would win twenty-four seats, Johnson commented that the results were 'satisfactory' to his party. He further declared, 'Despite the efforts of Fianna Fail and Cumann na nGaedheal, assisted by the newspapers, to make the treaty and the oath the dominant issue once again' the election had shown that 'many thousands of voters were determined to force social and economic issues to the forefront'. It was the view of Senator O'Farrell that Labour 'has now definitely established itself in the public life of the country'.

Four factors helped Labour in this election. First, the party was one of the beneficiaries of the widespread discontent with the failure of the Cosgrave government to create favourable social and economic conditions. Second, the public responded to Labour's constructive and serious programme of action. A third factor was the respect won by the party for its able and responsible opposition in the Dail. Finally, the considerable effort devoted to building up the 'grass roots' party organization had its reward.

The party recognized that its failure to put forward a sufficient number of candidates to form a possible alternative government was a severe handicap to its hopes of eventually growing to be the principal opposition party. But, the party could not do so because it could not raise enough money to finance wider political activity.[24] It was not in a position to pay for nomination deposits in districts where its candidates would have little chance of election and where the party could not finance adequate campaigns. It was estimated that Fianna Fail spent £30,000 in the election,[25] while Cumann na nGaedheal demonstrated that it also had plenty of money to spend. By comparison, the Labour Party was poverty stricken. It relied heavily on the trade unions for contributions and support and by the late twenties the unions were losing members. The party hoped that its success in the election would stimulate the unions to renewed growth, but the decline in membership continued.

Another factor which very likely militated against Labour's electoral chances was that its programme was too restrained, too responsible. Johnson held the view that Labour would have won many more seats and, correspondingly, would have deprived Fianna Fail of a 'big

23 The successful candidate was John Daly, County Cork. J. Butler, the Labour deputy from Waterford who resigned from that party in Jan. 1927, stood as an independent labour candidate but was defeated.

24 I.L.P. & T.U.C., *1927 report*, p. 41.

25 *Round Table*, Sept. 1927.

proportion' of its vote, if 'we had gone through the country with the propaganda of the extremists'.[26] Certainly the other major parties were considerably less restrained in both their speeches and their proposals. Labour's admittedly 'hum-drum' programme did not succeed in capturing the public imagination.

The Labour Party attained the success in June 1927 that it had expected to achieve in 1923. The party saw its advance in this election as an important step towards future growth. Unfortunately for Labour, this election was the high water mark of the party fortunes for decades. The party was not even to equal this performance until 1965, thirty-eight years later.

THE BUSINESS OF GOVERNMENT: THE SHORT DAIL

As a result of the election, the Cosgrave government found itself without majority support in the new Dail. In the last Dail it did have a majority of the sitting members—60 members out of a total of 105, 55 being a majority (with 47 elected deputies abstaining). In the new Dail the government party had only 47 members out of a total of 101, 51 being a majority (with 51 members not taking their seats). The possibility of stable government was slight; indeed, this Dail was to last barely two months.

Shortly after the election, reports circulated that Cumann na nGaedheal would not attempt to form a new government but would leave this decision up to the Dail. Other reports said that the Cosgrave government would not attempt to form a coalition ministry with any other party. The Labour Party denied rumours that it might seek to enter a coalition with Cumann na nGaedheal.[27] At meetings held on 20 and 22 June, immediately before the opening of the Dail, Labour decided to nominate its leader for the presidency only if Cosgrave refused to form a government. The party took the opportunity to re-elect Johnson and the other party leaders. William O'Brien, who was returned for Tipperary, assumed no party position but was definitely considered part of the leadership. On the eve of the inauguration of the new Dail, it appears that Labour made no attempt to seek agreement with the other non-government parties concerning an alternative government.

The period between the election and the meeting of the Dail was one of considerable activity for Fianna Fail. It was seeking to gain the support of other non-government parties for its attempt to enter the Dail without taking the oath of allegiance. In its issue of 18 June the *Nation* complained that Johnson and his party were not being co-operative, that without Fianna Fail in the Dail, Labour would be hopelessly outvoted on social and economic issues. With Fianna Fail in the body, it declared, the two parties could put through the many social and eco-

26 *Dail Eireann deb.*, xx, 177–78.

27 *Irish Independent*, 21 June 1927. *Dublin Evening Mail*, 15 June 1927; *Cork Examiner*, 22 June 1927.

nomic measures on which they were in agreement. The *Irish Independent* on 23 June reported that de Valera's party approached Labour, as well as other parties, with the request that it abstain from the Dail for a few days as a protest against the oath, but that this plea was refused.

Opening day of the Dail saw the abortive attempt of the Fianna Fail deputies to take their seats. They were turned away when they refused to take the oath. Following this rebuff, de Valera announced that his party would begin the necessarily long and difficult campaign to put the oath issue to a referendum.[28] Again the *Nation* took the Labour Party to task: it charged that Labour had connived with the Cosgrave government to exclude Fianna Fail because 'Johnson does not want the balance of power. He prefers the comfortable role as head of the Opposition which does not oppose.' At the same time, it continued to proclaim that Fianna Fail would lend significant support to Labour's socio-economic proposals if it were in the Dail.

Meanwhile, in the Dail Cosgrave once again was nominated for the presidency of the executive council. Upon nomination he acknowledged that his party no longer had a majority in the House and declared his willingness to adjourn the Dail if the other parties were prepared to form an alternative government. These other parties must have 'visualized' the probability of a coalition government when they attacked his government during the election, he declared, but 'they took good care that they could not command a majority.' He then pointed to the 'somewhat conflicting views and promises' of the other parties. Before anyone could take his offer seriously, Cosgrave proceeded to lay down the conditions under which he would form another government.[29]

The Labour Party did not put forward either an alternative government or an alternative national policy; it remained content to simply vote against another Cosgrave government. Johnson explained that his party had not attempted to form a coalition with other parties. It appears that there was a general expectation that Labour would present an alternative. The National League leader William Redmond, who was outspoken about coalitions during the campaign, said that he expected Johnson to offer an alternative, but 'on the contrary, his proposition amounts to nothing but a direct negative'. Patrick Baxter of the Farmers Party expressed a similar view. Several of the new independent members also called on Labour to propose an alternative.

When no replacement to the Cosgrave ministry was offered, Kevin O'Higgins castigated the other parties for 'irresponsibility' in seeking the defeat of the government in the election. O'Higgins said: 'We have here an admission of collective bankruptcy from the opposition Parties,

28 75,000 signatures were required to force Dail action on the initiative provision before a referendum could be held. *Dublin Evening Mail*, 24, 29 June 1927.

29 The conditions were firstly, the government must be able to put forward its programme, not just maintain law and order; secondly, there must be no tampering with the treaty or with the oath. *Dail Eireann deb.*, xx, 12.

disclaiming any idea that they could or would form a government'; the Labour Party, for example, was not looking for a majority. He warned that if the Cumann na nGaedheal government was not re-elected there would only be an 'ad hoc government' formed to dissolve the Dail and call new elections. He obviously understood that the smaller parties and the independents would shudder at the likelihood of another election so soon.

Labour's only reply to O'Higgins' onslaught was to declare that the government, having put proportional representation into the constitution, should have realized that the probable result would be a multiplicity of small parties. In any case, the Labour Party would continue to oppose the social and economic policies of the Cosgrave government. Offering no encouragement to the Fianna Fail deputies outside, Johnson declared that his party would refuse to be drawn into the oath controversy because this was 'a matter of very subordinate interest'. The failure of the Labour Party to offer an alternative government at this time can be best explained by the fact that there did not exist a majority in the Dail that would support it. It might have offered an alternative as a means of exposing new members to its policies and of maximizing the vote against the Cosgrave regime from the very beginning of the Dail. That it did not do so shortly proved to be a serious handicap.

Only Labour voted against the re-election of Cosgrave. The National League abstained, while the Farmers Party and the independents supported Cosgrave. As the top Labour priority in the new Dail was the unemployment problem, its first initiative was to put forward a motion which would restore uncovenanted unemployment benefits. The purpose of Labour's motion, which, it said, was 'drafted in mild terms . . . at the lowest possible level', was to 'provide a simple test of the spirit and intentions' of the new Dail. The motion was given considerable support, gaining the votes of the National League and several independents; the vote was thirty for and fifty-four against.[30]

On 30 June the Dail turned its attention to the usual task of passing on the estimates, and on 8 July it adjourned for a week. Two days later the ephemeral quiet of Irish political life was shattered by the assassination of Kevin O'Higgins, an act which has never been directly connected to any political party, anti-treatyite or otherwise. Indeed, the murder was never solved. Ernest Blythe, for one, harbours the view that the assassins were motivated by a desire to overthrow the Cosgrave regime: 'No attempt had been made on O'Higgins's life until Cumann na nGaedheal had suffered a serious setback which made it seem probable that it could speedily be driven from office if its strongest man were removed.'[31] All political parties immediately condemned the assassination.

The next day the Labour leaders offered the shaken Cosgrave ministry the prospect of a national coalition government of all Dail

30 Ibid., 36–38, 73–74; *Irishman*, 25 June, 9 July 1927.

31 *Irish Times*, 18 April 1966.

parties, 'if it was necessary to counteract the serious consequences' to financial stability and discipline in the police and armed forces. Johnson further proposed that such a government could attempt to forge a national agreement between workers, employers and investors for increased productivity and improved wages. After consideration, Cosgrave declined the offer.[32]

On 20 July the Cosgrave government presented as its response to the murder a legislative package of three bills. The first of these was a new, more extreme public safety bill. The second proposed to remove the initiative provision from the constitution, thereby depriving the anti-treatyites of its use in their attempt to abolish the oath. The third bill would require Dail candidates to take a pledge that they would take their seats upon election. The obvious purpose of this measure was to force the anti-treatyites either into the Dail or out of public life. The overall intention of these bills was to strike not only at illegal military organizations, but also at Sinn Fein and Fianna Fail, both legal political parties which had not been connected with the O'Higgins killing.

The Labour Party strongly opposed all three bills. In a heated debate on the second reading of the bills, Johnson roundly criticized the government's reaction to the assassination:

> The policy of the Government seems to have been that, having had a blow by the assassin, it is a rightful, necessary action of the State to respond by a hundred times severer blow at nothing. . . . The result is the introduction of a Bill ostensibly aimed at the secret military forces and other Bills openly aimed at the suppression of a rival political party.

Characterizing the government's action in introducing the bills as 'blind' and 'impotent', he declared that these measures would not 'add to the quietude of the State nor to 'the growing sense of political responsibility'. Defending Fianna Fail, he said that by Cosgrave's own statement the members of this party 'have clearly disassociated themselves from revolution by armed force and are . . . turning their attention to what they think to be a constitutional right'.

The Labour leader warned that the powers sought by the government would have the effect of annulling the rights guaranteed to individual citizens. Johnson declared the willingness of his party to support any 'necessary' legislation for public safety and state stability, but he held that the present situation 'is not anything like so bad as the President would have us believe'. He pointed out that the government already possessed great powers, which had proven to be sufficient to crush its opponents in the civil war. Finally, he declared, 'The general public opinion of detestation against crime and criminals is the best means of bringing to nought any such criminal conspiracy.' He moved that the second reading of the bills be delayed for a fortnight to allow

32 *Irishman*, 6 Aug. 1927; Johnson papers, N.L.I. MS 17162.

for 'discussion, opinion and criticism' of the proposals and for calm reconsideration by the government.[33] But Johnson's proposals had the contrary effect of angering the government's front bench.

Obviously sensing that its prestige was at stake, the government declared that the bills must be pushed forward immediately. The other parties, however, supported Labour's call for delay. The debate on the three bills, which lasted from 26 July to 4 August, reached levels of passion unequalled since the civil war and heights of personal abuse and contumely hitherto unknown in the Free State Dail. It appears that the government's response to Johnson's speech was not merely based on their desire for strict action in retaliation for the O'Higgins assassination. Their reaction included far too much personal abuse of Johnson for this to be the case. Seemingly, the government speakers were alarmed and resentful of Johnson's increased power in the Dail as demonstrated by the support he received from the other parties at this time.

Patrick McGilligan charged that the Labour Party was composed of 'weaklings' and that Johnson was running away from his responsibilities. Continuing, McGilligan declared: 'For five years we have had the spectacle of Deputy Johnson, daily, in session and after session, lusting after humanitarianism.' When McGilligan stated that Johnson had taken the same approach to government legislation at the height of the civil war, Labour deputy Daniel Morrissey pointed out that McGilligan was not in the Dail at that time and had not shared the dangers faced by Johnson and the Labour Party when he entered the Dail amidst threats of death from the republican forces. Another Labour member, Patrick Hogan, retorted that no one on the Labour benches would ever accuse McGilligan of 'hankering after humanitarianism'. He went on to charge the ministers with being consumed with 'bloodlust' and 'rage'. But the ministers congratulated themselves for 'courage' in proposing these bills. Critics of the legislation were accused of attempting to gain protection for themselves, while endangering others.[34] Fear of the gunman hovered over the government benches.

On the second day of the debate, the minister for education, Professor O'Sullivan, following a heated exchange with a Labour deputy concerning civil war executions and reprisals, declared that he could not help feeling that the Labour members 'are trying to make the biggest political capital they can' out of the situation caused by the assassination. He added that the Labour members were making speeches that would ensure their own safety but which could endanger the safety of McGilligan. The Labour Party immediately demanded that O'Sullivan

33 *Dail Eireann deb.*, xx, 840–50. Among the powers sought was authority to allow Gardai to stop and search citizens and take away papers without warrants, power to declare a group seditious, power to expel citizens from the country, suppression of 'dangerous' newspapers, and the power to establish special courts at the pleasure of the government.

34 Ibid., 899–909, 910–11, 924, 1350.

withdraw his statement. O'Sullivan's assertions obviously reflected Cosgrave's thinking because he leapt into the uproar with the request that O'Sullivan not withdraw his remarks. When O'Sullivan refused to withdraw, the Labour Party, for the first time since it entered the Dail five years before, marched out amidst mutual recriminations. As the *Irish Statesman* commented, the Free State Dail had had its first real scene.[35]

After the Labour Party had left, the Dail continued to debate the bill to abolish the initiative. The leaders of both the Farmers Party and the National League opposed this bill as well as the bill to require a pre-nomination pledge.[36] The Labour Party returned to the Dail the next day, but tempers did not abate. (Johnson resigned as chairman of the public accounts committee as a protest of O'Sullivan's charges.) On the second reading of the pre-nomination pledge bill, Richard Corish, who had been the only Labour deputy in the second Dail, brought up the subject of the treaty debate. He declared that acceptance of the treaty 'hinged around the oath' and that

> everybody there admitted, including deputies like myself who voted for the treaty, that we would only be prepared to take the oath under duress, but everybody there said that the first opportunity presenting itself to remove the oath would be taken advantage of.

Three ministers who had voted for the treaty—Cosgrave, Hogan and Lynch—immediately declared this had not been their position at the time of the treaty debate. However, none of these said anything in the treaty debate that would lead one to believe that they felt otherwise about the oath. A reading of the treaty debate would convince one that Corish's assertion reflected the general opinion of those who addressed themselves to the question of the oath. But now Cosgrave made it plain that he would not budge on the oath: he had not attempted to gain the approval of the British government to remove the oath and he would not so so. The second reading of the pre-nomination pledge bill was passed over significant opposition—fifty-one for, thirty-seven against.[37] (The bill finally became law the following November but because of intervening events, it was never implemented.)

The Dail then proceeded to the committee stage of the public safety bill. Tempers flared again. The leader of the Farmers Party Patrick Baxter charged Johnson with 'exciting' the Labour members to 'obstruct' the passage of the bill by calling on them to speak to amendments. Although the Labour Party spoke to each amendment, it did not attempt to obstruct this measure, as it had done during consideration of a similar measure in 1923. Not satisfied with merely accusing

35 Ibid., 947–50; *Irish Statesman*, 6 Aug. 1927.

36 *Dail Eireann deb.*, xx, 985–87, 993–94.

37 Ibid., 1088–94, 1111–12.

Johnson of obstructing the public safety bill, Baxter proceeded to place the entire responsibility for the bill on the Labour leader:

> This measure is as drastic as it is because the attitude of the Labour Party made it so. The course of this measure has undoubtedly been regulated by the conduct of the Labour Party. . . . The whole position changed when the Labour Party left the House.

Baxter said that it then became clear to him that there could be no consensus on the bill, that Labour would offer no constructive alternative to the government proposal. He further declared that Johnson and his party were responsible for the 'foreign atmosphere' that had come into the Dail. It was Baxter's view that the Labour Party was unwilling to grant the government any effective power.[38]

Certainly there was a 'foreign atmosphere' in the Dail at this time. Johnson clashed with the Ceann Comhairle (Speaker) on two occasions, something that had not happened in the previous five years. As the debate drew to a close, Johnson exclaimed that he was astonished by the animus arising from the public safety bill. On 4 August the public safety bill and the pre-nomination pledge received final passage.[39] The bill to abolish the initiative was left at the second stage when the Dail adjourned for eight days. But, as during the last adjournment, an event was to occur which transformed the political situation.

Political Confrontation and Combination

Since the time that Fianna Fail had been denied entrance into the Dail, the party had busied itself with a campaign to force a public vote on the question of abolition of the oath. The O'Higgins murder upset this effort. Now Fianna Fail was confronted with the government's legislative reaction to the assassination. The bill to abolish the initiative would prevent de Valera's party from removing the oath by means of an appeal to the electorate; soon this avenue would be cut off. Furthermore the pre-nomination pledge bill would have the effect at the next election of forcing the anti-treatyites to either commit themselves to entering the Dail or standing down in the election. Recognizing that the situation was critical, Fianna Fail again began manoeuvering for a means to get into the Dail without the humiliation of taking the oath. It could see that it was presented not merely with a dilemma, but also with an opportunity: if it could get into the Dail there was the clear probability that it could overthrow its arch-opponents—the party which had accepted the treaty.

The first move in the new Fianna Fail effort was, predictably, made by de Valera. In a speech in Dublin on 26 July he wooed the opposition parties with the prospect that if the Cosgrave government was voted out of office a coalition government may follow. He made the following offer:

38 Ibid., 1445, 1585–86, 1591.

39 Ibid., 1095, 1211, 1584. In order to make the legislation immediately effective, an emergency resolution was attached to the bill. Ibid., 1601–04.

> In the event of a coalition Government being formed and succeeding in securing that all representatives of the people be free to enter the twenty-six county Assembly without subscribing to any political test, the Fianna Fail Party will not press any issue involving the Treaty to the point of overthrowing such Government during the normal lifetime of the present Assembly.[40]

De Valera's statement undoubtedly was designed, in part, as a reply to Johnson's query during the campaign as to Fianna Fail's willingness to accept merely the removal of the oath for a period of five years, with no further alteration of the treaty. De Valera's statement, it should be noted, only made his offer to apply during 'the normal life of the present Assembly'. It was apparent that, due to the multitude of parties and the volatile situation, the present Dail was most unlikely to last very long. Further, de Valera did not say that his party would take the oath in order to oust the government, and without this bloc of votes it was quite certain that a majority could not be found to overturn Cosgrave.

The Labour Party did not reply to this suggestion, the most probable reason being that Fianna Fail had not said it would come into the Dail at this time. However, help came from an unexpected source. On 3 August James Larkin, still an outcast from the 'official' labour movement, held a public meeting outside his union headquarters in Dublin. At that time, Larkin called for a 'conference of parties and organizations' to oppose what he called the tyrannical measures of the government and 'to find a common denominator in defence of the lives, liberties and the rights of the common people'. Most interesting, Larkin proposed that the conference be summoned by the 'leader of the second largest party elected to the Dail'. De Valera accepted Larkin's proposals immediately and proceeded to invite two members each from the Labour Party, the Farmers Party, the National League, Fianna Fail, Sinn Fein, the Transport Union and Larkin's Workers Union of Ireland. The Fianna Fail leader declared that the purpose of the meeting was to decide what 'joint national action' was necessary to save the country from the government's repressive legislation.

The conference, which met on 5 August, was attended only by Larkin and de Valera. The Labour Party, together with the other invited organizations, refused to participate. In his reply to de Valera's invitation, Johnson stated that the best way for Fianna Fail to check the government would be for its members to take their seats in the Dail. The conference thus proved a failure. It is hard to resist the idea that Larkin and de Valera had agreed to the conference proposal before Larkin made his speech; certainly the language of each of their statements was very complimentary to the other. Both were leaders of organizations which were outside the recognized bodies in their respective fields and both wanted to gain admission. Beginning at this time,

40 *Nation*, 6 Aug. 1927.

and for the next two months, Larkin and de Valera's party enjoyed close and harmonious relations.[41]

While de Valera and Larkin were bandying about the conference proposal, important negotiations were taking place privately. On 1 August, Gerald Boland, a Fianna Fail leader, asked Johnson for a meeting to discuss a 'matter of urgency'; the meeting took place that night. Having intimated that Fianna Fail was on the verge of entering the Dail, Boland wanted to know what would be the position of the Labour Party in regard to the oath if it were to form a coalition government. Johnson immediately declared in a memorandum that it would be 'my duty to make every effort to get the Oath clause of the Treaty altered or deleted at the earliest possible moment', but this was to be done 'by agreement with the British Government'. To emphasize his commitment to this position, Johnson stated that he would resign from the proposed coalition government if he found that he could not secure alteration or deletion of the oath clause 'within a reasonable time'.[42] This commitment is somewhat surprising in the light of the statement he had made in the Dail just days before. At that time Johnson had again stated his belief that the oath should only be removed when it had become a hindrance to national development and that he had no evidence that this had yet occurred.[43] Johnson obviously decided that Boland's offer to bring Fianna Fail into the Dail if the Labour Party would attempt to get rid of the oath was a matter of such magnitude as to justify a sudden change on the oath question: in exchange for the creation of a large measure of political normality in the Free State, the Labour Party would undertake to destroy an important provision of the treaty settlement.

Two days after Johnson made his offer, Fianna Fail declared it unacceptable on the grounds that his position on the oath was not strong enough and that 'the small margin there is over the Free State Government supporters renders it [the coalition proposal] too doubtful a proposition'. This was followed by a series of meetings, from 6 to 9 August, between the leaders of the two parties. These resulted in the Labour leadership making definite commitments. In a memorandum drawn up by Johnson, Labour promised to support the withdrawal of the pending government legislation and the implementation of the initiative and referendum provisions of the constitution. The party now agreed that it would seek to get rid of the oath not only through negotiations with the British government but, that failing, a referen-

41 In his biography of Larkin, Emmet Larkin, in listing Big Jim's accomplishments, declares: 'Larkin did as much as one man could do to persuade Eamonn de Valera and his Republicans to take up an active political opposition in the Irish Parliament.' *James Larkin*, p. xvii.

42 Letter from Boland to Johnson, 1 Aug. 1927, Johnson memorandum, 1 Aug. 1927, *Thomas Johnson papers*, National Library of Ireland MS 17168; O'Brien diary, 1 Aug. 1927, *O'Brien papers*, MS 15705. See also ibid., MS 15704(1).

43 *Dail Eireann deb.*, xx, 1056; see also ibid., 16.

dum.[44] These terms being acceptable to Fianna Fail, the leaders of the two parties agreed that, following the entrance of Fianna Fail into the Dail, the Labour Party would form a coalition government with Fianna Fail providing support but not joining the ministry.[45]

As a matter of tactics, the Labour leaders decided not to reveal the commitments they had made. The probability that the two parties had made agreements which they chose to conceal was seized upon by the Cosgrave government. Yet the Labour commitment remained such a well-guarded confidence that the party leader from October 1927 to 1932, T. J. O'Connell, who was then outside the country, has declared that he never heard of such an agreement following his return.[46]

The Labour leaders had two important tasks to accomplish before the scheme to oust the Cosgrave government could be put into operation. First they had to secure approval of their plan from the Labour executive and the parliamentary party. Their second and far more difficult task was to win the National League over to their plan and to gain the support of a few of the fourteen independent members of the Dail. Although the National League held only eight seats in the Dail, its support was vital to Labour's effort to achieve a majority against the Cosgrave government.

With one member dissenting, the Labour executive approved of the agreement with Fianna Fail. The dissenter was Louie Bennett, who for long had been critical of what she saw as the pre-occupation of the party-congress with political affairs to the detriment of the trade union side of the movement. Miss Bennett opposed the proposal on the grounds that 'it was never right or wise to co-operate with another party with fundamentally different principles: coalition', she declared, 'meant a compromise on fundamental principles'. At a meeting held on 11 August, the parliamentary party, without apparent dissension, supported the proposal of its leadership.[47]

The leader of the National League had committed himself to the idea of a coalition government during the election campaign. Would Redmond support Labour with its Fianna Fail involvement? Without waiting for the consent of his party members, Redmond committed the National League to the coalition proposal. At meetings held the day before and the day of the resumption of the Dail, only one of the eight party deputies refused to support Redmond's initiative. But the group was concerned that the proposed government would be dominated directly by the Labour Party or indirectly by Fianna Fail; they

44 Johnson notes, 6, 8, 9 Aug. 1927; *Johnson papers* MS 17168; O'Brien diary, 1, 5, 6, 8, 10, 11 Aug. 1927, O'Brien papers MS 15705; interview with James Everett, 24 June 1964.

45 I.L.P. & T.U.C., *1928 report*, p. 24.

46 Interview with T. J. O'Connell, 3 Nov. 1965.

47 I.L.P. & T.U.C., *1928 report*, p. 24; O'Brien diary, 15 Aug. 1927, O'Brien papers MS 15705.

therefore demanded 'proper' National League representation in the cabinet.[48]

By 9 August it had become public knowledge that Fianna Fail was planning to enter the Dail and to join forces with the Labour Party to overthrow the government. Two days later, when confronted by the press, Johnson simply declared, 'If responsibility is imposed upon us, we will take it and not shirk our duty.' On 12 August, the day the Dail resumed, he unfolded his plan for a government composed of 'those elements in political life who were not active parties in the strife of the recent past'. He also revealed that under such a government the 'full and immediate realization' of Labour's social and economic programme could not be expected. When the Dail met, forty-three Fianna Fail deputies took the hated oath and filled the opposition benches. The melodrama of abstention had ended, but more dramatic events followed. Johnson immediately called for a vote of confidence in the government; debate on the motion was set for 16 August, four days later.[49]

The immediate reaction of the national press was that the government would be turned out of office. The *Dublin Evening Mail* reported that the government might resign even before the vote was taken, assuming the role of opposition to the coalition government. The *Irish Independent* declared that 'there is every reason to believe that the Cumann na nGaedheal Administration will be defeated' by a margin of about four votes. The political correspondent of the Sunday edition of that paper said that 'it is almost certain that Mr. Johnson will carry his vote of no confidence', while its editorial assumed that the Cosgrave regime would fall but advised that its overthrow would not necessarily lead to national disaster.[50]

The national press immediately assumed a critical stance towards the attempt to supplant the Cosgrave ministry with a coalition. The *Cork Examiner* on 17 August for example, pointed to the left wing of the Labour Party as presenting a danger to the stability of a coalition government; Mr. Johnson had a

> left to contend with, who if it suits their purposes would be prepared to associate with the Fianna Fail left. There is no adequate guarantee that the moderates of the Labour movement could keep the immoderates in order now, no more than when the red flag was raised over creameries and other industries.

More was to be heard about red flags later. The *Irish Independent* (16 August) held that the differences in the programmes of the proposed partners in the coalition would prevent the maintenance of stable

48 For correspondence between Johnson and Redmond, and on meeting of National League deputies, see Johnson papers, N.L.I. MS 17165.

49 *Irish Independent*, 12 Aug. 1927; *Dail Eireann deb.*, xx, 1645–46.

50 *Dublin Evening Mail*, 11 Aug., *Irish Independent*, 12 Aug., *Sunday Independent*, 14 Aug. 1927.

government, and that although the country could benefit from a lessening in legislative output, a coalition government would produce a 'do-nothing' policy. In its issue of 13 August the *Dublin Evening Mail* voiced its indignation:

> Only a few months ago, before the General Election, Labour speakers referred to Mr. de Valera in the most contemptuous terms and the National League owes seats in the Dail to votes which were never intended to help Fianna Fail. . . . The three parties indeed have had to go back upon almost everything they have said in the past.

Only George Russell's *Irish Statesman* (20 August) voiced confidence in the proposal.

The four days between Johnson's call for a motion of confidence and the debate on the motion were filled with intense consultations among the deputies. Reports of the proposed cabinet appeared in the press. It was generally assumed that Johnson would be president and Redmond vice-president. The executive council would be composed principally of Labour men, with one or two ministries going to the National League and one or two to the independents. Indeed, this was the composition of the proposed cabinet that Johnson, O'Brien and Mortished put together on 14 August.[51]

As the day of the debate approached it became apparent that the independent deputies would hold the balance of power. The Labour Party claimed that it did not 'make any promises or offer any inducements, or compromises . . . in any way in order to obtain support for the motion'. Evidence for this assertion is found in the fact that none of the independents supported the no-confidence motion. The balance shifted to the independents when the National League split on the issue of the no-confidence motion. Redmond had committed his party before he had consulted with it. One of its members, Vincent Rice, immediately resigned from the League and declared in favour of Cosgrave. Other members of his party continued to be upset by Redmond's commitment.[52]

Further factors working against the success of the motion soon came to light. One of the Labour members, T. J. O'Connell, was absent in Canada at this time. The loss of Kevin O'Higgins' vote ironically was cancelled out by the untimely death of Constance Markievicz, a Fianna Fail deputy. There is no evidence of dissension in the ranks of the Labour Party, although there was a report of some uneasiness about the effect that the alliance would have on the party in country areas. Up to the time of the vote, the party remained confident the motion would pass, albeit by a reduced margin. The margin was now 'two or three votes', allowing for 'anticipated defections'. Johnson's confidence is seen in the telegram that he sent O'Connell asking him to accept the

51 O'Brien diary, 14 Aug. 1927, O'Brien papers, MS 15705, 15704(1).

52 *Irish Independent*, 12, 13 Aug. 1927.

ministry for education. On the night before the motion was to be debated, Cosgrave, believing that his government would be defeated by a single vote, held a farewell party for his staff.[53]

The tripartite alliance of Labour, the National League and Fianna Fail appears, at first glance, to be an unusual or unlikely combination. The Labour Party, whose *raison d'être* was social and economic reform, had agreed to lay aside a major part of its programme upon the establishment of the coalition. Its leader had often had hard words for the anti-treatyites and had had at least one clash with Redmond. However, now that Fianna Fail was on the constitutional road and in the Dail, Labour had no objection to accepting its support. The alliance was sensible for de Valera's party because Fianna Fail had an overwhelmingly desire to oust the pro-treaty government, even if the former was not the immediate beneficiary. For his part, Redmond, as the heir to the defunct Irish Parliamentary Party, had been the recipient of many bitter remarks from the government front bench. Further, he did not view the coalition as undermining either the treaty or the constitution, to both of which his party was completely committed.

The debate on the no-confidence motion, lasting five hours, was surprisingly devoid of passion, due in part to the expected close vote and to the emotional excesses of the past few weeks. Another factor in the relative calm was Fianna Fail's token participation in the proceedings. Initiating the debate, and speaking under obvious strain, Johnson declared that 'from some public comments one would imagine there never had been a vote of this kind' before, but he reminded the Dail of the Labour Party's long record of opposition to the Cosgrave government. The difference, of course, was that previously Labour had been in no position to bring down the government. Johnson proceeded to censure both the government's socio-economic and political policies, while he also presented a picture of the positive value of a coalition government at that juncture. Dealing with the political aspect, Johnson contended that the government's retaliatory proposals to the O'Higgins murder 'indicated a state of mind in the Executive Council which was more likely to lessen the prospects of good order and good government than to improve them'. In castigating the government's approach in socio-economic matters, he asserted that it had 'not made the most' of the opportunities presented by existing legislation in dealing with long-standing public problems. He took as an example the government's failure to use its power to initiate 'public opportunities for employment'. But what was truly damning, he declared, was that the government had made clear that 'it intends to carry on as they have been carrying on in the past'.

Broaching the subject of coalition, Johnson declared that some deputies had said in June that there was no alternative to the present government. The entrance of forty-three deputies had changed that

53 *1928 report*, p. 25; interview with O'Connell; article by E. A. Lawlor, *Sunday Inde-dependent*, 11 Nov. 1965; T. P. Coogan, *Ireland since the rising*, pp. 65–66.

situation, he declared, and now several alternatives were possible. He proceeded to mention the various combinations which could compose a coalition government, but he urged the Dail to put aside the question of the composition of a new government until the issue of confidence in the present government had been decided. This was to ask too much of the Dail; every deputy certainly knew what would be the principal components of the proposed coalition.

Johnson's leading argument for the removal of the government was that 'there should be a party or combination of parties in office which will exclude from office for a time both those parties who have been in fierce contention.' He argued that if the present government remained in office, faced by the republicans as the principal opposition, 'the possibility of carrying on Parliamentary Government successfully and with a successful issue for the cause of peace and development are very much less'. A coalition government would not necessarily be weak and disunited, he contended, because it would not be less homogenous 'than the present coalition, known as the Cumann na nGaedheal Party'. He recalled that this party liked to boast that it was a 'perfect coalition'. While he criticized the government for interpreting narrowly the powers granted by the treaty, he declared that his party was completely committed to both the treaty and the constitution; his party differed from the government in that Labour desired 'the fullest interpretation' of the treaty. Without referring to the question of the oath, Johnson held that if either the treaty or the constitution 'prove to be of such a nature as to prevent the development of this State and this people, then let us change [them] by any means or all means'.[54]

All press reports described Johnson's speech as a poor effort. He was said to be 'nervous, ill at ease', with abrupt pauses for words'. and his manner 'halting and indecisive'. The most serious criticism of his speech was that it failed to make clear the nature and composition of the alternative to the existing ministry.[55] Granted that the national press was hostile to the coalition proposal, its reaction to Johnson's statement appears to be justified.

In his statement, Redmond declared that his party was supporting the motion on the political grounds stated by Johnson: that 'continued conflict' between the two major parties 'would further postpone peace and prosperity'. On the constitutional question, Redmond said that although his party was 'absolutely wedded to the fundamentals of the Anglo-Irish settlement', he did not doubt the right of either side to change the constitution. The National League, he declared, had secured two conditions for its support of the proposed alternative: firstly, there should be 'firm and efficient enforcement of ordinary

54 *Dail Eireann deb.*, xx, 1670–76.

55 The *Sunday Independent* (21 Aug. 1927) commented: 'Had he been less ruthless in suppressing his excitement he would probably have spoken better. As it was, his speech added to the tenseness of feeling . . . '.

law', and, secondly, there should be no attempt, either through legislative or administrative action, 'to put into operation the more contentious doctrines' in any party programme. He made clear that this included Labour's collectivist proposals. Fianna Fail's only contribution to the debate was a short supporting statement in Irish by Sean T. O'Kelly in which he declared that his party's hostility to the present government was well known.[56]

The only speaker for the government side was President Cosgrave. (Kevin O'Higgins undoubtedly would have relished this occasion.) Cosgrave's speech was, in the words of one observer, 'not so much a vindication of the Ministry's record as an onslaught upon Mr. Johnson'.[57] He began by recalling Johnson's willingness to enter a coalition government with Cumann na nGaedheal a few weeks before. Since economic conditions had not changed since then, Cosgrave declared, Johnson's desire to bring down the government was not based on a 'question of economy'. Passing to the question of what would follow if the government were defeated, the president declared: 'That was kept from us a sacred, guarded secret. . . . Have there been agreements secretly arrived at?'. Although he said that his party would lend support to any coalition government upon its establishment, he ridiculed Johnson's attempt to play the peacemaker.

Cosgrave saw other weaknesses in the coalition proposal. Recalling Johnson's message of support to the British trade unions during the 1926 general strike, he questioned whether Johnson, as head of government, would have 'his eyes on this country alone'. Further, he declared that the proposed alternative government was bound to be weak and unstable because the Labour Party and the National League represented only a small fraction of the Dail. Concluding his spirited statement on an emotional note, Cosgrave asked the Dail if the assassins of O'Higgins would 'feel easier if this motion is passed'. In rebuttal, Johnson accused Cosgrave of distorting the purpose behind the Labour Party's offer to enter a coalition government immediately after the killing of O'Higgins. Labour made the offer, he said, because it believed that a 'national government' of all parties would demonstrate stability at that time. Johnson further stated that his party had made no secret bargains to gain support for the motion.[58]

The Farmers Party then declared its support for the government. The party leader Patrick Baxter held that the peace and stability required by the country would best be secured by the present ministry. Continuing, he declared that his party, which mainly represented the bigger farmers, was opposed to the social and economic theories of the Labour leader, who had 'the mind of the industrial worker of the city'. He recalled the recent farm labourers' strike and the factory seizures of

56 *Dail Eireann deb.*, xx, 1682–88.

57 *Irish Independent*, 17 Aug. 1927.

58 *Dail Eireann deb.*, xx, 1678–81, 1745.

1920–22, and queried the Labour Party as to its position on these events.[59]

The commitment of the Farmers Party to the government was expected, but the failure of any independent deputy to support the motion was a serious blow to the coalitionists. Even such as Alfred Byrne, a frequent critic of the the government for its failure to deal effectively with the unemployment problem and a member who was expected to support the motion, did not rise to speak. Two new independent deputies, J. O'Hanlon and Jaspar Wolfe, declared that they would not vote to oust the government because if the motion was passed it would mean that an Englishman, Johnson, would become head of an Irish government. (Wolfe, an official under the British regime, had a grievance against Johnson arising out of a labour dispute.) Cosgrave's remark on Johnson's offer of support during the British general strike could be interpreted as a guarded reference to Johnson's English background. In any case, Johnson's Englishness had become an explicit factor in the debate. Concluding the debate, Johnson cited the citizenship clause in the constitution, and declared that he had 'lived in Ireland, worked in Ireland and served in Ireland for a longer number of years than most deputies', adding that 'the working people of this country had entrusted me with confidence and leadership.'[60]

The vote on the no-confidence motion resulted, surprisingly, in a tie—seventy-one for and seventy-one against. The Ceann Comhairle (Speaker), who had been returned automatically, proceeded to cast his vote for the government. The Cosgrave regime was saved and the coalition proved abortive.

It was generally believed that the Cosgrave government survived this challenge as a result of the abstention of John Jinks, a member of the National League. The Sligo alderman, a newly-elected member of the Dail, had agreed, according to the Labour Party, to vote for its motion; indeed at his party meeting he had seconded the motion which approved of Redmond's commitment of the party to the coalition proposal.[61] It is well to remember, however, that the National League was not an organized, disciplined party, but, rather, a collection of past supporters of the old Irish Parliamentary Party. Further, the members had not readily accepted Redmond's action. Jinks's own background would not suggest that he was likely to support such a combination—he had been a supporter of the British war effort, had been friendly towards Cosgrave in the past and had been the object of abuse by both the Labour and the republican press.[62]

There were various reports concerning Jinks's absence. Redmond declared darkly that Jinks 'might have been spirited away'. Mrs.

59 Ibid., 1691–98.

60 Ibid., 1700, 1726, 1745–46.

61 *1928 report*, p. 25; memorandum on meeting of National League deputies, 12 Aug. 1927, Johnson papers, N.L.I., MS 17165.

62 *Irish Worker*, 28 Nov., 5 Dec. 1914; *Nationality*, 16 June 1917; *Eire*, 28 July 1923.

Thomas Johnson believes that Bryan Cooper, ex-unionist supporter of Cosgrave, got Jinks drunk and locked him in a room in Buswell's Hotel, across from the Dail; but Jinks was in the chamber until shortly before the vote was taken. A popular story had Jinks standing in O'Connell Street looking at Nelson's Pillar at the time of the vote. His own explanation is probably most believable: he said that he had decided not to vote because two-thirds of the constituents who had contacted him asked that he vote for the government.[63] In an apparent spasm of relief that the Cosgrave government had been spared, the national press lionized Jinks; one newspaper called him 'the most famous man in Europe'. Jinks resigned and was expelled from his party and his brief Dail career ended when he was defeated in the September election.

The Labour Party itself was partly responsible for the defeat of its motion. Following the assassination of O'Higgins, Johnson had given Deputy O'Connell permission to attend a teachers' conference in Canada. Johnson believed that Fianna Fail was not about to enter the Dail and that the political situation would remain unchanged for a time.[64] This clearly was an error in judgement.

The principal reason for the failure of the coalition was that its proponents did not gain the support of any of the independent deputies. As has been seen, two of these declared that they would not vote for the no-confidence motion because it would mean that an Englishman would become head of the government. Possibly to mute this criticism the proponents had not made clear whether Johnson or Redmond would become president. It was generally assumed, however, that Johnson would have been the government leader.[65] Johnson's English background, therefore, did contribute to the defeat of the party's aspiration.

Other independent members had their own reasons for not supporting the motion. One of these was G. Hewson, who a few days before had been denounced by Cosgrave, as exhibiting a 'slave mind', and by the minister for agriculture who asserted that Hewson was a spokesman for a small group that was sorry that the English had left the country. Obviously subordinating personal feeling, Hewson decided to vote for Cosgrave because the proposed alternative 'was not sufficiently formed, both in personnel and policy'. Another independent member, M. Brennan, declined to support the coalition due to the fact that it would have been put into power by the vote of a third party which would remain outside the government. A third, John Daly of Cork, an independent labour member, bore Johnson a grudge arising from Johnson's

63 Interview with Mary Johnson, 22 June 1964. T. P. Coogan states that Bertie Smyllie; the editor of the *Irish Times*, was involved in this episode. Coogan, *Ireland since the rising*, p. 65, *Irish Independent*, 18 Aug. 1927.

64 Interview with T. J. O'Connell.

65 Mrs Thomas Johnson has stated that, in order to avoid the Englishman issue, O'Connell, not Johnson, would have become president. At that time, however, Johnson was in Canada. Interview with Mary Johnson, 22 June 1964.

refusal to allow Daly to be a Labour Party nominee four years before.[66] Most importantly, the independents were alike in one important respect—they were all constitutionalists and, therefore, were antagonistic towards Fianna Fail for its long period of abstention. Their hostile posture extended to any scheme involving Fianna Fail. Another factor was that almost all were new members and probably feared being responsible for a governmental upheaval.

The Labour Party assumed that because most of the independents had voted against the government's legislative package following O'Higgins's murder, these members would support the motion to oust the government. As events showed, however, the independents were simply opposed to the government's rash legislation at this time. It should be further recalled that the independent members had voted for the Cosgrave ministry at the beginning of the Dail after the Labour Party had failed to propose either an alternative government or policy. Was it not asking too much to expect them to turn about and expel the government they had voted to install but two months earlier?

Having suffered this reverse, Labour declared darkly, 'What menaces or promises were held out by the Government or others to these deputies, between Friday and Monday, is not known.' It is hardly surprising that the government did everything it could to stave off defeat. Apparently it offered Alfred Byrne, originally a supporter of the coalition, some action to relieve unemployment in Dublin in return for his vote.[67]

Had the Dail been elected on a wholly democratic basis, the no-confidence motion almost certainly would have passed. Under the 1922 constitution the universities were allowed six seats—three for the National University and three for Dublin University. By means of this provision the pro-treaty government was assured additional support; throughout the 1920's five of the six university deputies were consistent supporters of the Cosgrave government; indeed, three of them served as ministers. On the no-confidence motion five such deputies voted for Cosgrave, while the sixth, an abstentionist but independent republican, had not taken his seat.[68] The Labour Party had always opposed university representation in the Dail. Later, under a Fianna Fail government, this representation was abolished in the popular house.

66 G. Hewson statement, *Dail Eireann deb.*, xx, 1742; M. Brennan statement, ibid., 1743–44; Hogan statement, ibid., 1408; see also statement of Cosgrave, ibid., 1407; Daly statement, *Cork Examiner*, 15 Sept. 1927.

67 I.L.P. and T.U.C., *1928 report*, p. 25; O'Connell has said that Byrne had agreed to vote against Cosgrave. Interview with O'Connell. Immediately following the no-confidence vote, Byrne was on his feet asking what the government proposed to do about the Dublin unemployment situation. *Dail Eireann deb.*, xx, 1751.

68 In the June 1927 election Patrick McGilligan, government minister, Michael Hayes, the speaker, and P. Clery, abstentionist republican, were elected for the National University. Three 'independents', W. E. Thrift, Sir James Craig and E. H. Elton, were re-elected for the Dublin University; they were constant supporters of the Cosgrave government. *Irish Times*, 17 June 1927.

Was the coalition government proposal viable? Had this government been formed it clearly would have been in a weak parliamentary position—a government of two parties, representing less than 30 votes, supported by a party of 44 votes, this out of a total membership of 152. This government might have been able to conduct a stable administration for a time, but new elections could not be far away. The much-heralded period of non-contention and peace would not have lasted very long. The coalition was almost certainly committed to one major objective—the abolition or modification of the oath by means of negotiation with the British government. It does not seem likely that the Conservative government of the time would have agreed to changes in the treaty; it would be even less likely to agree to such at the urging of a weak and unstable coalition government.

If, by supporting the coalition proposal, the Labour Party hoped to see political issues subordinated and social and economic questions brought to the forefront, it was bound to be disappointed. Even if the oath had been abolished, there remained several other political issues—the governor-generalship, the land annuities and the treaty itself. From the standpoint of the welfare of the Irish working class, the coalition had little to offer. Labour had agreed not to press contentious legislation upon the coalition. Johnson had said that social and economic progress could have been made through administrative action, rather than by legislation, but the results, no doubt, hardly would have been major steps forward.

The Labour Party might have gained considerable political advantage had the coalition government been formed and had it effectively carried on the affairs of state until a new election was called. A successful, if brief, term in office would have given the party and its leaders public attention and approval. Perhaps this was what the Labour newspaper meant when, on 27 August, it declared:

> Labour would not have been able to place all its programme on the Statute book at once, but it would not have sacrificed its programme. It would have given the country the peace it needs, realizing that a period of sane politics would be the best preparation of the minds of the electorate for consideration of much more radical Labour needs as could be given effect.

On the other hand, had the coalition failed to maintain stability and security, the Labour Party probably would have been ruined.

Following the no-confidence vote, Cosgrave moved that the Dail adjourn until 11 October. There were two by-elections pending, both in Dublin, which could tip the scale either way. He therefore asked the Ceann Comhairle to call the Dail together one month after the by-elections if the government party lost both seats. By that time the missing Labour deputy would have returned. Perhaps one or two Sinn Feiners could have been coaxed into the Dail or support won from one or two of the independent members. Thus, there remained the possibility that the coalition government might yet be formed.

The national press was unanimous in condemning the alliance to overturn the Cumann na nGaedheal government; the *Irish Times* termed the effort a coup that failed. The *Irish Statesman* (27 August) was alone in seeing some good arising out of the whole situation: 'At least war of manoeuvre has now replaced trench warfare in Irish politics.' Under a barrage of critical comment, both Labour and the National League strove to prove their independence of Fianna Fail. Johnson declared that his party would not vote Fianna Fail into office; if a Fianna Fail government was formed, it would have to be installed either by the vote of the people or by the other parties. He based this decision on the party's commitment to end the situation which had 'divided the nation into two fiercely contending sections'. Meanwhile, the Labour newspaper devoted considerable space to an exposition of the reasons why the party had decided to enter the coalition.

Claiming that its resources were exhausted, Labour decided against entering candidates in the crucial by-elections. The *Irishman* emphasized that the party had reached no understanding with Fianna Fail concerning these contests; it declared that Labour's decision to stand down 'was a necessary declaration of independence'. Conversely, the party's failure to contest these seats could be viewed, and was presented, as a demonstration of subordination to Fianna Fail, rather than a show of independence. The party did make one final gesture of co-operation with Fianna Fail. Both parties signed a petition to force the electorate amendment law to a referendum.

The attempt to overthrow the government almost inevitably formed the main issue in the by-elections. Cumann na nGaedheal speakers charged that the Labour Party had not put forward candidates because it had 'thrown in its lot with Fianna Fail'. Cosgrave spoke darkly of 'secret agreements, secretly arrived at and kept from the people of the country'. Patrick McGilligan, adopting a more stringent position, attacked the Labour Party leader as an Englishman and asserted that in the immediate aftermath of the O'Higgins assassination, Johnson proposed that the seats of the abstentionists be declared vacant. The Labour newspaper responded with a lengthy article, 'All about the Englishman', which cited Johnson's long career in Ireland and in the Irish labour movement.[69] Adopting the abuse previously employed by the antitreatyites, one government party spokesman claimed that the Labour Party was the 'Empire Labour Party'. With a turnout of only fifty per cent of the voters, Cosgrave's party won both seats. Two days later, on 26 August, the president secured the dissolution of the Dail from the governor-general; a new election was set for 18 September.

Thus ended the first attempt to form a coalition government in the Free State. This failure and the controversy surrounding it was probably a major factor in the decline of the smaller parties over the next decade. The coalition proposal was not raised again until sixteen

69 *Irish Times,* 19 Aug. 1927; *Irishman,* 27 Aug. See also Mortished's reply for Labour in *Irish Times,* 19 Aug. 1927.

years later, during the 1943 election,[70] and the first coalition government was not formed until 1948. The coalition governments of 1948–51 and 1954–57 differed from the coalition proposed in 1927 in that they were representative of a majority of the Dail and were formed to keep the then dominant Fianna Fail Party out of office.

70 In the 1943 election Fine Gael, successor to Cumann na nGaedheal, proposed that a coalition government should be formed; Labour was non-committal. See correspondence of Michael Hayes, Johnson and Seamus Davin concerning the 1927 proposal. *Irish Independent*, 14–17 June 1943.

11
A Decade of Decline

The September 1927 election marked the beginning of a period of decline for the Labour Party that was to last a decade. Cosgrave argued that a new election was necessary because 'the work of the nation cannot be done', that a stable government must be achieved to ensure the success of a new government loan to be floated in November. It was apparent that the government, even with its two new seats, would not have a stable parliamentary majority. One of these seats would have been cancelled out by the return of the absent Labour deputy, and the government could not expect consistent support from the Farmers Party and from all the independents.

The other parties expressed surprise at Cosgrave's move. The Labour Party held that the president had no constitutional right to advise the governor-general to dissolve the Dail; only the Dail itself could order disolution. This had been the practice in 1923 and May 1927, but the constitution was not clear on this point.[1] An article, 'President Cosgrave and H.M. The King', in the 3 September issue of the *Irishman* declared that Cosgrave was following the British interpretation in this matter: 'Mr. Cosgrave has acted, not as a Minister responsible to the Dail, but as a wielder of the prerogative of the King.' To Labour, it was 'a tricksters' scheme to win a flashy political game'; de Valera saw it as 'sharp practice'.[2]

The sudden election did not find the two major parties, Cumann na nGaedheal and Fianna Fail, without adequate financial resources. Both put forward about the same number of candidates as in June and both carried on the same massive advertising campaign.[3] The smaller parties, however, were in no position to launch a new campaign. All of them put forward many fewer candidates than in June, except for Sinn Fein and Clann Eireann, which stood down. Only twenty-eight Labour candidates went forward, as compared to forty-five in June.

The extreme poverty of the Labour Party is evidenced by the fact that the national executive raised and spent only £1,200 in the campaign. The Transport Union remained the bulwark of the party, spending £4,800, £1,400 of which went for deposits for candidates sponsored by the union. Each candidate also attempted to raise funds for his campaign. Because of its beggared condition, the party found

1 N. Mansergh, *Irish Free State*, p. 185.

2 I.L.P. and T.U.C., *1928 report*, p. 26; *Irish Independent*, 26 Aug. 1927.

3 Cumann na nGaedheal put forward eighty-seven candidates in September, as opposed to ninety-six in June. Fianna Fail nominated eighty-eight in September, eighty-seven in June. *Irish Times*, 14 Sept. 1927. The National League ran only six candidates in September as opposed to thirty in June; the Farmers Party nominated nineteen instead of thirty-eight and the number of independent candidates was reduced from fifty-three to thirty-one. *Evening Herald*, 3 Sept.; *Irish Independent*, 5 Sept. 1927.

it impossible to compete with the 'money spent lavishly' by the two big parties.[4]

Campaign Issues

In the other elections of the decade, Labour had complained continuously that political and constitutional issues had been given much more attention than had social and economic questions. In this election, however, social and economic matters were almost completely ignored by all parties. Although its programme received scant attention, the Labour Party found itself in the centre of controversy. Not surprisingly, the party was forced to defend its role in the attempt to overthrow Cosgrave. The government party's attack was mostly on the level of personal abuse of the Labour Party's leadership. Another factor working against Labour was the rising demand by the press that voters elect a stable government, which in the circumstances meant voting for one or the other of the two major parties. Urging 'a definite decision', the *Dublin Evening Mail* (30 August) warned that under proportional representation 'the country may find itself with a small party (Labour, perhaps) of twenty or twenty-two holding the balance of power'.

One of the principal themes of the government party campaign was that Labour (as well as the National League), by its parliamentary alliance with Fianna Fail, had 'betrayed' both its party supporters and the treaty itself. On one occasion the minister for external affairs Desmond FitzGerald employed this theme:

> The Labour Party had betrayed the Labour men who voted for them and the treaty, in being prepared to throw the country into the melting-pot again and risk a recrudescene of anarchy in the country, which must necessarily be followed by unemployment and misery.[5]

The Labour executive later admitted that many party supporters saw the party's involvement in the coalition proposal as conflicting with Labour's long-held posture of independence.[6] In a similar vein, the Cumann na nGaedheal journal, the *Freeman*, declared that the charge made by Johnson that the government intended to declare Fianna Fail an unlawful assembly was 'merely an attempt to help Fianna Fail in its campaign for indemnity to assassins'. Cumann na nGaedheal speakers hammered home the assertion that the coalition proposal was merely a plot to put de Valera in power.[7]

Only once did the government party raise an issue which had a socio-economic bearing. This occurred when Cosgrave warned the voters that greatly increased government expenditure would result if

4 I.T.G.W.U., *1927 report*, p. 11; I.L.P. and T.U.C., *1928 report*, pp. 26, 59. See editorial comment *Dublin Evening Mail* 26 Aug. 1927 on Labour's unpreparedness.

5 *Dublin Evening Mail*, 14 Sept. 1927.

6 *1928 report*, pp. 24–25.

7 *Freeman*, 3 Sept. 1927; *Irish Times*, 12 Sept. 1927.

a Labour government was returned. He said that such a government would provide unemployment benefit at the 'English' level, restore old-age pension reductions and introduce widow and orphan pensions, at a total cost of £1 million. The *Irishman* (17 September 1927) made haste to reply that Cosgrave 'conveniently forgets that last April his colleague, Mr. Blythe, remitted tax to the extent of half a million for the benefit, not of the struggling middle class family, but of the wealthy income tax payers.'

For the first time in this decade, Cumann na nGaedheal attempted to make an issue of Labour's socialist beliefs. That it was done at this time is an indication of the attention that the government party focused on Labour in this election. Cosgrave charged that the Labour Party sought to establish state socialism, but that the Irish people, 'wouldn't stand for it'. The anti-socialist crusade was carried forward by other government party speakers and supporters, including at least two priests.[8] The 10 September issue of the *Nation*, Fianna Fail's organ, questioned Cosgrave's change of front:

> The Labour Party, which he could not praise too highly at the last election, is, it appears, tainted with Socialism and is therefore abhorrent to this great upholder of Christian principles.

The Labour Party busily defended itself. Johnson took the lead in defending the ill-fated coalition proposal. He declared that inter-party governments were assumed under proportional representation; he also pointed to the many successful coalition governments in other countries. But his party did not call anew for a coalition ministry; rather, it attempted to assert that it was independent of all other parties and would remain so.[9] Interestingly, de Valera made clear that he had not turned away from the idea of another coalition; 'Fianna Fail were prepared to support any alternative government while waiting for the Irish people to give them a majority.'

Labour countered Cumann na nGaedheal's attack with charges that the government was seeking to create a dictatorship by means of a 'rushed election', that it was attempting to smother 'independent criticism' and 'crush the possibility of an alternative government'. Labour further held that the government party 'was counting on the power of the purse', that is, Cumann na nGaedheal's financial backing, 'to wipe out the Labour Party'. On the constitutional question, Labour reiterated that it supported the treaty and 'nothing less than the Treaty'. At this time, however, it became slightly more radical on this issue by stating that it 'did not accept the Treaty as the final settlement of Ireland's needs'. The party had already accused Cosgrave of standing

8 Cosgrave's statement in *Irish Independent*, 6 Sept. 1927. Statements of Very Rev. C. McNamara, P.P. and Dean Doyle of Ossory in ibid., 6, 15 Sept. 1927; *Irish Times*, 12 Sept. 1927.

9 Sen. M. Duffy was the only Labour speaker to advocate another attempt at coalition government. *Cork Examiner*, 13 Sept. 1927.

on the prerogatives of the British king on the dissolution of the Dail. Now Johnson challenged the minister for external affairs to state the government's policy for the Free State should Britain go to war. The Labour leader asserted that the Cosgrave regime had become 'the instrument of . . . anti-national elements in the country'. The Labour Party's tendency towards radicalism on national issues at this time can be explained, in part, by Cumann na nGaedheal's attack on the party for being 'anti-national'.

A significant development was the abuse heaped on the heads of the Labour leaders, especially Johnson, by both the supporters of the government and the ministers themselves. Previously, of course, the abuse had come from the anti-treatyites. Contradicting his earlier words of praise, Cosgrave now condemned Johnson's leadership; he declared, for example, 'In no crisis during the last five years did Mr. Johnson ever exhibit the qualities of statemanship.' But this criticism was mildness itself beside the statement of one Cumann na nGaedheal candidate who called Johnson 'an Atheist and head of an organization allied with English Freemasons and Moscow'. Johnson delcared that this sort of accusation was spread not only in his constituency, but throughout the country.[10]

Attacks on Johnson for being English became the stock in trade for many Cumann na nGaedheal campaigners. This matter had been raised in every campaign since 1918, but this was the first time that it was used by the government party. Now that Johnson was considered to be fully on the side of the enemy, however, the Cumann na nGaedheal enthusiasts apparently decided the time had come to beat Johnson with this club. Mid-way through the campaign, the *Freeman* declared that it had heard enough of the 'Englishman' argument:

> We have heard a good deal . . . of the argument that Mr. Johnson, being an Englishman, is unfit to be President of the Free State. It is an argument with which we have no sympathy and of which we hope no more will be heard. Mr. Johnson's record in the last ten years is as good as that of most Irishmen.

But this rebuke did not prevent various Cumann na nGaedheal candidates from continuing to make use of the matter. Referring to Johnson and Redmond, one of these declared, 'The country was not so bankrupt of intelligence and common sense that they would send into the Dail to lead the country an English Socialist and an English Imperialist.'[11] De Valera, of course, had to put up with similar abuse in the early years of his career. John Daly, now drawn to the bosom of Cumann na nGaedheal, said that de Valera, an 'Irish-Italian', 'pretended he hated the English, but he was ready to install an Englishman as

10 Statement of W. O'Donnell, Mayo, who withdrew his assertions upon Johnson's demand. *Cork Examiner*, 15 Sept. 1927; *Evening Herald*, 14 Sept. 1927.

11 Statement of J. J. Byrne, Dublin north. *Irish Independent*. See also statement of Denis Gorey, ibid., 1 Sept. 1927.

President'. Even Patrick Hogan, the minister for agriculture and a decent man, felt compelled to raise the 'Englishman' issue. Johnson's party vigorously defended its leader, citing his long record of service to the nation, both in the labour movement and in the national struggle; T. J. O'Connell praised him as a 'Protestant serving Ireland'.[12]

In marked contrast to previous electoral contests, Fianna Fail did not attack the Labour Party. It could hardly have done so after having just finished working with Labour in the Dail. There is evidence that Fianna Fail supporters gave Labour a bit of help in some constituencies.[13] For its part, Labour had nothing critical to say about Fianna Fail. While the two parties observed a truce, attack on the Labour Party came from a new, or rather, an old source.

James Larkin had been curiously inactive in the June election. Now he more than made up for this. As has been seen, Larkin had co-operated with Fianna Fail in certain tactics before that party had entered the Dail. Now Big Jim decided to enter the political arena, using his previously somnolent Irish Workers League as the vehicle. Although there was no formal alliance between Fianna Fail and Larkin's group, there is good evidence that the two organizations enjoyed most friendly relations in the election. It soon became clear that one of Larkin's objectives was to secure the defeat of the Labour candidates in the Dublin area, especially Johnson.

The Irish Workers League put forward three candidates: Larkin for Dublin north, John Lawlor for Dublin south, and Larkin's son James for Johnson's district, County Dublin (Larkin originally said that the league would also contest Tipperary, the district of his opponent O'Brien, Cork City and Limerick). Larkin declared that his organization had decided to participate in the election because of the unsettled political conditions existing since the murder of O'Higgins, and because the position of the workers was growing worse hourly. He blamed not only the Cosgrave government, but also 'the allegedly official Labour Party and many of the Trade Union leaders who represented British unions in Ireland'. Larkin's entrance into the political fray at this time could also be explained by his Labour opponents' view that he was consumed by envy and would attempt to destroy anything not of his own making—in this case the Johnson-led Labour Party. Also, he may have been resentful of Johnson's prominence in national affairs.[14] But perhaps Larkin simply did not want to miss out on a good fight.

The Labour Party took the position that Larkin was not seeking to achieve better representation for the workers, but was only trying to undermine the party. It pointed out that Larkin could not take his seat if elected because he was an undischarged bankrupt; the other two

12 Statement of O'Connell, *Irishman*, 17 Sept.; Norton, *Irish Times*, 7 Sept.; J. T. O'Farrell, *Irish Independent*, 7 Sept. 1927.

13 Interview with William McMullen, 30 Nov. 1965.

14 *Irish Times*, 1 Sept. 1927; interviews with Archie Heron and Frank Robbins.

Larkinite candidates, it said, were only going forward in order to draw away Labour votes. Grossly underestimating Larkin's appeal in this election, R. J. P. Mortished, a Labour candidate in the same district as Big Jim, declared that the Larkinite candidates 'won't subtract a score of votes from us'.[15]

Although the Larkinite candidates went forward under the banner of the Irish Workers League, they were sometimes referred to as independent labour, but more often as Communist candidates. As the Workers League was affiliated to the Communist International, there was justification for this label: Johnson, for one, held to this view. When Larkin brought in Willie Gallacher, the Communist member of the British Parliament, to speak for him, the impression was solidified. The government party attempted to make political capital out of Fianna Fail—Larkin co-operation by publishing advertisements connecting 'Fianna Fail and the Communist Party'.[16]

Larkin concentrated his fire on Johnson, charging that under Johnson's leadership the Labour Party had failed to forward the workers' interests and had been taken over by 'place hunters'. Reaching to the past, the man of 1913 alleged that Johnson had failed to support certain strikes and had said that Connolly was wrong to stage the 1916 rising. With near-demonic intent, Larkin sought Johnson's political destruction; perhaps all the frustration of a deposed leader was coming out. Larkin's son, then twenty-one, was not a serious candidate in County Dublin but his name was James Larkin. Larkin himself toured the constituency, heaping contumely not only on Johnson but on his wife as well. These activities culminated in a scuffle between Larkin and Johnson's son, from which the former emerged with a black eye. Larkin also found time to charge R. J. P. Mortished, the Labour Party assistant secretary, with being a member of the Black and Tans during the national struggle.[17]

That Larkin was working closely with Fianna Fail is beyond doubt. The leading Fianna Fail candidate in Larkin's district, Eamonn Cooney, urged Fianna Fail voters to support Larkin because he 'stood for militant Irish nationalism just as much as Fianna Fail'.[18] Larkin predicted that de Valera would be elected 'Premier'; Larkin's brother Peter declared that only the Workers League and Fianna Fail were opposed to Imperialism'. A League advertisement openly urged support for de Valera's party. After the election, Larkin declared that Fianna Fail

15 *Irishman*, 10 Sept.; *Irish Independent*, 31 Aug. The Transport Union unsuccessfully attempted to prevent Larkin's nomination because of his inability to take his seat if elected. *Evening Herald*, 1 Sept. 1927.

16 *Irish Independent*, 15 Sept. 1927.

17 Larkin's son has agreed that he was not a serious candidate. Interview with James Larkin, Jr. For abuse of Johnson's wife, interview with Mary Johnson, 22 June 1964. 'Clan Larkin and Clan Johnson clashed in Rathfarnham', *Irish Independent*, 12 Sept. 1927; interview with Fred Johnson, 14 Oct. 1965.

18 The next day Cooney declared that he had spoken personally, not for his party. *Irish Independent*, 13 Sept. 1927.

leaders told him that 'thanks to his whirlwind campaign . . . he got them two or three seats they did not expect.' In the event, Larkin got nothing out of the election, except perhaps, revenge.

Election Results

The Labour Party maintained a brave front concerning the outcome of the election; Johnson commented that his party 'may gain a seat or two and we have no reason to anticipate any losses', but it was quite apparent that Labour was on the defensive. T. J. O'Connell, for example, acknowledges that he was forced to ride out the storm in his constituency.[19] When the returns were in, the results showed that the Labour Party had suffered a major set-back, holding only thirteen seats. In the number of Dail seats, Labour was back to its 1923 level; in the number of first preference votes, it was below the 1923 figure.

In the overall result, the two major parties gained at the expense of the smaller parties. Cumann na nGaedheal won sixty-one seats, just enough to continue as the government, but this was a significant advance compared to the forty-seven seats it won in June. Fianna Fail was close behind, winning fifty-seven seats; in June it had won forty-four and Sinn Fein seven. The Farmers Party continued its decline, securing only six seats as opposed to eleven in June. The National League was slashed from eight to two. Thirteen independents were elected, one fewer than in June. The three Irish Workers League candidates polled an impressive 12,000 first preference votes and Larkin was elected in Dublin North. His victory proved to have only token value, as he was disqualified from taking his seat. When the Larkinite vote is combined with that of the Labour Party in Dublin, the total shows that the 'labour' vote in this area had declined from that of June.[20]

The most serious loss for the Labour Party was the defeat of the party leader in his County Dublin constituency. All the other Labour men in the Dail since 1923 were returned. The party had assumed that since Johnson's running mate in County Dublin, William Norton, had stood down in this election, Johnson's return was nearly assured. The intervention of Larkin, together with the candidacy of his son, certainly was partially responsible for Johnson's defeat. However, the combined 'labour' vote in the district was greatly below that of June. This suggests that Johnson had lost the votes of some former supporters, including ex-unionists, who had previously supported him for his moderate,

19 Interview with O'Connell.

20 First preference votes.

	September election	June election
Labour Party	106,000	143,000
Cumann na nGaedheal	453,000	312,000
Fianna Fail	411,000	219,000
Farmers Party	74,000	101,000
National League	19,000	83,000
Independents	104,000	154,000

Irish Independent, 15 June; 20, 21 Sept. 1927. The *Irishman*, 15 Oct. 1927, reported 'official jubilation' in the Communist International upon Larkin's victory.

responsible posture in the Dail and for his support of the treaty; these same voters now reacted against his co-operation with de Valera and the anti-treatyites.[21]

The Labour Party did not lose strength uniformly over the country; in some districts it held its position and in some it gained votes over its June performance. It won one new seat—in Donegal, where for the first and only time it achieved a victory in that county, but it had had a near-miss there in June. But, repeating the pattern of 1923, the party polled disastrously in Dublin and Cork, the two major cities in the state, winning but one seat (in Cork) out of twenty.[22] In an election analysis in the 23 September issue of the *Irishman,* R. J. P. Mortished attributed Labour's debacle in the urban centres to trade unionist 'inertia' concerning Labour political action, but he gave no reasons for the existence of this condition. Certainly the Larkin split and the resulting inter-union war was a continuing factor in the party's weakness in Dublin. In Cork, the party had never achieved a firm footing. What Mortished found impressive was the continuing strength of Labour outside these two cities:

> It is noteworthy that the Labour representatives who were elected in 1923, with, of course, the outstanding exception of Mr. Johnson, were able, in spite of the attempt to crush them out completely, to retain their seats. Their success must be attributed, first, to the irreducible minimum of Labour strength in the country, but in part also to a reward of good service. . . . If we can retain a dozen seats under every conceivable handicap, then at a normal election we ought to be able to win many more.

The national press generally attributed Labour's reversal to its involvement in the coalition proposal and its co-operation with Fianna Fail.[23] It would appear that the party did lose some support as a result of its actions in August. But the principal reason for the Labour reverse at this time was that the voters generally supported one or other of the major parties in order to ensure stable government. Had a relatively effective coalition government been established, the public might not have felt compelled to choose between the two big parties, but this was not the situation. True, the two parties who would have formed the coalition government suffered heavily in the election, but this happened to all the smaller parties. Moreover, Johnson's defeat cannot be explained solely by his actions in the Dail in August. Patrick Baxter, the leader of the Farmers Party, and Denis Gorey, the former leader and a

21 Johnson polled 3,700 first preference votes and young Larkin 2,100, the combined vote being 5,800; in June Johnson and Norton polled a total of 9,600 votes. *Irish Independent,* 19 Sept. 1927; *1928 report,* p. 27.

22 The Labour vote was down in Dublin, Cork city, Carlow-Kilkenny, Leix-Offaly and Meath. Labour held its vote in Leitrim-Sligo, Longford-Westmeath, Tipperary, Wexford and Wicklow. *1928 report,* p. 27.

23 *Irish Independent,* 19 Sept., *Sunday Independent,* 23 Sept., *Cork Examiner,* 21 Sept., *The Kerryman,* 24 Sept. 1927.

convert to Cumann na nGaedheal, both of whom supported Cosgrave on the no-confidence motion, suffered defeat, as did John Jinks, who, of course, did not vote. The entrance into the Dail of Fianna Fail had created a new political situation, and it appears that the electorate had decided to discard some of the figures who had comprised the opposition in the initial period of the Free State. The September 1927 election was a turning point for the Labour Party as well as for the other small parties. It marked the beginning of a period of decline that was not reversed for twenty years.

THE PARTY AND THE CONGRESS SEPARATE

When the Labour Party was established in 1912, it was considered by its founders to be the political arm of the trade union movement. Until 1930 both the political and industrial branches of the labour movement were contained in one organization—the party-congress. Although it was recognized that this form of organization was unique among the labour movements of Europe, the Labour leadership in the early and mid-1920s held that combining both functions in one body provided security to the movement in a troubled period.

Until 1928 there was practically no demand in the labour movement for the separation of political and trade union branches. There was, however, the assertion of the small Irish Women Workers Union that the party-congress was devoting too much attention to political affairs and not enough to the trade union movement. Beginning at the 1924 Labour conference, and at every annual meeting through 1927, the union raised this question. The Labour executive did attempt to strengthen and stimulate trade union organization in this period, but its efforts were unsuccessful; union membership began to decline by mid-decade. In 1926 Louie Bennett, the leader of the womens' union, initiated a debate in the pages of the *Voice of Labour* concerning the desirability of separating the two arms of the movement. Archie Heron, the political organizer, told the Labour meeting that year that the existing set-up, with both branches under the control of a single executive, 'was a decided strength and it would be fatal to do anything that would create two separate and distinct organizations'.[24] The question of division was not raised again until after the political upheavals of 1927.

In each of the three national elections from 1923 to 1927 Labour Party spokesmen had complained of lack of support from the trade union movement. This criticism extended to the unions (and until 1925 to the trades councils) as well as to individual trade unionists.[25] It was generally held within the party that this lack of support was due to the preoccupation of the average trade unionist with the political and constitutional issues then raging in the country. Furthermore, the

24 *Voice of Labour*, 3 Sept.—2 Oct. 1926; *1926 report*, p. 140.

25 *1924 report*, pp. 88–89; *1927 report*, pp. 9–12, 57–58; *Irishman*, 30 July 1927; *1928 report*, pp. 116–17.

Larkin split did much to cripple the growth of the party in Dublin. Once the party realized that trade unionist support was unreliable, it began to establish political groups independent of the unions. Its principal move in this direction was the creation of local party branches, beginning in 1925. At the same time, the Labour executive declared that the trade union side of the organization should not be concerned about the party-congress being swamped by non-trade unionists. Problems arising out of the presence of local Labour groups at the annual conference, it proposed, should 'be left for solution until the political side of the organization has been well developed'. Time was to prove that the danger of political activists dominating the party-congress was more apparent than real. The local party groups did not achieve significant growth, had no effect on party-congress policy and, after 1927, declined to almost nothing.

Following the misfortunes of 1927 the prospects of the party-congress looked bleak; both the industrial and political branches of the movement were in decline. Further, the defeat of Thomas Johnson in the September election marked the end of his remarkable leadership of the organization. Johnson's effectiveness in keeping both sides of the movement working smoothly together is evidenced by the disintegration of party-congress harmony once he left the leadership.

Johnson did not attempt to regain his position. He never contested another Dail seat, and in 1928 he resigned as the party-congress secretary. But he remained active in the labour movement, acting as party legislative advisor for the next several years while serving in the senate from 1928 to 1936. The exigencies of Irish politics found him a colleague of James Larkin in the mid-1940s, in the trade union congress. When the Labour Court was established in 1946, Johnson was appointed a member and served until 1955.

Johnson's position as both leader of the Dail party and secretary of the party-congress was unique. No attempt was made to continue this arrangement. Johnson's successor as Dail party leader was T. J. O'Connell, deputy party leader since 1923 and secretary of the Irish National Teachers Organization since 1916. A man from the west (representing first Mayo north and then Galway), O'Connell was in the Johnson mould, being a careful, cautious leader of great dedication and integrity, but with limited popular appeal. The new party-congress secretary was R. J. P. Mortished.

Evidence of mounting friction between the political and trade union sides occurred at the 1928 Labour conference. There were complaints by trade unionists that the Dail party was not following the policy of the party-congress and that the Labour deputies were disinterested in the affairs of that body. This meeting also saw an unsuccessful attempt to introduce 'card' voting, which would have assured domination by the larger unions. The next year's meeting saw both the executive and the new secretary criticized for inactivity and lack of policy direction.[26]

26 *1928 report*, pp. 89–90, 96. *1929 report*, pp. 84–90; *Irishman*, 10 Aug. 1929.

Before the 1929 Labour conference those interested primarily in political activity proposed that the two branches be separated into independent organizations. The first concrete plan for separation was put forward a month before the meeting by the Post Office Workers Union and its secretary William Norton.[27] At the annual conference there was general agreement that the branches should separate; no voice was raised in opposition to this proposal. It should be borne in mind that for long there had been an assumption in the labour movement that the party would eventually establish a separate organization. This was to occur when the party had become strong enough to stand on its own. As it was, the separation took place in very different circumstances.

The act of division was a case of the party seceding from the trade union congress; the congress maintained its organization as it was before the party was founded. The operation was carried out with dispatch. A committee appointed by the 1929 Labour conference approved the separation scheme. A special conference was held from 28 February to 1 March 1930 at which the division was achieved; only two delegates opposed this action. Separation came at this time for several reasons. One factor was that the party could no longer hope for substantial financial and organizational help from the industrial side of the movement. The trade unions were in decline and the party-congress revenue had fallen. Moreover, the unions had proved to be ineffective instruments for political activity; William Norton told the 1929 meeting, 'Not one of the thirteen Labour Deputies held his seat by Trade Union votes.' Another factor was the weakened leadership of the party-congress executive. Dissension was growing and neither the members of the executive nor Mortished had ready answers to the criticism of their leadership.

The most important reason for separation at this time was that those persons who were principally concerned with political activity believed that the party could appeal to a wider spectrum of the electorate only if it were free from the image of being a trade unionist party. This viewpoint was put forward in the 6 July 1929 issue of the Labour weekly. The *Irishman* argued that although the long range goals of the unions and of the party were the same, 'their immediate objectives are not the same and their methods and appeal cannot be the same'. Since there was only a minority of wage earners in the state, what was needed, it said, was 'a political party which can appeal to every citizen, irrespective of whether he or she is or is not a wage earner in need of a trade union'. The chairman of the 1929 meeting, L. J. Duffy, told the delegates that the party's programme was 'democratically sound' but 'if that programme is to unfold freely, it should rest, not on the Trade Union movement as such, but on the individual men and women who support it.'[28]

27 *Irishman*, 6 July 1929. The first suggestion of separation after the September 1927 election was made by Victor Hall in the Labour weekly, 29 Oct. 1927.

28 *1929 report*, pp. 67–106; *Irish Times*, 1 March 1930.

The separated party did not develop a programme that was markedly different from what went before; the party generally held to the proposals of the 1920s. Some minor changes were made in its constitution; for example, a liberal appeal for social reconstruction replaced the labour demand for workers' control. Neither did a separate party mean that the unions would no longer participate in political affairs; the unions were eligible to join the party as corporate members. The Transport Union and its leader William O'Brien continued to have great influence in party affairs. Some of the other unions, however, did not affiliate with the new party. The separation of the party and the trades congress was made very clear when no machinery for joint consultation was established. Further, officers of the congress could not be officers of the party. But informal contact between the two would be maintained due to the fact that 'Trade Union representatives will be present at annual meetings of both organizations.' The party decided that the congress would not have the power to decide which unions could affiliate with the party, but it would have the right to object to the admission of unions that did not belong to the congress.[29]

The all-Ireland facade of the Labour Party was maintained. The proudest assertion of the labour movement was that since 1921 it was one of the few organizations which encompassed the thirty-two counties. A joint council was set up with the Labour Party (Northern Ireland) and bi-annual meetings were held alternatively in Dublin and Belfast. Due to the differing political situations in the two areas, little co-ordination and unity actually developed.[30]

The new party plunged into the struggle to develop its organization. While it attempted to revive the local party scheme, it declared that it would put forward eighty candidates at the next general election, thus negating the standing criticism that it did not put forward enough candidates to form a possible government.[31] The party organization effort had indifferent successess and throughout the 1930s the party never put forward more than thirty-one candidates in any election. Not until 1943 did it put forward enough candidates to form a possible government. Further, the party attracted very few nominees who were not trade unionists. In the early 1930s the party failed to develop new support, failed even to hold it support, for a variety of reasons. Among these was the party's inability to develop new issues; adhering to the pattern of the 1920s, it remained on old but unprofitable ground on political and constitutional issues. This was at the same time that Fianna Fail, already demanding radical constitutional changes, was continuing to develop social and economic policies comparable to those of Labour. An overriding factor in the inability of a smaller party such as Labour to

29 *Irish Times*, 3 March 1930; Irish Trade Union Congress, *1930 report*, p. 127; Irish Labour Party, *1931 report*, p. 3; *Irishman*, 8 March, 19 July 1930.

30 I.T.U.C., *1930 report*, p. 144; I.L.P., *1931 report*, pp. 3–4.

31 *Irish Independent*, 28 Feb. 1930. By 1931 the party claimed to have 112 local branches. *The Watchword*, 25 April 1931. *Irishman*, 22 March 1930.

grow in the early thirties was the public's concern for stable government. The September 1927 election had shown the electorate that either Fianna Fail or Cumann na nGaedheal would be strong enough to form a possible government at the next election. Hence, most voters were drawn towards voting for either of the two major parties, with the smaller parties suffering accordingly.

Seemingly in uncanny imitation of the situation created by the 1922 division of Sinn Fein, the personalities and quarrels of the 1923 split in the labour movement continued to be a dominant feature of Labour Party politics for the next two decades. The Larkin-Transport Union controversy lasted a lifetime. Had Larkin been able to take his seat in the Dail in 1927, doubtlessly he would have found himself supporting the same social and economic position as did the Labour Party. This situation would have gone some way towards healing the breach between himself and the party. (Larkin finally found his way into the Dail in 1937; his gradual return to the party can be dated as beginning that year.[32]) In 1928 Larkin again raised his proposal for a new workers' party but he never attempted to organize it. In the same year he rejected suggestions offered by third parties that the political sides of the labour movement be re-united. Larkin held that political unity could only follow industrial unity, and neither he nor his opponents in the Transport Union were prepared to settle their union differences.[33]

Larkin's Communist affiliation was another difficulty in any unity scheme.[34] Even when he dropped this connection in the early 1930s, he was kept out of the Labour Party and his union out of the trade union congress. The group chiefly responsible for the continuing opposition to Larkin was, not surprisingly, William O'Brien and his colleagues in the Transport Union leadership. Using his position in the party and the power of the Transport Union in the congress, O'Brien fought against any suggestion that past sins should be forgiven. In the mid-1940s he was prepared to splinter both the party and the congress rather than treat with Big Jim. This entirely fruitless conflict ended only with the compulsory retirement of O'Brien from the Transport Union in 1946 and the death of Larkin a year later.

32 Interview with James Larkin, Jr.

33 *Irish Worker*, 12 May 1928; interview with James Larkin, Jr. See also Larkin, *James Larkin*, p. 292.

34 Larkin was a delegate to the 1928 meeting of the Communist International and his Irish Workers League continued to be affiliated with that body. Larkin, *James Larkin*, pp. 290–92.

12
Conclusion

> *'Certainly it is true that preoccupation with political issues has overshadowed consideration of social and economic problems. The bland assumption of critics that this indicates a lack of realism on the part of the Irish electorate should not, however, pass unquestioned. Is it not the case that political problems in Ireland have been fundamental over the last twenty-five years? Is it not the case that until they were settled, concentration on economic and social issues would have been unrealistic? . . . To Aristotle, man was a political animal, but contemporary critics affect to believe that an electorate, primarily concerned with political problems, is for that very reason to be dismissed as immature.'*
>
> Nicholas Mansergh, *The Commonwealth and the nations* (London 1948), p.182.

'It is an extraordinary thing', declared the economic historian George O'Brien in 1936, 'that, in the Free State, with the long Irish tradition of aggressive trade unionism in the towns and aggressive agrarian association in the country, the labour party should be so insignificant.'[1] This was at a time when the socialist parties of the other European democratic countries were making rapid strides, having already achieved power in Scandinavia. The most important factor responsible for the anaemic political thrust of the Irish Labour Party by the third decade of this century was the dominance of the issue of self-government. The predominance of the national question did not hinder the growth of the trade union side of the labour movement (indeed, it greatly contributed to the spread of Irish-based unions), but it did present near-insurmountable difficulties for the development of a strong Labour Party.

Other difficulties stood in the way of the party: its straddling on the question of home rule, a party structure of narrow appeal, the small industrial vote, partition and the powerful influence of the Catholic Church. To take the last point first, the Catholic Church throughout

1 G. O'Brien, *The four green fields* (Dublin 1936), p. 100.

Europe fifty years ago generally took a conservative position on social and economic questions. Church spokesmen appeared preoccupied with the fear of Marxism and the threat of violent revolution rather than with the existing social conditions. The Church in Ireland drew the great majority of its priests from small farmer and lower-middle classes; thus it had a bias towards the values and experiences of rural society. From time to time a few priests addressed themselves to the problems of the workers, but always they advised moderation and more moderation. Larkin and all his works were roundly condemned by many a cleric. The sway of political radicalism in the country had the effect of making the Church ultra-cautious on social and economic questions. A powerful and conservative church conditioned the ground against social experimentation. Yet, because of the influence and example of the British trade unions, the labour movement in Ireland was always wholly secular although in every other European country with a major Catholic population, Church-sponsored unions were created to combat the rise of socialist-dominated workers' organizations.

Even before the creation of the Labour Party, its parent, the Irish Trade Union Congress had decided that the organized labour movement should not take a position on either the general question of the legitimacy of Irish nationalism or on the specific question of home rule. Although a majority of Irish trade unionists were nationalists, the congress also represented large numbers of northern Protestant and Unionist workers. By avoiding commitment on the question of Irish self-government, the congress attained its primary objective: the maintenance of an all-Ireland trade union movement. This was a considerable achievement, as few organizations encompassing the whole country continued to exist once partition became a fact. When the decision to form a political party was made, however, the refusal of the congress to commit itself on the national question eventually proved to be a severe handicap to the fledgling party.

For the decade after 1902 continuous debate occurred within the congress concerning firstly, whether it should create a political party and, secondly, what its composition and affiliations should be. The rise of industrial unionism, in Ireland appropriately termed 'Larkinism', provided a powerful impetus towards the construction of a nationally-based party. But it was the seemingly imminent achievement of home rule in 1912 which tipped the balance in favour of an Irish-based party, independent of any British connection.

The two groups who had led the struggle for this type of party—the strongly nationalist and socialist bloc led by James Larkin and James Connolly and dominated by Dubliners, and a smaller group, unconcerned with nationalism, less vocally socialist and more trade union orientated—both agreed that the party should be combined, at least in the initial period, with the country's representative labour body—the trades congress. This position was sensible at the time, earlier labour political bodies unconnected to the trade unions had foundered. Further, throughout Europe the support of the trade unions was a necessary condition for the growth of labour parties.[2] But in no other country in Europe was the party united with the union congress. This arrangement, which gave the party an exclusive trade unionist-appearance, eventually hindered its development. The over-possessive parent stunted its child's growth. In 1912 the need to preserve unity within the congress was uppermost in the mind's of the congress-party leaders. They therefore decided that the first party programme should avoid commitment to either nationalism or socialism; what was advocated was far-reaching social and economic reforms. In this way the founders of the party sought to avoid alienating their basically more conservative constituencies while they were seeking to achieve their initial political goal: the creation of a modest Labour bloc in the home rule parliament.

Two events disrupted the plans of the party's founders. First came the British Parliament's decision to divide Ireland and to divide it in such a way as to separate industrial Belfast from the rest of the country. Here the labour movement faced a dilemma: while all sections opposed separation, the bulk of northern labour opinion was opposed to inclusion in a Dublin parliament. It was clear to all political observers that the severing of the industrial heart of Ireland from the rest would be a crippling blow to the new party. The second event, and one that had even more serious immediate consequences, was the outbreak of the European war and the consequent shelving of home rule. The destruction of the early prospect of home rule undermined the logic on which the party was founded.

With the suspension of home rule it is not surprising that little was done to develop the party structure. But a vigorous local political organization had long existed in Belfast and beginning in 1911 a similar structure emerged in Dublin. From that date until the suspension of local elections during the war it was Labour, not Griffith's tiny Sinn Fein group, which was the principal opponent of the United Irish League in the Dublin municipal elections. It was here that Labour made its first attempt to win a parliamentary seat from the hitherto all-dominant Irish Parliamentary Party, a challenge that came much closer to success than corresponding Sinn Fein efforts in the few years before the war. Further, Labour members were serving on local bodies in all parts of the country, while the Transport Union had established a widely-read and provocative weekly newspaper. Liberty Hall was known in the far corners of the land.

The Labour executive was keenly critical of Irish involvement in the war, but because of the differing views of the workers on the matter, not only in the north but throughout the country, it did not go so far as to directly oppose Irish participation. It is noteworthy that the congress-party stood alone among the representative labour bodies of the countries involved in the war in being neutral on the war issue. It should

2 L. D. Epstein, *Political parties in western democracies* (New York 1967), p. 150.

also be noted, however, that the Irish Labour stance was not based primarily on the pre-war position taken by the European socialist movement—that the workers of Europe should not fight each other. Its position was based on national consideration, as was the commitment of the other European labour movements to the war, the difference being that in Ireland there was a submerged nationality seeking fulfilment.

If the immediate prospect of the creation of an effective party was ended by the war, a significant and militant labour force was maintained and strengthened in Dublin. The origins and development of a force, that had such an important influence not only on the labour movement but on the country itself, demands assessment. The excitement and turmoil which gripped industrial Ireland in the period 1910–14 was not due simply to James Larkin and his brand of militant unionism. These were years of unprecedented industrial conflict in Britain as well. From his arrival in Ireland in 1907, Larkin shaped and led a series of challenges to Irish employers, culminating in the great Dublin labour struggle of 1913. It was Larkin's charismatic personality which disguised the fact that at this time Ireland was demonstrating that not only politically but economically it was part of the United Kingdom. The workers' revolt began in Britain and spread to Ireland. Despite the Irish parentage of both Larkin and Connolly, and their determination to win acceptance in Ireland, they were ideological imports from Britain.

There is, however, at least one important difference between the labour upheavals in the two islands. In Britain it was the workers who took the initiative, with the trade union leaders reluctantly following, while in Ireland the revolt was led by the union leaders or at least the most active of them, principally Larkin and his colleagues in the Transport Union and the Dublin Trades Council. The reason why the militants were able to seize the leadership of Irish Labour was that, unlike the situation in the British movement, a comprehensive union structure was lacking. The militants built their own power base when they began to organize the unskilled workers. A further factor in the rise to dominance of the militants was the absence of an established, parliamentary Labour Party which would be expected to act as a restraining, moderating influence. This meant that radical practices, such as the sympathetic strike, were approved, indeed fostered, by the Labour leadership.

The difference in the character of the leaderships of the two movements helps to explain the difficulty with which they co-operated in the 1913 struggle in Dublin. It is sometimes mooted that the British movement did little to support the Dublin workers, but by any standard the help given by the British movement could be termed generous. The British movement did not call a general strike to support the Dublin cause, but neither did the Irish movement. (It seems strange that the Irish congress-party was not employed to mobilize support in other parts of Ireland. This was an indication that it had little influence at at this time.) Further, the Irish trade unions nearly twenty years before had left the British congress to establish their own, while the new Irish Labour Party had rejected any ties to its British counterpart. Mention should also be made that of all British parties, the Labour Party had the best record in regard to Irish matters.

The period of the revolution in Ireland was heralded by the Dublin struggle of 1913. A sullen and embittered segment of the Dublin working class was destined to do more than disturb the operation of William Martin Murphy's tramway company. It became clear to them that social justice could only be achieved when the foreign oppressive regime had been replaced by self-government. One concrete product of the struggle was the Citizen Army, originally formed to protect workers from police attack, but soon to be transformed into a weapon for political revolution. It was through this small but potent force that the militants in the Irish labour movement added their weight to the fateful balance at Eastertide 1916. Thus the connection between 1913 and the rebellion is direct and causal.

From shortly after the beginning of the European war until the rising, the leadership of the labour movement was not to be in the hands of Larkin. Indeed, due to the action of the British Government, his absence in America was to extend to nearly nine years. In the year and a half to April 1916 a leader with vision and audacity—Connolly—ably filled this role. The question has often been raised as to whether or not Larkin would have led the Citizen Army into rebellion as did Connolly. During his seven years in Ireland to 1914 he had demonstrated that he was an activist, a man who seized opportunities. Combined with this are his assertions of the need to use the war period to attempt to gain Irish independence. Both of these factors lead to the conclusion that he would have trodden the same path as Connolly. But with the death of Connolly such qualities were not to be found in his successors. Larkin was to be very much a missing ingredient in the labour movement after 1916. Further, his long exile prevented him from regaining his old leadership in the face of the opposition of the new leaders.

Connolly, of course, was both a nationalist and a socialist; as a citizen of a subject nation, he saw the two as a piece. In a period of imperialist war, he did the only thing logical for him: he struck for national freedom. The great majority of Dublin trade unionists, as well as union members elsewhere in the country, did not ascribe to his revolutionary views and were not in any way involved in the rising. Further, the organized Labour movement as such had nothing to do with it. The loss of Connolly was an irreparable blow to the movement. A leader who combined utter determination with revolutionary principles was missing in the next half decade when these very qualities, possessed by the Sinn Fein leaders, won for their movement so very much.

The arrest of the Dublin trade union leaders and the disruption of union organization, threw responsibility for patching together the movement on to those members of the congress-party executive (principally Thomas Johnson and D. R. Campbell), who were not known nationalists and who therefore could not be suspected of complicity in the revolt. They were soon joined by the released Dublin labour leaders—William O'Brien, Thomas Foran and Thomas Farren, of whom only Farren had taken part in the rising. These men comprised the leadership of the labour movement for the next decade, with the chief figures being Johnson and O'Brien.

In regard to both men, it was a case of less talented subordinates moving into positions of leadership in the wake of disaster. A relatively immature movement had been most fortunate to have men of the calibre of Connolly and Larkin as leaders; but luck does not always last. Now its leadership would reflect the actual state of development of the movement. Johnson had been neither a leader of a local political organization nor of a trade union. He emerged from the congress-party apparatus (he was chairman of the executive in 1916) as a leader when the situation required a businesslike binder-of-wounds; he maintained this leadership by his complete devotion to the labour movement and his clear, reasoned socialist philosophy. O'Brien brought an unrivalled experience in socialist and trade union bodies to his new responsibility. With Connolly gone, the Transport Union desperately required a man of driving administrative ability. O'Brien accepted the union's invitation to fill this need and quickly became the domineering figure in the organization as he directed it through a period of spectacular expansion.

The great question confronting the new leaders of the congress-party was what direction the labour movement should take. Caution and reasonableness governed their decision: they determined that it would be best to rebuild the movement on the same basis on which it had been organized in 1912–14, rather than to pursue the links that Connolly had forged with the advanced nationalists. In doing so they were simply recognizing the fact that Connolly's commitment to national revolution was not shared by the great majority of trade unionists. They apparently underestimated the extent to which the Irish political climate had changed since the party was created. The European war, the resort to physical force, the upsurge of nationalism following the ruthless suppression of the rebellion—all these factors did not alter their decision to build the party almost exclusively on social and economic issues, leaving the national question to be settled by others, and hopefully soon. By taking this road, they chose to overlook Connolly's pronouncement that 'political and social freedom are not two separate and unrelated ideas but are two sides of one great principle, each being incomplete without the other.'

By reason of being chairman of the 1916 conference where he presented the leadership's policy decision, Johnson has been credited with being both the author and the primary force behind the policy. Undoubtedly he strongly urged this approach, but responsibility for the decision was shared by the Labour leadership as a whole. By fact of his English upbringing and his Belfast residence, Johnson could not be expected to understand fully the force of nationalism in Irish politics; in the years after 1916 he only gradually came to grasp this. What is surprising is that men like O'Brien, Farren and Foran apparently underestimated the power of the national idea. One gets the impression that they did not consider that it was necessary for the movement to devote attention to this. They appear to be prisoners of the Marxist belief that the working class would inevitably come to power; the Russian revolution and the rapid development of the labour movement throughout Europe provided evidence for this belief.

The combined congress-party structure was partially responsible for the leaders' decision not to be involved in the revived militant national movement. Many of the trade unionists were not nationalists and probably would have split away from the congress-party had it committed itself to Irish nationalism. There was also a division among the workers between the supporters of constitutional action and those who believed in revolution. Also, the spread of trade unionism probably would have been hampered had the national labour body taken stands on purely political questions. With the exception of Johnson, all of the leaders were first and foremost trade union officials; accordingly, their greatest fear was that the trade union movement would be overtaken by division and stagnation. Returning to the 1912 formula, the leadership decided that social and economic reform was the only practicable basis consistent with trade union interests on which to seek worker political support.

Initially, this policy appeared to work well. Both the party-congress and the Dublin labour movement were re-organized and strengthened. Helped by nationalist feeling, Irish-based unions, especially the Transport Union, grew by leaps and bounds in all parts of the country. In the political arena, where the dominating issue was Irish self-government, the Labour Party was forced to compete with a party whose primary appeal was based on this issue. Sinn Fein offered some promises of social reform following Irish independence, but it gained its basic support from the nationalist feeling engendered by or at least revived by the rebellion.

In its competition with Sinn Fein and the crumbling Irish Parliamentary Party, the Labour Party did not seek political supremacy; carrying on its outlook of 1914, rather it sought only a portion of political power. In this it was recognizing that it could make no claim to speak for anything like a majority of the electorate. Even with this modest objective, Labour was clearly at a disadvantage compared with its principal rival. It was attempting to bring a new issue before the country—that of social and economic transformation, while Sinn Fein simply added an extremist twist to the well-established issue of nationalism. Further, while the Labour Party's structure restricted its appeal to working men, Sinn Fein could appeal to all classes. Finally, Labour very much took into account views of the northern Protestants who as a group rejected Irish nationalism, while Sinn Fein, largely ignoring the existence of this large element, sought the support of the nationalist majority in the rest of the country.

Despite its lack of radicalism on political questions, the congress-party became increasingly more advanced on socio-economic matters until it arrived at a comprehensively socialist position in its 1918 constitution. One gets the impression that the Labour leaders gave greater attention to the creation of a party programme than it did to the formation of constituency organizations. The party's adoption of radical positions on socio-economic questions might be assumed to mean that it was attempting to match the extremism of Sinn Fein on political issues, but the trend at this time in all European labour movements was towards an open commitment to socialist ideology.

In its struggle with Sinn Fein, Labour failed to secure the necessary minimum of support largely because it felt that it could not clearly support Irish independence. Under the onslaught of the militant nationalists, the Labour Party did go as far as to support self-determination and the removal of all class privileges, but this was not enough. Sinn Fein's argument that independence necessarily must precede socio-economic reform overwhelmed Labour's plea that reform was required immediately, independence or not. Further, the extravagant nationalist doctrine of Sinn Fein completely overshadowed Labour's assertion that a sense of national unity could not be created by nationalist slogans and threats, but only by a programme of social and economic advancement for the mass of the Irish people, regardless of their political beliefs.

The result was that the Labour Party was forced out of the 1918 election, undoubtedly the most important Irish election in this century: a massive new electorate was having its first experience in politics and Labour was absent from the lists. The failure of the party to attain even a limited political foothold at this juncture has had grave consequences for both the party and the labour movement itself. Hoping for the best, the Labour leadership declared that the party's retirement from the contest would help to bring about a speedy settlement of the national question, but this proved to be a wish in vain. Political and constitutional issues were almost inevitably destined to remain the prime topics of debate for the foreseeable future. Was not partition clearly a prospect? How likely was it that Sinn Fein could achieve an independent republic in the face of an imperial Britain, fresh from victory in the European war? The Labour leaders were, at the least, unrealistic in expecting a quick resolution of this question.

Having been shoved out of this crucial election, the Labour Party was outside the leadership of the national struggle. It played no part in the construction of the rebel government of Dail Eireann. This arrangement was satisfactory to both Sinn Fein and the congress-party. A labour movement not directly tied to or supportive of the revolutionary government was used to give the appearance of a non-aligned organization driven to active condemnation of British policy and practice in Ireland. It did things that the insurgent movement could not do, such as organize strikes, appeal to the international labour movement, etc. For its part, the Labour organization's non-recognition of Dail Eireann allowed it to maintain unity in a time of great political stress. The adoption of the Labour-inspired democratic programme by the underground parliament, immediately upon its formation, gave the appearance that Sinn Fein was prepared to accept sweeping socio-economic changes. Had these principles been implemented from the very beginning of effective self-government, they would have resulted in a nearly complete transformation of Irish society. As it was, the Labour leaders were again to be disappointed, as almost nothing was done, either during the national struggle or for a decade after, to put the programme into effect.

The labour movement provided massive support for the independence struggle, but in doing so it was acting largely as a subordinate to the Sinn Fein leadership. At the same time, the Labour leadership refused to take a revolutionary plunge of its own. In a period of violence and upheaval, with the trade unions at the peak of their strength, it did not use the disorganized conditions to attempt a socialist revolution. Why was this? In rural areas there was evidence of serious socio-economic discontent, as seen in the land seizures, cattle drives and factory occupations. At the same time, however, the land purchase acts and the establishment of old age pensions had done much to create a more contented rural population. What of the cities? Here the direct brunt of the British military was felt. If the tightly organized I.R.A. had difficulty surviving in this situation, what chance would the more-loosely organized workers' bodies have of developing a revolutionary vehicle?

A further consideration is that although the Labour leaders loudly heralded the Russian revolution and talked about the advent of soviets and workers' control in Ireland, they did not believe in violence. Also, they were aware that they did not possess the support necessary to stage any sort of social revolution. Irish trade unionists, although fairly prone to strikes, were not socialists; they looked to their unions to provide for their economic betterment and that was all. It is probable that the national question diverted potential revolutionary tendencies among the workers. According to one veteran of the labour movement, the Left in Ireland was simply extreme nationalism. The Labour leaders were prepared to employ the weapon of the general strike but this was used exclusively to further the cause of self-government. Perhaps the comment of the British socialist Willie Gallacher could be applied to the Irish Labour leaders: 'We were carrying on a strike when we ought to have been making a revolution.'[3]

The Labour Party based its hopes on the assumption that it would attain an immediate position of power in Irish politics once the troublesome question of self-government had finally been resolved by others.

3 W. Gallacher, *Revolt on the Clyde* (London 1936), p. 221.

Yet during the period of the national struggle and its bitter aftermath political allegiances were being forged that were to last a lifetime. Being basically a rural society, loyalty counts for much in Ireland. Great popular figures were emerging from both the political and military sides of the national movement. Because the Labour Party failed to claim the workers' political allegiance on the hustings from the beginning, the rule was established in Irish politics that a man could be a good trade unionist and yet cast his vote for a nationalist (or Unionist) party.

In both the treaty controversy and in the ensuing civil war, the party could rightly disclaim responsibility. But in its policy of non-involvement, the party leadership demonstrated a failure to understand that political issues often have a crucial bearing upon socio-economic matters. It failed to recognize that certain provisions of the treaty would severely limit the powers of an Irish government, and thereby continue the constitutional controversy to the detriment of economic and social questions. The party could no longer avoid taking positions on major issues before the country and still hope to shortly attain a powerful position in the new state. As a result of its tactics and posture between 1916 and 1922 Labour leadership achieved the least possible both for itself and for the labour movement.

In the treaty election of 1922 Labour received its reward for its consistently neutral stance on the national question. In that contest the party obtained a share of votes from peace-makers and moderates; at the next election Labour lost these votes to the treaty party. The immediate prospect facing Labour was civil war. No situation could have been less favourable for the achievement of the party's programme of socio-economic reform and development. Inside the Dail the party was confronted by a largely preoccupied government with an artificially created majority, while outside the parliament were one-third of those elected, many of whom would have supported much of Labour's programme. Another factor which restricted Labour's political influence was the separation of the only major industrial area from the rest of Ireland. In the Dail the party was forced to play the role of a tiny opposition with no hope of victory.

With great energy and considerable skill the Labour Party criticized, indeed exposed, the Cosgrave government's failure to take full advantage of the treaty, especially in regard to the Boundary Commission, the council of Ireland, the financial agreements and the annuity payments. Yet the political group which was the principal beneficiary of these exposures was not the Labour Party but the anti-treatyites. Labour's position was further eroded when Fianna Fail appropriated much of the party's distinctive social and economic policy. At the same time, the anti-treatyites refusal to enter the Free State assembly delayed for years the implementation of the very proposals they had appropriated, thereby adding to Labour's legislative frustration.

At no time in the 1920s did Labour succeed in becoming the focus of radical and progressive activity. This was due largely to the party's structure. It was a trade unionist party, united with the Trade Union Congress; its leadership and Dail membership was trade unionist. Although the party created machinery to give a place to non-trade unionists, it is not surprising that the overwhelmingly trade union image of the party discouraged all but a few from joining. The trade union outlook and personnel of the party also prevented it from developing major support from the small farmers and farm labourers. Yet the party gained little from its trade union composition as it was weakest where the unions were the strongest—in the large urban areas of Dublin and Cork.

The inability of Labour to develop significant support in Dublin can be explained in part by the fact that most Dublin workers were strongly nationalist and the party did not satisfy them on this issue. Then there was the long-lasting conflict between Larkin and the O'Brienite leadership of the Transport Union which began when Larkin returned to Ireland in 1923. The bitter opposition which Larkin fostered against everybody who sided with O'Brien was a chronic handicap for the party in the capital. The Larkin split was Ireland's equivalent to the divisions which occurred in every European labour movement after the Bolshevik revolution. Larkin's volatile personality largely disguised the basically ideological nature of the division in Ireland.

Another factor which hindered the development of the Labour Party was its commitment to a socialist reconstruction of Irish society. In a state as strongly Catholic and agricultural as the Free State this was not a politically attractive goal. An additional factor was the widespread revulsion from the excesses of the Russian revolution and the fear that similar explosions could occur, even at home. In these circumstances, the party wisely restricted its specific proposals for nationalization to industries, such as transportation and communication, where state ownership would be obviously most beneficial. From the point of view of political advantage, however, the plethora of Labour proposals for social and economic reform had the effect of largely cancelling each other out. The party would have done better to fasten itself to a few vital and popular issues. It did not choose to exploit issues that were not directly related to its socio-economic concerns. Inside the Dail Labour was a severe critic of the Cosgrave goverment on constitutional and political matters, but it failed to take command of such issues as the annuity payments in the country. Had it done so, there is every likelihood that it would have won the support of many who otherwise would not have been attracted to the party. The fact that the party was eventually drawn into involvement with strictly political matters—in the coalition scheme of 1927—is evidence that its belief that it could avoid such involvement was unrealistic.

What of Johnson's term as principal spokesman of Irish Labour? By reason of his English and Belfast background, Johnson was one of the few leaders in the Free State with experience outside nationalist Ireland; in the labour movement he was the only one. For several years he was both the secretary of the congress-party and leader of the Dail Labour Party. This was an embarrassing dual capacity, which Johnson himself recognized. It would have been egotism if other able men were available to take one of these posts, but none were. He was not a popular leader; he was also an Englishman who only slowly came to comprehend the force of Irish nationalism. How then did he hold the two leading positions in the labour movement? Certainly complete devotion to duty was a factor, but there were other devoted men. The principal reason was that there was no one else who could articulate the socialist position as well as Tom Johnson. He was needed to speak for his party as well as to explain what socialism was to its members. But, as William O'Brien and Cathal O'Shannon later concluded, he was not essentially a politician, that is, a leader capable of simplifying ideas and developing broad, appealing issues. As well, he was a dedicated parliamentarian, when the party needed a leader who could rally public support.

The other leading figure was William O'Brien. A shrewd, careful man of unquestioned administrative ability, O'Brien never completely rose above the level of a manipulator of Dublin Trades Council elections. He was a gifted committeeman and organizer as well as a sincere advocate of socialism, but he was not an able leader of the labour movement. In a phrase, O'Brien lacked positive imagination. It is likely that his physical disability—a lame leg—had the effect of making him somewhat withdrawn and self-conscious. At any rate, like Johnson he had little popular appeal. He determinedly worked his way up the Labour ladder to two power positions—secretary of the Transport Union and leading member of the congress-party executive, and he determinedly held on to these positions. A bachelor of simple tastes, he found his love in power. Within his limitations, however, O'Brien contributed much to the labour movement during his long career—from organizing the return of Connolly to Ireland in 1910 to his courageous leadership of his union during the perilous years of the national struggle.

O'Brien also deserves most of the credit for the rapid growth of the Transport Union in the five years after 1916; by 1921 it claimed over 100,000 members. But with the depressed conditions of the early 1920s, the union began to lose its new-found members, and by the end of the decade it was down to less than half its peak strength. The general decline was not due to any failing of O'Brien, but the conflict with Larkin, which resulted in the loss of two-thirds of the union's Dublin membership, was partly due to him. Also, O'Brien must bear a major share of the responsibility for the resulting lasting division in the labour movement. Time demonstrated (especially the events of the early 1940s when Larkin was prepared to put the old quarrel aside) that O'Brien was a narrow, coldly unforgiving figure, an excluder and not a healer.

To compare different periods with their varying conditions is dangerous and often meaningless, but a comparison of the Transport Union leadership of Larkin and O'Brien shall be hazarded. In the five years that Larkin led the union it was a dynamic, life-generating force; moulded of the unskilled labour mass of Dublin, it courageously challenged the social and economic assumptions of pre-war Ireland. During the thirty years of O'Brien's direction the union could not be described thus. But O'Brien came to leadership of the union when there was a pressing need for administrative control and consolidation. E. J. Hobsbawm has pointed to two factors that drive a labour movement to the right: first, the mere technicalities of recognized trade union and political activities (collective bargaining, appointment of labour officials to government boards, etc.); second, the efforts of government and business to strengthen the moderates and weaken the radicals.[4] Both of these factors undoubtedly influenced the policy of the Transport Union under O'Brien's leadership, but he was naturally a cautious and careful man.

In fairness, it should be remembered that there is another period of Larkin's activity in Ireland, one that is usually overlooked by the many admirers of the man who led the workers' revolt of 1913. This is the ten years after 1923. To Larkin life was largely a case of rule or ruin. A colossal egoist, he failed to acknowledge the major contributions that others had made in expanding the union during his long absence. He expected the immediate and total restoration of his old powers. After he failed to regain these, and consequently was driven out of the union he founded, he employed slander, libel and violence not only against O'Brien and the Transport Union executive, but also against anyone in the labour movement who stood with them. He did great harm.

Having said so much that is critical and censorious of the leaders of Irish Labour after 1916, it is now wholly appropriate to cite their achievements. While Sinn Fein virtually ignored the problem of the existence of a million Unionists in the north, the Labour Party firmly clung to an all-Ireland outlook. Mainly through the consistent moderation of men such as Johnson and O'Brien, a united national Labour organization was maintained not only through a most dangerous period but long after partition had severed many connections between the two parts of the island. Hanging over Ireland throughout the last years of the European war was the threat of conscription, and when the issue was finally fought, the labour movement was in the forefront of the struggle. The utilization of the congress-party in the general strike, the 'first example of a successful general strike in Western Europe', according to Warre B. Wells, was a major factor in ending this threat.

The labour movement also contributed greatly to the attainment of national self-government for most of Ireland, and it did so in a variety of ways. An important factor in Labour's support for the national movement was the realization by the national leadership that the men of the congress-party executive were both dependable and circumspect. Later, when the treaty controversy erupted the Labour Party attempted

4 E. J. Hobsbawn, *Labouring men; studies in the history of labour* (New York 1967), p. 396.

to be a peacemaker. It offered its own compromise solution and worked tirelessly to head off the civil war. Remaining consistent to its constitutional approach to politics, and notwithstanding threats to its members, the party entered the Free State Dail. There it made a major contribution towards the creation of effective democratic government in the twenty-six counties. It must be remembered that without the Labour Party the first Free State assembly would have been almost entirely a one-party body. By its vigorous commitment to parliamentary government, Labour could claim a considerable part of the credit for establishing the Dail as the representative political body of the nation, the recognition of which eventually forced the anti-treatyites to enter.

With little over a dozen members, the party for five years provided a remarkable opposition to the Cosgrave government. From the viewpoint of a reasoned and demanding examination of a government's policy and practice, the Labour Party did an outstanding job. Much of this was the personal achievement of Tom Johnson, who was well termed a one-man opposition. Johnson immersed himself in legislative affairs, speaking forcefully and intelligently on a wide range of subjects; his attendance was constant as he missed only a handful of roll calls during this time. Both Johnson and his party took the business of government seriously. It can be claimed that Johnson left a permanent mark on the Dail, for as the first leader of the opposition, he was instrumental in creating a prevailing mood of dignity and restraint during the body's proceedings.

As the principal opposition party during a strange interregnum, the Labour Party was unable to rally the other non-government elements to its side. One reason for this was that the Farmers Party deputies and almost all of the independent members were extremely cautious and conservative. Stubbornly uninformed about the wider issues of the period and the affairs of the Cosgrave government, they defended their narrow interests and left their responsibility rest. Also, they found most unpalatable the socialist-influenced proposals of the Labour Party.

All of the many social and economic proposals put forward by the party had the mark of being properly researched, rationally argued and forward looking. They covered the fields of education, economic development, social services, housing, transportation, agriculture and fisheries. All this from a small and underfinanced party. Most of the Labour proposals have been either largely adopted by successive governments or been recognized as objectives still to be achieved.

Johnson's socio-economic philosophy, based on socialist principles and largely unoriginal, was considerably advanced for its time, certainly in Ireland. He held that government, as society's agent, must be fully committed to the furtherance of its people's welfare. To achieve this end, the government would be required to undertake programmes of national planning in all fields; it would also be required to employ a variety of fiscal measures to achieve national self-sufficiency and economic development. Committed to the traditional role of minimal state responsibility as well as to the conventional capitalist thought of the day, the Cosgrave government dismissed Johnson's ideas as utopian and impracticable. T. J. Barrington, for one, has pointed out the abuse which greeted proposals for planning and programming in this period.[5] Johnson was a prophet, and he met the prophet's fate.

Had the Labour Party, given its mistaken outlook concerning political issues during the national struggle and later, been able to achieve its initial objective—a stable Dail with a membership of about twenty—it would have been vastly more effective in pressing for progressive legislation in the 1930s. The party also would have laid the base for future growth. It came very close to achieving this objective, but by the end of the 1920s the party's development had been circumscribed and its image restricted to that of a trade union pressure group. The lack of success of the political side of the Irish movement by 1930 should be seen in the perspective of Europe of that time. Among European labour movements there were many greater failures; the destruction of the Italian movement after the world war, to be followed by that of the Spanish movement in the 1930s. Then there was the inability of the German and British movements to gain effective control of government in the 1920s, each to face greater failure in the next decade.

Forty years later the oldest party in the State still survives and indeed in recent years has prospered. During four difficult decades, when it suffered many reverses and few victories, the Labour Party never came close to eradication. This was principally because it has had a continuing function in Irish politics: it has been the defender of the interests of the weakest members of industrial society and it has offered, in no matter how diluted a form, the untried alternative of socialism. It offered not the approach of state-sponsored bodies created haphazardly and reluctantly, but a programme and philosophy of community and co-operative organization of the social and economic life of the nation.

Beginning in the mid-1960s, the party began to attract the vital elements it formerly lacked: reformist or progressive members of the middle class, young people and intellectuals. Although the trade unions have remained basically preoccupied with the matters of wages, hours and conditions, the two largest unions in the Republic have become affiliated. The increased social concern and broader vision that has come into the Catholic Church with Pope John undoubtedly has altered the attitudes of many Irishmen concerning socialism. The Common Market experience will expose the country to continental ideas and models. More immediately, the upheaval in the north, which began with the civil rights movement of 1968-69, has had the effect of generating new interest in socialism; it has also forced a re-examination of the social policies of the Republic.

The steady rise of the party's voting strength, both in local and parliamentary elections has been a most hopeful sign in a business

5 T. J. Barrington, 'Public administration, 1927–36', in *The years of the great test, 1926–39,* F. McManus, ed., p. 90.

where votes are almost everything. It has given every appearance that it has left the minor party stage and is capable of continuing growth. At last the Labour Party can justly claim to be the focus of the Left in Ireland.

Bibliography

1 INTERVIEWS

Blythe, Ernest *10 August 1971*
Boland, Gerald *9 August 1967*
Connolly, Roderick *1 October 1965*
Everett, James *24 June 1964*
Gilmore, George *14 November 1966*
Hayes, Michael *19 April 1967*
Heron, Archie *30 November 1964*
Johnson, Fred *14 October 1965*
Johnson, Mary *22 June 1964*
Larkin, James, the younger *3 February 1966*
McMullen, William *30 November 1965*
Nolan, John *1 December 1963*
O'Connell, Thomas J. *3 November 1965*
O'Donnell, Peadar *21 November 1964*
O'Reilly, Michael W. *25 July 1970*
O'Shannon, Cathal *1 June 1964*
Robbins, Frank *28 November 1964*
Ryan, Desmond *22 May 1964*
Sinclair, Betty *25 August 1970*
Swift, John *11 August 1970*

2 COLLECTIONS OF PRIVATE PAPERS

Thomas Johnson, National Library of Ireland
William O'Brien, National Library of Ireland

3 NEWSPAPERS AND PERIODICALS

a. *National newspapers and periodicals*

Belfast Newsletter
Belfast Telegraph
Contemporary Review
Cork Examiner
Dublin Evening Mail
Dublin Saturday Post
Evening Herald
Evening Telegraph
Freeman's Journal
Irish Catholic
Irish Economist
Irish Homestead
Irish Independent
Irish Life
Irish Monthly
Irish News (Belfast)
Irish Review
Irish Rosary
Irish Statesman
Irish Times
Journal of the Statistical and Social Inquiry Society
Kerryman
Leader
Manchester Guardian
Quarterly Review
Round Table
Spark
Studies
Tipperary Star

b. *Labour newspapers*

An Dion, 1926–30
Distributive Workers, 1927–30
Dublin Trade and Labour Journal, 1909 (only four issues)

Irish Hammer and Plough, 1926
Irishman, 1927–30
Irish Opinion, 1917–18
Irish Worker, 1911–14
—— 1923–27 (Larkinite, published irregularly)
Irish Workers Voice, 1932–36
New Way, 1917–19
Red Hand, 1919
Voice of Labour, 1918–19, 1921–27
Watchword, 1930–32
Watchword of Labour, 1919–20
Worker, 1914–15
Workers' Republic, 1898–1903 (published by the Irish Socialist Republican Party) 1914–16 (published by the Irish Transport and General Workers Union) 1921–23 (published by the Communist Party of Ireland)
—— March–December 1927 (published by the Workers Party of Ireland)
Workers Voice, 1930–32

c. *Other party newspapers*

Eire, 1923–24
Freeman, 1922–23, 1927–28
Free State, 1922
Irish Bulletin, 1919–23
Irish Citizen, 1912–15
Irish Freedom, 1912–14, 1926–30
Irishman, 1917–18
Irish Nation, 1907–10
Irish Peasant, 1905–07
Irish War News, 1922–23
Irish World and Industrial Advocate, 1917
Liberator and Irish Trade Unionist
Nation, 1922, 1924, 1927
Nationality, 1915–19
New Ireland, 1917–19, 1922
Poblacht na hEireann, 1922
Phoblacht, An, 1925–30
Plain People, The, 1922
Sinn Fein. 1912–14, 1923–25
Star, 1929
Toiler, 1913
United Ireland, 1890
United Irishman, 1898–1903
Weekly Summary, 1919–21

4 LABOUR REPORTS AND PUBLICATIONS

Belfast and District Trades Union Council. *Belfast and District Trades Union Council, 1881–1951 : a short history*. Belfast 1951.
Belfast Trades and Labour Council. *Souvenir of the Trade Union Congress at the Grosvenor Hall, Belfast*. 1929.
Dublin Trades Council. *Minutes*. 1913–27.
Irish Labour Party. *Annual report*. 1930–70.
—— *The nation organized*. 1932
—— *Planning for the crisis*, 1940
—— *Labour's programme for a better Ireland*, 1943
—— *The disaffiliation from the Labour Party of the Irish Transport and General Workers Union*, 1944.
Irish Labour Party and Trade Union Congress. *Annual report*. 1918–29
—— [O'Rahilly, Alfred?]. *Who burnt Cork city?*. 1920.
—— *Ireland at Berne*.1919.
Irish Trade Union Congress. *Annual report*. 1894–1911, 1930–45
Irish Trade Union Congress and Labour Party. *Annual report*. 1912–17
Irish Transport and General Workers Union. *Annual report*. 1918–55
—— *Rules*. 1918
—— *Some pages from union history*. 1924
—— *The attempt to smash the Irish Transport and General Workers Union*. 1924.
——*P. T. Daly's libel suit*. 1925.
—— *Thomas Johnson's libel suit*. 1925
—— *Fifty years of Liberty Hall*, edited by C. O'Shannon, Dublin, 1959
——*Liberty* (monthly publication). 1952–
Labour Party (British). *Annual report*. 1911–26
—— *Report of the Labour Party commission on Ireland*. London, 1921
Labour Party (Northern Ireland). *Annual report*. 1924–30
Workers Union of Ireland. *Rules*

5 PARLIAMENTARY REPORTS

Chief Secretary's Office Registered Papers, 1919–21, State Papers Office, Dublin.
Dail Eireann debates, vols. i–xx, 1922–27.
——. *Constructive works of the first Dail*. Dublin, 1921.
——. *Proceedings of the first Dail*. 1919–21. Dublin, 1921.
——. *Proceedings of the second Dail*. 1921–22. Dublin, 1921.
——. *Debate on the treaty between Great Britain and Ireland signed in London on 6th December 1921*. Dublin, 1922.
——. Dail Eireann papers, 1919–21, State Papers Office, Dublin.
Seanad Eireann debates, vols. i–x.
British government white paper, 'Documents relative to the Sinn Fein movement.' H.M.S.O., 1921 [Cmd. 1108].
——'Intercourse between Bolshevism and Sinn Fein.' H.M.S.O., 1921 [Cmd. 1326].
Provisional government, Irish Free State, blue paper, 'Correspondence of E. de Valera and others.' 1922.

6 BOOKS, ARTICLES AND PAMPHLETS

American Commission on conditions in Ireland. *Report*. New York 1920.
Barker, Ernest. *Ireland in the last fifty years*. Oxford 1919.
Barry, Tom. *Guerrilla days in Ireland*. Tralee n.d. (1962?).

Bealey, F., and Pelling, Henry. *Labour and politics, 1900–1906: a history of the Labour Representation Committee*. London 1958.

Beaslai, Piaras. *Michael Collins and the making of a new Ireland*. 2 vols. Dublin 1926.

Beckett, James C. *The making of modern Ireland, 1603–1923*. New York 1966.

Beecher, Liam. 'Tadhg Barry.' *Liberty* 26, nos. 4, 5 (Nov.–Dec. 1971).

Bell, J. Bowyer. *The secret army: a history of the I.R.A., 1916–1970*. London 1970.

Bleakley, David. 'Trade union beginnings in Belfast and district, with special reference to the period 1881–1900 and to the work of the Belfast and District Trades Council during that period'. M.A. thesis. Queen's University of Belfast, 1955.

Boyd, Andrew. *The rise of the Irish trade unions, 1929–1970*. Tralee 1971.

Boyle, John W. 'The rise of the Irish labour movement, 1888–1907', Ph. D. dissertation. Trinity College, Dublin, 1961.

——, editor. *Workers and leaders*. Cork 1966.

Brady, Thomas. *The historical basis of socialism in Ireland*. New York 1919.

Breen, Dan. *My fight for Irish freedom*. Rev. and enl. ed. Tralee 1964.

Brennan, Robert. *Allegiance*. Dublin 1950.

Briggs, Asa. *Chartist studies*. London 1959.

—— and Saville, John eds. *Essays in labour history*. London 1960.

Briollay, Sylvain. *Ireland in rebellion*. Dublin 1922.

Bromage, Mary. *De Valera and the march of a nation*. New York 1956.

Clarkson, Jesse D. *Labour and nationalism in Ireland*. New York 1925.

Chubb, Basil. *The government and politics of Ireland*. Stanford, California 1970.

——. 'The republic of Ireland.' In *European political parties*, edited by S. Henig and J. Pinder. London 1969.

——. *The Constitution of Ireland*. Dublin 1966.

Clayton, Bertram. 'Sinn Fein and Labour.' *Quarterly Review*, (January 1918).

Cole, G. D. H. *British working class politics, 1832–1914*. London 1941.

——. *Communism and social democracy, 1914–31*. London 1961.

Collins, Michael. *The path to freedom*. Dublin 1922.

Connolly, James. *Labour in Irish history*. Dublin 1956.

——. *Socialism and nationalism*. Edited by Desmond Ryan. Dublin 1948.

——. *Labour and Easter week*. Edited by Desmond Ryan. Dublin 1949.

——. *The axe to the root and old wine in new bottles*. New ed. Dublin 1934.

——. *Erin's hope: the end and the means*. Dublin 1897.

——. *Labour, nationality and religion*. Dublin 1910.

——. *The reconquest of Ireland*. Dublin 1972.

——. *Socialism made easy*. Dublin, 1968, 1971. Introduction by D. R. O'Connor Lysaght.

——. *The new evangel*. New ed. Dublin 1917.

Coogan, Timothy Patrick. *Ireland since the rising*. New York 1966.

——. *The I.R.A.* New York 1970.

Cosgrave, William T. *Policy of the Cumann na nGaedheal Party*. Dublin 1927.

Costigan, Giovanni, *A history of modern Ireland with a sketch of earlier times*. New York 1969.

Craig, Edward T. *The Irish land and labour question, 1882*. London 1882.

Dangerfield, George. *The strange death of liberal England*. New York 1961.

D'Arcy, Fergus. 'Skilled tradesmen in Dublin, 1800–50: a study of their opinions, activities and organizations.' M.A. thesis. University College, Dublin 1968.

Davitt, Michael. *The fall of feudalism in Ireland*. New York 1904; reprint Shannon 1971.

Dawson, Richard. *Red terror and green*. London 1920.

Deasy, Joseph. *The fiery cross: the story of Jim Larkin*. Dublin 1963.

de Blacam, Aodh. *What Sinn Fein stands for*. Dublin 1921.

——. *Towards the republic*. Dublin 1918.

de Valera, Eamon. *The national policy of Fianna Fail*. Dublin 1926.

Eason, J. C. M. 'Comparative government expenditure, 1924–25 through 1929–30.' *Statistical and Social Inquiry Society of Ireland*. Dublin 1930.

Edwards, Owen Dudley. *The sins of our fathers: facts of conflict in Northern Ireland*. Dublin 1970.

——. *The mind of an activist: James Connolly*. Dublin 1971.

——., and Pyle, Fergus. *1916: the Easter rising*. London 1968.

Ellis, P. Berresford. *The making of the Irish working class*. London 1972.

Epstein, Leon D. *Political parties in western democracies*. New York 1967.

Farley, Desmond. *Social insurance and social assistance in Ireland*. Dublin 1964.

Farrell, Brian. *The founding of Dail Eireann*. Dublin 1971.

——. 'Labour and the Irish political system: a suggested approach to analysis.' *Economic and Social Review* 1, no. 4 (July 1970), pp. 477–502.

Fianna Fail. *The land annuities*. Dublin 1932.

——. *The story of Fianna Fail*. Dublin 1960.

Figgis, Darrell. *Recollections of the Irish war*. London 1927.

FitzGerald, Desmond. *Memoirs of Desmond FitzGerald, 1913–1916*. London 1968.

Flynn, William J. *Free State parliamentary companion*. Dublin 1932, 1939.

——. *Irish parliamentary handbook*. Dublin 1945.

——. *Oireachtas companion and Saorstat guide*. Dublin 1928, 1929.

Fox, Ralph. *Marx, Engels and Lenin on Ireland*. New York 1940.

Fox, Robert M. *Green banners*. London 1938.

——. *The history of the Irish Citizen Army*. Dublin 1943.

——. *James Connolly, the forerunner*. Dublin 1946.

——. *Jim Larkin and the rise of the underman*. London 1957.

——. *Labour in the national struggle*. Dublin n.d. (1945?).

——. *Louie Bennett*. Dublin 1958.

Galenson, Walter. *Comparative labor movements*. New York 1952.

Gallacher, Willie, *Revolt on the Clyde*. London 1936.

Gallagher, Frank. *The Anglo-Irish treaty*. London 1965.

——. *Days of fear*. Cork 1967.

——. *King and constitution*. Dublin 1932.

——. [David Hogan]. *Four glorious years*. Dublin 1953.

Garnier, Charles, M. *A popular history of Ireland*. Cork 1961.

Goldring, Douglas. *Odd man out: the autobiography of a 'propaganda novelist'*. London 1935.

Greaves, C. Desmond. *The life and times of James Connolly*. London 1961.

——. *Liam Mellows and the Irish revolution*. London 1971.

Green, J. R. *The government of Ireland, 1921*. Dublin 1922.

Gwynn, Denis. *The Irish Free State, 1922–27*. London 1928.

Harbinson, J. 'A history of the Northern Ireland Labour Party, 1891–1949'. M. Econ. thesis. Queen's University of Belfast 1966.

Harrison, Henry. *Ireland and the British Empire, 1937*. London 1937.

Hayes, Michael. 'Dail Eireann and the Irish civil war.' *Studies*, (Spring 1969).

Healy, Timothy M. *Letters and leaders of my day*. London 1928.

Henig, S. and Pinder, J., eds. *European political parties*. London 1969.

Hennelly, M. F. *The church, the champion of the working man*. Dublin 1937.

Henry, Robert M. *The evolution of Sinn Fein*. New York 1920.

Hobsbawm, E. J. *Labouring men: studies in the history of labour*. New York 1967.

Hogan, James. *Could Ireland become communist*? Dublin 1935.

Holt, Edgar, *Protest in arms: the Irish troubles, 1916–23*. New York 1961.

Horn, P. 'The National Agricultural Labourers Union in Ireland, 1873–9.' *Irish Historical Studies* 17, no. 67 (March 1971), pp. 340–52.

Irish political leaflets. National Library of Ireland, Dublin.

Irish Times, Weekly. *Sinn Fein rebellion handbook*. Dublin 1916.

Irwin, Wilmot. *Betrayal in Ireland*. Belfast n.d.

Jackson, T. A., *Ireland her own*. New York 1970.

Johnson, Thomas. *A handbook for rebels*. Dublin 1918.

——. *A workers republic, socialist or distributist?* Dublin 1938.

Judge, Jerome J. 'Trade union organization in the republic of Ireland.' M.Econ. Sci. dissertation, University College, Dublin, 1951.

——. 'The labour movement in Ireland'. Ph.D. dissertation, University College, Dublin, 1955.

Kettle, Thomas. *The day's burden*. London 1937.

King, Clifford. *The orange and the green*. London 1965.

Larkin, Emmet. *James Larkin, Irish labour leader, 1876–1947*. London 1965.

Lenin, V. I. *Collected works*. Moscow 1964.

Longford, (Frank Pakenham) Earl of, and O'Neill, Thomas P. *Eamon de Valera*. London 1970.

Lynch, Patrick. 'The social revolution that never was.' In *The Irish struggle, 1916–1926*, edited by T. Desmond Williams. London 1966.

——. 'William Thompson and the socialist tradition.' In *Leaders and workers*, edited by John W. Boyle. Cork 1966.

Lyons, Francis S. L. 'The economic ideas of Parnell.' In *Historical studies: papers read before the third conference of Irish historians*, edited by M. Roberts. London 1959.

——. *The fall of Parnell, 1890–91*. London 1962.

——. *Ireland since the famine*. London 1971.

——. *The Irish parliamentary party, 1890–1910*. London 1951.

——. *John Dillon, a biography*. London 1968.

——. *Ireland since the famine*. New York 1971.

Lysaght, D. R. O'Connor. *The making of Northern Ireland*. Dublin 1969.

——. *The republic of Ireland: a hypothesis in eight chapters and two intermissions*. Cork 1970.

Mac Donagh, Michael. 'Sinn Fein and

Macardle, Dorothy. *The Irish republic*. London 1937.

McCaffrey, Laurence J. *The Irish question, 1800–1922*, Lexington, Kentucky 1968.

McCracken, J. C. *Representative government in Ireland: a study of Dail Eireann 1919–48*. Oxford 1958.

McDonald, Walter. *Some ethical aspects of the social question: some suggestions for priests*. London 1920.

MacDonagh, Oliver. *Ireland*. Englewood Cliffs, New Jersey 1968.

MacDonagh, Michael. 'Sinn Fein and labour in Ireland.' *Contemporary Review*, (April 1918).

McDowell, Robert B. *The Irish convention, 1917–18*. London 1970.

MacGiolla Choille, Brendan, ed. *Chief secretary's office, Dublin Castle, intelligence notes, 1913–16, preserved in the State Papers Office*. Dublin 1966.

McHugh, Roger, ed. *Dublin 1916*. New York 1966.

McInerney, Michael. Articles on the 'democratic programme' of 1919. *Irish Times*, 28 November 1966, 15 March 1967, 21 January 1969.

——. 'The Irish labour movement.' *Hibernia*, March 1963.

——. 'Peadar O'Donnell.' *Irish Times*

——. *The riddle of Erskine Childers*. Cork 1971.

McKenna, Laurence, S.. T. *The social teachings of James Connolly*. Dublin 1920.

McKenna, Rose. *A plea for social emancipation in Ireland*. Manchester 1917.

McManus, Francis, ed. *The years of the great test, 1926–39*. Cork 1967.

McMullen, William. *With James Connolly in Belfast*. Dublin n.d.

Macready, Nevil. *Annals of an active life*. 2 vols. London 1924.

Malone, Andrew E. [L. P. Byrne]. 'Irish labour in wartime.' *Studies*, (June 1918).

——. 'Party government in the Irish Free State' in *Political Science Quarterly*, vol. 44, no. 3 (September 1929), pp. 363–78.

Mansergh, Nicholas. *The Irish Free State, its government and politics*. London 1934.

——. *The Irish question, 1840–1921*. London 1965.

Marreco, Anne. *The rebel countess: the life and times of Constance Markievicz*. London 1967.

Martin, Francis X., ed. *Leaders and men of the Easter rising: Dublin 1916*. Ithaca, New York 1967.

Meenan, James. *The Irish economy since 1922*. Liverpool 1970.

Mellows, Liam. *Notes from Mountjoy jail*. London 1966.

Mitchell, Arthur. 'A brief history of the Irish Labour Party.' *Irish Times*, 27 February–2 March 1967.

——. 'The economic philosophy of George Russell.' *Irish Times*, 17 April 1967.

——. 'The Irish labour movement and the civil war.' *Capuchin Annual*, 1972.

——. 'Labour and the national struggle, 1919–21.' *Capuchin Annual*, 1971.

——. 'Thomas Johnson, 1872–1963, a pioneer labour leader.' *Studies* 58, no. 232 (Winter 1969), pp. 396–404.

——. 'William O'Brien, 1881–1968, and the Irish labour movement.' *Studies* 60, no. 239 (Winter 1971) pp. 311–331.

Moody, Theodore W. 'Michael Davitt and the British labour movement.' *Transactions of the Royal Historical Society*, 5th series, 3 (1953), pp. 53–76.

——, and, Martin, F. X., ed. *The course of Irish history*. Cork 1967.

Moss, Warner. *Political parties in the Irish Free State*. New York 1933.

Musgrave, Patrick. *A socialist and war*. London 1940.

Neeson, Eoin. *The civil war in Ireland*. Cork 1966.

Nevin, Donal. 'The Irish Citizen Army.' In *1916: the Easter rising*, edited by O. Dudley Edwards and F. Pyle. London 1968.

——. 'Labour and the political revolution.' In *The years of the great test, 1926–39*, edited by F. MacManus.

——. 'Labour in the Easter rising.' *Irish Times 1916 supplement*, April 1966.

Nevinson, Henry W. *Last changes, last chances*. New York 1929.

Nugent, John D. *The case for constitutionalism*. Dublin 1918.

——. *Labour and the new parliament*. Dublin 1918.

O'Briain, Barra. *The Irish constitution*. Dublin and Cork 1929.

O'Brien, Conor Cruise. *Parnell and his party, 1880–90*. Oxford 1957.

——, editor. *The shaping of modern Ireland*. London 1960.

O'Brien, George. *The four green fields*. Dublin 1936.

O'Brien, Nora Connolly. *Portrait of a rebel father*. Dublin 1935.

O'Brien, William. *Forth the banners go*, edited by Edward MacLysaght. Dublin 1969.

O'Casey, Sean. *Drums under the windows*. London 1945.

——. *I knock at the door: swift glances back at things that made me*. London 1939.

——. *Inishfallen, fare thee well*. London 1949.

——. *Pictures in the hallway*. London 1942.

——. [P. O Cathasaigh] *The history of the Irish Citizen Army*. Dublin 1919.

O'Connell, Thomas J. *History of the Irish National Teachers Organization, 1868–1968*. Dublin 1968.

O'Connor, Art. *Notes on national economy*. Dublin 1924.

O'Connor, Frank. *Michael Collins: the big fellow*. London 1937.

O'Connor, Ulick. *The times I've seen: Oliver St. John Gogarty*. New York 1963.

O'Donnell, Peadar. *There will be another day*. Dublin 1963.

O'Donoghue, Florence. *No other law*. Dublin 1934.

O'Faolain, Sean. *Constance Markievicz; or, the average revolutionary*. London 1934.

——. *De Valera*. Dublin 1933.

O'Hegarty, Patrick S. *A history of Ireland under the union, 1801 to 1922*. London 1952.

——. *The victory of Sinn Fein: how it was won, and how it used it*. Dublin 1924.

O'Higgins, Kevin. *The civil war and the events which led up to it*. Dublin n.d. [1922?].

——. *Three years hard work*. Dublin 1924.

O'Higgins, Rachel. 'Ireland and Chartism.' Ph. D. dissertation, Trinity College, Dublin, 1959.

O'Leary, Cornelius. *The Irish republic and its experiment with proportional representation*. South Bend, Indiana 1961.

O'Malley, Ernie. *On another man's wound*. London 1935.

O'Neill, Brian. *The war for the land in Ireland*. London 1933.

O'Shannon, Cathal. Articles on the 'democratic programme' of 1919. *Irish Times*, 31 January, 1 February 1944.

——, editor. *Fifty years of Liberty Hall*. Dublin 1969.

——. 'Some personal memoirs of Connolly.' *Voice of Labour*, 10 May 1924.

O'Sullivan, Donal. *The Irish Free State and its senate*. London 1940.

Pakenham, Frank. *Peace by ordeal*. London 1935.

Pearse, Patrick. *The sovereign people*. Dublin 1916.

——. *Collected works*. Dublin 1922.

Pelling, Henry. *The origins of the Labour Party, 1800–1900*. London 1954.

——. *A short history of the Labour Party*. London 1961.

——, and Bealey, F. *Labour and politics, 1900–1906*. London 1958.

Pollard, Hugh B. C. *The secret societies of Ireland*.

Pomfret, J. *The struggle for the land in Ireland*. Princeton, New Jersey 1930.

Pyne, Peter. 'The third Sinn Fein Party, 1923–26'. *Economic and Social Review* i, nos. 1 and 2 (October 1969, January 1970).

Rawson, D. W. 'The life-span of labour parties.' *Political Studies*, 17, no. 3 (September 1969).

Reed, Donald, and Glasgow, Eric. *Feargus O'Connor, Irishman and chartist*. London 1969.

Robbins, Frank. Unpublished recollections.

'Ronald'. *Freedom's road for Irish workers*. Manchester 1917.

Ross, J. F. S. *The Irish electoral system*. London 1959.

'Russell, Charles'. *Should the workers of Ireland support Sinn Fein?* Dublin 1918.

Russell, George W. [AE]. *The national being*. Dublin 1920.

——. *Co-operation and nationality: a guide for rural reformers from this to the next generation*. Dublin 1912.

——. *Letters from AE*, edited by Alan Denson. London 1961.

Ryan, Andrew P. *Mutiny at the Curragh*. London 1956.

Ryan, Desmond. *Benevolent dictator: a study of Eamon de Valera*. London 1936.

——. *James Connolly, his life, work and writings*. Dublin 1924.

——. *The man called Pearse*. Dublin and London 1919.

——. *The phoenix flame: a story*. London 1937.

——. *Remembering Sion: a chronicle of storm and quiet*. London 1934.

——. *The rising: the complete story of Easter week*. Dublin 1949.

——. 'When the spectre haunted Cork, 1872.' *The Bell*, vol. 12, no. 4, pp. 317–24, July 1946.

Ryan, William P. *The Irish labour movement from the twenties to our own day*. Dublin 1919.

——. *The labour revolt and Larkinism.* London 1913.
——. *The pope's green island.* London 1912.

Sheehan, Daniel D. *Ireland since Parnell.* London 1921.
Sheehy Skeffington, Francis. *Michael Davitt: revolutionary agitator and labour leader.* Dublin 1908.
Sigerson, Selma. *Sinn Fein and socialism.* Dublin n.d. [ca 1918].
Sinn Fein Re-organizing Committee. *Sinn Fein's economic programme.* Dublin 1924.
'Spalpin'. *Sinn Fein and the labour movement.* Dublin n.d. [1918?].
Stephens, James. *The insurrection in Dublin.* 3rd edition. Dublin 1965.
Strauss, Emil. *Irish nationalism and British democracy.* London 1951.
Street, Cecil J. C. [I.O. pseud]. *The administration of Ireland, 1920.* London 1921.
——. *Ireland in 1921.* London 1922.

Taylor, Rex. *Michael Collins.* London 1958.
Thornley, David. 'The development of the Irish labour movement.' *Christus Rex* 18, no. 1 (January–March 1964).
——. Introduction to *The government and politics of Ireland,* by Basil Chubb. Stanford, California 1970.
——. 'Ireland, the end of an era?' *Studies* 53, no. 209 (1964), pp. 1–17.
——. *Isaac Butt and home rule.* London 1964.

Ulster Unionist Labour Association. *Labour Party commission on Ireland: analysis and criticism.* Belfast 1921.
Ulster trade unionists and home rule. Belfast. n.d. [*c.* 1914].

Van Voris, Jacqueline. *Costance deMarkievicz in the cause of Ireland.* Amherst, Massachusetts 1967.

Webb, Sidney, and Webb, Beatrice. *A history of trade unionism.* London 1920.
Wells, Ware B. *Irish indiscretions.* Dublin 1923.
——, and Marlowe, N. [pseud.]. *The Irish convention.* London 1917.
——, and——. *A history of the Irish rebellion of 1916.* Dublin and London 1916.
White, James Robert. *Misfit: an autobiography.* London 1930.
White, Terence deVere. *Kevin O'Higgins.* London 1948.
Whyte, John. *Church and state in modern Ireland, 1923–70.* Dublin 1971.
Williams, Thomas Desmond, ed. *The Irish struggle, 1916–1926.* London 1966.
Wright, Arnold. *Disturbed Dublin: the story of the great strike of 1913–14, with a discription of the industries of the Irish capital.* London 1914.

Younger, Calton. *Ireland's civil war.* London 1968.

Index